Winning Authors

POPULAR AUTHORS SERIES

Winning Authors

Profiles of the Newbery Medalists

Kathleen Long Bostrom

Popular Authors Series

UNLIMITED

A Member of the Greenwood Publishing Group

Westport, Connecticut • London

Library of Congress Cataloging-in-Publication Data

Bostrom, Kathleen Long.
    Winning authors : profiles of the Newbery medalists / by Kathleen Long Bostrom.
       p. cm. — (Popular authors series)
    Includes bibliographical references.
    ISBN 1–56308–877–0 (alk. paper)
    1. Children's literature, American—History and criticism. 2. Children's literature,
American—Bio-bibliography. 3. Authors, American—20th century—Biography.
4. Newbery Medal. I. Title. II. Series.
    PS490.B67   2003
    810 9'9282—dc21   2003053878
    [B]

British Library Cataloguing in Publication Data is available.

Copyright © 2003 by Kathleen Long Bostrom

All rights reserved. No portion of this book may be
reproduced, by any process or technique, without the
express written consent of the publisher.

Library of Congress Catalog Card Number: 2003053878
ISBN: 1–56308–877–0

First published in 2003

Libraries Unlimited, 88 Post Road West, Westport, CT 06881
A Member of the Greenwood Publishing Group, Inc.
www.lu.com

Printed in the United States of America

The paper used in this book complies with the
Permanent Paper Standard issued by the National
Information Standards Organization (Z39.48–1984).

10 9 8 7 6 5 4 3 2 1

Copyright Acknowledgments

All photograph permission credits can be found in the Appendix on page 312.
All quotes from Newbery Awards acceptance speeches are reproduced by permission of
The Newbery & Caldecott Medal Books, 1986–2001, American Library Association
(Association for Library Services to Children), 2001.

Excerpts from Kunitz, Stanley J., and Howard Haycraft, eds. 1951. *The Junior Book of
Authors.* Second Edition. New York: The H. W. Wilson Company, used with permission
of the publisher.

Every reasonable effort has been made to trace the owners of copyright materials in this
book, but in some instances this has proven impossible. The editor and publisher will be
glad to receive information leading to more complete acknowledgments in subsequent
printings of the book and in the meantime extend their apologies for any omissions.

This book is dedicated to:

The authors,
Who weave worlds with their words;

The librarians,
Who put these worlds in our reach;

The readers,
Who make it all worthwhile.

I would also like to thank the staff
at Libraries Unlimited, past and present,
who made the dream of this author come true.

Contents

Acknowledgments

This book would not have been possible without the help and encouragement of a variety of people. In particular, I would like to thank the Newbery Medal authors who granted me interviews by phone, e-mail, or in person. They are, in alphabetical order, Joan Blos; Susan Cooper; Sharon Creech; Karen Cushman; Russell Freedman; Jean Craighead George; Virginia Hamilton and her husband, Arnold Adoff; Irene Hunt and her sister, Shirley Beem; Madeleine L'Engle and her staff, especially Charlotte Jones; Lois Lowry; Patricia MacLachlan; Robin McKinley; Phyllis Reynolds Naylor; Linda Sue Park; Katherine Paterson; Jerry Spinelli; and Maia Wojciechowska. You have made me glad to be an author who writes for children.

I also thank those who helped me secure photographs and copyright permissions for this book. I thank Eve Cotton of the American Library Association; Lauren Raece from *The Horn Book;* Jackie Jones from the Gale Group; Kristin Marley from Harcourt Trade Books, Children's Books Division; Allison Devlin, Laura Ferrell, Colleen Leonardi, Dana Schwartz, and Rebecca Grose from HarperCollins Publishers; Marjorie Naughton, Adrienne Waintraub, Megan Fink, and Alison Root from Random House; Sarah Henry from Penguin Putnam; and Alexis Burling and Stephanie Wimmer from Scholastic, Inc. My apologies to anyone I have neglected to mention.

I thank my husband, Greg, who believed in this book from the start and who helped edit my manuscript. I thank my children, Christopher, Amy, and David, who graciously allowed me to spend hours at the computer and did not begrudge the time.

I am grateful to Betty Morris and to Barbara Ittner, Emma Bailey, Margaret Maybury, and the rest of the staff at Libraries Unlimited and to the team at Impressions Book and Journal Services, Inc. for their direction and guidance and for publishing what I hope will be a valuable resource for many years to come.

Preface

When I first began writing books in the early 1990s, I became fascinated with the lives and techniques of other authors. Because I was writing for children, I focused on learning about the Newbery Medalists. Many of my favorite books from childhood were Newbery Medal books, although I didn't know it at the time. All I knew was what I liked and how much I valued an author who could captivate a young reader.

I went to the local libraries to find a single book with biographies of the Newbery Medal winners, but could not find any. The librarians and the authors all agreed that a book such as the one I envisioned would be a wonderful resource for children and for others interested in Newbery authors.

I started interviewing Newbery Medalists. Whenever an author came to town, or within driving distance, I arranged to meet and do a live interview. Sometimes I interviewed an author over the telephone or through the mail. All the authors were helpful, kind, and willing to take time with me. As I researched this book, I made many new friends along the way and have discovered what is certainly no surprise: that people who write for children are wonderful, amazing, creative, and terrific people.

In the many cases where I was unable to interview the author directly, I used a number of valuable resources found in the library, including the series *Something About the Author* and the collections of Newbery Medal acceptance speeches and biographies from the *Horn Book* and published by the American Library Association. The bibliography at the back of this book gives full information on all resources utilized in the writing of these biographies.

While this book is written to reach the interest of children, it is my hope that people of all ages will find in these pages the motivation to learn more about the lives of these marvelous authors and to read their books. Words are only words until they come to life by being read—by you, the reader.

The Rev. Dr. Kathleen Long Bostrom
July 2003, Wildwood, Illinois

To the Reader

You are about to embark upon a marvelous adventure into the lives of some of the greatest authors of all time. Be forewarned: these authors are more than just terrific writers. They're terrific people, too. Once you meet them in these pages you will find that your list of friends has grown, for these authors are real people and they truly love what they do: writing for you!

Winning Authors: Profiles of the Newbery Medalists is written specifically for

- Readers in grades 4 through 8

- Students researching and writing reports on the Newbery authors

- Those who wish to become writers or who simply want to find out more about a favorite author

- Educators (teachers/librarians) who can use the profiles for author studies and to supplement discussions on particular books

The biographies can also be used as read-alouds for younger readers.

This book is organized for ease of reading and research. Following a brief explanation of the origin of the Newbery Medal and other crucial information, the book is divided into chapters, one for each author. The authors are listed chronologically, according to when they received the award, from the winner of the first Newbery Medal in 1922 through the Newbery Medalist for 2002. For each medal winner, the genre of the book, in parentheses, follows the title.

For each author, information is included about both his or her personal and writing life. In the case of the earlier authors, finding information proved to be difficult. There is less written about the first Newbery Medal winners simply because at the time, the Newbery Medal was not as well known as it is today and the winners did not receive as much publicity. Therefore, information on these early winners is not as available.

Along with each author's biography is a listing of the other honors and awards he or she has received. The focus is on the major literary awards given to authors of books for children. Some of the lesser-known awards may not be listed. You are encouraged to check the resources listed in the bibliography for more information about each author.

A list of each author's books is also included so as to encourage the reader to discover more about the author than just the book that won the Newbery Medal. Some of the authors have written an amazing number of books, others just a few. It helps in learning more about the author to view the types of books each has written during his or her writing career.

During the course of writing this book, inconsistencies were discovered in previous research. For instance, in several cases, different birth or death dates were given for the same author. Whenever such discrepancies were discovered, further research was done to try and determine the correct date. If there are errors, they are solely my responsibility.

A number of the authors in this book were still living at the time of this printing. This makes it impossible to have complete biographies for these authors. Please check with your local library to find out information on the continued writing careers of these authors and to learn about the Newbery Medal winners who have been named since this book was written.

As for author Web sites, they tend to change frequently. Web sites for several authors can be found under "For More Information About/by" at the end of each chapter. The best way to find information about an author's Web site is to go to the Web site of the publisher and find out more about the author through them. Another way is to search the World Wide Web using the author's name. Many Web sites are "unofficial"; that is, they are put together by fans of the author rather than the author him- or herself. These sites can be a helpful source of information, but remember, they are not the official Web sites of the authors and may contain misinformation.

Above all, enjoy yourself as you read about these wonderful authors of children's books. Who knows, your name may be listed among them some day!

Introduction

One Man's Vision: The Whole World's Gain

John Newbery: A Man with a Vision

On a bright spring day in 1744, a revolution began. No gunshots were fired, no battle lines drawn, and no lives lost. Best of all, there were no losers in this revolution, only winners.

Triggered by a much-admired London bookseller, the revolution began quietly and with little fanfare. The only inkling that a history-making event was about to occur came in the form of an announcement that appeared on the back page of a London newspaper on June 18, 1744:

> This Day is publish'd According to
> Act of Parliament (Neatly bound and gilt)
> *A Little Pretty Pocket-Book,*
> intended for the Instruction and Amusement of
> little Master Tommy and pretty Miss Polly . . .
> Printed for J. Newbery, at the Bible and Crown,
> near Devereux Court.

The key word in this advertisement is the word *Amusement.* When John Newbery published *A Little Pretty Pocket-Book* in 1744, "amusement" was not a word associated with books for children. Until that time, the sole purpose of books was to teach strict moral and religious values, and anything that might be considered "amusing" or "entertaining" was not in the picture at all. John Newbery changed that with one small book.

Although some people felt that Newbery's books were not proper for children, the actions of the majority spoke louder than the words of protest from a few. Children and adults alike bought Newbery's merry little books as if they'd discovered buried treasure, and indeed, they had. The world of children's literature would never be the same.

If only John Newbery could see the results of his gentle revolution, what a proud and delighted man he would be!

The Birth of the Newbery Medal

Although John Newbery died in 1767, his name lives on thanks to Frederic G. Melcher. Melcher, a Midwestern bookseller and editor who lived in the early part of the twentieth century, believed that publishers and booksellers needed to do a better job of promoting books for children. In 1921, Melcher made a proposal to the American Library Association that a special medal be given each year to honor the author of the most distinguished book for children. Melcher recognized the impact that John Newbery had had on children's book publishing, so he suggested that the award be named for Mr. Newbery. René Chambellan designed the medal.

Melcher made his final proposal on June 21, 1921, 176 years after the publication of Newbery's first book. In 1922, the first Newbery Medal was awarded to Hendrik van Loon for his history book *The Story of Mankind.*

The Newbery Medal was the first children's book award in the world. Since 1922, the Newbery Medal has been awarded annually, following the guidelines set by Frederic Melcher, who stated that the purpose of the medal was to

- Encourage original and creative work in the field of books for children

- Emphasize to the public that contributions to literature for children deserve recognition similar to poetry, plays, or novels

- Give those librarians who make it their life's work to serve children's reading interests an opportunity to encourage good writing in this field

The Newbery Medal is considered by many to be the highest honor given in the field of children's books. The author who receives this award has the satisfaction not only of being recognized for top quality writing but also of knowing that his or her book will achieve the status of a classic, set apart from the thousands of other books published each year.

What It Takes to Be a Winner

The requirements for eligibility as a Newbery Medal–winning book are very specific. All books considered for the award must be

- Original; no reprint of a previously published book or compilations from more than one book are eligible

- Published within the previous calendar year

- Published in the United States of America

- Of interest to children through the age of fourteen

- Outstanding in quality of writing and significance to the world of literature

The book can be fiction, nonfiction, or poetry. The author must be a citizen or resident of the United States.

Who Makes the Choice?

Each year, a Newbery Award Committee is appointed by the Association for Library Service for Children (ALSC), a division of the American Library Association (ALA). Fifteen committee members are nominated, seven by the ALSC and seven by the president-elect of the ALA; the chair is elected by the ALSC membership from a slate submitted by the nominating committee. Committee members serve a one-year term and cannot be reelected to a Newbery Award Committee for another five years.

How Are the Books Selected?

ALSC members and book publishers can recommend a book for consideration by the committee. However, final nominations have to come from a member of the committee. Books are voted on twice in the fall, so that the committee members can start to focus on the books that are most likely to be potential award winners. Committees may end up reading and reviewing between 300 and 400 books, an average of one or more books per day. That's a lot of reading!

During the voting, each committee member votes for three books, and points are assigned. To win the Medal, a book must receive at least eight first-place points as well as have eight more points than the other books being considered. The award committee for each year decides if any books will be named honor books, and if so, how many. The honor books are those that earn a majority of votes but not enough to receive the Newbery Medal.

The revolution that began on that spring day in 1744 has made all of us winners because we are the ones who have the joy and privilege of reading the many marvelous books. Thank you, John Newbery and Frederic Melcher and all the wonderful authors who write for the young and for the young at heart.

The Randolph Caldecott Medal

In 1937, fifteen years after the Newbery Medal was established, Frederick G. Melcher suggested that a second annual medal for children's books be awarded, this one specifically for picture books. The medal, named in honor of the nineteenth-century English illustrator Randolph J. Caldecott, is given to the artist who has illustrated the most distinguished picture book for the year. The winner of the Caldecott Medal must meet many of the same requirements as the nominees for the Newbery Medal. The ALSC also has the responsibility of choosing the winner of the Caldecott Medal and administering the award.

1922: Hendrik van Loon

Born	January 14, 1882
	Rotterdam, Holland, the Netherlands
Married	Eliza Bowditch, June 1906 (children: Henry and Gerard)
	Helen Criswell, August 1920
	Frances Goodrich Ames, 1927
	Remarried Helen Criswell, 1930
Died	March 11, 1944

Awards and Honors

Newbery Medal (History): *The Story of Mankind* (Boni & Liveright, 1921)

About the Author and His Writing

What would it be like to be the first person to ever win the Newbery Medal? That honor belongs to Hendrik van Loon, who was awarded the newly established Newbery Medal in 1922 for his book *The Story of Mankind* (Boni & Liveright, 1921). He not only wrote this book; he illustrated it as well, with sketches and drawings unlike the usual ones found in history books of the time.

The Story of Mankind began as a series of eight history books for children. Later, this idea was changed and the book became a single volume of history. It's a good thing, too, because otherwise it might not have won the Newbery Medal.

Hendrik van Loon was born in Rotterdam, Holland. As a child, he enjoyed going to museums and drawing pictures. The home he grew up in was quite unique. "No two rooms were on the same floor," he wrote. "Short and long staircases ran every which way. My own little room (as soon as I was allowed to enjoy such a luxury) seemed to hang suspended in mid-air, since the space below it belonged to another house" (Commire 1980, 18:288).

The strangely built house contained more than just odd rooms; there was also a great deal of unhappiness within. Hendrik's father was especially cruel. "If, as a child, we made ourselves a little boat out of a piece of cork and an old rag, he would wait until we had finished our craft and then he would smash it underneath the heel of his boot" (Commire 1980, 18:288). After van Loon's mother died when he was nineteen years old, he was sent to a boarding school so he could get away from the influence of his father. One year later, he sailed for America.

(On seeing the skull of a prehistoric man as a child) What if this head had been the head of one of my ancestors? It made life so much more interesting to imagine your ancestors fighting mastodons and tigers instead of going to dull offices as everyone I knew did every day of the year. (Commire 1980, 18:288)

Hendrik studied law at Cornell University, in Ithaca, New York, even though he did not wish to be a lawyer. Of much more interest to him were journalism and history. "From my tenth year I wanted more than anything to be a very famous historian," he wrote (Commire 1980, 18:288). Writing about history seemed the perfect match for his interests and abilities. He taught history at Cornell University and Antioch College in Yellow Springs, Ohio. Hendrik also lectured extensively in the United States and many other countries.

Hendrik's personal life was anything but steady. He married four times, twice to the same woman. He had two children, Henry and Gerard, with his first wife, Eliza Bowditch.

> I loved my mother but never had any sincere affection for my father. This aversion has gone so far that when occasionally a sincere lover of one of my books asks me for a photograph, I will send him a picture, not of my face, but of my hands, for those hands are the hands of my mother. (*The Story of Mankind,* p. x)

In his adult years he enjoyed going to the Central Children's Room of the New York Library. The red-tiled floors and low ceilings reminded him of his native Holland. He kept in touch with the staff of the library throughout his entire adult life.

Hendrik was a hard worker. His addiction to work troubled him but also gave him relief. He wrote about his compulsion, "It is a pest, a plague, it ruins everything. I have all the money I need, and I don't know why I work except perhaps that it has been my refuge for so long that it was a sort of jail, and I did not dare look outside for fear I might be lost" (Commire 1980, 18:291).

After winning the Newbery Medal, van Loon was able to give up his teaching job and concentrate on writing and illustrating. His favorite subject to write about was history. He spent many years as a press correspondent and journalist, lectured on history at universities, and worked as a radio commentator. During World War II, van Loon hosted a radio broadcast as his contribution to the war efforts and established a shortwave radio station from Boston to the Netherlands.

Van Loon's travels allowed him to meet famous and interesting people, including the physicist Albert Einstein. The two enjoyed playing their violins together during the ocean voyage on which they met.

In 1942, the first recipient of the Newbery Medal received the highest honor he could have hoped for from his native country: The Order of the Netherlands Lion, which was conferred upon him by Queen Wilhelmina.

Only two years later, Hendrik van Loon died of heart failure. At the time of his death, nearly six million copies of his books had been sold.

A Word to My Readers:

History is the mighty Tower of Experience, which Time has built amidst the endless fields of bygone ages. It is no easy task to reach the top of this ancient structure and get the benefit of the full *view*. There is no elevator, but young feet are strong and it can be done. (*The Story of Mankind,* p. x)

Books by Hendrik van Loon

America (Boni & Liveright, 1927).

Ancient Man: The Beginning of Civilizations (Boni & Liveright, 1922).

*The Arts (Simon & Schuster, 1937, 1939; Liveright, 1974).

*The Fall of the Dutch Republic (Houghton Mifflin, 1913, 1924).

*Fighters for Freedom: Jefferson and Bolivar (Dodd, Mead, 1962).

The Golden Book of the Dutch Navigators (Century, 1916; D. Appleton Century, 1938).

*History with a Match, Being an Account of the Earliest Navigators and the Discovery of America (David McKay, 1917).

How to Look at Pictures: A Short History of Painting (Modern Age Books for National Committee for Art Appreciation, 1938).

Invasion (Harcourt, Brace & Co., 1940).

Life and Times of Johann Sebastian Bach (G. G. Harrap, 1942).

Life and Times of Pieter Stuyvesant (H. Holt & Co., 1928).

The Life and Times of Rembrandt van Rijn (Garden City, 1930; Liveright, 1943).

The Life and Times of Simon Bolivar (Dodd, Mead, 1943).

The Message of the Bells; or, What Happened to Us on Christmas Eve (Garden City, 1942).

Observations on the Mystery of Print and the Work of Johann Gutenberg (Second National Book Fair/Book Manufacturer's Institute, 1937).

Our Battle: Being One Man's Answer to My Battle, by Adolf Hitler (Simon & Schuster, 1938).

R. v R., the life of Rembrandt van Rijn (For the Members of the Heritage Club, 1939).

Report to Saint Peter, Upon the Kind of World in Which Hendrik Willem van Loon Spent the First Years of His Life (Simon & Schuster, 1947; G. G. Harrap, 1948).

Rise of the Dutch Kingdom, 1795–1813 (Doubleday, Page & Co., 1915).

*Romance of Discovery, Being an Account of the Earliest Navigators and the Discovery of America (Carlton House, 1937).

Ships and How They Sailed the Seven Seas (5000 B.C.—A.D. 1935) (Simon & Schuster, 1935).

Story of America (Liveright, 1942).

Story of Inventions: Man, the Miracle Maker (Garden City, 1934).

*The Story of Mankind (Boni & Liveright, 1921, 1926; Macmillan, 1923; Garden City, 1938; Liveright, 1951, 1972, 1984, 1999).

*illustrated by the author

The Story of Mankind: Including a New Final Chapter Which Brings the Material Up to the European War of 1938 (Pocket Books, 1939).

The Story of the Bible (Boni & Liveright, 1923; Garden City, 1936; Liveright, 1946; Grosset & Dunlap, 1966; Bell/Crown, 1985).

The Story of the Pacific (Harcourt, Brace & Co., 1940).

Story of Wilbur the Hat: Being a True Account of the Strange Things Which Sometimes Happen in a Part of the World Which Does Not Exist: Written and Drawn for the Fun of It by Hendrik Willem van Loon (Liveright, 1925).

Thomas Jefferson (Dodd, Mead, 1943).

Tolerance (Boni & Liveright, 1925,1927; Garden City, 1933; Liveright, 1940).

Van Loon's Geography: The Story of the World We Live In (Simon & Schuster, 1932).

Van Loon's Lives (Simon & Schuster, 1942).

A World Divided Is a World Lost (Cosmos, 1935).

For More Information About/by Hendrik van Loon

Autobiography: 1940. *Invasion.* Harcourt, Brace & Co.

Autobiography: 1947. *Report to Saint Peter, Upon the Kind of World in Which Hendrik Willem Van Loon Spent the First Years of His Life.* Simon & Schuster.

Commire, Anne, ed. 1980. *Something About the Author: Facts and Pictures About Contemporary Authors and Illustrators of Books for Young People.* Vol. 18. Gale Research.

van Loon, Gerard Willem. 1972. *The Story of Hendrik Willem van Loon.* Lippincott.

van Loon, Hendrik Willem. 1921. *The Story of Mankind.* Boni & Liveright.

1923: Hugh Lofting

Born	January 14, 1886
	Maidenhead, Berkshire, England
Married	Flora Small, 1912 (died 1927) (children: Elizabeth and Colin)
	Katherine Harrower-Peters, 1928 (died 1929)
	Josephine Fricker, 1935 (children: Christopher)
Died	September 26 (27?), 1947
	Santa Monica, California

Awards and Honors

Newbery Medal (Animal Stories, Adventure): *The Voyages of Doctor Dolittle* (Frederick A. Stokes, 1922)

About the Author and His Writing

There are many people who can speak more than one language. But how many people can understand the language of animals and speak it as well?

Hugh Lofting couldn't talk to animals, but out of his imagination sprang a doctor who could do just that. Doctor Dolittle may be the best-known doctor of all time, at least to anyone who loves a good story.

Hugh John Lofting was born in England to an Irish father and an English mother. Besides Hugh, his family included four brothers and a sister. Hugh was an imaginative child and loved to create stories to tell his brothers and sisters. He also loved animals and had many pets as a child. He even kept a miniature zoo in his mother's linen closet, with toy animals, of course.

> I make no claim to be an authority on writing or illustrating for children. The fact that I have been successful merely means that I can write and illustrate in my own way. (Commire 1979, 15:183)

At the age of eight, Hugh was sent to a boarding school. He rarely saw his family after that. He studied engineering and became an engineer. Although he hated his job and didn't think he made a very good engineer, it did allow him to do a lot of traveling to various parts of the world. Many of the places where he traveled later became the settings for Doctor Dolittle's adventures.

In 1912, Hugh married Flora Small of New York. The newlyweds settled in the United States and had two children, Elizabeth and Colin.

Then came World War I. Hugh joined the British Army, serving in France and Flanders. Many things about the war upset him. The violence deeply troubled him, and he became a great believer in working for peace. He thought that the best way to achieve a lasting peace for all people was through the education of children.

During the time he spent fighting in the war, Hugh became more and more disturbed by the tremendous amount of hatred between people of different races. In the same way,

Hugh thought that the animals were treated unfairly. "However seriously a soldier was wounded, his life was not despaired of: all the resources of a surgery highly developed by the war were brought to his aid," Hugh wrote. "A seriously wounded horse was put out by a timely bullet. This did not seem quite fair. If we made the animals take the same chances as we did ourselves, why did we not give them similar attention when wounded?" (Commire 1979, 15:182).

> Another trouble with the average writing for children is that authors always seem to think they must "write down" to them. I have found that the intelligent children (and I'm afraid the intelligent children are the only kind I am interested in) resent nothing so much as being written down to or talked down to. (Kunitz and Haycraft 1951, 199)

Hugh's concern for the animals, along with his children's request that he write them letters about his experiences, led to the creation of Doctor Dolittle. "My children at home wanted letters from me—and they wanted them with illustrations rather than without. There seemed very little of interest to write to youngsters from the Front: the news was either too horrible or too dull. And it was all censored. One thing, however, that kept forcing itself more and more on my attention was the very considerable part the animals were playing in the World War. That was the beginning of the idea: an eccentric country physician with a bent for natural history and a great love of pets, who finally decides to give up his human practice for the more difficult, more sincere, and for him, more attractive therapy of the animal kingdom" (Commire 1979, 15:182). A new hero, Doctor Dolittle, was born.

After being wounded in the war, Hugh was discharged from the army. His wife encouraged him to try and publish the Doctor Dolittle letters as a book. During the voyage that took Hugh back to America, he met an author, Cecil Roberts, who learned of the Dolittle stories. He read them and liked them so much he gave Hugh the name of his publisher in New York. In 1920, *The Story of Doctor Dolittle* (Frederick A. Stokes, 1920) was published and became an instant hit.

Hugh then wrote and illustrated *The Voyages of Doctor Dolittle,* published in 1922. Not only was this book a popular success like the first, it was awarded the second Newbery Medal in 1923. From that point on, Hugh's new career was established: that of an author and illustrator.

Doctor Dolittle began as a cheerful, charming doctor who became more serious as his adventures continued. This was perhaps a parallel to Hugh's life. His adulthood was marked with several sorrows. His first wife died in 1927, only four years after his great success in winning the Newbery Medal. He married Katherine Harrower-Peters in 1928, but she died less than a year later. In 1935, Hugh married Josephine Fricker, and they had a son, Christopher.

Eleven years after the birth of Christopher, Hugh John Lofting died at the age of 61. In the twenty-seven years that followed the publication of his first Doctor Dolittle book, Hugh wrote thirteen other books about the kindly doctor, as well as a number of other books for children. The Doctor Dolittle stories are still some of the best loved of all time.

A Word to My Readers:

If we make children see that all races, given equal physical and mental chances for development, have about the same batting averages of good and bad, we shall have laid another very substantial foundation stone in the edifice of peace and internationalism. (Commire 1979, 15:183)

Books by Hugh Lofting

Doctor Dolittle: A Treasury (Lippincott, 1967; London: Capte, 1968).

Doctor Dolittle and the Green Canary (Lippincott, 1950).

Doctor Dolittle and the Secret Lake (Lippincott, 1948).

Doctor Dolittle in the Moon (Frederick A. Stokes, 1928; Lippincott, 1956; Penguin, 1968).

Doctor Dolittle's Caravan (Frederick A. Stokes, 1926; Delacorte Press, Dell, 1988).

Doctor Dolittle's Circus (Frederick A. Stokes, 1924; Delacorte Press, 1988).

Doctor Dolittle's Garden (Frederick A. Stokes, 1927).

Doctor Dolittle's Post Office (Frederick A. Stokes, 1923; Lippincott, 1960; Dell, 1988).

Doctor Dolittle's Puddleby Adventures (Lippincott, 1952).

Gub Gub's Book (Simon & Schuster Books for Young Readers, 1992).

Gub Gub's Book: An Encyclopedia of Food (Frederick A. Stokes, 1932).

Noisy Nora (Frederick A. Stokes, 1929).

Porridge Poetry, Cooked, Ornamented, and Served Up by Hugh Lofting (Frederick A. Stokes, 1924).

The Story of Doctor Dolittle (*Dover, 1997; William Morrow, 1997).

The Story of Doctor Dolittle, Being the History of His Peculiar Life at Home and Astonishing Adventures in Foreign Parts (*Frederick A. Stokes, 1920; Delacorte Press, 1988).

The Story of Mrs. Tubbs (Frederick A. Stokes, 1923; Lippincott, 1968).

Tommy, Tilly and Mrs. Tubbs (Frederick A. Stokes, 1936, 1937).

The Twilight of Magic (Frederick A. Stokes, 1930; Lippincott, 1967; Simon & Schuster Books for Young Readers, 1993).

The Voyages of Doctor Dolittle (*Frederick A. Stokes, 1922; *Lippincott, 1950; *Delacorte Press, 1988; Grosset & Dunlap, 1998).

*illustrated by the author

For More Information About/by Hugh Lofting

Commire, Anne, ed. 1979. *Something About the Author: Facts and Pictures About Contemporary Authors and Illustrators of Books for Young People.* Vol. 15. Gale Research.

Kunitz, Stanley J., and Howard Haycraft, eds. 1951. *The Junior Book of Authors.* 2d ed. H. W. Wilson.

1924: Charles Boardman Hawes

Born	January 24, 1889 Clifton Spring, New York
Married	Dorothea Cable, 1916 (children: Pete and another son)
Died	July 15, 1923

Awards and Honors

Newbery Medal (Action and Adventure): *The Dark Frigate* (Atlantic Monthly Press, 1923)

Newbery Honor Book for 1922: *The Great Quest: A Romance of 1926* (Atlantic Monthly Press, 1921)

About the Author and His Writing

Charles Boardman Hawes, the third person to win the Newbery Medal, never even knew he had received such a high honor. He died shortly after the publication of his winning book, *The Dark Frigate*. Ironically, the hero of *The Dark Frigate* was a sailor who fought for the king at Newbury in England, where John Newbery—the man for whom the Newbery Medal was named—had lived.

The Newbery Medal wasn't the first one of Hawes's books to win an award, however. *The Great Quest* won a Newbery Honor Medal in 1922, the first year that this award was given.

> From curious old books, many of them forgotten save by students of archaic days at sea, I have taken words and phrases and incidents. The words and phrases I have put into the talk of the men of the Rose of Devon; the incidents I have shaped and fitted anew to serve my purpose. (Miller and Field 1955, 32)

As a teenager, Charles, or "Carl" as he was called by close friends and family, enjoyed going for long walks. He had trouble finding people to join him on these walks, because most of his friends considered a long walk to be no more than five or ten miles. Carl's definition of a long walk: twenty or thirty miles. Only that kind of distance qualified as a real, honest-to-goodness walk in his mind.

In 1916, Carl married his wife, Dorothea; they had two sons. He loved being a father to his boys. When his first child was born, Carl's mother asked him what name he wanted the children to call him. "The Old Man," he replied, and from then on, that was how he was known by his boys.

The Old Man spent many hours reading poetry to his little sons. "Do they understand it?" he said. "Probably not, though how do we know? At least they love the rollicking rhythms. And if they learn the whole music of it now, later they will come into their inheritance" (Miller and Field 1955, 31).

Carl wrote books but also worked as a teacher and a staff member on the journal *Youth's Companion.* He served as an assistant editor of *Open Road* magazine and volunteered for the library committee in his hometown.

Except for finding walking partners, Carl never had a problem making friends. His honesty, warmth, deep laugh, and courteous nature made him well liked wherever he went. He always spoke the truth, even when his opinion differed from that of everyone else, but everyone respected him because they knew he was a man of good character.

There is little else known about this man who left a mark on the literary world even though his life was brief. The Old Man was a young man when he died in his early thirties. His wife, Dorothea, gave the Newbery Medal acceptance speech in place of her late husband.

Charles "Carl" Boardman Hawes would have been honored to know that his book *The Dark Frigate* had received so great a tribute as to win the Newbery Medal. In Dorothea's speech, she said that "Today, receiving that Medal for my husband, I dare to hope that you are telling me, and telling American children the country over, that he has made, with *The Dark Frigate,* what only I know how much he wanted to make, a contribution, however small, to the truth that shall set us all free. In his name, I thank you" (Miller and Field 1955, 32).

> Is fact the only truth? Does not imagination—the seeing eye—sometimes strike far beyond fact, to the very heart of truth? (Dorothea Hawes, in the Newbery acceptance speech given on behalf of her husband; from the preface to *The Dark Frigate*)

> **A Word to My Readers:**
>
> (In a conversation with his two year old, Pete)
> "Come on, Pete, let's go for an adventure."
> "Where is adventure, Old Man?"
> "Around every corner."
> (Miller and Field 1955, 30)

Books by Charles Boardman Hawes

The Dark Frigate (Atlantic Monthly Press, 1923; Little, Brown, 1996, 1971).

The Great Quest: A Romance of 1826 (Atlantic Monthly Press, 1921).

The Mutineers (Atlantic Monthly Press, 1920; Little, Brown, 1941).

For More Information About/by Charles Boardman Hawes

Hawes, Charles. *The Dark Frigate* (Atlantic Monthly Press, 1923).

Miller, Bertha Mahony, and Elinor Whitney Field, eds. 1955. *Newbery Medal Books: 1922–1955.* Horn Book.

1925: Charles Joseph Finger

Born	December 25, 1869 Willesden, Sussex, England
Married	Nellie B. Ferguson, June 7, 1902 (children: Hubert Philip, Charles Joseph, Herbert Eric, Helen, and Kitty)
Died	January 7, 1941

Awards and Honors

Newbery Medal (Action and Adventure): *Tales from Silver Lands* (Doubleday, Page & Co., 1924)

About the Author and His Writing

From musician to prospector, sailor to writer, Charles Joseph Finger lived life to the fullest. In everything he did he gave his best and was never short on enthusiasm or energy.

Born December 25, 1869, in Willesden, Sussex, England, Charles Joseph Finger grew up in London and was educated in the finest private schools. His childhood was a pleasant one, and his memories of Christmastime were especially vivid. "Glorious were the festivals of my boyhood," he wrote. "As if it were yesterday I see, with my mind's eye, the glittering tree, thickly hung with shining things. Poor would have been the Christmas that did not bring a new Jules Verne, a Boy's Annual, a Henty, a Kingstone, or some other book brilliantly illustrated." He read often. "The day was barren on which I did not have a book in hand, and I read riding, walking in crowded streets, at mealtimes" (Commire 1985, 42:79).

> The idea of becoming a cogwheel in the world's machinery stuck with me, but I wanted to be a wheel, not a point on the rim of one. (Commire 1985, 42:80)

The spirit of adventure took Charles to the sea before he even reached the age of twenty. In his late teens, he became a merchant seaman. He traveled to South America, Mexico, Canada, and then to Alaska, where he prospected for gold. Charles spent a number of years living in South America, and it was the stories he learned from the Indians there that later became the basis for his Newbery winning book, *Tales from Silver Lands*.

Charles attended King's College in London and studied music in Germany. He chose to settle in the United States in 1887. He became a naturalized citizen nine years later, in 1896. On June 7, 1902, he married Nellie B. Ferguson. They had three sons and two daughters. His daughter Helen remembers him as "a tremendously vital man, physically and mentally" (Miller and Field 1955, 37).

He first published an article for a magazine called *Youth's Companion* and earned twenty-five dollars for it. It would be many years before he wrote again. He became

11

director of the Conservatory of Music in San Angelo, Texas, and then worked for the railroad. In 1920, he turned to editing and wrote and published a one-man magazine, *All's Well.*

At the age of fifty, Charles began to realize how much more time he spent on his job than on his family. "It came to me with all the force of a blow that my five children were growing up, and, except for seeing them at the week-end, I was a stranger to them" (Commire 1985, 42:84). He gave up his career in the business world and moved his family to Arkansas, where he bought a run-down old farm. When Finger could not keep up with the bills, he turned to writing as a way of supporting his family. He used an old stone building on a wooded hillside near his home as his office.

> I cannot separate enjoyment from writing. (Commire 1985, 42:85)

A friend suggested that Charles write a book about all his adventures as a young man. The stories for *Tales from Silver Lands* were first heard by his children. During the evenings, the family gathered around the big fireplace, and Charles told the tales that would later become his Newbery Medal–winning book. After winning the Newbery Medal, Finger went on to write close to two dozen more books. Although his early writing was mostly for adults, he turned to children's books as his own grandchildren were born and grew.

It was not only his children who enjoyed hearing his stories. Charles loved to entertain friends by reading to them from the many books that lined the walls of his living room. The visitors who came to the Finger household included authors and poets, critics and editors.

Charles Joseph Finger died from influenza on January 7, 1941, at the age of seventy-one. He wrote thirty-five books in the years he devoted to his writing. He lived a life of adventure and traveled to many parts of the world. But, as his daughter Helen wrote, "Perhaps it is in the role of weaver of fairy tales that we like to remember him best" (Miller and Field 1955, 38).

A Word to My Readers:

A man has to cultivate somehow a sort of zest. He has to be interested. He must go through life with a lilt, not trudge along. Above all, he must believe in himself, not seeing failure in what are, after all, merely stumbling blocks and quite in the routine of things, but trying his experiment to the end. (Commire 1985, 42:85)

Books by Charles Joseph Finger

Adventure Under Sapphire Skies (William Morrow, 1931), with sketches by his wife, Helen Finger.

Affair at the Inn as Seen by Philo the Innkeeper & the Taxgatherer of Rome (Richard W. Ellis, Georgian Press, 1931).

Boswell's Life of Johnson (Haldeman Julius, 1923).

Bushrangers (McBride & Co., 1924).

Courageous Companions (Longmans, Green & Co., 1929), illustrated by Newbery Medal–winner James Daugherty.

The Distant Prize: A Book About Rovers, Rangers, and Rascals (D. Appleton Century, 1935).

Foot-loose in the West (W. Morrow, 1932), with sketches by his wife, Helen Finger.

Free Fantasia on Books and Reading (Haldeman Julius, 1924).

Frontier Ballads, Heard and Gathered by Charles J. Finger (Doubleday, Page & Co., 1927).

Highwaymen: A Book of Gallant Rogues (Books for Libraries Press, 1970).

Historic Crimes and Criminals (Haldeman Julius, 1922).

In Lawless Lands (M. Kennerly, 1924; Books for Libraries Press, 1971).

Joseph Addison and His Time (Haldeman Julius, 1922).

Life of Barnum, the Man Who Lured the Herd (Haldeman Julius, 1924).

Life of Theodore Roosevelt (Haldeman Julius, 1924).

Lost Civilizations (Haldeman Julius, 1922).

Magellan and the Pacific (Haldeman Julius, 1924).

Mahomet (Haldeman Julius, 1923).

Romantic Rascals (McBride & Co., 1927; Books for Libraries Press, 1969).

Sailor Chanties and Cowboy Songs, compiled by C. J. Finger (Norwood Editions, 1974; Folcroft Library Editions, 1977; R. West, 1978).

Seven Horizons (Doubleday, Doran & Co., 1930).

Spreading Stain: A Tale for Boys and Men with Boys' Hearts (Doubleday, Page & Co., 1927).

Tales from Silver Lands (Doubleday, Page & Co., 1924).

Tales Worth Telling (Century, 1927).

Valiant Vagabonds (D. Appleton Century, 1936; Books for Libraries Press, 1968).

When Guns Thundered at Tripoli (H. Holt & Co., 1937).

For More Information About/by Charles Joseph Finger

Commire, Anne, ed. 1985. *Something About the Author: Facts and Pictures About Contemporary Authors and Illustrators of Books for Young People.* Vol. 42. Gale Research.

Miller, Bertha Mahony and Elinor Whitney Field, eds. 1955. *Newbery Medal Books: 1922–1955.* Horn Book.

1926: Arthur Bowie Chrisman

Born	July 16, 1889
	West Brook, Virginia
Died	February 24, 1953
	Shirley, Arkansas

Awards and Honors

Newbery Medal (Action and Adventure): *Shen of the Sea: A Book for Children* (Dutton, 1925)

About the Author and His Writing

Arthur Bowie Chrisman was a born storyteller. He learned to read as soon as he could crawl and to write as soon as he could walk. Perhaps this explains his later success as an author.

The sixth child and third son born to Isaac Arthur and Mary Louis Bryarly Chrisman, Arthur was descended from one of the thirteen original pioneer families who had come to the Shenandoah Valley in 1732. He grew up on a large farm, doing his share of the daily chores, milking cows, chopping wood, and everything in between. He attended a one-room schoolhouse where all the grade levels were taught in one large room.

Whenever he had time, Arthur told stories to his brothers and sisters and anyone who would listen. In good weather, he often sat up in a tree, weaving tales about animals, especially his favorite character, "Little Pig." When the weather forced him inside, he spent hours in an old, abandoned building that had been the home of slaves many years before. "Here I kept all of my treasures," he wrote. "Clay men and clay jugs, sailing ships, and bows and arrows, sand mills and wind mills, water mills and heat mills, sleds, wagons, fishing poles and many other contrivances, all made by my own hands. I never owned more than a half dozen bought toys in my life, but made my own toys in the thousands" (Miller and Field 1955, 42).

> I never have written with the idea of making a fortune, I merely decided to write and let fate take care of all subsequent happenings. (Miller and Field 1955, 42)

Arthur enjoyed hearing the stories that others had to tell. One friend, Mr. Burke, had been an Indian fighter and told young Arthur stories of his western adventures. Mr. Looky, another companion, filled his imagination with tales of wild animals. He also loved the stories of Edgar Allan Poe. Arthur never tired of hearing stories or of writing his own.

It wasn't until Arthur turned eighteen that he began to write down his stories with the intention of trying to sell them. It took him six years before even a short poem was published, for which he did not receive any pay. This didn't bother him. He never wrote with the goal of making lots of money. He wrote because he loved stories.

For a time, Arthur explored California, traveling on foot. He studied history and wrote. While working on one story, he went to a Chinese shop to learn about the foods his Asian character might eat. In the process, Arthur struck up a friendship with the Chinese shopkeeper. This increased his fascination with China, and he began to focus on stories from this land. He published one of the stories that later became a part of *Shen of the Sea*. It took seven more years before he finished the collection of sixteen Chinese folktales that made up this classic book that won the Newbery Medal in 1926. He published only two more books after this.

In the 1930s, Arthur returned to his hometown farm. The children of the town, including several of his own nieces, realized what a treasure they had in this man who could keep them spellbound with his wonderful tales. They watched for him to walk to the post office, then insisted that he tell them stories. Arthur liked to lie down under an old black walnut tree, cracking nuts as he talked.

Arthur Bowie Chrisman once wrote, "it is one of my weaknesses always to babble of the old times, which were the good times, and say very little of myself" (Kunitz and Haycraft 1951, 69). Although he was shy about talking of his own life, thankfully he left behind a few wonderful books to remember him by. He died in 1953.

A Word to My Readers:

My favorite motto has always been an old Chinese proverb: "Walk slowly, perhaps the river will have receded when you come to it." (Miller and Field 1955, 43)

Books by Arthur Bowie Chrisman

Shen of the Sea: A Book for Children (Dutton, 1925, 1968).

Treasures Long Hidden: Old Tales and New Tales of the East (Dutton, 1941).

The Wind That Wouldn't Blow: Stories of the Merry Middle Kingdom for Children, and Myself (Dutton, 1927).

For More Information About/by Arthur Bowie Chrisman

Kunitz, Stanley J., and Howard Haycraft, eds. 1951. *The Junior Book of Authors.* 2d ed. H. W. Wilson.

Miller, Bertha Mahony, and Elinor Whitney Field, eds. 1955. *Newbery Medal Books: 1922–1955.* Horn Book.

1927: Will James

Born	June 6, 1892
	near Great Falls, Montana
Died	September 3, 1942
	Hollywood, California

Awards and Honors

Newbery Medal (Western): *Smoky, the Cowhorse* (C. Scribner's Sons, 1926)

About the Author and His Writing

On June 6, 1892, Will James arrived in the world on a quilt spread out in the middle of a prairie where his mother gave birth. "My first squint at sunlight was under a canvas flap and the first sounds that come to my ears was the jingling of my dad's spurs, the nickering of horses, and the bellering of cattle" (Kunitz and Haycraft 1951, 170).

Will's rugged beginning set the stage for several years of tough times. His mother died when he was only one year old. His father, a cowman, suffered a fatal injury three years later while handling cattle. Before he died, he asked that his good friend, a French Canadian trapper and prospector named Jean Beaupre, adopt and raise his little boy. "He turned out to be as mighty fine a foster father to me as any real father could ever been," Will remembered. "I know I must of been a daggone nuisance plenty of times but he sure never showed that I was" (Kunitz and Haycraft 1951, 170).

> I know a lot of things I'd rather do than write or talk about myself: I'd a heap rather be roping or branding, or just mix in a corralful of good horses. (Kunitz and Haycraft 1951, 169)

Jean and Will traveled into Canada during the fur trapping seasons. Will didn't like to go that far because it meant leaving behind his beloved horse until spring came and they returned south.

While Will was a young teen, his adopted father drowned in a river. From then on, the boy was on his own. He decided to follow in his birth father's footsteps and become a cowboy.

From an early age, Will liked to draw, but he might never have developed this talent if he hadn't wound up in jail, serving time for stealing cattle. He passed the hours by doodling and drawing. He became serious about illustrating while recovering from a horseback riding accident. He sold a few drawings to a magazine. Will's first published illustration was of a horse, Smoky, which he sold to *Sunset* magazine for twenty-five dollars. *Time* magazine later wrote that Will James "was a cowboy until a bucking horse threw him into writing" (Kunitz and Haycraft 1951, 171).

A friend suggested that Will write stories to go along with his drawings of horses. Although he had never attended school, Will had learned to read and write from his adopted father and from old magazines he picked up at various cow camps. He followed his friend's advice and wrote a short article and sent it to a publisher in the east, who bought the story. Before long Will was writing books.

Will actually wrote his Newbery award–winning book *Smoky, the Cowhorse* for adults, so the announcement that he had won a medal for the best children's book of the year came as a shock. "I don't know about that medal, but it's fine with me," he said (Miller and Field 1955, 42). Some criticized the book for its use of language and improper grammar, but children loved the story of the cowhorse who is stolen and later reunited with his beloved owner.

> I write for everybody in general, like I would talk to friends who are interested in what I have to say. (Kunitz and Haycraft 1951, 171)

As well as being a writer and illustrator, Will worked in a rodeo and on a ranch and even as an extra in Western movies. When the rodeo came to New York City, Will rode down Fifth Avenue on a horse. The rodeo stopped in front of the Scribner Building, home of Will's publisher. Will's friends gathered at the windows and waved excitedly at this unique man who had found his way into the homes and hearts of so many readers.

Will died in 1942. From his birth on the prairie to his death in Hollywood, California, Will remained down to earth, unaffected by his fame, and happy to be known as a cowboy who wrote wonderful books.

A Word to My Readers:

I hope I have a chance to talk to you sometimes through them books of mine and that you enjoy riding along with me. (Kunitz and Haycraft 1951, 171)

Books by Will James

All in the Day's Riding (C. Scribner's Sons, 1933; Mountain Press, 1998).

Big Enough (C. Scribner's Sons, 1931; Mountain Press, 1997).

Cowboy in the Making (C. Scribner's Sons, 1937).

Cowboys, North and South (C. Scribner's Sons, 1924; Arno Press, 1975; Mountain Press, 1995).

Cow Country (C. Scribner's Sons, 1927; Mountain Press, 1995).

The Dark Horse (C. Scribner's Sons, 1939).

Drifting Cowboy (C. Scribner's Sons, 1925; Mountain Press, 1995).

Flint Spears: Cowboy Rodeo Contestant (C. Scribner's Sons, 1938).

Home Ranch (C. Scribner's Sons, 1935; Mountain Press, 1999).

In the Saddle with Uncle Bill (C. Scribner's Sons, 1935; Mountain Press, 2001).

*illustrated by the author

Lone Cowboy: My Life Story (C. Scribner's Sons, 1930; University of Nebraska Press, 1985; Mountain Press, 1996).

Look-See with Uncle Bill (C. Scribner's Sons, 1938).

My First Horse (C. Scribner's Sons, 1940).

Sand (C. Scribner's Sons, 1929; Sun Dial Press, 1941; Mountain Press, 1996).

Scorpion, A Good Bad Horse (C. Scribner's Sons, 1936; University of Nebraska Press, 1975; Mountain Press, 2001).

Smoky, the Cow Horse (C. Scribner's Sons, 1926, 1929; Aladdin Books, 1987; Aladdin Books, Maxwell Macmillian International, 1993; Mountain Press, 2000).

Sun Up: Tales of the Cow Camps (C. Scribner's Sons, 1931; Mountain Press, 1997).

Tenderfoot (Niggard & Elliot, 1993).

The Three Mustangeers (C. Scribner's Sons, 1933; Mountain Press, 1999).

Uncle Bill: A Tale of Two Kids and a Cowboy (Mountain Press, 1998).

The Will James Cowboy Book (C. Scribner's Sons, 1938).

Young Cowboy (arranged from *Big Enough* and *Sun Up;* C. Scribner's Sons, 1935; Mountain Press, 2000).

For More Information About/by Will James

Autobiography: 1930. *Lone Cowboy: My Life Story.* C. Scribner's Sons.

Kunitz, Stanley J., and Howard Haycraft, eds. 1951. *The Junior Book of Authors.* 2d ed. H. W. Wilson.

Miller, Bertha Mahony, and Elinor Whitney Field, eds. 1955. *Newbery Medal Books: 1922–1955.* Horn Book.

1928: Dhan Gopal Mukerji

Born	July 6, 1890
	Calcutta, India
Married	Ethel Ray Dugan, 1918 (children: Dhan Gopal II)
Died	July 14, 1936
	New York

Awards and Honors

Newbery Medal (Historical Fiction): *Gay Neck, the Story of a Pigeon* (Dutton, 1927)

About the Author and His Writing

Dhan Gopal Mukerji was a man of many different words. Along with the language of his native country of India, he learned to speak Japanese, French, and English. Dhan treasured the value and power of words. Not one who cared for chitchat and trivial conversation, he preferred to delve into deeper questions. Dhan loved to talk about intellectual and spiritual issues, and often asked people he met for the first time, "What is your religion?" or "What is your conception of God?" (Miller and Field 1955, 56). His intensity sprang from his profound interest in people and their lives and in discovering what was important to them. Yet along with his intensity, Dhan was a man with a quick wit and a vibrant sense of humor.

Born near Calcutta, Dhan was the son of Brahmin parents who were priests in a Hindu temple near Calcutta. Their ministry was, in a way, a "family business," as Dhan's ancestors had served in that same temple for centuries. It's hard to imagine any business these days that has been in a person's family for such a long time. Dhan studied to be a Hindu priest, and although he did not pursue this vocation, it surely was an influence in his life and in his writing.

> In every one of my books hides a lesson. (Miller and Field 1955, 60)

Dhan spent his childhood immersed in religion and in the folktales native to his culture. In his own words, "Because stories were told to me, I in turn developed the habit of storytelling" (Miller and Field 1955, 62). When he grew up, Mukerji spent many hours telling stories to schoolchildren and taught Hindu folklore and culture. He once said that the major preoccupation of all his writing centered around translating his beloved Hindu folktales into English so they could be shared with a larger audience. This was no easy task. Dhan often had to work hard to arrange words that could translate the concepts and flow of the Hindu language into English.

At the age of eighteen, Dhan spent a year in Japan. From there, at the age of nineteen, he moved to the United States where he lived the remainder of his life. He married Ethel Ray Dugan in 1918, and they had one son.

In 1928, Dhan's book *Gay Neck, the Story of a Pigeon* was awarded the Newbery Medal. The title minimizes what is a powerful book. Gay Neck is no ordinary pigeon but a particular breed: the carrier pigeon, a remarkable bird that is now extinct.

Carrier pigeons played a significant role during World War I. In a time before radio, television, and computers, carrier pigeons were used to send messages back and forth to troops in various parts of battle. Without the carrier pigeons, many more human lives may have been lost during the war.

> The habits that our children are forming today will largely determine the character of their leadership tomorrow. (Miller and Field 1955, 62)

Dhan wrote *Gay Neck, the Story of a Pigeon* during the war. The facts of the story are based on Dhan's own childhood encounters with carrier pigeons. "Most of it is a record of my experiences with about forty pigeons and their leader. Alas, as I went on writing the book I had to go beyond my experiences, and had to draw upon those of the trainers of army pigeons" (Miller and Field 1955, 62). Thus the story of Gay Neck, though fiction, is authentic in its details.

Gay Neck is fascinating not only because it depicts the life of a bird now extinct but also because of its strong antiwar message. Dhan hoped to clearly illustrate the tragedy of war. Within that goal, he sought to show the strong connection between people and animals and how each depends upon the other for protection and life.

Dhan died in 1936, not long after his forty-sixth birthday and less than a decade after winning the Newbery Medal. He had written other books in that time in an ongoing effort to bring the life and legends of India into the lives of young readers everywhere.

A Word to My Readers:

Until a nation appreciates the common culture of another nation it will not be able to understand the value of international peace . . . If we know early in life how good our neighbor's culture can be, we shall think twice before we decide to destroy it by warfare. (Miller and Field 1955, 64)

Books by Dhan Gopal Mukerji

Bunny, Hound and Clown (Dutton, 1931).

Caste and Outcast (Dutton, 1923; J. M. Dent & Sons, 1929).

The Chief of the Herd (Dutton, 1929).

Daily Meditation; or, The Practice of Repose (Dutton, 1933).

Devotional Passages from the Hindu Bible, Adapted into English (Dutton, 1929).

Disillusioned India (Dutton, 1930).

The Face of Silence (Dutton, 1926; Servire, 1973; Borgo Press, 1985).

Fierce-Face: The Story of a Tiger (Dutton, 1936).

Gay Neck, the Story of a Pigeon (Dutton, 1927, 1968).

Ghond, the Hunter (Dutton, 1928).

Hari, the Jungle Lad (Dutton, 1924, 1937).

Hindu Fables, for Little Children (Dutton, 1929).

The Song of God: Translation of the Bhagavad-Gita (Dutton, 1931).

For More Information About/by Dhan Gopal Mukerji

Autobiography: 1923. *Caste and Outcast.* Dutton.

Miller, Bertha Mahony, and Elinor Whitney Field, eds. 1955. *Newbery Medal Books: 1922–1955.* Horn Book.

1929: Eric P. Kelly

Born   March 16, 1884
                 Amesbury, Massachusetts

Married   Katherine Collins Merrill, 1924

Died   January 3, 1960

Awards and Honors

Newbery Medal (Historical Fiction): *The Trumpeter of Krakow, a Tale of the Fifteenth Century* (Macmillan, 1928)

About the Author and His Writing

During the first ten years after Eric won the 1929 Newbery Medal for *The Trumpeter of Krakow,* it seemed to him as if "pen were never tranquil nor typewriter silent" (Miller and Field 1955, 66). Eric wrote ten books in the decade following his Newbery Medal and worked as a teacher at the same time.

Those whirlwind years reflected Eric's life up to that point. Born in Amesbury, Massachusetts, Eric's family moved to Denver, Colorado, in the late 1880s, when he was five. The family returned east and settled in New York when Eric was in high school. After graduation, he moved from home to attend college at Dartmouth.

> I don't know if you call it a song exactly, but it's a kind of vibration that issues from this city of Krakow that arouses a very tumult in my heart. (Miller and Field 1955, 70)

That was not the end of his travels. Kelly worked as a journalist, first in Massachusetts, then in New Jersey, New York, and Boston. When World War I broke out, Eric taught French to servicemen on their way overseas and later went to France to live and to work with French soldiers. While in France, Eric met many Polish exiles who encouraged him to come to Poland to organize a welfare system that would offer food and supplies to the many people who had been left destitute after the war.

Eric became so enamored of Poland and its people that he learned Polish and traveled throughout the countryside, exploring the culture and getting acquainted with the people. He was captivated by the depth and sincerity of the Polish spirit and by the people's enthusiasm and deep respect for creativity, especially in art and music. Eric shed much of the stuffiness that he felt had been part of his New England upbringing. "I found my style, I found myself, I found an expression other people seemed to like" (Kunitz and Haycraft 1951, 177).

After three years doing this work, Eric returned to the United States, taught, and wrote. He returned to Poland in 1925 to teach and study at the University of Krakow. It was during this time that he wrote *The Trumpeter of Krakow.* The book was in part inspired by an old church in the area, about which Eric wrote, "I did not let one day pass without spending some time within the walls of the church" (Miller and Field 1955, 71).

The book is a medieval story that takes place during the 1400s in Krakow. A young boy, Joseph, and his family have been entrusted with guarding Poland's most precious jewel, the Great Tarnov Crystal. The title of the book refers to the position held by Joseph's father: to trumpet a particular tune from the tower of the church during the hours of the night. Joseph learns to play the song and fills in for his father on various occasions. He saves the town from destruction one night by changing the end of the song, and sending a warning to the townspeople.

> That a fast moving world has swept me through scenes of indescribable change is something I rejoice at. (Kunitz and Haycraft 1951, 176)

When World War II began, Eric went to Mexico to work with Polish refugees who had fled their native land. He helped build a refuge for homeless Poles, a majority of whom were children. He took great pride in his work with the people whose country had won a place in his heart. "With all these people coming to a strange land, most of them suffering from malaria, undernourished, mentally distressed at separation from the other members of their families whom many were never to see again; I really am rejoiced in this, that I brought them all through without losing a single soul" (Miller and Field 1955, 67–68). His efforts on behalf of these children made Eric Kelly something of a "trumpeter of Krakow" himself.

Eric served as professor of journalism at Dartmouth College from 1929–54. He died on January 3, 1960.

A Word to My Readers:

Outside the changes and the loss of many whose generation is my generation, I am really quite happy in the existence which is mine. (Miller and Field 1955, 69)

Books by Eric P. Kelly

The Blacksmith of Vilno: A Tale of Poland in the Year 1832 (Macmillan, 1930).

From Star to Star, a Story of Krakow in 1493 (Lippincott, 1944).

A Girl Who Would be Queen: The Story and Diary of the Young Countess Krasinska (A. C. McClurg & Co., 1939).

The Golden Star of Halich: A Tale of the Red Land in 1362 (Macmillan, 1931).

The Hand in the Picture, a Story of Poland (Lippincott, 1947).

In Clean Hay: A Christmas Story (Frank D. Fortney, 1940; Macmillan, 1953).

The Land and People of Poland (Lippincott, 1964).

The Land of the Polish People (Frederick A. Stokes, 1943).

On the Staked Plain (Macmillan, 1940).

Polish Legends and Tales (Polish Publication Society of America, 1971).

The Trumpeter of Krakow, a Tale of the Fifteenth Century (Macmillan, 1928, 1966; Chatto & Windus, 1968; Aladdin Books, Maxwell Macmillan International, 1992).

For More Information About/by Eric P. Kelly

Kunitz, Stanley J., and Howard Haycraft, eds. 1951. *The Junior Book of Authors*. 2d ed. H. W. Wilson.

Miller, Bertha Mahony, and Elinor Whitney Field, eds. 1955. *Newbery Medal Books: 1922–1955*. Horn Book.

1930: Rachel Field

Born	September 19, 1894 Stockbridge, Massachusetts
Married	Arthur Pederson, 1935 (children: Hannah)
Died	March 14, 1942 Beverly Hills, California

Awards and Honors

Newbery Medal (Historical Fiction): *Hitty, Her First Hundred Years* (Macmillan, 1929)
Newbery Honor Book for 1932: *Calico Bush* (Macmillan, 1931)
Booksellers' Award: *Time Out of Mind* (Macmillan, 1935)

About the Author and Her Writing

Imagine a person who didn't learn to read until she was ten years old, and who then grew up to win the Newbery Medal for her skills as a writer. That person is Rachel Field, and the book, *Hitty, Her First Hundred Years* (Macmillan, 1929), made Rachel the first woman ever to win the Newbery Medal.

Rachel's early interest was not in writing but in the theater. She attended a little country school in Massachusetts where different grades were taught in the same classroom. Despite her inability to read, Rachel managed to get the leading roles in several of the plays produced by the school. "I couldn't read then but the parts were read aloud to me and I knew all the other children's lines as well as my own long before the dress rehearsals," she wrote. "Of course, I decided then and there to become a great actress" (Kunitz and Haycraft 1951, 123).

> It seems to me far more important to be able to remember exactly how a thing impressed you when you were a child than to guess how it may impress another child. (Commire 1979, 15:110)

When Rachel was eleven, her mother decided that it was time for her daughter to expand her education. The family moved to Springfield, Massachusetts. Rachel did not enjoy being in the public schools. "I never did catch up with my age in school work, and I never liked studying again till I got to college," she admits. "Report card day was a terror to me every time" (Kunitz and Haycraft 1951, 123–24).

Then in high school, Rachel won first prize for an essay. Along with the prize, she won twenty dollars. The winning essay led to her being accepted to Radcliffe College as a special student.

After college Rachel lived in New York, where she worked in several editorial jobs. In her spare time she wrote poetry and plays. Her first published book, *The Pointed People,* came out in 1924. Rachel illustrated the book of poems with silhouettes that she cut from black paper.

25

Although her first adult novel was turned down by a number of editors, several of them told Rachel that they liked the first part of the book, which described the childhood of the main character. The editors suggested that Rachel write books for children.

Rachel's curious mind and keen eye for details made her books interesting and delightful. "I was always able to take in details. I loved old houses, and I never entered one for the first time that I did not get an exact picture in my mind of at least one of the rooms" (Commire 1979, 15:113). This attention to detail, and her interest in history, served her well when it came time to write *Hitty*.

> There is one thing that Hitty and the Medal have in common and that is the past. I never get over that such things as old samplers, toys, and little tattered children's books should be here for us to see and touch long after those who made and handled them are gone. (Miller and Field 1955, 87–88)

Hitty was an actual doll that Rachel and her friend, Dorothy Lathrop, found in an antique shop. They both loved the doll and later returned to the antique shop to buy her. Dorothy suggested that Rachel write the story of the doll's life, while Dorothy agreed to illustrate the book. Writing a story that covered one hundred years of American history was more work than Rachel had expected, although she said that "I feel as if I, myself, had very little to do with it. It is as if Hitty took things into her own mountain ashwood hands right from the start" (Miller and Field 1955, 86). Hitty even attended the Newbery Medal award ceremony, perhaps the first and only doll to do so.

Rachel spent her summers on a small, wooded island off the coast of Maine. "I suppose it, more than any one other thing in my life, has helped me with my writing. For it means roots and background to me. It creeps into nearly everything I write and I never want to be anywhere else when summer comes around" (Kunitz and Haycraft 1951, 125).

In 1935, Rachel married Arthur Pederson. They adopted a daughter, Hannah, in 1939. Rachel continued to write books, plays, and poems and started to focus her efforts on novels for adults. Her first such book, *Time Out of Mind* (Macmillan, 1935), was published in April 1935. She dedicated the book to her husband. It became an immediate best-seller. The novel also received the Booksellers' Award as the most distinguished novel of its year. Her next novel, *All This, and Heaven Too* (Macmillan, 1938), was also a great success and even became a motion picture.

It seemed as though Rachel Field's career as an author would be long and prosperous. But her health began to fail. In 1942 Rachel developed a severe case of pneumonia after having surgery and died. She was only forty-eight years old.

> ### A Word to My Readers:
> (About the writing of Hitty) I tried to select every word and phrase carefully, for I think people don't give words half enough credit. Yet they are what really affect readers, children most of all because they are the most impressionable. (Miller and Field 1955, 87)

The little girl who could not read grew up to inspire many children with her writing, particularly with the story of the wooden doll who is forever an important part of American history.

Books by Rachel Field

All This, and Heaven Too (Macmillan, 1938, 1940).

All Through the Night (Macmillan, 1940, 1955).

An Alphabet for Boys and Girls (Doubleday, Page & Co., 1926).

American Folk and Fairy Tales, selected by Rachel Field (C. Scribner's Sons, 1929).

And Now Tomorrow (Macmillan, 1942).

The Bird Began to Sing (William Morrow, 1932).

Branches Green (Macmillan, 1934).

Calico Bush (Macmillan, 1931, 1966; Aladdin Paperbacks, 1998).

Christmas in London ([Aldus?] , [1946?]).

The Cross-Stitch Heart, and Other Plays (C. Scribner's Sons, 1927).

Eliza and the Elves (Macmillan, 1926).

Fear Is the Thorn (Macmillan, 1936).

First Class Matter, a Comedy in One Act (S. French, 1936).

General Store (Greenwillow Books, 1988; Little, Brown, 1998).

God's Pocket: The Story of Captain Samuel Hadlock, Junior, of Cranberry Isles, Maine (Macmillan, 1934).

Hepatica Hawks (Macmillan, 1932).

Hitty, Her First Hundred Years (Macmillan, 1929).

If Once You Have Slept on an Island (Caroline House, Boyds Mills Press, 1993; Mulberry Books, 1995).

*Just Across the Street (Macmillan, 1933).

A Little Book of Days (Doubleday, Page & Co., 1927).

*Little Dog Toby (Macmillan, 1928).

The Magic Pawnshop: A New Year's Eve Fantasy (E. P. Dutton & Co., 1927).

*Patchwork Plays (Doubleday, Doran & Co., 1930).

Pocket-Handkerchief Park (Doubleday, Doran & Co., 1929).

*Poems (Macmillan, 1957).

Points East, Narratives of New England (Brewer & Warren, 1930).

Polly Patchwork (Doubleday, Doran & Co., 1928).

Prayer for a Child (Macmillan, 1944).

*illustrated by the author

The Rachel Field Storybook (Doubleday, 1958).

Rise Up, Jennie Smith: A Play in One Act (S. French, 1918).

A Road Might Lead to Anywhere (Little, Brown, 1990).

Six Plays (C. Scribner's Sons, 1924).

Susanna B. And William C. (William Morrow, 1934).

*Taxis and Toadstools (Doubleday, Page & Co., 1926).

Time Out of Mind (Macmillan, 1935).

To See Ourselves (Macmillan, 1937).

*The Yellow Shop (Doubleday, Doran & Co., 1931).

For More Information About/by Rachel Field

Commire, Anne, ed. 1979. *Something About the Author: Facts and Pictures About Contemporary Authors and Illustrators of Books for Young People*. Vol. 15. Gale Research.

Kunitz, Stanley J., and Howard Haycraft, eds. 1951. *The Junior Book of Authors*. 2d ed. H. W. Wilson.

Miller, Bertha Mahony, and Elinor Whitney Field, eds. 1955. *The Newbery Medal Books: 1922–1955*. Horn Book.

1931: Elizabeth Coatsworth

Born	May 31, 1893 Buffalo, New York
Married	Henry Beston, June 18, 1929 (children: Margaret and Catherine)
Died	August 31 or September 2, 1986 (sources vary)

Awards and Honors

Newbery Medal (Fantasy): *The Cat Who Went to Heaven* (Macmillan, 1930)

About the Author and Her Writing

It took Elizabeth Coatsworth one week to write, type, and illustrate *The Cat Who Went to Heaven,* winner of the 1931 Newbery Medal. The idea for the book, however, developed over the years of Elizabeth's childhood, in which she traveled to many exotic places and experienced a variety of different cultures.

Elizabeth was born in Buffalo, New York, in 1893. At that time, Buffalo was a large town where everybody knew everybody else, where people took the time to sit on their front porches and wave at friends as they passed by in horse-drawn carriages or on foot. Before Elizabeth was even a year old, her family traveled to California, stopping along the way to visit the Indian pueblos, a great fascination to the little girl.

> I love to write, but like any other craft, there are hours of correcting, polishing, and rewriting that a writer must be ready to put in as well as the wonderful hours of writing, when the pen seems to be running away with the story. (Hopkins 1974, 97–98)

By the age of five, Elizabeth had climbed various parts of the Alps and ridden donkeys across the desert in Egypt with her family. During the years when she was twelve and thirteen, the Coatsworth clan lived in southern California, traveling to Mexico and visiting the ancient Aztec ruins.

Although Elizabeth's family did a great deal of traveling when she was growing up, most of her years were spent in Buffalo. For eight months of each year she was consumed with her schoolwork. The school she attended required long hours in the classroom, and the two-mile walk home ensured that Elizabeth rarely arrived before the sun went down.

Summer vacations made up for the long school year. The family spent each summer at a beach on the Canadian shore of Lake Erie. The days were full of swimming in warm water, playing in the sand, climbing the trees, and exploring the vast woods. Those summers fed Elizabeth's love of the outdoors, a love she later shared with her husband, Henry Beston, an author and a naturalist.

Elizabeth's venture into writing books for children began with a challenge. Louise Seaman, a classmate of hers from her days at Vassar, had become an editor at Macmillan.

At the time Macmillan was in the process of starting up one of the first children's publishing departments in the country. Elizabeth and Louise were visiting one day when Elizabeth made a few critical comments about one of the newly published books. Louise countered her criticisms with the comment that if Elizabeth felt that way, why didn't she write a better book? Elizabeth took up the challenge and wrote *The Cat and the Captain* (Macmillan, 1927) her first published book for children.

Elizabeth's travels in her early years made a deep impression on her, but it was the year after she earned her master's degree from Vassar that sparked the flame that led her to write *The Cat Who Went to Heaven.* During that year, she traveled with her mother and sister throughout the Orient. They visited China and Korea, staying in monasteries where they were often the first white women that the people had ever seen. They also spent a month in Kyoto, Japan, where they visited several old Buddhist temples.

In one of the temples, they saw a picture depicting the death of Buddha. The picture included several animals, including a cat. Cats were not usually shown in a holy place such as a temple because of their reputation for being creatures who lacked humility. While traveling in Java, the family visited another old Buddhist temple. In this one, many of the carvings on the walls included animals. After their return home, a friend sent Elizabeth a print that showed a cat mourning the death of Buddha.

Elizabeth tucked away these experiences and their strange connections and let them take root for the next ten years. Then one day she sat down and in a week's time wrote the book about an artist, a painting, a cat, and a miracle.

Two of Elizabeth's picture books were illustrated by individuals who also won the Newbery Medal for their own books: *The Golden Horseshoe* (Macmillan, 1935), illustrated by Robert Lawson (Newbery Medal winner in 1945 for *Rabbit Hill* and Caldecott Medal winner in 1941 for *They Were Strong and Good*), and *Alice-All-By-Herself* (Macmillan, 1937), illustrated by Marguerite de Angeli (Newbery Medal winner in 1950 for *The Door in the Wall*).

Above all else, Elizabeth was a marvelous poet. Her first book was a collection of poetry for adults. She often wove poems throughout her many books of prose, inserting her graceful lyrics between the chapters as well as within.

Elizabeth Coatsworth died in 1986 at the age of ninety-three. Over the course of her long lifetime, she wrote nearly 100 books for both children and adults. A colleague wrote of Elizabeth that her "special contribution to children's books of our time lies in the never-failing, superior intelligence of her style, and next in her ever-present sense of the poetry of the situation in hand, whether it is expressed in verse or prose; and finally in her choice of interesting subject matter, a worthy challenge for the imaginative reader, young or old" (Miller and Field 1955, 98).

A Word to My Readers:

Vulgarity and cruelty are the only two things of which I can think that are unsuitable in books for children. I don't mean that stories should always be happy or that they should avoid poverty, sickness, and death, if these are necessary for the carrying on of the plot, but they should avoid sadism or lingering over the details. They should avoid the suggestion of dark things left to stir uneasily in the imagination. (Coatsworth 1948, 392)

Books by Elizabeth Coatsworth

Alice-All-By-Herself (Macmillan, 1937), illustrated by Newbery Medal–winner Marguerite de Angeli.

All of a Sudden Susie (Macmillan, 1974).

American Adventures, 1620–1945 (Macmillan, 1924).

Atlas and Beyond (Harper & Brothers, 1924).

Aunt Flora (Macmillan, 1953).

Bess and the Sphinx (Macmillan, 1967).

The Big Green Umbrella (Grosset & Dunlap, 1944).

Bob Bodden and the Good Ship Rover (Garrard, 1968).

Bob Bodden and the Seagoing Farm (Garrard, 1970).

The Boy with the Parrot, a Story of Guatemala (Macmillan, 1930).

The Captain's Daughter (Macmillan, 1950).

The Cat and the Captain (Macmillan, 1927, 1974).

The Cat Who Went to Heaven (Macmillan, 1930, 1958; Aladdin Books, Maxwell Macmillan International, 1990).

The Cave (Viking Press, 1958).

Cherry Ann and the Dragon Horse (Macmillan, 1955).

The Children Come Running (Golden Press, 1960).

Compass Rose (Coward McCann, 1929).

Country Neighborhood (Macmillan, 1944).

Country Poems (Macmillan, 1942).

Creaking Stair (Poems) (Coward McCann, 1949).

Cricket and the Emperor's Son (Macmillan, 1932).

Daisy (Macmillan, 1973).

Dancing Tom (Macmillan, 1938).

Daniel Webster's Horses (Garrard, 1971).

Desert Dan (Viking Press, 1960).

The Dog from Nowhere (Row, Peterson, 1958).

Dollar for Luck (Macmillan, 1951).

Door to the North, a Saga of Fourteenth Century America (Winston, 1950).

Down Half the World (Macmillan, 1968).

Down Tumbledown Mountain (Row, Peterson, 1958).

The Enchanted: An Incredible Tale (Pantheon, 1951, 1968).

The Fair American (Macmillan, 1940).

First Adventure (Macmillan, 1950).

Forgotten Island (Grosset & Dunlap, 1942).

Fox Footprints (A. A. Knopf, 1923).

The Fox Friend (Macmillan, 1966).

George and Red (Macmillan, 1969).

The Giant Golden Book of Cat Stories (Simon & Schuster, 1953).

Giant Golden Book of Dogs, Cats, and Horses: 61 Stories and Poems (Simon & Schuster, 1957).

The Golden Horseshoe (Macmillan, 1935), illustrated by Newbery and Caldecott Medal winner Robert Lawson.

Good Night (Macmillan, 1972).

Grandmother Cat and the Hermit (Macmillan, 1970).

The Hand of Apollo (Viking Press, 1965).

Hide and Seek (Pantheon, 1956).

Indian Encounters: An Anthology of Stories and Poems (Macmillan, 1960).

Indian Mound Farm (Macmillan, 1969).

Jock's Island (Viking Press, 1963).

Jon the Unlucky (Holt, Rinehart & Winston, 1964).

Knock at the Door (Macmillan, 1931).

The Last Fort: A Story of the French Voyageurs (Winston, 1952).

Lighthouse Island (W. W. Norton, 1968).

The Little Haymakers (Macmillan, 1940).

The Littlest House (Macmillan, 1940).

Lonely Maria (Pantheon, 1960).

The Lucky Ones: Five Journeys Toward a Home (Macmillan, 1968).

Maine Memories (S. Greene Press, 1968; Countryman Press, 1991).

Maine Ways (Macmillan, 1947).

Marra's World (Greenwillow Books, 1975).

Mountain Bride, an Incredible Tale (Pantheon, 1954).

Mouse Chorus (Pantheon, 1955).

Night and the Cat (Macmillan, 1950).

The Noble Doll (Viking Press, 1961).

Old Whirlwind: A Story of Davy Crockett (Macmillan, 1953).

The Peaceable Kingdom, and Other Poems (Pantheon, 1958).

The Peddler's Cart (Macmillan, 1956).

Personal Geography: Almost an Autobiography (S. Greene Press, 1976; G. K. Hall, 1979; Countryman Press, 1994).

Pika and the Roses (Pantheon, 1959).

The Place (Holt, Rinehart & Winston, 1966).

Plum Daffy Adventure (Macmillan, 1947).

Poems (Macmillan, 1957).

The Princess and the Lion (Pantheon, 1963).

Pure Magic (Macmillan, 1973).

Ronnie and the Chief's Son (Macmillan, 1962).

The Secret (Macmillan, 1965).

Silky, an Incredible Tale (Pantheon, 1953).

The Snow Parlor, and Other Bedtime Stories (Grosset & Dunlap, 1971).

The Sod House (Macmillan, 1954).

Song of the Camels: A Christmas Poem (North South Books, 1997).

South Shore Town (Macmillan, 1948).

The Sparrow Bush: Rhymes (W. W. Norton, 1966).

The Sun's Diary: A Book of Days for Any Year (Macmillan, 1929).

Sword of the Wilderness (Macmillan, 1936).

They Walk in the Night (W. W. Norton, 1969).

A Toast to the King (Coward McCann, 1940).

Tonio and the Stranger, a Mexican Adventure (Grosset & Dunlap, 1941).

Toutou in Bondage (Macmillan, 1929).

Troll Weather (Macmillan, 1967).

Trudy and the Tree House (Macmillan, 1944).

The Trunk (Macmillan, 1941).

Twelve Months Make a Year (Macmillan, 1943).

Under the Green Willow (Macmillan, 1971; Greenwillow Books, 1984).

Up Hill and Down (A. A. Knopf, 1947).

The Wanderers (Four Winds Press, 1972).

Werefox (originally published as *Pure Magic*) (Collier Books, 1975).

The White Horse (Macmillan, 1942).

The Wishing Pear (Macmillan, 1951).

The Wonderful Day (Macmillan, 1946).

You Say You Saw a Camel? (Row, Peterson, 1958).

You Shall Have a Carriage (Macmillan, 1941).

For More Information About/by Elizabeth Coatsworth

Autobiography: 1976. *Personal Geography: Almost an Autobiography.* S. Greene Press.

Coatsworth, Elizabeth. 1948. Upon Writing for Children. *Horn Book Magazine* 24 (September): 392.

Hopkins, Lee Bennett. 1974. *More Books by More People: Interviews with Sixty-Five Authors of Books for Children.* Citation Press.

Miller, Bertha Mahony, and Elinor Whitney Field, eds. 1955. *Newbery Medal Books: 1922–1955.* Horn Book.

1932: Laura Adams Armer

Born   January 12, 1874
          Sacramento, California

Married   Sidney Armer, 1902 (children: Austin)

Died   March 16, 1963

Awards and Honors

Newbery Medal (Historical Fiction): *Waterless Mountain* (Longmans, Green & Co., 1931)

About the Author and Her Writing

Laura Adams Armer didn't write her first book until she was fifty-seven years old. That book, *Waterless Mountain,* earned her the Newbery Medal in 1932. Not only was this her first published book it was also the first she had ever heard of the Newbery Medal. Coming late into writing, Laura never concerned herself with literary awards. In her acceptance speech she said she was glad she had been unaware of the award. "I do not believe in working consciously for awards. I believe in singing the song in one's own heart, and singing it as well as possible" (Miller and Field 1955, 105).

> I believe that every boy and girl born into the world comes trailing clouds of glory, which most grown-ups have forgotten. (Kunitz and Haycraft 1951, 8)

For Laura that song in her heart began in her childhood, growing up in northern California. Her father, Charles Wilson Adams, had come to California in 1859, driving a team of oxen across the Great Plains and Rocky Mountains. Laura, the third and youngest child, entered the world on January 12, 1874.

Laura was a sickly child. She spent many hours alone at home, in fragile health. Rather than allow her ailments to turn her bitter or reclusive, Laura instead became a dreamer. She later wrote, "Perhaps there are some children who dream as I dreamed when a very little girl, about all the things grown-ups laugh at. I am sure that everyone has dreamed of flying, of soaring so easily in the air and being sure that he could teach others how to do it" (Kunitz and Haycraft 1951, 9).

Before she began writing, art was the outlet for Laura's creative "song." She attended the California School of Design in San Francisco, studying drawing and painting. There she met Sidney Armer, the man who became her husband. They had one son, Austin, and Laura devoted her time and energies to raising her son and caring for the household, although she did find brief occasions to continue her study of painting.

At the age of fifty, Laura journeyed to the Navajo Reservation in northern Arizona. Her heart soared at the beauty of mountain and sky. The lifestyle and folklore of the Navajo people made her feel as though she had finally found the promised land her father had been searching for when he left New Hampshire and traveled West over half a century before.

So inspired was she by the Navajo people that she painted thirty canvases. She also recreated one hundred sand paintings for the House of Navajo Religion in Santa Fe, New Mexico, while residing on the reservations or in the villages for months at a time.

Waterless Mountain is told through the eyes of an eight-year-old Navajo boy. His story clearly portrays the domestic and religious life of the Navajo people. Laura's descriptions of the life, ceremonies, legends, and symbolism of the Navajo culture provide the reader with a realistic picture of the life of these Native Americans. Laura and her husband, Sidney, illustrated the Newbery–winning book. Either Laura, Sidney, or the pair of them illustrated all six of Laura's books.

> . . . dreams of beauty are more real than acts that are ugly and sorrowful. (Kunitz and Haycraft 1951, 9)

When Laura got word that she had won the Newbery Medal, she was living in the wilderness of Navajo and Hopi countryside. The nearest railroad was seventy-eight miles away. A vicious sandstorm kept her stranded in the village for four days. Finally, however, she made the train trip to New Orleans to accept the Medal. After the awards ceremony, Hendrik van Loon, the winner of the first Newbery Medal in 1922, sent Laura flowers and a note thanking her for not having written her book ten years earlier, when she would have been his competitor for the Medal!

Despite the poor health of her childhood, Laura lived to be eighty-nine years old. Her life, her art, and her writing combine to create a wonderful song of life that continues to be heard.

A Word to My Readers:

There were no flying machines when I was a child, but men were trying to invent them. There were no horseless carriages, but men did make them. So I have seen many dreams of the impossible come true. That is why I still hope that men will learn how not to go to war, how not to be so greedy for money that they enslave their brothers to toil and grow sick with producing for profit instead of making what they need for happiness. (Kunitz and Haycraft 1951, 9)

Books by Laura Adams Armer

Farthest West (Longmans, Green & Co., 1939), illustrated by her husband, Sidney Armer.

*The Forest Pool (Longmans, Green & Co., 1938).

In Navajo Land (David McKay, 1962), illustrated with photos by Laura, Sidney, and Austin Armer.

*Southwest (Longmans, Green & Co., 1935).

*Trader's Children (Longmans, Green & Co., 1937).

*Waterless Mountain (Longmans, Green & Co., 1931).

*illustrated by the author

For More Information About/by Laura Adams Armer

Kunitz, Stanley J., and Howard Haycraft, eds. 1951. *The Junior Book of Authors.* 2d ed. H. W. Wilson.

Miller, Bertha Mahony, and Elinor Whitney Field, eds. 1955. *Newbery Medal Books: 1922–1955.* Horn Book.

1933: Elizabeth Foreman Lewis

Born	May 24, 1892
	Baltimore, Maryland
Married	John Abraham Lewis, 1921 (children: John Fulton Lewis)
Died	August 7, 1958

Awards and Honors

Newbery Medal (Historical Fiction, Adventure): *Young Fu of the Upper Yangtze* (Winston, 1932)

About the Author and Her Writing

When Elizabeth Foreman Lewis was born, the nurse informed her mother that the baby had two crowns on her head. According to the nurse this meant that she was destined to live in two different countries. What seemed like a strange prediction eventually came true.

Elizabeth spent her childhood years in the farm country near Baltimore, Maryland, surrounded by books and the joys of rural life: lots of animals, good food, laughter, singing, and hospitality. Although she and her sister were educated in public schools, much of their learning came from the church. Elizabeth's young life was shaped by many of the proverbs she learned, especially one in particular: "If worth doing at all, it is worth doing well." This proverb became a model for the way Elizabeth lived her life.

> In 1917 I crossed the Pacific to a land where I was not for a number of years to see a library, but where I discovered books to be in themselves of an importance exceeding anything I had ever known. (Miller and Field 1955, 112)

As a young woman, Elizabeth attended the Maryland Institute of Art in Baltimore. For a time, she worked as an architectural designer of dollhouses. She also kept statistics for the railroad and gave many hours of effort to the work of the Methodist Church. It was through the church that Elizabeth found her way to China, the country that would become her second home.

In 1917, the Methodist Women's Board sent Elizabeth to China as a missionary. There she taught English literature, physical education, and commercial law. She also studied and immersed herself in the Chinese culture, which had many connections to her own beliefs about life. Elizabeth was delighted to discover that the Chinese enjoyed proverbs as much as she did.

While in China, Elizabeth met John Abraham Lewis, the son of a Methodist bishop. They married in Nanking, China, and later had one son, John Fulton Lewis, who grew up to be a newspaper reporter.

One of Elizabeth's favorite proverbs was, "Read good books; speak good words." She grew up reading many books but may not have realized how precious books truly were until her years in China. There, the young schoolgirls were enchanted by her small collection of books and believed that she must be very rich to own any books at all.

Although Elizabeth loved her life in China, illness soon forced the Lewis family to return to the United States. But she brought home her deep love for China and its people. Telling the stories of what she had seen and the people she had met became a focus of her life. She could not say enough good things about China to anyone who would listen.

Elizabeth never thought about writing a book until a friend suggested she write about her beloved China. Immediately inspired by this thought, Elizabeth wrote *Young Fu of the Upper Yangtze,* which was awarded the Newbery Medal in 1933. Elizabeth wrote several more books for children and for adults, all set in China.

Lewis believed that winning the Newbery Medal was a great honor. In her acceptance speech, she said that "the award will be for me in the future not only a constant source of encouragement, but a stimulus as well to do always the best work of which I am capable" (Miller and Field 1955, 111).

Elizabeth always remembered what she learned from the Chinese about the priceless gift of the written word. She ended her Newbery acceptance speech by saying that "today I owe a special happiness to the thought that this award in memory of John Newbery is conferred, by those whose life it is to exalt books, on a volume that comes out of a land where the printed page ranks above all other treasure" (Miller and Field 1955, 113).

After winning the Newbery Medal, the author spent her time giving her best to writing about the people of her second homeland. Elizabeth Foreman Lewis died on August 7, 1958. The prediction made at her birth had been fulfilled.

A Word to My Readers:

My own opinion is that youth is much the same the world over, regardless of race or color. Differences there are in ways of thinking and habits of living, but for the most part these seem artificial. (Miller and Field 1955, 111)

Books by Elizabeth Foreman Lewis

China Quest (Winston, 1937).

Ho-Ming, Girl of New China (Winston, 1934).

When the Typhoon Blows (Winston, 1942).

Young Fu of the Upper Yangtze (Winston, 1932; Holt, Rinehart & Winston, 1973).

For More Information About/by Elizabeth Foreman Lewis

Miller, Bertha Mahony, and Elinor Whitney Field, eds. 1955. *Newbery Medal Books: 1922–1955.* Horn Book.

1934: Cornelia Meigs

Born	December 6, 1884
	Rock Island, Illinois
Died	September 10, 1973
Pseudonym	Adair Aldon

Awards and Honors

Newbery Medal (Biography): *Invincible Louisa: The Story of the Author of* Little Women (Little, Brown, 1933)

Drama League Prize, 1916: *The Steadfast Princess: A Play for Young People* (Macmillan, 1916)

Newbery Honor Book for 1922: *The Windy Hill* (Macmillan, 1921)

Beacon Hill Bookshelf Prize, 1927: *The Trade Wind* (Little, Brown, 1927)

Newbery Honor Book for 1929: *Clearing Weather* (Little, Brown, 1928)

Newbery Honor Book for 1933: *Swift Rivers* (Little, Brown, 1932)

About the Author and Her Writing

In her own words, Cornelia Meigs "grew up on the shore of a great blue river; she had a big garden to play in, with hiding places in the overgrown lilac bushes, with cherry trees of fairy-like beauty and rich red harvest, with tall pines whose comfortable branches seemed to have grown especially for children's climbing" (Miller and Field 1955, 117–18). This setting proved to be an ideal one for a young girl with a vivid imagination and a cheerful, upbeat spirit.

Cornelia came from a long line of storytellers. Many of young Cornelia's imaginary adventures sprang from the stories she'd heard through the years about her famous seafaring ancestors. Her great-grandfather, Commodore John Rodgers, commanded three of the six first great sailing ships built for the United States: the *Constellation,* the *President,* and the *Constitution.* It's no wonder that as a child, Cornelia spent many hours in the tops of the pine trees, pretending that they were the tall masts of ships. From her post, she watched for pirates and make-believe vessels, all the while inventing colorful stories that may never have made their way into books but that oiled the wheels of a young girl's mind and prepared her for the day when she would become a published author.

> It is in that impact, I think, in the question of how long and how deeply it touches its reader, that the worth of a book really lies. (Miller and Field 1955, 122)

Cornelia's own connection to real-life history may have instilled in her a love for all history. She described her favorite subject as "that boundless world of the past crowding with its message up to the very door of the present" (Miller and Field 1955, 118).

Much of Cornelia's adult life paralleled that of the heroine of her Newbery Medal book, *Invincible Louisa* (Little, Brown, 1933), a biography of Louisa May Alcott. Cornelia suffered from health limitations and kept house for her widowed father until his death. She was a second mother to her many nieces and nephews, bringing them to live with her during the summer months and playing a vital role in their upbringing. For eighteen years she taught writing and American literature at her alma mater, Bryn Mawr College, located in Pennsylvania. During her tenure she took a three-year leave of absence during World War II and worked for the War Department. Cornelia's life was full of demands, but through it all she never lost her zest for living and her optimistic outlook. Her own biography could easily be titled "Invincible Cornelia," for that she was.

For a writer who loved history, it is fitting that Cornelia be the one to initiate the writing of a book that became a landmark in the field of children's literature: *A Critical History of Children's Literature* (Macmillan, 1953, 1969). She cowrote the book and served as its editor in chief. Cornelia did not realize the importance of her own role in the history of children's literature as a winner of the Newbery Medal and as a writer of over twenty books. Prior to winning the Newbery Medal, three of her books were named Newbery Honor books: *The Windy Hill* (Macmillan, 1921), *Clearing Weather* (Little, Brown, 1928), and *Swift Rivers* (Little, Brown, 1932). It was not her desire so much to be a part of history as to tell it. She did this with great skill.

Cornelia's humility regarding her own place in the history of children's literature can best be displayed in the words she spoke during her Newbery Medal acceptance speech. "What you have done today," she said, "is, in effect, to bestow the Newbery Award upon Louisa Alcott. She has deserved it for a very long time." Cornelia concluded her speech by saying, "If I could stretch my voice across the years, I would say, 'Louisa, this medal is yours,' and I do assure you that Louisa and I both thank you from the bottom of our hearts" (Miller and Field 1955, 124).

Cornelia Meigs died on September 10, 1973, nearly forty years after winning the Newbery Medal. In that time, she continued to be a productive author and contributor to the world of literature for children as well as adults.

A Word to My Readers:

I learned . . . two very important things which have to do with authorship: one, that you must have sufficient confidence in your project to make time for it no matter what are the demands and distractions; the other, that inspiration has to be attended by intensively hard work, sometimes even replaced by it, apparently, to bring a writing enterprise to its proper end. (Kunitz and Haycraft 1951, 218)

Books by Cornelia Meigs

As the Crow Flies (Macmillan, 1927).

At the Sign of the Two Heroes (Century, 1920), published under her pseudonym, Adair Aldon.

Call of the Mountain (Little, Brown, 1940), illustrated by Newbery Medal winner James Daugherty.

Clearing Weather (Little, Brown, 1928).

The Covered Bridge (Macmillan, 1936).

A Critical History of Children's Literature (Macmillan, 1953, 1969).

The Crooked Apple Tree (Little, Brown, 1929).

The Dutch Colt (Macmillan, 1952).

Fair Wind to Virginia (Macmillan, 1955).

The Great Design: Men and Events in the United Nations from 1945–1963 (Little, Brown, 1964).

Helga and the White Peacock (Macmillan, 1922).

Hill of Adventure (Century, 1922), published under her pseudonym, Adair Aldon.

Invincible Louisa: The Story of the Author of Little Women (Little, Brown, 1933).

Jane Addams, Pioneer for Social Justice: A Biography (Little, Brown, 1970).

The Kingdom of the Winding Road (Macmillan, 1915).

Louisa M. Alcott and the American Family Story (London: Bodley Head, 1970; H. Z. Walck, 1971).

Master Simon's Garden: A Story (Macmillan, 1916).

Mother Makes Christmas (Grosset & Dunlap, 1940), illustrated by Newbery Medal–winner Lois Lenski.

Mounted Messenger (Macmillan, 1943).

Mystery at the Red House (Macmillan, 1961).

The New Moon: The Story of Dick Martin's Courage (Macmillan, 1924), illustrated by Newbery Medal–winner Marguerite de Angeli.

The Pirate of Jasper Peak (Macmillan, 1918).

The Pool of Stars (Macmillan, 1919).

Railroad West: A Novel (Little, Brown, 1937).

Rain on the Roof (Macmillan, 1925).

The Scarlet Oak (Macmillan, 1938).

The Steadfast Princess: A Play for Young People (Macmillan, 1916).

Swift Rivers (Little, Brown, 1932, 1937; Walker, 1994).

The Trade Wind (Little, Brown, 1927).

The Two Crowns, a Story (Macmillan, 1949).

Vanished Island (Macmillan, 1941).

The Violent Men, a Study of Human Relations in the First American Congress (Macmillan, 1949).

What Makes a College? A History of Bryn Mawr (Macmillan, 1956).

Wild Geese Flying (Macmillan, 1957).

The Willow Whistle (Macmillan, 1931).

Wind in the Chimney (Macmillan, 1934).

The Windy Hill (Macmillan, 1921).

The Wonderful Locomotive (Macmillan, 1928).

Young Americans: How History Looked to Them While It Was in the Making (Junior Literary Guild and Ginn, 1936).

For More Information About/by Cornelia Meigs

Kunitz, Stanley J., and Howard Haycraft, eds. 1951. *The Junior Book of Authors.* 2d ed. H. W. Wilson.

Miller, Bertha Mahony, and Elinor Whitney Field, eds. 1955. *The Newbery Medal Books: 1922–1955.* Horn Book.

1935: Monica Shannon

Born	March 1905(?)
	Canada
Died	August 13, 1965

Awards and Honors

Newbery Medal (Historical Fiction): *Dobry* (Viking Press, 1934)

About the Author and Her Writing

Monica Shannon was born in Canada, but her family moved to Seattle while she was still an infant. One of the future author's playmates as a child was a bear cub from the Rocky Mountains where Monica's family lived. Playing with a bear cub in the mountains seemed a natural enough thing to do for a young child who loved the great outdoors and spent hours of time among the sequoias and pines, near mountain springs and in fields of glowing gold grain.

And it wasn't a bit unusual either for Monica to end a summer day sitting among the Flathead Indians who camped near the hills by her home or watching the cattlemen cook their pancakes and share them with a flock of pet robins. Monica's dog, Lenore, a St. Bernard brought from Switzerland by her father, served as a friend and guardian as the young girl roamed the vast lands.

Monica's love of nature is reflected in the poem she wrote and recited in her Newbery acceptance speech:

> A weed puts out the poorest flower that grows
> And ages later rivals any rose.
> A butterfly appears of Chinese blue,
> Which used to be a slug upon a yew.
> A cloud flies by and flashes wings afire—
> But yesterday foul water in a mire.
> And all man's dreams are birds above old trees
> While God and man go listening to these.
> (Miller and Field 1955, 133)

In fact, her entire speech proclaimed the wondrous beauty of nature and the remarkable character of animals.

Monica's writing skills were recognized as early as elementary school. In one assignment the students had to write about their favorite Bible character. Monica chose the Old Testament character Joseph because he was once a shepherd and Monica knew a shepherd who lived on their ranch. Her teacher was so pleased with the story that she displayed it for the other students and teachers to see, and Monica received a special medal for her story.

Several years later, she wrote a story about the American Revolution. Again the teacher recognized the young girl's talent. She had Monica copy the story in a white leather book the teacher called an "Honor book," bought for just such an occasion. As Monica recalled later, "Writing has its downs as well as its ups," for she had to stay in and write in the book while her classmates went ice skating (Kunitz and Haycraft 1951, 272).

In her adult years it was not surprising for visitors to Monica's home to find scraps of writing tucked in vases, bowls, behind a picture, or under a book. Monica did much of her writing on a large, screened veranda where she could view the countryside she so deeply loved.

> All animals are more worthy of respect than people who see little of them imagine. (Miller and Field 1955, 133)

How did a woman born in Canada and raised in the western United States come to write a book about a Bulgarian boy? Monica's inspiration for her Newbery Medal–winning book, *Dobry*, came from two sources. One was the Bulgarian tales she learned as a child, told to her by the Bulgarian ranch hands employed by her father. The other was the illustrator of the book, a Bulgarian named Atanas Katchamakoff, who shared his childhood memories with Monica. Out of these two sources of inspiration, Monica wove a lovely, poetic story about a young Bulgarian boy who dreams of being an artist and who is encouraged by his kindly grandfather despite the fact that nobody in Dobry's family had ever done such a thing.

When *Dobry* was named the Newbery Medal book for 1935, Monica and a friend, Jasmine Britton, traveled to Denver where the award ceremony was held. Jasmine's job was to keep Monica calm and to help her get ready to receive the medal. Both women were so excited by the honor of Monica winning the Medal that as they prepared for the dinner and speech, they put Monica's dress on backward! They barely had time to get it reversed before the taxi arrived to take them to the award ceremony.

The reverence Monica showed for life and for the gift of creation is illustrated in many instances in her Newbery–winning book and eloquently portrayed in this excerpt, where Dobry complains to his grandfather about having to carry the heavy bag of wheat seeds:

> "What are you carrying there under your arm?" his grandfather asks.
> "I said, 'The wheat seeds, heavy,' and Dobry hunched up his shoulder as he remembered.
> "And Grandfather said to me, 'No, you carry there under your arm a whole field of tall blowing wheat. A whole wheat field! Every little seed is alive, all of life in it.'" (p. 68)

Monica Shannon's writing career lasted less than ten years. She published six books between 1926 and 1935, of which *Dobry* was the next to last. Although she lived another 28 years after the publication of her final book, whatever writing she may have done was more for pleasure than for the public. Monica died on August 13, 1965.

A Word to My Readers:

When a body really lives apart with mountains, there are moments, hours, days of beauty that can only be pondered in the heart before partaking of that sacrament which is a complete oneness with nature. (Miller and Field 1955, 134)

Books by Monica Shannon

California Fairy Tales (Doubleday, Page & Co., 1926; Stephen Daye Press, 1953, 1957).

Dobry (Viking Press, 1934; Puffin Books, 1993).

Eyes for the Dark (Doubleday, Doran & Co., 1928).

Goose Grass Rhymes (Doubleday, Doran & Co., 1930).

More Tales from California (Doubleday, Doran & Co., 1935; Stephen Daye Press, 1960).

Tawnymore (Doubleday, Doran & Co., 1931).

For More Information About/by Monica Shannon

Kunitz, Stanley J., and Howard Haycraft, eds. 1951. *The Junior Book of Authors.* 2d ed. H. W. Wilson.

Miller, Bertha Mahony, and Elinor Whitney Field, eds. 1955. *Newbery Medal Books: 1922–1955.* Horn Book.

1936: Carol Ryrie Brink

Born	December 28, 1895
	Moscow, Idaho
Married	Raymond W. Brink, 1917 (children: David and Nora)
Died	August 15, 1981

Awards and Honors

Newbery Medal (Historical Fiction): *Caddie Woodlawn* (Macmillan, 1935), illustrated by
   Newbery Medal–winner Kate Seredy
Friends of American Writers Award, 1956: *The Headland* (Macmillan, 1955)
Lewis Carroll Shelf Award, 1959: *Caddie Woodlawn*
Irvin Kerlan Award, 1978: *Four Girls on a Homestead* (Latah County Museum Society,
   1977)

About the Author and Her Writing

There are times when a tragedy becomes an opportunity with far-reaching conse-
quences for good. Such was the case with Carol Ryrie Brink's life. Her father died when
she was five years old, her mother when she was eight. Left orphaned, with no brothers
or sisters, Carol went to live with her grandmother and an aunt. Although some people
would have been scarred forever by such tragic beginnings, Carol Ryrie Brink never felt
sorry for herself. Neither did she allow her loss to define her as a human being.

> Winning the Newbery Award made me very proud and happy, and it has certainly done much to make the book well-known and popular. The medal is one of my prized posses-sions, and I shall always be thankful for it. (Hopkins 1974, 57)

Carol's grandmother, Caddie Woodhouse, lived in a
large farmhouse with a barn, an orchard, and lots of animals. Carol's favorite pet was a little pony, upon which
she rode all over the Idaho hills. Riding the pony, gazing
at the mountains, and daydreaming stories brought a lot
of happiness to the orphaned child. It was during this
time that Carol told herself that one day, she would grow
up and write books.

Her most famous book, *Caddie Woodlawn*, is more
fact than fiction. The book is based on her grandmother's
tales of her own growing-up years in Wisconsin. Carol's
grandmother, whom she lovingly called "Gram," grew up
in a large family in Wisconsin when that area of the
United States was still very much wild and unsettled.
Carol loved hearing Gram's stories of her pioneer days and of the adventures she and her
brothers and sisters lived out in real life. Carol said that she could be convinced to do
about anything if Gram promised to tell her a story about her childhood.

Gram was a steadfast, kindhearted, and practical woman. Carol's aunt became a
second mother to her niece and filled the little girl's days with fun and interesting adven-

tures and ideas. The two women raised Carol to know that she was loved and cherished. The hardships they faced served only to make them stronger and more caring.

Carol graduated from the University of Idaho in 1917 and soon after married Raymond W. Brink, a mathematician and college professor. They had two children, David and Nora. It was through her children that Carol first began to write in earnest. She was disappointed in the quality of the Sunday school materials the children brought home each week and decided that she could do a better job herself. She wrote a couple of stories and sent them to a publisher, where they were received and welcomed by the editors. Thus began Carol's foray into the publishing world.

Most of Carol's stories were based on real life: her grandmother's, her own, and the people she met along the way. When writing, Carol liked to begin with a person, place, or experience that evoked in her an emotional response. She would fictionalize the story to some degree, but even then the deeper truths remained vivid and real. Once Carol began to write, she did so quickly, because prior to writing she spent a great deal of time thinking through her stories and characters. She was a writer who could easily get in touch with her own childhood memories, which made her stories enjoyable for the children for whom she wrote.

During the writing of *Caddie Woodlawn,* Brink corresponded regularly with her grandmother. She went to visit the area of Wisconsin where Gram had lived and was astonished to discover how accurately the older woman remembered the details of the place. Brink credited the book's authenticity to her grandmother's remarkable gift for storytelling. Yet the stories would have been lost if Carol had not written them down in book form.

In 1970, the Dunn County Historical Society of Menomonie, Wisconsin, dedicated the Caddie Woodlawn Memorial Park. The family's old farmhouse was restored as a historical landmark. Visitors are welcome to come and see what life was like in Wisconsin in the early 1800s. The park is built on a corner of property that once belonged to Carol's grandfather.

Carol's admiration for the pioneer qualities lived by her beloved Gram and portrayed in her Newbery Medal–winning book modeled her life and thought. In her Newbery acceptance speech, she spoke clearly about the need for all generations to remember and to claim the traits that helped form our country:

> If we can just keep hold of some of the sturdy pioneer qualities of these grandparents to hand down to our children, perhaps our children will be better fitted to meet courageously the difficult problems of our modern world. It is an entirely different world, but, after all, the pioneer qualities of courage, willingness to go to meet the unknown, and steadfastness under difficulties are the things most needed today, as they were then. (Miller and Field 1955, 144)

A Word to My Readers:

[A writer should] begin laying up riches in childhood and never to cease learning and experiencing and storing away, so that the older the writer becomes the richer the hidden mine will be. (Silvey 1995, 84)

Carol Ryrie Brink published more than thirty books during her writing career, including sixteen novels for children and short stories, articles, poems, plays, and novels for adults. Of all these, *Caddie Woodlawn* remained her favorite and the one that readers loved the best as well. She died on August 15, 1981.

Books by Carol Ryrie Brink

All Over Town (Macmillan, 1939, 1968).

Andy Buckram's Tin Men (Viking Press, 1966).

Anything Can Happen on the River! (Macmillan, 1934).

Baby Island (Macmillan, 1937; Aladdin Books, Maxwell Macmillan International, 1993).

The Bad Times of Irma Baumlein (Macmillan, 1972; Aladdin Books, Maxwell Macmillan International, 1991).

Buffalo Coat: A Novel (Washington State University Press, 1933; Macmillan, 1944; Latah County Historical Society, 1980).

Caddie Woodlawn (Macmillan, 1935, illustrated by Newbery Medal–winner Kate Seredy; Macmillan, 1973; ABC Clio, 1988; Aladdin Books, Collier Macmillan Publishers, 1990; Aladdin Paperbacks, 1997).

A Chain of Hands (Washington State University Press, 1993).

Family Grandstand (Viking Press, 1952).

Family Sabbatical (Viking Press, 1956).

Four Girls on a Homestead (Latah County Museum Society, 1977).

Goody O'Grumpity (North South Books, 1994).

Harps in the Wind: The Story of the Singing Hutchinsons (Macmillan, 1947; De Capo Press, 1980).

The Headland, a Novel (Macmillan, 1955).

The Highly Trained Dogs of Professor Petit (Macmillan, 1953).

Lad with a Whistle (Macmillan, 1941).

Louly (Macmillan, 1974).

Mademoiselle Misfortune (Macmillan, 1936), illustrated by Newbery Medal–winner Kate Seredy.

The Magical Melons (Macmillan, 1944; Aladdin Books, Collier Macmillan, 1990).

The Pink Motel (Macmillan, 1959; Aladdin Books, 1993).

Queen of Dolls, a Pantomimed Reading (Eldridge Entertainment House, 1928).

Snow in the River (Macmillan, 1964; Washington State University Press, published in cooperation with the Latah County Historical Society, 1964).

Stopover (Macmillan, 1951).

Strangers in the Forest (Macmillan, 1959; Washington State University Press, 1993).

Twin Cities (Macmillan, 1961).

Two Are Better than One (Macmillan, 1968).

For More Information About/by Carol Ryrie Brink

Hopkins, Lee Bennett. 1974. *More Books by More People: Interviews with Sixty-Five Authors of Books for Children.* Citation Press.

Miller, Bertha Mahony, and Elinor Whitney Field, eds. 1955. *Newbery Medal Books: 1922–1955.* Horn Book.

Silvey, Anita, ed. 1995. *Children's Books and Their Creators.* Houghton Mifflin.

1937: Ruth Sawyer

Born	August 5, 1880
	Boston, Massachusetts
Married	Albert C. Durand, 1911 (children: David and Margaret)
Died	June 3, 1970

Awards and Honors

Newbery Medal (Contemporary Life): *Roller Skates* (Viking Press, 1936)
Catholic Library Association Regina Medal, 1965
Laura Ingalls Wilder Award, 1965

About the Author and Her Writing

As a young child, Ruth Sawyer had one word that summed up how she felt about herself: failure. An eager, energetic, willful child, Ruth was never content with just "being." She yearned to "do," whatever that might be: skating, swimming, dancing, singing, anything she admired in someone else. Because she could not do everything as perfectly as she wished, as easily as she wanted, she thought of herself as a failure.

Ironically, the skill in which she eventually succeeded was in a vocation she never imagined for herself: a writer. "What I finally did accomplish, writing books, I never dreamed of doing when I was young. And I am sure my teachers never dreamed of it, either. I never passed English grammar; and to this day I have very queer ideas about spelling and punctuation" (Kunitz and Haycraft 1951, 266).

> Make use of (experience) and it serves you bountifully; hoard it, and it turns to dust. (Miller and Field 1955, 149)

Ruth was the last of five children born to older parents, and the only girl. Although her older brothers teased her a good deal, they also allowed her to join them on their camping, hunting, and sailing trips, and little Ruth did her best to keep up with the boys. Although Ruth came along later in her parents' lives, they did not let her birth disrupt their rigid routines. A daily schedule was pinned to the wall above her bed. The hours of the day were marked with bells and whistles, rules and regulations. Ruth despised all this and longed to be as free as the fairies in the folktale told to her by her beloved Irish nanny, Johanna.

As she listened to Johanna's tales of Ireland, Ruth discovered her own imagination set free from the strict routines of her life. When she turned ten years old, her family went abroad, leaving her at home under the care of her extended family and of Johanna. That year, Ruth discovered the outside world that had been denied her for so long.

Roller Skates, the book that won the Newbery Medal in 1937, tells the story of that year in Ruth's life. Although the main character of the book is named Lucinda, the events and experiences are those lived by Ruth herself. Finally free from the routines imposed upon her by her busy family, Ruth found her fairy wings in the form of a pair of roller skates, which took her to parts and places of New York City she had never imagined. The

51

rebellious spirit with which she had been born, and which had been cultivated through the first ten years of her life, finally burst forth like a butterfly from a cocoon.

Throughout her long life, Ruth believed very strongly that children needed to have freedom to live, to explore, and to experience life. When she accepted the Newbery Medal in 1937, she spoke about her unyielding belief that children should be allowed to express themselves openly. "Children," she said, "make a far more direct approach if we would let them; and by a far more advantageous highroad. A free child is a happy child; and there is nothing more lovely; even a disagreeable child ceases to be disagreeable and is liked" (Miller and Field 1955, 155).

Although Ruth did not excel in English and grammar, the love of folktales that had been instilled in her by Johanna propelled her forward in her career as a writer, much as that pair of roller skates sent her flying up and down the streets of New York. She studied to be a teacher, majoring in folklore and storytelling at New York's Teacher's College. But classroom learning was not enough for Ruth. In 1905, she traveled to Ireland, sent by her employer, a local newspaper, to do a series of articles on Irish folklore and festivals. Her time in Ireland, coupled with the magic of Johanna's childhood tales, sealed Ruth's career as a writer. After being recognized for her own gifts as a storyteller, she was encouraged by others to write down the stories she so beautifully told.

Ruth focused her writing on the retelling of folktale from many lands, some of which she visited: Cuba, Ireland, and Spain; and others she knew only from books: Hungary, Serbia, Arabia, and Austria. Ruth's greatest love, however, lay in collecting and writing Christmas stories. For twenty-five years straight, Ruth told the same Christmas folktale to groups of young children, many of them Irish immigrants, who gathered at the New York Public Library.

In 1911, Ruth married Dr. Albert C. Durand, an optometrist. They had a son, David, and a daughter, Margaret or "Peg." Peg married Robert McCloskey, an artist and writer who won the Caldecott Medal in 1942. Ruth and her son-in-law collaborated on a book, *Journey Cake, Ho!* (Viking Press, 1953), which won a Caldecott Honor Award in 1954.

In 1965 at the age of eighty-five, Ruth received the Laura Ingalls Wilder Award and the Regina Medal for her lifetime contribution to children's literature. The girl who felt herself to be a failure grew up to be a woman who was anything but that.

Ruth died in 1970, two months shy of her ninetieth birthday. She never lost touch with the spunky child within.

A Word to My Readers:

As adults, I think, we are so incapable of measuring values for childhood. And so, if this book has any point at all it lies in that fact of freedom for every child, in his own way, that he, too, may catch the music of the spheres. (Miller and Field 1955, 154)

Books by Ruth Sawyer

*Annabel (Falmouth Publishing House, 1941).

Christmas Anna Angel (Viking Press, 1944; Aldus Printers, 1949), illustrated by Newbery Medal–winner Kate Seredy.

*illustrated by the author

A Cottage for Betsy (Harper, 1954).

Daddles, the Story of a Plain Hound Dog (Little, Brown, 1964).

Doctor Danny (Harper & Brothers, 1918).

The Enchanted Schoolhouse (Viking Press, 1956).

Folkhouse, the Autobiography of a Home (D. Appleton, 1932).

The Gold of Bernardino (Aldus Printers, 1952).

Herself, Himself & Myself: A Romance (Harper & Brothers, 1917).

Journey Cake, Ho! (Viking Press, 1953; Puffin Books, 1978; Viking Press, 1982), illustrated by Caldecott Medalist Robert McCloskey.

Leerie (Harper & Brothers, 1920).

The Little Red Horse (Viking Press, 1950).

The Long Christmas (Viking Press, 1941).

Maggie Rose, Her Birthday Christmas (Harper, 1952).

My Spain: A Storyteller's Year of Collecting (Viking Press, 1967).

Old Con and Patrick (Viking Press, 1946).

The Primrose Ring (Harper & Brothers, 1915).

The Remarkable Christmas of the Cobbler's Sons, told by Ruth Sawyer (Viking Press, 1994).

Roller Skates (Viking Press, 1936; Puffin Books, 1986; Viking Press, 1995).

Seven Miles to Arden (Harper & Brothers, 1916).

The Silver Sixpence (Harper & Brothers, 1921).

The Tale of the Enchanted Bunnies (Harper & Brothers, 1923).

This Is the Christmas, a Serbian Folk Tale (Horn Book, 1945).

This Way to Christmas (Harper & Brothers, 1924; Harper & Row, 1952).

Tono Antonio (Viking Press, 1934).

The Way of the Storyteller (Viking Press, 1942; Penguin, 1976).

The Year of Jubilo (Viking Press, 1940).

The Year of the Christmas Dragon (Viking Press, 1960).

For More Information About/by Ruth Sawyer

Kunitz, Stanley J., and Howard Haycraft, eds. 1951. *The Junior Book of Authors.* 2d ed. H. W. Wilson.

Miller, Bertha Mahony, and Elinor Whitney Field, eds. 1955. *Newbery Medal Books: 1922–1955.* Horn Book.

1938: Kate Seredy

Born	November 10, 1889
	Budapest, Hungary
Died	March 7, 1975

Awards and Honors

Newbery Medal (Folktale): *The White Stag* (Viking Press, 1937)
Newbery Honor Book for 1936: *The Good Master* (Viking Press, 1935)
Newbery Honor Book for 1940: *The Singing Tree* (Viking Press, 1940)
Lewis Carroll Shelf Award, 1959

Illustrated the following award-winning books:

Newbery Medal Book for 1936: *Caddie Woodlawn* (Macmillan, 1935), by Carol Ryrie Brink
Newbery Honor Book for 1936: *Young Walter Scott* (Viking Press, 1935), by Newbery Medalist Elizabeth Janet Gray
Newbery Honor Book for 1937: *Winterbound* (Viking Press, 1936), by Margery Bianco
Caldecott Honor Book for 1945: *Christmas Anna Angel* (Viking Press, 1944), by Newbery Medalist Ruth Sawyer
Newbery Honor Book for 1947: *The Wonderful Year* (Junior Literary Guild/Julian Messner, 1946), by Nancy Barnes

About the Author and Her Writing

Kate Seredy won the Newbery Medal in 1938 for *The White Stag,* a book she both wrote and illustrated. By that time, her name was already associated with the Newbery Medal. She illustrated the 1936 Newbery winner, *Caddie Woodlawn,* as well as the 1936 Newbery Honor Book *Young Walter Scott.* Seredy also wrote and illustrated the 1936 Newbery Honor Book *The Good Master* and illustrated the 1937 Newbery Honor Book *Winterbound.*

Kate Seredy never quite envisioned herself as an author, even after writing numerous books. " 'Out of nowhere' sums up my own attitude toward my career as an author," she once wrote. "I do not know anything about the craft of writing and the more I write, the less I know. Each time a story comes out of nowhere and, almost against my better judgment, I put it on paper and later see it in print, 'Written and illustrated by Kate Seredy,' I sigh: 'This is the last. I can never write again. I don't know how' " (Miller and Field 1955, 161).

Kate was born in 1889 in Budapest, Hungary. Her father, a respected teacher, brought many wonderful books and people into the family home. At the age of nine Kate, an only child, accompanied her father and a group of famous artists and scientists when they went to live in the countryside to study the life and art of the peasants. Although

Kate did not believe herself to be a careful observer of the lives of these poor farmers, they would later become the subjects of her first book.

Kate wanted to be a painter. She attended the Academy of Art in Budapest, where her teachers insisted she first learn to draw. She studied art during the summer months in Italy, France, and Germany. Her destiny as an artist seemed certain until World War I broke out. For two years Kate worked as a nurse, attending the men who had been severely injured while serving on the front lines. The massive amount of bloodshed, violence, and sickness got the best of her, and she spent months in recovery, suffering not only from physical illness but also from a wounded mind and spirit.

However, Seredy, ever the optimist, later said that even during that most difficult time in her life, she learned a valuable lesson about discipline: "I learned that it does not matter how tired you are in mind and body; as long as there is a job to be done, the job comes first. It has *got* to be done" (Miller and Field 1955, 164).

> Between the last words of a manuscript and the first copy of the finished book, I saw and felt helping hands, unselfish, friendly hands, ready always to make a book just a little bit better, more beautiful. (Miller and Field 1955, 165)

In 1922 Kate emigrated to the United States. These were hard years for the country and for Kate, as she struggled to support herself by stenciling greeting cards, painting lampshades, and eventually illustrating the covers for sheet music. She later recalled walking down Fifth Avenue one day in 1930 and seeing in the window a display of the Newbery Medal book that year, *Hitty* (Macmillan, 1929). "I said to myself: 'You are a very great artist, Dorothy Lathrop, but you wait . . . I am coming, too'" (Miller and Field 1955, 164).

Her break came in 1926 when she met another Hungarian, Willy Pogany. He introduced her to a publisher, who asked her to illustrate a textbook. Thus began her career as an illustrator of books. During the next nine years, she illustrated about fifteen textbooks and a number of children's trade books, among them *Caddie Woodlawn.*

Not having children of her own, Kate sensed the need to be around children as a way of learning what children thought and how they saw the world. She felt that this would help her be a better illustrator of children's books. In 1933, she opened a bookstore in her New Jersey home, the Story Book House. The bookstore failed after a year, but nonetheless provided her with the much-desired contact with children.

Then came the meeting that changed Kate's life forever, when she met May Massee, a children's editor at Viking House. Kate had hoped to be assigned a children's book to illustrate, but instead, Miss Massee, charmed by the young Hungarian woman, said to her, "I like the way you tell a story. Go home and write a book about your childhood in Hungary" (Hoffman and Samuels 1972, 380–81). Kate did just that. The book, *The Good Master,* became her first published book and was the one based on the peasant life of Hungary that she had experienced those many years before.

Kate's Newbery Medal book, *The White Stag,* was based on her father's favorite Hungarian folktale. It took her only three weeks to write the book. Considering that English was Kate's second language, this was a remarkable accomplishment.

After winning the Newbery Medal, Kate went on to illustrate one of the Caldecott Honor Books of 1945, *Christmas Anna Angel,* and a Newbery Honor Book for 1947, *The Wonderful Year.* By the time of her death in 1975, she had illustrated over fifty textbooks and children's books by other authors. And even though all her books started out as fully illustrated picture books, only one remained that way: *Gypsy* (Viking Press, 1951), the story of a cat. Whether she ever realized it or not, Kate Seredy had the gift of words as well as art.

> ## A Word to My Readers:
> The only way I can repay all that I have received all these years is to try to do better and better work as time goes on and to try to give more than I receive. (Miller and Field 1955, 165)

Books by Kate Seredy

A Brand New Uncle (Viking Press, 1961).

The Chestry Oak (Viking Press, 1948).

The Good Master (Viking Press, 1935; Puffin Books, 1986).

Gypsy (Viking Press, 1951).

Lazy Tinka (Viking Press, 1962).

Listening (Viking Press, 1936).

The Open Gate (Viking Press, 1943).

Philomena (Viking Press, 1955).

The Singing Tree (Viking Press, 1940; Puffin Books, 1990).

The Tenement Tree (Viking Press, 1959).

A Tree for Peter (Viking Press, 1941).

The White Stag (Viking Press, 1937; Puffin Books, 1965, 1979).

For More Information About/by Kate Seredy

Hoffman, Miriam, and Eva Samuels. 1972. *Authors and Illustrators of Children's Books: Writings on Their Lives and Works.* R. R. Bowker.

Kunitz, Stanley J., and Howard Haycraft, eds. 1951. *The Junior Book of Authors.* 2d ed. H. W. Wilson.

Miller, Bertha Mahony, and Elinor Whitney Field, eds. 1955. *Newbery Medal Books: 1922–1955.* Horn Book.

*illustrated by the author
Kate Seredy also illustrated books by other authors.

1939: Elizabeth Wright Enright

Born	September 17, 1909 Oak Park, Illinois
Married	Robert (Marty) Gillham, 1930 (children: Nicolas [Nicky], Robert [Robin], and Oliver)
Died	June 8, 1968

Awards and Honors

Newbery Medal (Contemporary Life): *Thimble Summer* (Farrar & Rinehart, 1938)
Newbery Honor Book for 1958: *Gone Away Lake* (Harcourt, Brace & Co., 1957)

About the Author and Her Writing

Elizabeth Wright Enright spent the last night before her wedding finishing the illustrations for a book. That's the kind of dedication she put into her career as an author and illustrator!

Both of Elizabeth's parents were artists. Her father, W. J. Enright, was a famous political cartoonist. Her mother, Maginel Wright Barney, was an illustrator and designed shoes for the world-renowned company Capezio. In fact, she was one of the innovators of the very first jeweled shoes. Elizabeth's family moved from Chicago to New York when she was one year old so that her parents could pursue their careers in art.

From the time Elizabeth turned three, it was not unusual to find the little girl drawing on whatever happened to be at hand. "I drew all over my school books, the telephone book, the blackboard, the sidewalk, my mother's best writing paper; and when I wore socks I even drew faces on my bare knees," she recalled. "In fact, whenever I had a pencil in my hand I was irresponsible and a menace" (Miller and Field 1955, 172).

One of Elizabeth's most vivid childhood memories was of pressing her face against the glass doors that led to her mother's study and watching her mother bent over her worktable, dishes of watercolors spread around her and pens and pencils stuck in her hair.

Elizabeth's parents divorced when she was eleven years old. She then attended boarding schools in Connecticut and studied dance with Martha Graham. She later remembered being enthralled as a child as she watched the famous dancer Pavlova. Elizabeth even aspired to be a dancer herself but eventually gave up that dream as she found other interests.

After finishing high school, Elizabeth studied for two years at the Art Students League in New York and afterward spent part of a year studying in Paris. She got her first

> I remember very well the glow of magic that illuminated the world for months after my mother had taken me to see Pavlova dance; and I remember the moment when my grandmother opened a book, and began to read me the first chapter of a story called *Treasure Island*. (Miller and Field 1955, 174)

job illustrating fairy tales, which she had always loved. The next book she illustrated turned out to be the one she finished right before her marriage in 1930 to Robert (Marty) Gillham. The couple raised three sons, Nicolas (Nicky), Robert (Robin), and Oliver.

Elizabeth's foray into writing came by an unexpected route. Having been around art all her life, and having studied art, it seemed natural that a career in artwork would be her destiny. But Elizabeth tired of illustrating books written by other people. She decided it would be more fun to write and illustrate her own book. *Kintu: A Congo Adventure* (Farrar & Rinehart, 1935) marked her debut as both writer and illustrator. Elizabeth drew the pictures first and then wrote the book, an unusual sequence for the formation of an illustrated book. During the writing of that book, Elizabeth discovered that she had both an aptitude and a talent for writing. She wrote her second book, *Thimble Summer,* while visiting the Wisconsin farm of her famous uncle, the architect Frank Lloyd Wright. One year during a terrible drought, Elizabeth wrote a book in between helping the other residents haul water from the farmhouse down to the withering vegetable garden. Writing about a thunderstorm in her book brought the young writer great joy. Even if the weather wouldn't cooperate in reality, she could make storm clouds do whatever she wanted in her own story.

Along with her children's books, Elizabeth also wrote for adults. Her favorite genre was the short story, and she had many of these published in well-known magazines such as *Harper's,* the *New Yorker, Cosmopolitan,* and others. She published several books that contained collections of her short stories and also published several fairy tales.

Elizabeth never lost her gift for remembering the feel of being a child. With each book she wrote, the memories became sharper and more colorful. "As I wrote I discovered that phenomenon which most of us discover in writing, particularly in writing of childhood: the curious way in which memories come to light, fresh and unexpected and intact, from the deep hiding-place where we had thought them lost forever" (Miller and Field 1955, 170).

Elizabeth remains one of the youngest people to ever win the Newbery Medal. The award made her feel both proud and humbled. Nineteen years later, she won the Newbery Honor Award for her book *Gone-Away Lake,* which some critics believe to be her best book ever. She died eleven years later, in 1968.

A Word to My Readers:

There is a peculiar joy in writing about children for children. One naturally goes back to one's own childhood to find things. To me the astonishing thing is in the way one took life during those years. It was as though a thin, but tough, membrane had not yet grown between oneself and the rest of the world. A child sees everything sharp and radiant; each object with its shadow beside it. (Miller and Field 1955, 174)

Books by Elizabeth Wright Enright

A Christmas Tree for Lydia (Rinehart, 1951).

Doublefields: Memories and Stories (Harcourt, Brace & World, 1966; London: Heinemann, 1967).

The Four Story Mistake (Farrar & Rinehart, 1942; Puffin Books, 1997).

Gone-Away Lake (Harcourt, Brace & Co., 1957; Harcourt Brace Jovanovich, 1987, 1990; Harcourt, 2000).

Kintu: A Congo Adventure (Farrar & Rinehart, 1935).

The Melendy Family (Rinehart, 1947).

The Moment Before the Rain (Harcourt, Brace & Co., 1955).

Return to Gone Away (Harcourt, Brace & World, 1961; Harcourt Brace Jovanovich, 1987, 1990).

The Riddle of the Fly, & Other Stories (Harcourt, Brace & Co., 1959; Books for Libraries Press, 1970).

The Saturdays (Farrar & Rinehart, 1941; H. Holt & Co., 1969; Puffin Books, 1997).

The Sea Is All Around (Farrar & Rinehart, 1940).

Spiderweb for Two, a Melendy Maze (Rinehart, 1951; Puffin Books, 1997).

Tatsinda (Harcourt, Brace & World, 1963).

Then There Were Five (Farrar & Rinehart, 1944; Puffin Books, 1997).

Thimble Summer (Farrar & Rinehart, 1938).

Zeee (Harcourt Brace Jovanovich, 1963; Harcourt, Brace & World, 1965; London: Heinemann, 1966).

For More Information About/by Elizabeth Wright Enright

Miller, Bertha Mahony, and Elinor Whitney Field, eds. 1955. *Newbery Medal Books: 1922–1955*. Horn Book.

*illustrated by the author
Elizabeth Wright Enright also illustrated books by other authors.

1940: James Daugherty

Born	June 1, 1889 Asheville, North Carolina
Married	Sonia Medvedeva, 1913 (children: Charles)
Died	February 12, 1974

Awards and Honors

Newbery Medal (Non-Fiction, Biography): *Daniel Boone* (Viking Press, Junior Literary Guild, 1939)

Caldecott Honor Book for 1939: *Andy and the Lion* (Viking Press, 1938)

Illustrated the 1957 Caldecott Honor Book *Gillespie and the Guards* (Viking Press, 1956), by Benjamin Elkin

About the Author and His Writing

It started with a picture book. James "Jimmy" Daugherty (DAW-er-tee) illustrated a book about Daniel Boone several years before he wrote the biography of this American hero, the book that won the Newbery Medal in 1940.

> I always have a feeling of receiving a unique personal favor when borrowing books at libraries. I say to myself, how generous is this charming person to lend me, a perfect stranger, this valuable book, this priceless treasure. (Miller and Field 1955, 185)

May Massee, an editor at Doubleday, Page & Co., had asked him to illustrate Stewart E. White's book *Daniel Boone, Wilderness Scout* (Allyn & Bacon, 1926). Ms. Massee handed him the manuscript with these encouraging words: "Do what you like, have a good time, and God bless you" (Miller and Field 1955, 90). Jimmy, deeply inspired by the stories of the American frontier, already had the enthusiasm and eagerness to follow through with Ms. Massee's request.

Jimmy's love for and knowledge of American history came not from school and books as much as from the stories his father and grandfather told him during his growing-up years. Jimmy and his father had an extremely close relationship, and one of the best memories of Jimmy's life were the hours spent listening to his father tell stories while he sat and drew pictures. It is a tribute to both father and son that one day, the stories and the illustrations would come together to create wonderful books for children and adults.

Jimmy's writing career blossomed only after he became a well-known illustrator. In 1939 he won the Caldecott Honor Award for the book *Andy and the Lion,* a wonderful example of his exuberant and free-flowing artistic style. He won another Caldecott Honor Award in 1957 for *Gillespie and the Guards* (Viking Press, 1956), written by Benjamin Elkin.

Daugherty became known for his beautiful murals, which were highly regarded for their quality. Painting murals and writing books may seem to require two vastly different skills, but there are significant similarities. Lynd Ward, an artist, illustrator, and author, wrote that "both of these media imply talking to a large audience and saying something to that audience that shall be both articulate and meaningful. This is precisely what Daugherty does and his work in each form gains sustenance from his experience in the other" (Miller and Field 1955, 181).

Inspired by the writing of Walt Whitman and Whitman's vision of America, Jimmy wrote biographies of a number of American heroes besides Daniel Boone, including Benjamin Franklin, Abraham Lincoln, and Lewis and Clark. He once described early America as "so beautiful—very poised, very searching, and very patient with a blundering elder generation" (Kunitz and Haycraft 1951, 90). Born in the same century as the Civil War, later living through both world wars, Jimmy often agonized over the destruction and violence of war, feeling empathy not only for his fellow Americans but for people all over the globe.

Jimmy married Sonia Medvedeva, a writer of books and plays for children. Jimmy illustrated most of her books during her career. They were colleagues as well as husband and wife. Jimmy said that when one of his books is completed, "I *inflict* it on my loving wife, Sonia, who is an author, my best friend, and severest critic" (Hopkins 45–46).

The Daughertys had one son, Charles. The boy often served as a model for his father's illustrations. Indeed, anyone who came into contact was fair game for the artist/author's creative expression.

Jimmy had much to say about the important role of children's literature in the culture of American society. In the acceptance speech he gave after winning the Newbery Medal, he said, "I do think that somewhere between sappiness and sourness children's books can go along courageously and frankly and gaily with the forward-marching masses of young people to tackle with imagination and good cheer the tough problems they may have ahead" (Miller and Field 1955, 189).

He did not believe that children should be forced to write to authors, still a frequent school assignment. Rather, Jimmy thought the authors should write, teachers should teach, and children should be left to "be their naturally joyous selves" (Hopkins 1969, 46).

A friend once described Jimmy Daugherty in these words: "Tall, muscular, straggling, possessed of arms and legs that defy all dancing school theories of grace but that never appear awkward, alive with a vitality and a rhythm that color and shade his personality, he might have stepped from any one of the number of books he has illustrated" (Kunitz and Haycraft 1951, 90).

James Daugherty illustrated more books than he wrote, but that does not lessen the impact of his stories. He died on February 12, 1974.

A Word to My Readers:

Wit and taste, beauty and joy are as much a necessary part of the democratic heritage as economics and the utilities. It is the function of the arts to delight and heal us as children, of the dullness and bitterness of materialistic systems, of the weariness of meaningless routines. Children's books are a part of that art of joy and joy in art that is the certain inalienable right of free people. (Miller and Field 1955, 191)

Books by James Daugherty

Andy and the Lion (Viking Press, 1938; Puffin Books, 1989) (Caldecott Honor Book).

*Daniel Boone (Viking Press, Junior Literary Guild, 1939).

*The Landing of the Pilgrims (Random House, 1950, 1981, 1996).

*Lincoln's Gettysburg Address: A Pictorial Interpretation (A. Whitman, 1947).

*The Magna Charta (Random House, 1956).

*Marcus and Narcissa Whitman, Pioneers of Oregon (Viking Press, 1953).

Of Courage Undaunted: Across the Continent with Lewis and Clark (Viking Press, 1951; Marshall Cavendish, Grey Castle Press, 1991).

*Outline of Government in Connecticut (Prepared under the direction of the House Committee on Public Information of the Connecticut General Assembly, 1944).

The Picnic: A Frolic in Two Colors and Three Parts (Viking Press, 1958).

*Poor Richard (Viking Press, 1941; Marshall Cavendish, Grey Castle Press, 1991).

*Trappers and Traders of the Far West (Random House, 1952).

West of Boston (Viking Press, 1956).

The Wild, Wild West (E. M. Hale by arrangement with David McKay, 1948).

William Blake (Viking Press, 1960).

For More Information About/by James Daugherty

Hopkins, Lee Bennett. 1969. *Books Are by People: Interviews with 104 Authors and Illustrators of Books for Young Children*. Citation Press.

Kunitz, Stanley J., and Howard Haycraft, eds. 1951. *The Junior Book of Authors*. 2d ed. H. W. Wilson.

Miller, Bertha Mahony, and Elinor Whitney Field, eds. 1955. *Newbery Medal Books: 1922–1955*. Horn Book.

*illustrated by the author
James Daugherty also illustrated books by other authors.

1941: Armstrong Sperry

Born	November 7, 1897
	New Haven, Connecticut
Married	Margaret Mitchell, June 12, 1930 (children: Susan and John)
Died	April 28, 1976
	Hanover, New Hampshire

Awards and Honors

Newbery Medal (Adventure): *Call It Courage* (Macmillan, 1940)
Newbery Honor Book for 1936: *All Sail Set: A Romance of the "Flying Cloud"* (Winston, 1935)

About the Author and His Writing

Armstrong Sperry came from a lineage that could be traced back to the earliest American settlers. One side of the family included many farmers, and the other side was drawn to the sea. Both sides of this heritage came together in the person and work of Armstrong Sperry.

> Children of to-day, who are the men and women of to-morrow, will need the best we have to give. (Miller and Field 1955, 207)

Born and raised in the rocky hills of Connecticut, young Armstrong was spellbound by the wild tales of his great grandfather Sereno Armstrong, a sea captain, who told of pirates and cannibals and pearl-laden lagoons. Cap'n Armstrong's description of the island of Bora Bora particularly grabbed the attention of his great-grandson. "Prettiest little island I ever did see," the captain would tell him. "I'd like for *you* to see it some day, young 'un!" (Miller and Field 1955, 194).

It took Armstrong a while before his great-grandfather's wish came true. First, he tried his hand as an illustrator. He finished art school and was hired by an advertising agency for what was at that time a huge salary—twenty-five dollars a week. But after two years of drawing ads for vacuum cleaners, canned soup, and hairnets, Armstrong became disillusioned with what the world offered to a young, talented artist. It was then that he took Cap'n Armstrong's words to heart and set sail for the South Seas.

After a year of seafaring, Armstrong finally sailed to Bora Bora, planning to stay for an extended visit. He arrived on a beat-up sailing ship that carried bunches of red bananas swinging from the rails and pigs and chickens interspersed among the other passengers. He never forgot his first glimpse of the island, which, from a distance, looked like no more than a cloud. As the sailing ship drew closer Armstrong saw the huge volcanic mountain rising into the clouds, sparkling waterfalls glistening in the sunlight and wild goats leaping among the peaks. To Armstrong, the island represented a perfect world.

63

Unused to having long-term visitors, the entire population of the island, including the chief, greeted the young seafarer upon his arrival. The chief invited Armstrong to live in his own home with his wife and four children. The house, made of bamboo walls and rising above the ground on stilts, looked to Sperry more like a birdcage than a home. As the people of the island welcomed the newcomer into their lives, he began to learn the culture, language, and traditions of the people. He loved it all.

In the year that Armstrong was in Bora Bora, the island underwent a remarkable transition. One of the major crops, vanilla, suddenly became extremely valuable when a blight destroyed the vanilla vines on the other islands. People from all over the world poured onto Bora Bora seeking to capitalize on the value of its vanilla crop. Crime, which had never before existed on the island, became rampant. It grieved Armstrong to see the idyllic island life destroyed by selfishness and greed.

In that same year the value of the vanilla beans dropped as the crop became available on the other islands again. The islanders sank into despair. Then another tragedy hit when a hurricane blasted the island, destroying homes and land and further plunging the people into hopelessness.

Under the faithful guidance of the chief, the people rebuilt their lives. Eventually they were able to reestablish life as it had been when Armstrong first arrived on the island.

After returning to the United States, Armstrong married another author, Margaret Mitchell, and they had two children, Susan and John. The family made its home on a farm in Vermont, hearkening back to the side of Armstrong's ancestors that made their home on land. His year in Bora Bora, coupled with the time he spent traveling the South Seas, eventually led Armstrong to writing and illustrating books whose themes often centered around the South Sea Islands. This included the Newbery Medal winner for 1941, *Call It Courage,* about a young Polynesian boy who shows his courage in the face of great challenges. Armstrong found inspiration in the beauty of that particular part of the world but even more in the bravery he had witnessed through the people as they faced tremendous hardship.

The love of the sea remained in his soul, a love that lives on in his books that were initially inspired by the stories of his great grandfather, Cap'n Armstrong. Sperry died on April 28, 1976.

A Word to My Readers:

In each of these books I have given to the major character some challenge he must meet, some great obstacle he must overcome, some ideal toward which he must aspire. Children identify themselves with the characters they read about, and so it becomes an obligation on the part of the author to create the kind of people with whom we want our children to be identified. (Miller and Field 1955, 206)

Books by Armstrong Sperry

All About the Arctic and Antarctic (Random House, 1957).

All About the Jungle (Random House, 1959).

All Sail Set: A Romance of the "Flying Cloud" (Winston, 1935; D. R. Godine, 1984).

The Amazon, River Sea of Brazil (Garrard, 1961).

*Bamboo, the Grass Tree (Macmillan, 1942).

*Black Falcon, a Story of Piracy and Old New Orleans (Winston, 1949).

*Call It Courage (Macmillan, 1940; Cornerstone Books, 1989; Aladdin Books, 1990).

*Captain Cook Explores the South Seas (Random House, 1955).

*Coconut, the Wonder Tree (Macmillan, 1942).

*Danger to Windward (Winston, 1947).

*Frozen Fire (Doubleday, 1956).

*Great River, Wide Land: The Rio Grande Through History (Macmillan, 1967).

*Hull Down for Action (Doubleday, Doran & Co., 1945).

*John Paul Jones, Fighting Sailor (Random House, 1953).

*Little Eagle, a Navajo Boy (Winston, 1938).

*Lost Lagoon: A Pacific Adventure (Doubleday, Doran & Co., 1939).

No Brighter Glory (Macmillan, 1942).

*One Day with Jambi in Sumatra (Winston, 1934).

*One Day with Manu (Winston, 1933).

*One Day with Tuktu (Winston, 1935).

*Pacific Islands Speaking (Macmillan, 1955).

*The Rain Forest (Macmillan, 1947).

River of the West: The Story of the Boston Men (Winston, 1952).

*South of Cape Horn: A Saga of Nat Palmer and Early Antarctic Exploration (Winston, 1958).

*Storm Canvas (Winston, 1944).

*Teri Taro from Bora Bora (A. A. Knopf, 1940).

*Thunder Country (Macmillan, 1952).

The Voyages of Christopher Columbus (Random House, 1950).

*Wagons Westward: The Old Trail to Santa Fe (Winston, 1936; D. R. Godine, 1990).

For More Information About/by Armstrong Sperry

Kunitz, Stanley J., and Howard Haycraft, eds. 1951. *The Junior Book of Authors.* 2d ed. H. W. Wilson.

Miller, Bertha Mahony, and Elinor Whitney Field, eds. 1955. *Newbery Medal Books: 1922–1955.* Horn Book.

*illustrated by the author
Armstrong Sperry also illustrated books by other authors.

1942: Walter Dumaux Edmonds

Born	July 15, 1903 Boonville, New York
Married	Eleanor Livingston Stetson, 1929 (died 1956) (children: Peter, Eleanor, and Sarah) Katherine Baker-Carr, 1956
Died	January 24, 1998 Utica, New York

Awards and Honors

Newbery Medal (Historical Fiction): *The Matchlock Gun* (Dodd, Mead, 1941)
National Book Award, 1976: *Bert Breen's Barn* (Little, Brown, 1975)

About the Author and His Writing

Although the Newbery Medal is given in the field of children's literature, Walter Edmonds did not write his Newbery Medal–winning book, *The Matchlock Gun,* for children. He wrote all of his books for adults. Indeed, many of his books began as stories published in adult magazines, including *The Matchlock Gun.* But sometimes fate intervenes in our plans, and that's what happened to Walter Edmonds.

> The criterion of any child's book should be whether it has enough stuff, humor, reality, wisdom, excitement to be interesting to an adult mind. (Miller and Field 1955, 221)

Walter grew up in New York, dividing his time between winters spent in New York City, where he went to school, and summers on the family dairy farm, where he learned far more about real life. Many of Walter's stories took place near the farm in the area of New York known as the Mohawk Valley.

Walter did not intend to be a writer. He attended college at Harvard. His father hoped he would become a chemical engineer, but that dream ended when Walter failed his first course in chemistry. He wrote and worked for the school magazine, the *Harvard Advocate,* and even served as president of the journal. In part because of his work with the *Advocate,* Walter decided to major in English.

While still a student at Harvard, Walter submitted a story for a course requirement. The professor encouraged him to submit the story to *Scribner's Magazine,* and it was accepted for publication. Walter decided then and there to make a career as a writer.

The idea for *The Matchlock Gun* came from the transcript of a true family story sent to him by a man named Thomas Shepherd, whom Walter had never met. Walter pondered the incident for several days and very quickly found that the material lent itself to being told as a short story. He wrote Mr. Shepherd and asked for permission to write a short story based on the facts that Mr. Shepherd had written to him and received the go-ahead. It only took Walter a couple of days to write the story, which was then published by the *Saturday Evening Post.*

An editor named Dorothy Bryan contacted Walter and told him that she thought the story would make an excellent book for children. Eventually, Walter was persuaded to write *The Matchlock Gun,* originally titled *The Spanish Gun.* When the book won the 1942 Newbery Medal as the most outstanding book written for children, Walter must have been doubly surprised: first, that his book won such a prestigious award; and second, that the award was for a children's book.

> The business of books is to inspire, and instruct, and entertain; and the proper inspiration and instruction has to do with the world the child is preparing for. (Miller and Field 1955, 222)

Walter quickly learned that being named the winner of the Newbery Medal brought with it great prestige but some complications as well. Shortly after the award was announced, Walter's editor shipped him 1,000 books to autograph and return. The post office of the small town where Walter lived was not equipped for such a massive shipment of books. The mail carrier delivered several of the boxes in an old car. The boxes were then dropped off on the roadside by Walter's driveway, and he had to lug the heavy load up the hill to his house and then back to the road for pickup. Unwilling to make the mail carrier go through so much effort on his behalf, Walter bought a truck for use in hauling future shipments of the book.

Although most of the ideas for Walter's books came from his childhood in New York state, he also gleaned ideas from a variety of other sources, including old newspapers, books, and letters from his readers. Perhaps it was his training as an English major or his work with the *Harvard Advocate,* but whatever the reason, Walter rarely had to rewrite. He felt obligated to keep working on a paragraph until he got it just right before going on to the next one.

Walter married Eleanor Livingston Stetson, in 1929. They had three children: Peter, Eleanor, and Sarah. After his first wife died in 1956, he married Katherine Baker-Carr.

The Newbery Medal was not the only award Walter received in his lifetime. In 1976, he won the prestigious National Book Award for *Bert Breen's Barn.* Another of his books, *Drums Along the Mohawk* (Little, Brown, 1936), was made into a movie. Walter died in 1998 at the age of ninety-four.

> ## A Word to My Readers:
> You cannot grow ambition and you cannot grow ideas any more than you can grow grain without fertilizer, and the first element of thought is discipline . . . This is especially true of books, for it is in reading to himself that a child first begins to know himself. (Miller and Field 1955, 220)

Books by Walter Dumaux Edmonds

Beaver Valley (Little, Brown, 1971).

Bert Breen's Barn (Little, Brown, 1975; Syracuse University Press, 1991).

The Big Barn (Little, Brown and Company, 1930).

*illustrated by the author

The Boyds of Black River (Dodd, Mead, 1953; Syracuse University Press, 1988).

Cadmus Henry (Dodd, Mead, 1949).

Chad Hanna (Little, Brown, 1940).

Corporal Bess: The Story of a Boy and a Dog (Dodd, Mead, 1952).

Drums Along the Mohawk (Little, Brown, 1936, 1937; Globe Book Co., 1954; Syracuse University Press, 1997).

Erie Water (Little, Brown, 1933).

Hound Dog Moses and the Promised Land (Dodd, Mead, 1954).

In the Hands of the Senecas (Little, Brown, 1947; Syracuse University Press, 1995).

The Matchlock Gun (Dodd, Mead, 1941; Putnam's, 1989).

Mostly Canallers: Collected Stories (Syracuse University Press, 1987).

Mr. Benedict's Lion (Dodd, Mead, 1950).

The Musket and the Cross: The Struggle of France and England for North America (Little, Brown, 1968).

The Night Raider and Other Stories (Little, Brown, 1980).

Rome Haul (Little, Brown, 1929; Syracuse University Press, 1987).

Seven American Stories (Little, Brown, 1970).

The South African Quirt (Little, Brown, 1985).

The Story of Richard Storm (Little, Brown, 1974).

Tales My Father Never Told (Syracuse University Press, 1995).

*They Fought with What They Had: The Story of the Army Air Forces in the Southwest Pacific, 1941–1942 (Little, Brown, 1951; Zenger, 1982; Center for Air Force History, 1992; Time Life Books, 1993).

They Had a Horse (Dodd, Mead, 1962).

Time to Go House (Little, Brown, 1969; Syracuse University Press, 1994).

Tom Whipple (Dodd, Mead, 1942).

Two Logs Crossing: John Haskell's Story (Dodd, Mead, 1943).

Uncle Ben's Whale (Dodd, Mead, 1955).

The Wedding Journey (Little, Brown, 1947).

Wilderness Clearing (Dodd, Mead, 1944).

Wolf Hunt (Little, Brown, 1970).

Young Ames (Little, Brown, 1942).

For More Information About/by Walter Dumaux Edmonds

Miller, Bertha Mahony, and Elinor Whitney Field, eds. 1955. *Newbery Medal Books: 1922–1955*. Horn Book.

1943: Elizabeth Janet Gray (Vining)

Born	October 6, 1902 Philadelphia, Pennsylvania
Married	Morgan Vining, January 31, 1929
Died	November 27, 1999

Awards and Honors

Newbery Medal (Historical Fiction): *Adam of the Road* (Viking Press, 1942), illustrated
    by Newbery Medal–winner Robert Lawson
Newbery Honor Book for 1931: *Meggy MacIntosh* (Viking Press, 1930)
Newbery Honor Book for 1936: *Young Walter Scott* (Viking Press, 1935), illustrated by
    Newbery Medal–winner Kate Seredy
Newbery Honor Book for 1939: *Penn* (Viking Press, 1938)

About the Author and Her Writing

Elizabeth Janet Gray sold her first story to a publisher in 1915. The acceptance letter she received began, "Dear Mrs. Gray . . . " The editor had no idea that the new author wasn't married, or that she was only thirteen years old. The publisher, "Young Churchman," paid Elizabeth a whopping two dollars for her efforts. The thrill of being published and being thought of as a grown woman gave Elizabeth an early start on the road to becoming an author.

Ten years after Elizabeth published that first story in a church Sunday school magazine, she published her first book, *Merediths' Ann* (Doubleday, Page & Co., 1927). During the decade between those publications, much happened in Elizabeth Gray's life.

Born to a Quaker mother and a Scottish-born father, Elizabeth came along years after her parents expected to have any more children. Her childhood was happy, filled with the stories and songs of her parents and a rich heritage that would later find expression in many of her stories.

> History, after all, is people.
> (Miller and Field 1955, 240)

Elizabeth was a bright and beautiful child. She entered Bryn Mawr College near Philadelphia at the tender age of sixteen years old. Following graduation, Elizabeth took on teaching jobs to pay the bills. She continued to send stories to publishers but received a number of rejection letters, which she once said she used to wallpaper a corner of her bedroom.

Along with the rejection letters came acceptances as well, for Elizabeth continued to have stories published in Sunday school magazines. While waiting for her big break publishing books, Elizabeth began teaching English, ancient history, and community civics. The high school where she taught was situated in a New Jersey seaside resort. The setting was perfect for a young woman who loved to write. Every afternoon after school she walked to the beach, wrapped herself in a rug, and curled up on the boardwalk, staring out at the wide gray sea, writing, writing, writing.

Those winter afternoons resulted in Elizabeth's first book. May Massee, an editor who encouraged many other writers whose books won the Newbery Medal, invited Elizabeth to New York to talk over a manuscript that Elizabeth had sent to her. Ms. Massee's enthusiasm and friendship provided a welcome change from the rejection letters that had discouraged but not defeated the young author. With Ms. Massee's constant support, Elizabeth's career as an author was underway.

> . . . the sense of history that gives us a perspective on the present may help us to chart the future. It gives us a profound sense of being part of a long chain of life that went on years before us and will go on years after us. (Miller and Field 1955, 239)

Although Elizabeth's first love was writing, she didn't depend solely on the income from her books as a means of support. She worked in a library and continued to teach. On January 31, 1929, she married Morgan Vining, a member of the faculty at the University of North Carolina. Elizabeth and her husband built a home on an acre lot filled with trees, and amid everything else she did, Elizabeth wrote books.

Sadly, the happy marriage ended in tragedy when her husband was killed in an automobile accident in 1933. The grief-stricken widow moved back to Philadelphia to live with her mother and sister and to continue to write and travel.

In 1946, after giving several years of service to the peace efforts during World War II, Elizabeth was hired by the emperor of Japan to come to his country and teach English to the crown prince. She held this position for four years and later wrote a book about her experiences, *Windows for the Crown Prince* (Lippincott, 1952).

Elizabeth never remarried, but she occasionally used her married name, Elizabeth Gray Vining, on her later books, mostly adult novels, biographies, and her autobiographical work. Although she never had children of her own, she loved writing for children best of all. "Why do I write for children?" she once wrote. "I rather think because they enjoy their books so much, read and reread them instead of tossing them aside after a cursory skimming, which is satisfying to a hardworking author. Or perhaps I might ask myself why I write at all, and that is easier to answer. I write because I can't help it" (Kunitz and Haycraft 1951, 145).

Elizabeth's love for writing, and writing for children, was rewarded many times. She won the Newbery Honor Medal three times: in 1931 for *Meggy MacIntosh,* in 1936 for *Young Walter Scott,* and in 1939 for *Penn.*

Elizabeth's greatest honor came in 1943 when her book *Adam of the Road* was awarded the Newbery Medal. This story of a young minstrel boy living in the 1200s was illustrated by Robert Lawson, who had already won the Caldecott Medal in 1941 and who later won the Newbery Medal himself in 1945 for *Rabbit Hill.* Elizabeth's book began as a collection of retold minstrel tales, but she became so captivated by the thought of the minstrels themselves that she cast aside her first inclination and wrote a very different book altogether.

Even as Elizabeth Janet Gray Vining wrote many books about historical characters, so she, too, has taken her place in history as an author, beloved by many. All in all, she wrote over sixty books for children and adults. She began her writing career at the tender age of thirteen and lived another eighty-four years before her death in 1999.

> ## A Word to My Readers:
> The knowledge that certain endowments which we enjoy or have even been accepting dully without appreciation have been won for us with difficulty in the past and saved for us over and over at a cost, may teach us that it is our part to cherish and preserve them and to hand them on to those who come after us larger and stronger than they were when we got them. (Miller and Field 1955, 239)

Books by Elizabeth Janet Gray (Vining)

Adam of the Road (Viking Press, 1942; Puffin Books, 1987), illustrated by Newbery Medal–winner Robert Lawson.

Anthology with Comments (Pendle Hill, 1942).

Being Seventy: the Measure of a Year (G. K. Hall, Viking Press, 1978).

Beppy Marlowe of Charles Town (Viking Press, 1936).

The Cheerful Heart (Viking Press, 1959).

The Fair Adventure (Viking Press, 1940).

Flora MacDonald: Her Life in the Highlands and America (London: Bles, 1967).

Friend of Life: The Biography of Rufus M. Jones (Lippincott, 1958).

Harnessing Pegasus: Inspiration and Meditation (Pendle Hill, 1978).

I, Roberta (Lippincott, 1967).

I Will Adventure (Viking Press, 1962).

Jane Hope (Viking Press, 1933).

May Massee Collection: Creative Publishing for Children (William Allen White Library, 1972).

Meggy MacIntosh (Viking Press, 1930).

Merediths' Ann: An Out of Doors Story for Girls (Doubleday, Page & Co., 1927; Sun Dial Press, 1937; Doubleday, 1946).

Mr. Whittier (Viking Press, 1974).

Penn (Viking Press, 1938; Philadelphia Yearly Meeting of the Society of Friends, 1986).

A Quest There Is (Pendle Hill, 1982).

Quiet Pilgrimage (Lippincott, 1970).

Return to Japan (Lippincott, 1960).

Take Heed of Loving Me (Lippincott, 1964).

The Taken Girl (Viking Press, 1972; G. K. Hall, 1973).

Tilly-Tod (Doubleday, Doran & Co., 1929).

The Virginia Exiles (Lippincott, 1955).

William Penn: Mystic, as Reflected in His Writings (Pendle Hill Publications, 1969).

Windows for the Crown Prince (Lippincott, 1952).

The World in Tune (Pendle Hill, 1952; Pendle Hill/Harper, 1954).

Young Walter Scott (Viking Press, 1935), illustrated by Newbery Medal–winner Kate Seredy.

For More Information About/by Elizabeth Janet Gray (Vining)

Autobiography: 1978. *Being Seventy: The Measure of a Year.* G. K. Hall, Viking Press.

Kunitz, Stanley J., and Howard Haycraft, eds. 1951. *The Junior Book of Authors.* 2d ed. H. W. Wilson.

Miller, Bertha Mahony, and Elinor Whitney Field, eds. 1955. *Newbery Medal Books: 1922–1955.* Horn Book.

1944: Esther Forbes

Born	June 28, 1891
	Westborough, Massachusetts
Married	Albert Learned Hoskins, 1926
Died	August 12, 1967

Awards and Honors

Newbery Medal (Historical Fiction): *Johnny Tremain, a Novel for Old and Young* (Houghton Mifflin, 1943)

Pulitzer Prize in History, 1942: *Paul Revere and the World He Lived In* (Houghton Mifflin, 1942)

About the Author and Her Writing

Esther Forbes first became well known as an author of books for adults when she won the 1942 Pulitzer Prize in History for her book *Paul Revere and the World He Lived In* (Houghton Mifflin, 1942). This was only the second time that a woman won the Pulitzer Prize in History. Two years later, Paul Revere's life would again bring Esther fame when she won the 1944 Newbery Medal for *Johnny Tremain,* the story of a young boy caught up in the events of the Revolutionary War. In fact, it was while writing the Pulitzer Prize–winning book that the seeds for the Newbery Medal–winning book first took root.

History was always very much a part of Esther's life. Both her parents were historians. Her father was a judge, and her mother a writer. Esther lived most of her life in the same house in Massachusetts where she was born, the youngest of five children. As a child, Esther read a lot, but not just books for children. She read Shakespeare and Rudyard Kipling and Thomas Hardy. She even memorized the *Iliad.* At the age of thirteen, Esther attempted to write a novel about the Greek god Achilles, perhaps motivated by her memorization of Homer's classic.

> No matter how much external things change, the human emotions do not seem to change much. (Miller and Field 1955, 248)

As with many other people born in the first half of the twentieth century, Esther grew up on the true-life tales of her ancestors, told to her by parents and grandparents. Among these were stories of great uncles captured by Native Americans and taken to Canada; whether or not these stories can be verified, they fueled Esther's imagination.

History came alive within her own home: one of the beds was graced with a beautiful bedspread embroidered by the mother and grandmother of Samuel Adams, an important figure in the American Revolution and a family ancestor. Esther's name came from a family member who had died generations before in a Cambridge jail, accused of witchcraft in a time when many people were falsely accused by frightened townspeople and sentenced to death.

Esther learned a love of the land during the many hours she spent riding her pony around the New England hills. This love was later cultivated when she lived for a year as a farmhand on a large farm in Virginia. She earned the esteemed position of working with the horses, beyond the usual chore of picking apples assigned to most of the girls. Esther so deeply loved this time of her life and the farm work so well that she returned two more times to help bring in the fall harvest.

After college, Esther joined the editorial staff of Houghton Mifflin Company, a publishing house. She worked there for six years, then married and traveled abroad. The marriage only lasted seven years, and then Esther was on her own again, delving into the subjects of life that intrigued her the most.

Along with her fascination with history, Esther was always interested in why people do what they do. She worked to create true-to-life characters in her books, detailing the events and circumstances from which they found motivation. Esther gave even her fictional characters personalities that reflected the truth of human nature: unpredictable, ever changing, and always, to Esther, immensely fascinating.

Esther didn't need to invent situations in which to place her characters. She believed that history itself provided the necessary excitement, thrill, and suspense needed in any good story. She wove these elements into all her stories in a way that made her books accessible and interesting. Anyone reading her books will find that their knowledge of history has been enriched. *Johnny Tremain* is often used in schools as a welcome component in the teaching of American history.

Esther lived the final years of her life with a brother and sister in the New England area that was both her home and the inspiration for her writing. Although she didn't write many books following her Newbery Medal book, she enjoyed gardening, traveling, and being with people. Her books continue to connect their readers to a time long past, a time that, because of this author, does not seem so far away after all.

A Word to My Readers:

One thing I knew I wanted to do was to show the boys and girls of today how difficult were those other children's lives by modern standards; how early they were asked to take on the responsibilities of men and women. They were not allowed to be children very long. (Miller and Field 1955, 253)

Books by Esther Forbes

America's Paul Revere (Houghton Mifflin, 1946; Marshall Cavendish, Grey Castle Press, 1991).

The Boston Book (Houghton Mifflin, 1947).

Johnny Tremain, a Novel for Old and Young (Houghton Mifflin, 1943, 1945, 1998; ABC Clio, 1987).

A Mirror for Witches (Houghton Mifflin, 1928; Academy Chicago, 1985).

Miss Marvel (Houghton Mifflin, 1935).

O Genteel Lady! (Houghton Mifflin, 1926; Academy Chicago, 1986).

Paul Revere and the World He Lived In (Houghton Mifflin, 1942, 1988; American Past, Book of the Month Club, 1983).

Rainbow on the Road (Houghton Mifflin, 1954).

The Running of the Tide (Houghton Mifflin, 1948).

For More Information About/by Esther Forbes

Miller, Bertha Mahony, and Elinor Whitney Field, eds. 1955. *Newbery Medal Books: 1922–1955*. Horn Book.

1945: Robert Lawson

Born	October 4, 1892
	New York City
Married	Marie Abrams, 1922
Died	May 26, 1957

Awards and Honors

First (and only) person to win both the Newbery Medal and the Caldecott Medal.
Newbery Medal (Animal Stories): *Rabbit Hill* (Viking Press, 1944)
Wrote and illustrated the Caldecott Medal book for 1941: *They Were Strong and Good* (Viking Press, 1940)
Illustrated the 1943 Newbery Medal book: *Adam of the Road* (Viking Press, 1942) by Elizabeth Janet Gray (Vining)
Newbery Honor Book for 1958: *The Great Wheel* (Viking Press, 1957)

About the Author and His Writing

Robert Lawson didn't set out to be an author or an illustrator. He did not spend his childhood writing and drawing, as many of the other Newbery Medal–winning authors before him had done. But he did win first prize in high school for a poster he illustrated, which earned him one dollar and perhaps a bit of recognition. That moment of fame became far overshadowed as the years went by, and Robert became the first and still the only person to win both the Newbery and Caldecott Medals.

> This is a great country and we are a great and tough people. No one has ever gotten us down yet. (Hoffman and Samuels 1972, 263)

Robert came from an unusual family. His father was a young teenager when the Civil War broke out, and he joined the armed services. Robert's mother was raised among Native Americans and lumberjacks in Minnesota and was fluent in several languages. Robert, born in New York City in 1892, had the benefit of two loving parents who told him stories and valued the worth of a good book. Robert's mother, especially, encouraged her son to read. She didn't care so much about what he read so long as he read, but she subtly made sure that Robert had access to books that were so well written and beautifully illustrated that he gravitated away from "sculch," his mother's term for what she considered to be "trashy" books.

Mrs. Lawson was a writer and painter, and once a year she took Robert to New York City's Metropolitan Museum of Art. They wandered through the halls filled with paintings and sculptures, soaking in the beauty of the art and enjoying lunch together in the museum's restaurant.

Robert wanted to be an engineer, to build railroads and bridges and be part of the adventures he read about in books, but in order to do that, he needed skills in mathematics, which he did not have. His father wanted him to go into the dry goods business, but that didn't interest Robert. Instead, after high school Robert attended the New York School of Fine and Applied Arts (later renamed the Parsons School), encouraged by his mother, who recognized his potential for a career in art. Robert studied at the school for three years and won scholarships for his drawing and illustrations.

When World War I broke out, Robert served in France in the camouflage division, painting camouflage scenes. After the war, he returned home, and in 1922 he married Marie Abrams, also an author and illustrator. They earned a living during their first years together by designing greeting cards, but the Great Depression halted their career in that field.

Robert turned to etchings, and although his talent shone, he could not make a living with this craft. He illustrated his first book in 1930, and the quality of his work brought him more and more requests to do book illustrations, so this is where he focused his efforts.

Robert and Marie built a home in Westport in 1936. They named the place Rabbit Hill due to the large population of rabbits that lived in the area. Husband and wife worked side by side and lived in the same house for the rest of their lives. Robert even built models of the animals he wrote about and placed them in the garden of their home.

In 1939, Robert wrote his first book, *Ben and Me* (Little, Brown, 1939), which he also illustrated. From then on, although Robert continued to illustrate books for others, he concentrated on both writing and illustrating his own material. *Ben and Me* also started a tradition for Robert of writing books about famous people as seen through the eyes of their pets. In this case, the story of Benjamin Franklin is told by Amos, a mouse.

A friend of the Lawson's, Munro Leaf, decided to write a manuscript for Robert that would show the rest of the world what he knew: that Robert had a special gift as an illustrator. The result of their teamwork, a book about a peace-loving bull called *The Story of Ferdinand* (Viking Press, 1938), catapulted both men into the limelight. They teamed up again for *Wee Gillis* (Viking Press, 1938), which was named a Caldecott Honor Book in 1939.

In 1941, Robert won the Caldecott Medal for a book he wrote and illustrated, *They Were Strong and Good* (Viking Press, 1940), based on the stories of his ancestors. When Robert won the Newbery Medal in 1945 for *Rabbit Hill,* he became the first and still the only person ever to win both the Caldecott and the Newbery Medals. All along the way, the success of *Rabbit Hill* seemed to be announced by the rabbits themselves. On the way to the mailbox one day, he spotted a small rabbit just like the one in the book. In the mailbox, he found a letter from his editor, May Massee, telling him how much she loved the book. Shortly before he received a good review on the book, or a check for the sales, a horde of rabbits would suddenly be present in the yard.

Most amazing, however, is that after a two-month illness during which time Robert didn't get to his studio to work, he spotted through the widow one day a young rabbit, again just like the one in his book. The rabbit sat and sat for ten minutes before hopping away. Robert hadn't seen a rabbit in the area for a long time. But the next day, in the mail, came the letter telling him that his book had been awarded the Newbery Medal.

When Robert made his acceptance speech, he said he wished he could divide the Medal like a pie and give a piece to everyone who deserved it, including his editor, May Massee, and his wife, Marie. *Rabbit Hill,* he said, was the one book he wrote of which he had little to do with the writing of it. "I pushed the pencil and pecked at the typewriter, but someone else certainly must have written it. With every other book I've ever done I have always made a complete outline and had everything planned up to the last line, but for this one I had nothing at all" (Miller and Field 1955, 264).

Winning both the Newbery and Caldecott Medals gave Lawson a great feeling of responsibility for his young readers. He spent many of his later years teaching, reaching out to young readers and making every effort to never talk down to anyone, no matter how much younger than he. Robert Lawson died in 1957 at the age of sixty-four.

Whether written by the rabbits or by Robert himself, *Rabbit Hill* stands as a classic and one that will delight readers of all ages for years and years to come. His mother would have been proud of her son and of his many books, none of which anyone would dare call "sculch."

A Word to My Readers:

(On writing *They Were Strong and Good*) I have hoped that just presenting a simple picture of some of these people would give to the young people of this time, and perhaps to their parents, a feeling of pride in their country and their forbears and a feeling of great responsibility. (Hoffman and Samuels 1972, 262)

Books by Robert Lawson

Ben and Me: A New and Astonishing Life of Benjamin Franklin as Written by His Good Mouse Amos (Little, Brown, 1939, 1988).

Captain Kidd's Cat (Little, Brown, 1956, 1984).

Dick Whittington and His Cat (Limited Editions Club, 1949).

The Fabulous Flight (Little, Brown, 1949, 1984).

The Great Wheel (Viking Press, 1957; Walker, 1993).

I Discover Columbus (Little, Brown, 1941, 1991).

Just for Fun, a Collection of Stories and Verses (Rand McNally, 1940).

Mr. Revere and I (Little, Brown, 1953, 1981, 1988).

Mr. Twigg's Mistake (Little, Brown, 1947).

Rabbit Hill (Viking Press, 1944; Puffin Books, 1977; Penguin, 1978).

Robbut, a Tale of Tails (Gregg Press, 1981; Linnet Books, 1989).

They Were Strong and Good (Viking Press, 1940).

The Tough Winter (Viking Press, Junior Literary Guild, 1954; Puffin Books, 1979).

Watchwords of Liberty: A Pageant of American Quotations (Little, Brown, 1957).

*illustrated by the author
Robert Lawson also illustrated books by other authors, including the Newbery Award Medal Book for 1943, *Adam of the Road,* by Elizabeth Janet Gray.

For More Information About/by Robert Lawson

Hoffman, Miriam, and Eva Samuels. 1972. *Authors and Illustrators of Children's Books*. R. R. Bowker.

Miller, Bertha Mahony, and Elinor Whitney Field, eds. 1955. *The Newbery Medal Books: 1922–1955*. Horn Book.

1946: Lois Lenski

Born	October 14, 1893 Springfield, Ohio
Married	Arthur Covey, 1921 (children: Stephen)
Died	September 11, 1974

Awards and Honors

Newbery Medal (Contemporary Life): *Strawberry Girl* (Lippincott, 1945)
Newbery Honor Book for 1937: *Phoebe Fairchild: Her Book* (Frederick A. Stokes, 1936)
Newbery Honor Book for 1942: *Indian Captive: The Story of Mary Jemison* (Frederick A. Stokes, 1941)

About the Author and Her Writing

When Lois Lenski turned six years old, her family moved from Springfield, Ohio, to the small town of Anna, also in Ohio. The family's move raised the population of the town from 200 to 207.

Lois lived in Anna, Ohio, until she finished high school. Her father, a Lutheran minister, was strict with the family, and there were few luxuries, but growing up in a small town made up for any lack Lois might otherwise have felt. The close bonds developed among families and friends, the freedom to roam the countryside, and the feeling of safety and security; all these enveloped Lois as she grew from a child to a teenager and shaped her into a calm, confident, capable adult.

> My fundamental interest in both my historical and my regional books is always the same. It is an interest in people—especially children. I have a great curiosity to find out what people think, feel, say and do; to understand their behavior and the motives behind it. (Miller and Field 1955, 279)

After high school, Lois studied to be a teacher. Her high school English teacher encouraged her to specialize in English, for she felt certain that Lois had gifts in this area. Lois graduated from Ohio State University and the College of Education, all the while figuring that teaching would be her vocation. But despite her focus, Lois found that her heart was really in art and drawing, a love she first experienced as a little girl copying magazine covers and tracing the pictures from flower catalogs.

At the urging of another teacher, Lois decided to attend the Art Students' League in New York City for a year. Her father was greatly opposed to the idea. He wanted his daughter to settle into a secure job as a teacher. When Lois insisted on going to New York to study art, her father refused to offer any financial support. So Lois, after a year of full-time study, began taking art classes during half days and painting illustrations for Christmas cards and place cards so that she could earn a living.

After four years of working and going to school, Lois spent a year in Italy and London. Upon her return to the United States, she was given her first job as an illustrator, when she received a commission to illustrate a book. She did such a fine job that soon many publishers were coming to her and offering her more illustration opportunities.

In 1921, Lois married a famous mural painter, Arthur Covey, a widower who brought with him an instant family: a twelve-year-old daughter and a four-year-old son from his first marriage. Soon they added their own son, Stephen. Lois, always a careful observer of human nature and especially of children, was filled with the ideas for books as she watched her young son play. She decided to write and illustrate a series of books for very small children, with the title character being named, aptly enough, "Mr. Small." A series of different "Small" books were eventually published.

Lois enjoyed writing and illustrating her own books. She felt that doing the writing and the illustrating allowed the resulting book to be more cohesive. Lois also believed that children made the best critics, and often tried out her stories and illustrations on children before she submitted a final work. Once she changed an illustration of a cow standing in a field because a little child pointed out to her that the cow looked as if it were standing *on* the fence, not behind it!

Lois was a hard worker, but as her workload increased, her health began to fail. She and her family started spending winters in the South. Through this supposed interruption in Lois's life came the inspiration for many of her most popular books. Up until then, most of her research for her books, aside from the books written for little children, came from doing research from books others had written.

As she spent more and more time living among diverse people in different regions of the country, she became not only a keen observer but also a participant in their lives. It wasn't unusual for a flock of children to gather around her as she sat in a field with her drawing board and pencils, sketching a scene. This often led to a family inviting her into their home for a cup of coffee or a meal. Lois truly became a part of the lives of the people, and through these experiences, her love of humankind in all its shapes and forms became deepened even further.

When Lois spent time in a new region, she absorbed the local stories, listened to the music, and sketched the people and their way of life. So when she wrote her books, she accurately conveyed the attitudes, feelings, and experiences of the people. She began writing books for older children, books that told the stories of the mountain people of North Carolina; the French-speaking folks of the Louisiana bayou; and the Florida "Crackers," the very poorest white people, struggling to earn a living off the land. Lois's books set a new standard of excellence in children's literature by portraying the lifestyles found in the various regions of the United States.

A Word to My Readers:

Words, as listed in the dictionary, are dead. Words become alive only with use. A coat takes on the character of a man after he has worn it and shaped it to his person—it becomes truly his, and reflects his personality. Until words are used they are dead and lifeless. Through use, words become living speech, echoing the spirit within. Words need to be "worn" to attain beauty. There is poetry in the common speech of man. (Miller and Field 1955, 286)

Lois's book *Strawberry Girl* earned her the Newbery Medal in 1946. In her acceptance speech, she said that she hoped that the medal didn't just represent the merit of this one book but of the series of books she felt committed to writing about the children of the United States of America. She wrote over one hundred books and illustrated over fifty by other authors.

Lois and her husband lived for many years in an old farmhouse in Connecticut. Known as Greenacres and built in 1790, this home sounds like a perfect place for a woman who treasured the history of her country.

Books by Lois Lenski

Adventure in Understanding: Talks to Parents, Teachers, and Librarians, 1944–1966 (Friends of the Florida State Library, 1968).

Animals for Me (Oxford University Press, 1941; H. Z. Walck, [1959?]).

Arabella and Her Aunts (Frederick A. Stokes, 1932).

Bayou Suzette (Frederick A. Stokes, 1943).

Benny and His Penny (A. A. Knopf, 1931).

Berries in the Scoop, a Cape Cod Cranberry Story (Lippincott, 1956).

Big Little Davy (Oxford University Press, 1956).

Blue Ridge Billy (Lippincott, 1946).

Boom Town Boy (Lippincott, 1948).

Bound Girl of Cobble Hill (Frederick A. Stokes, 1938).

City Poems (H. Z. Walck, 1971).

Coal Camp Girl (Lippincott, 1959).

Corn Farm Boy (Lippincott, 1954).

Cotton in My Sack (Lippincott, 1949).

Cowboy Small (Oxford University Press, 1949; H. Z. Walck, 1960).

Davy and His Dog (Oxford University Press, 1957; H. Z. Walck, 1958).

Davy Goes Places (H. Z. Walck, 1961).

Davy's Day (H. Z. Walck, 1959).

Debbie and Her Dolls (H. Z. Walck, 1970).

Debbie and Her Family (H. Z. Walck, 1969).

Debbie and Her Grandma (H. Z. Walck, 1967).

Debbie and Her Pets (H. Z. Walck, 1971).

Debbie Goes to Nursery School (H. Z. Walck, 1970).

*illustrated by the author
Lois Lenski also illustrated books by other authors.

Debbie Herself (H. Z. Walck, 1969).

**Deer Valley Girl* (Lippincott, 1968).

A Dog Came to School (H. Z. Walck, 1955; Oxford University Press, 1955).

The Easter Rabbit's Parade (Oxford University Press, 1936).

Flood Friday (Lippincott, 1956).

**Florida, My Florida: Poems* (Friends of the Library, Florida State University, 1971).

**A Going to the Westward* (Frederick A. Stokes, 1937).

**Gooseberry Garden* (Harper & Brothers, 1934).

**Grandmother Tippytoe* (Frederick A. Stokes, 1931).

**High Rise Secret* (Lippincott, 1966).

Houseboat Girl (Lippincott, 1957).

I Like Winter (Oxford University Press, 1950; H. Z. Walck, 1960).

Indian Captive: The Story of Mary Jemison (Frederick A. Stokes, 1941; Harper-Collins, 1994).

Journey into Childhood. The Autobiography of Lois Lenski (Lippincott, 1972).

Judy's Journey (Lippincott, 1947).

Let's Play House (Oxford University Press, 1944; H. Z. Walck, 1961).

Little Airplane (Oxford University Press, 1938; H. Z. Walck, 1959).

Little Auto (H. Z. Walck, 1959).

Little Baby Ann (Oxford University Press, 1935).

The Little Family: A Little Book (Doubleday, Doran, 1932; Random House, 2002).

The Little Farm (Oxford University Press, 1942; H. Z. Walck, 1959, 1965).

The Little Fire Engine (Oxford University Press, 1946; H. Z. Walck, [1960?]).

**A Little Girl of Nineteen Hundred* (Frederick A. Stokes, 1928).

The Little Sail Boat (Oxford University Press, 1937; H. Z. Walck, 1960).

**Little Sioux Girl* (Lippincott, 1958).

The Little Train (Oxford University Press, 1940; H. Z. Walck, 1960).

Lois Lenski's Big Book of Mr. Small (H. Z. Walck, 1979; Derrydale Books/Crown, 1985).

**Lois Lenski's Christmas Stories* (Lippincott, 1968).

**Mama Hattie's Girl* (Lippincott, 1953).

More Mr. Small (H. Z. Walck, 1979).

Mr. and Mrs. Noah (T. Y. Crowell, 1948; Random House, 2002).

Now It's Fall (Oxford University Press, 1958; H. Z. Walck, 1948).

Ocean Born Mary (Frederick A. Stokes, 1939).

On a Summer Day (Oxford University Press, 1953; H. Z. Walck, 1959).

Papa Small (H.Z. Walck, 1951, 1966).

Peanuts for Billy Ben (Lippincott, 1952).

Phoebe Fairchild: Her Book (Frederick A. Stokes, 1936).

Policeman Small (H. Z. Walck, 1962).

Prairie School (Lippincott, 1951).

Project Boy (Lippincott, 1954).

Puritan Adventure (Lippincott, 1944).

San Francisco Boy (Lippincott, 1955).

Shoo Fly Girl (Lippincott, 1963).

Sing a Song of People (Little, Brown, 1987; Delmar, 1990).

Skipping Village: A Town of Not So Long Ago (Frederick A. Stokes, 1927).

Spinach Boy (Frederick A. Stokes, 1930).

Spring Is Here (Oxford University Press, 1945; H. Z. Walck, [1960?]).

Strawberry Girl (Lippincott, 1945).

Surprise for Davy (Oxford University Press, 1947; H. Z. Walck, 1959).

Surprise for Mother (Frederick A. Stokes, 1934).

Texas Tomboy (Lippincott, 1950).

To Be a Logger (Lippincott, 1967).

Two Brothers and Their Animal Friends (Frederick A. Stokes, 1929).

Two Brothers and Their Baby Sister (Frederick A. Stokes, 1930).

We Live by the River (Lippincott, 1956).

We Live in the City (Lippincott, 1954).

We Live in the Country (Lippincott, 1960).

We Live in the North (Lippincott, 1965).

We Live in the South (Lippincott, 1952).

We Live in the Southwest (Lippincott, 1962).

For More Information About/by Lois Lenski

Autobiography: 1972. *Journey into Childhood.* Lippincott.

Miller, Bertha Mahony, and Elinor Whitney Field, eds. 1955. *The Newbery Medal Books: 1922–1955.* Horn Book.

1947: Carolyn Sherwin Bailey (Hill)

Born	October 25, 1875
	Hoosick Falls, New York
Married	Dr. Eben Clayton Hill, 1936
Died	December 23, 1961

Awards and Honors

Newbery Medal (Fantasy): *Miss Hickory* (Viking Press, 1946)

About the Author and Her Writing

Apples played a large role in the life of Carolyn Sherwin Bailey. When she was six years old, a visiting physician handed her a large apple and told her to go for a long walk and not return until she had eaten the entire fruit. By the time little Carolyn returned home, she found that a baby sister had been born.

Carolyn married her husband, Dr. Eben Clayton Hill, in 1936. Dr. Hill was a well-known physician at Johns Hopkins University. The couple lived in an old farmhouse in New Hampshire, where they owned over four hundred apple trees.

> [Imagination] is a place of refuge all [our] lives, a guidebook to reality. (Miller and Field 1955, 297)

And in the book that won the Newbery Medal in 1947, the title character, a doll named *Miss Hickory,* was made from the branch of an apple tree.

Carolyn was educated at home until she reached the age of twelve. Her mother, Emma Blanchard Bailey, taught mathematics and was a writer. Her father, Charles Henry Bailey, was a pioneer in metallurgy, the chemistry of metals. He traveled for business in Canada and the United States as well as Central and South America. It's no wonder that Carolyn recalled many adventures from her childhood.

One of Carolyn's earliest memories (along with eating the apple that preceded the birth of her younger sister) was of riding her tricycle up and down the halls of an asylum for insane criminals. Her mother spent time there as a caseworker and volunteer writer and often brought her daughter along.

As a child, Carolyn loved making up stories. Before she could write, she dictated stories to her mother, who cheerfully wrote them down. Carolyn won twenty-five dollars at the age of five for one of her stories, a princely sum of money in 1880.

Carolyn trained as a teacher at Teachers College, Columbia University, as well as at the Montessori School in Rome and the New York School of Social Work. She worked as a teacher and a social worker, following in some degree in the footsteps of her mother. Once she published her first book in 1905, her career as a writer and editor of books for children superseded her other work and provided her with a career that combined her love of history with her gift for storytelling.

When Carolyn was just a girl, her grandmother created the first Miss Hickory doll. Carolyn and her little friend played for many hours outside under the lilac bushes. When Carolyn moved on to other interests, the little doll was forgotten.

Perhaps "forgotten" is too strong a word. Miss Hickory remained tucked away in Carolyn's memory until a time some sixty years later when Carolyn was in Florida. Battling a miserable case of hay fever, she longed to return to the small, mountain town where she had spent so much time during each fall. Without her trusty typewriter at hand, Carolyn took out a pad of paper and a pencil, and the story of Miss Hickory began. Later, Carolyn insisted that the feisty twig doll with a hickory nut head wrote the story herself, and that Carolyn served only as the secretary, much as her own mother had done for her years before.

Until the success of *Miss Hickory,* Carolyn had been best known for her books of Americana. She had researched the history and development of pioneer arts, crafts, and toys, all of special interest to her. Her collections of stories entitled *For the Children's Hour* had also gained recognition for the author. All in all, Carolyn wrote over seventy books for children.

Carolyn maintained a sense of whimsy and adventure throughout her long life. The old farmhouse where she and her husband lived had six fireplaces as well as a secret staircase, not to mention the acres of apple trees. Carolyn told visitors that a friendly "ghost" lived at the farmhouse, because every so often a door would unlatch itself. This didn't bother Carolyn. She claimed that "if any ghost loves the old house enough to come back to it, he or she is most welcome" (Miller and Field 1955, 290).

In her later years Carolyn lived six months of each year at the farmhouse and six months in New York City, on the edge of Grammercy Park. Although she enjoyed the view from the window of her New York apartment, a view that included lovely flower beds, trees, and children constantly at play, Carolyn's heart remained in the country, where she and *Miss Hickory* were born.

A Word to My Readers:

To our teachers, to far-seeing editors and publishers, mainly to our librarians do we owe the preservation, in a troubled world, of the rhapsodies of childhood. (Miller and Field 1955, 299)

Books by Carolyn Sherwin Bailey (Hill)

Bailey's In and Outdoor Play Games: Boys' and Girls' Book of What to Play and Make (A. Whitman, 1923).

Boys and Girls of Colonial Days (A. Flanagan, 1917).

Boys and Girls of Discovery Days (A. Flanagan, 1926).

Boys and Girls of Pioneer Days, from Washington to Lincoln (A. Flanagan, 1924).

Boys and Girls of Today: A First Book of Citizenship (A. Flanagan, 1928).

Broad Stripes and Bright Stars: Stories of American History (Milton Bradley, 1919).

The Children's Book of Games & Parties (M. A. Donohue & Co., 1913).

A Christmas Party: Poem (Pantheon, 1975).

Country Stop (Viking Press, 1942).

Daily Program of Gift and Occupation Work (Milton Bradley, 1904).

Enchanted Village (Viking Press, 1950).

Finnegan II, His Nine Lives (Viking Press, 1953).

Firelight Stories: Folk Tales Retold for Kindergarten, School and Home (Milton Bradley, 1907).

Flickertail (H. Z. Walck, 1962).

For the Children's Hour (Milton Bradley, 1906; Gale Research, 1974).

For the Story Teller: Story Telling and Stories to Tell (Milton Bradley, 1913; Gryphon Books, 1971; Gale Research, 1975).

Friendly Tales: A Community Story Book (Milton Bradley, 1923).

From Moccasins to Wings: Stories of Our Travel Ways (Milton Bradley, 1938).

Girls' Make-at-Home Things (Frederick A. Stokes, 1912).

Hero Stories (Milton Bradley, 1919).

Homespun Playdays (Viking Press, 1941).

In the Animal World (Milton Bradley, 1924).

The Little Rabbit Who Wanted Red Wings (Platt & Munk, 1945, 1961, 1987).

Little Readers Series (McLoughlin Brothers, 1934).

The Little Red Schoolhouse (Viking Press, 1957).

Merry Tales for Children: Best Stories of Humor for Boys and Girls (Milton Bradley, 1921).

Merry Tales for Children: Best Stories of Humor for Boys and Girls (Platt & Munk, 1943).

Miss Hickory (Viking Press, 1946; Penguin, 1978).

Old Man Rabbit's Dinner Party (Platt & Munk, 1949).

Once Upon a Time Animal Stories (Milton Bradley, 1918).

Pioneer Art in America (Viking Press, 1944).

Plays for the Children's Hour (Milton Bradley, 1931; Core Collections Books, 1978).

Read Aloud Stories (Milton Bradley, 1929).

Schoolroom Plans and Projects (ed.) (Milton Bradley, 1932).

Sixty Games and Pastimes for All Occasions (A. Whitman, 1928).

Stories Children Need (Milton Bradley, 1916).

Stories Children Want (Milton Bradley, 1931; Platt & Munk, 1943).

Stories for Any Day (Pilgrim Press, 1917).

Stories for Every Holiday (Abingdon Press, 1918; Abingdon Press, Gale Research, 1974; Omnigraphics, 1989).

Stories for Sunday Telling (Pilgrim Press, 1916).

Stories from an Indian Cave: The Cherokee Cave Builders (A. Whitman, 1924).

Stories of Great Adventures (Adapted from the Classics) (Milton Bradley, 1919).

Tell Me Another Story: The Book of Story Programs (Platt & Munk, 1943).

The Torch of Courage, and Other Stories (Milton Bradley, 1921).

Untold History Stories (F. A. Owen, 1927).

What to Do for Uncle Sam: A First Book of Citizenship (A. Flanagan, 1918).

When Grandfather Was a Boy (Ginn & Co., 1928).

Wonder Stories, the Best Myths for Boys and Girls (Milton Bradley, 1920).

The Wonderful Tree and Golden Day Stories (A. Whitman, 1925).

The Wonderful Window, and Other Stories (Cokesbury Press, 1926).

York Story League (Platt & Munk, 1934).

For More Information About/by Carolyn Sherwin Bailey (Hill)

Commire, Anne, ed. 1978. *Something About the Author: Facts and Pictures About Contemporary Authors and Illustrators of Books for Young People.* Vol. 14. Gale Research.

Miller, Bertha Mahony, and Elinor Whitney Field, eds. 1955. *Newbery Medal Books: 1922–1955.* Horn Book.

1948: William Pène du Bois

Born	May 9, 1916 Nutley, New Jersey
Married	Jane Bouché, 1943 Willa Kim, 1955
Died	February 5, 1993 Nice, France

Awards and Honors

Newbery Medal (Adventure, Fantasy): *The Twenty-One Balloons* (Viking Press, 1947)
Wrote and illustrated the 1952 Caldecott Honor Book *Bear Party* (Viking Press, 1951)
Wrote and illustrated the 1957 Caldecott Honor Book *Lion* (Viking Press, 1956)

About the Author and His Writing

As a child, William Pène du Bois (Pen Doo-BWA) loved the circus. He averaged thirty visits a year. His best friend's parents were a lion tamer and a tightrope walker, and his favorite game as a young child was to pretend that he was an elephant trainer, with his father serving as the elephant.

The circus offered Billy, as he was known to his family, a much-needed release from the regimen of his daily life. Both Billy and his sister, Yvonne, attended boarding schools during the week. The routine at Billy's school was such that the boys dressed at the same time, washed their hands and faces at the same time, dumped the water down the sink at the same time, and sat down to eat at precisely the same time. The weekends were quite different. Billy and Yvonne's mother would stuff them full of good food, unlike the morning bread and coffee that was their weekday breakfast. And every Saturday night during the winter, the family attended the circus.

Billy was not an avid reader as a child. He later attributed this to the fact that when he was eight years old and just learning to read English, his family moved to France. After Billy turned fourteen, the family returned to the United States. By then, he had forgotten most of his English.

But Billy's lack of reading skills did not keep him from loving books. His favorites were the ones with intricate illustrations, which he absorbed with great concentration. He also enjoyed the science fiction writings of Jules Verne, and even at the age of five, Billy spent hours with these books, poring over the drawings of inventions and mechanical devices that never ceased to amaze and delight him.

Artwork came naturally to Billy. His father was an acclaimed artist, and the boy learned many of his skills at home. Yet some of William Pène du Bois's best skills in art came from his sixth-grade mathematics teacher, Monsieur Diremaire.

Monsieur Diremaire, and many of the schoolteachers in France, believed that perfection and neatness were as important as figuring out the right answers. Every morning, when the boys brought their homework assignment to Monsieur Diremaire, they had to endure a painful ten minutes during which time the teacher held up and examined each paper. If the paper passed his scrutiny and was judged neat and flawless, it ended up in one pile on the desk. If there was even one small spot of ink or a misplaced line, Monsieur Diremaire tore the homework paper into four neat strips and set them on a separate pile on his desk.

The importance of neatness and clarity made a profound impression on William, and the lessons proved useful when he later turned to writing and illustrating. His own worktable was exemplary. Every pencil was kept sharp and lined up in neat rows, and the brushes were similarly arranged. William made it a goal to complete one perfect drawing per day. He felt that to do more than that would be to sacrifice the quality of his work. If, at the end of the day, the finished drawing or painting did not meet his standards, he would rip it up, much as his mathematics professor had done to his homework assignments many years before.

> In writing and illustrating children's books, I keep but one audience in mind, and that audience is myself as a child and the friends I used to play with. (Miller and Field 1955, 309)

The du Bois family returned to the United States when William was fourteen. The young boy set his mind on going to college. Two years later, when he was but sixteen years old, he was ready to attend Harvard University in Massachusetts when his parents told him they could not afford to pay his tuition to school. Instead of being disappointed, du Bois announced that he planned to write and illustrate books for children, for that was his plan whether or not he went to college.

William never regretted his decision. His first book, *Giant Otto,* was published when he was only nineteen. Two more books followed in quick succession. He then served in the United States Army during World War II and actually wrote the manuscript for *The Twenty-One Balloons* while in the service. He submitted the manuscript to his publisher the day he completed his tour of duty, and the book that resulted won the Newbery Medal in 1948. William later wrote and illustrated two Caldecott Honor books, *Bear Party* (1952) and *Lion* (1957).

When he wrote a book, William first spent so much time thinking about the story and working on the precise illustrations that by the time he sat down to write, the story wrote itself very quickly. The years of routine and discipline paid off in ways he might never have imagined when he was little Billy at the boarding school.

William's regimented life may also have led to his fascination with the thought of living on an island, a theme present in many of his books, including the 1948 Newbery Medal–winning book, *The Twenty-One Balloons.* He had first imagined the joy of sailing away in a hot air balloon back at school in France, when he and a friend discussed what they would do if the world came to an end. The two decided that they would sail off in a hot air balloon just as the world exploded into bits and pieces.

The years following the Newbery Medal were filled with writing, including a series of books for children on the seven deadly sins. He also continued an earlier series about

---

A Word to My Readers:

As a child I hardly read at all, although I loved to look at books. I was the sort of fellow who just looks at pictures. I try to keep such impatient children in mind in making my books. (Miller and Field 1955, 309)

a large dog named Otto. Otto had been the main character in du Bois's first published book.

William married twice: the first time in 1943 to Jane Bouché, the daughter of a famous painter, and the second time in 1955 to Willa Kim, a theatrical designer. In 1993, he died in a hospital in France after suffering a stroke.

Books by William Pène du Bois

*The Alligator Case (Harper & Row, 1965).

Bear Circus (Viking Press, 1971).

*Bear Party (Viking Press, 1951).

Call Me Bandicoot (Harper & Row, 1970).

*Elisabeth, the Cow Ghost (Viking Press, 1964).

*The Flying Locomotive (Viking Press, 1941).

The Forbidden Forest (London: Chatto & Windus, Harper & Row, 1978).

Gentleman Bear (Farrar, Straus & Giroux, 1985).

Giant Otto (Viking Press, 1936).

*The Giant (Viking Press, 1954).

*The Great Geppy (Viking Press, 1940).

*The Hare and the Tortoise & the Tortoise and the Hare (Doubleday, 1972).

The Horse in the Camel Suit (Harper & Row, 1967).

*Lazy Tommy Pumpkinhead (Harper & Row, 1966).

*Lion (Viking Press, 1956).

Mother Goose for Christmas (Viking Press, 1973).

Otto and the Magic Potatoes (Viking Press, 1970).

Otto at Sea (Viking Press, 1936).

Otto in Africa (Viking Press, 1961).

Otto in Texas: The Adventures of Otto (Viking Press, 1959).

Peter Graves (Cheshire, 1969).

*Porko von Popbutton (Harper & Row, 1969).

Pretty Pretty Peggy Mofitt (Harper & Row, 1968).

*Squirrel Hotel (Viking Press, 1952; Gregg Press, 1979).

*The Three Policemen; or, Young Bottsford of Farbe Island (Viking Press, 1938, 1960).

*The Twenty-One Balloons (Viking Press, 1947; Puffin Books, 1986).

*illustrated by the author
William Pène du Bois also illustrated books by other authors, including Sick Day, by Newbery Medal–winner Patricia MacLachlan.

For More Information About/by William Pène du Bois

Chicago Tribune. 1993. February 8, sec. 4, p. 8.

Kunitz, Stanley J., and Howard Haycraft, eds. 1951. *The Junior Book of Authors.* 2d ed. H. W. Wilson.

Miller, Bertha Mahony, and Elinor Whitney Field, eds. 1955. *Newbery Medal Books: 1922–1955.* Horn Book.

1949: Marguerite Henry

Born   April 13, 1902
              Milwaukee, Wisconsin

Married   Sydney Crocker Henry, 1923

Died   November 26, 1997
              Rancho Santa Fe, California

Awards and Honors

Newbery Medal (Animal Stories): *King of the Wind* (Rand McNally, 1948)
Newbery Honor Book for 1946: *Justin Morgan Had a Horse* (Wilcox & Follett, 1945)
Newbery Honor Book for 1948: *Misty of Chincoteague* (Rand McNally, 1947)

About the Author and Her Writing

For a person who grew up without any pets, Marguerite Henry knew a lot about animals, especially horses. In fact, her stories about horses are considered to be some of the best ever written.

Marguerite was born in Milwaukee, Wisconsin, the youngest of five children, three of whom were almost grown up by the time Marguerite was born. Her childhood was a happy one. On cold winter evenings the family would gather around the big table in the dining room. Her mother darned stockings and her father read and smoked his pipe, while Marguerite and her sister Gertrude did their homework.

> Putting a book to bed—that is, preparing it for the press—is as much fun to me as the writing of it. It provides the excitement of playing in an orchestra, with none of the dull hours of practicing. (Miller and Field 1955, 332)

Some of Marguerite's fondest childhood memories come from being in her father's printing shop. She once said, "Papa was a printer and his shop was a wondrous place. Presses whirred. Long sheets of paper streamed out of them. They went in clean and came out covered with words. Papa's desk was more exciting than Pandora's box. It yielded big, fat tablets in pink, green, yellow and blue, and bundles of pencils that wrote in a big black swathe." Marguerite was charmed by the stacks of paper tablets. When she daydreamed her father would say, "A tablet for your thoughts," instead of the usual "A penny for your thoughts" (Kunitz and Haycraft 1951, 156).

Perhaps it was the thrill of seeing words and paper being created that fueled Marguerite's love of writing. As a child, Marguerite wrote many of her own stories and poems on her father's colorful tablets. At the age of eleven, she sold her first story to the *Delineator Magazine*. She wrote often for her high school newspaper and continued to write while she studied at the Milwaukee State Teachers College.

When Marguerite was twenty-one years old, she married Sydney Crocker Henry, who encouraged her to keep writing. She sold many articles to various magazines.

Marguerite and Sydney hired a cook, Beda, who came from Finland. Beda and her husband, Effendi, told wonderful stories about their native country. Marguerite enjoyed these stories so much that she decided to write a book for children, with the main characters being two Finnish children, Auno and Tauno. The book became a big success, and Marguerite decided to invest her writing energies into creating books for children.

> Horses are honest always. Sometimes people are not. (Hoffman and Samuels 1972, 206)

The Henrys made up for all the pets that neither of them had had as children. They moved to the country and bought their first horse, Misty. Misty became the inspiration for many of Marguerite's most popular books, including *Misty of Chincoteague,* which was named a Newbery Honor Book for 1948. But that was not her first award: her book *Justin Morgan Had a Horse* had already won a Newbery Honor Award in 1946.

The two Newbery Honor Awards were just a prelude for her achievements in publishing books for children. In 1949, *King of the Wind* won the Newbery Medal.

> It takes an understanding reader to discover his own book. The writer is no more than the farmer with his bag of seeds. The reader is a field, new plowed in spring. The farmer scatters his seeds, but all the plants that grow from them do not come up alike . . . That's the way it is with books. Sometimes a book gives you a small moment of happiness; and sometimes when you close the cover, the books grows big within you. (Miller and Field 1955, 333)

King of the Wind began as a picture on a piece of letterhead stationery. Wesley Dennis, an illustrator and a friend of Marguerite's, designed the letterhead for a man who owned a famous Godolphin Arabian horse. Marguerite and Wesley became fascinated by the story of this particular breed of horse. They joined together to write and illustrate the book that went on to win the Newbery Medal.

Marguerite always spent a lot of time researching her stories. She traveled to places where the horses were born and raised and spoke to the people who owned them. Her stories are based on solid facts and real-life characters, so the readers of her books learn a great deal without even realizing it.

Marguerite said that her only "down" times were when she turned in a manuscript to her editor. "I am suddenly bereft. It is as if the sun had slid into the horizon and a cold curtain of rain had slapped across my face. A whole lifetime of emptiness seems to stretch out before me. And then, oh happy relief! In a little while the manuscript is back home,

> ### A Word to My Readers:
> I'm trying to write a book that you can crawl into as snugly as you do into your own bed, a book about which you can say, "This is mine. It fits around me. I fit into it. It fits under and over and around me. It warms me. It is mine, mine, *mine!"* (Miller and Field 1955, 333)

with blessed little question marks along the margins. Then once again I'm happy. I've got work to do!" (Miller and Field 1955, 334).

Marguerite never had any children. As far as the world of literature is concerned, her children are those who have read and loved her books. She died in 1997 in California.

Books by Marguerite Henry

Alaska in Story and Pictures (A. Whitman, 1941).

Album of Dogs (Rand McNally, 1970).

Album of Horses (Rand McNally, 1951; Aladdin Books, 1993).

All About Horses (Random House, 1962, 1967).

Always Reddy (Whittlesey House, 1947).

Argentina in Story and Pictures (A. Whitman, 1946).

Australia in Story and Pictures (A. Whitman, 1946).

The Bahamas in Story and Pictures (A. Whitman, 1946).

Benjamin West and His Cat Grimalkin (Bobbs Merrill, 1947; Collier Macmillan, 1987).

Birds and Home (M. A. Donohue & Co., 1942).

Birds at Home (Hubbard Press, 1972).

Black Gold (Rand McNally, 1957; Checkerboard Press, 1987; Aladdin Books, 1992).

Born to Trot (Rand McNally, 1950; Checkerboard Press, 1987; Aladdin Paperbacks, 1993).

A Boy and a Dog (Wilcox & Follett, 1944).

Brazil in Story and Pictures (A. Whitman, 1941).

Brighty of the Grand Canyon (Rand McNally, 1953; Checkerboard Press, [1987?]; Aladdin Books, 1991).

British Honduras in Story and Pictures (A. Whitman, 1946).

Brown Sunshine of Sawdust Valley (Simon & Schuster Books for Young Readers, 1996).

Canada in Story and Pictures (A. Whitman, 1941).

Cinnabar, the One O'Clock Fox (Rand McNally, 1956).

Dear Readers and Riders (Rand McNally, 1969).

Dominican Republic in Story and Pictures (A. Whitman, 1946).

Five O'Clock Charlie (Rand McNally, 1962; Aladdin Paperbacks, 1994).

Gaudenzia, Pride of the Palio (Rand McNally, 1960).

Geraldine Belinda (Platt & Munk, 1942).

Hawaii in Story and Pictures (A. Whitman, 1946).

The Illustrated Marguerite Henry (Rand McNally, 1980).

Justin Morgan Had a Horse (Wilcox & Follett, 1945; Rand McNally, 1954; Checkerboard Press, 1987, Aladdin Books, 1991).

King of the Wind (Rand McNally, 1948; Checkerboard Press, 1987; Thorndike Press, 1991; Simon & Schuster Books for Young Readers, 2001).

Little Fellow (Rand McNally, 1975).

Little or Nothing from Nottingham (Whittlesey House, 1949).

Marguerite Henry's Album of Horses (Aladdin Books, 1993).

Marguerite Henry's Misty Treasury (Rand McNally, 1982).

Misty of Chincoteague (Rand McNally, 1947; Checkerboard Press, 1987; Aladdin Books, 1991; Simon & Schuster Books for Young Readers, 2000; Thorndike Press, 2000).

Misty's Twilight (Macmillan, 1992; Aladdin Paperbacks, 1996).

Muley Ears, Nobody's Dog (Rand McNally, 1959).

Mustang, Wild Spirit of the West (Rand McNally, 1966; Checkerboard Press, 1987; Aladdin Books, 1992).

New Zealand in Story and Pictures (A. Whitman, 1946).

One Man's Horse (Rand McNally, 1977).

Our First Pony (Rand McNally, 1984; Aladdin Paperbacks, 1997).

Peter Lundy and the Medicine Hat Stallion (originally published under the title *San Domingo, the Medicine Hat Stallion*) (Rand McNally, 1972, 1976, 1977).

A Pictorial Life Story of Misty (Rand McNally, 1976).

Robert Fulton, Boy Craftsman (Bobbs Merrill, 1945, 1962).

San Domingo, The Medicine Hat Stallion (Rand McNally, 1972; Checkerboard Press, 1990; Aladdin Books, 1992).

Sea Star: Orphan of Chincoteague (Rand McNally, 1949; Checkerboard Press, 1987; Aladdin Books, 1991).

Stormy, Misty's Foal (Rand McNally, 1963; Checkerboard Press, 1987; Aladdin Books, 1991).

Virgin Islands in Story and Pictures (A. Whitman, 1946).

Wagging Tails: An Album of Dogs (Rand McNally, 1955).

West Indies in Story and Pictures (A. Whitman, 1941).

White Stallion of Lipizza (Rand McNally, 1964; Aladdin Books, 1994; Macmillan, 1994).

The Wildest Horse Race in the World (Rand McNally, 1960, 1976).

For More Information About/by Marguerite Henry

Hoffman, Miriam, and Eva Samuels. 1972. *Authors and Illustrators of Children's Books: Writings on Their Lives and Works.* R. R. Bowker.

Kunitz, Stanley J., and Howard Haycraft, eds. 1951. *The Junior Book of Authors.* 2d ed. H. W. Wilson.

Miller, Bertha Mahony, and Elinor Whitney Field, eds. 1955. *Newbery Medal Books: 1922–1955.* Horn Book.

1950: Marguerite de Angeli

Born	March 14, 1889 Lapeer, Michigan
Married	John Dailey de Angeli, April 2, 1910 (children: John, Arthur, Nina, H. Edward, and Maurice)
Died	June 16, 1987

Awards and Honors

Newbery Medal (Historical Fiction): *The Door in the Wall* (Doubleday, 1949)
Newbery Honor Book for 1957: *Black Fox of Lorne* (Doubleday, 1956)

About the Author and Her Writing

As a young girl, Marguerite de Angeli took piano lessons, but only for a short time. Her teacher thought she was hopeless, since she preferred playing by ear rather than learning the notes. That teacher might have been surprised years later to discover that his "hopeless" pupil had a gift for music, especially for song. While still a young girl, Marguerite was asked to sing in a church choir for pay. She soon decided she wanted to be an opera singer when she grew up.

> The idea for a book starts from such small beginnings that often it is difficult to tell just when it does begin. In a way, each book has grown out of the one before it. (Miller and Field 1955, 345)

Her early dream nearly came true. As a young adult Marguerite was offered a part in an opera by the famous Oscar Hammerstein. Then she met a man by the name of John de Angeli (de AN jel ee) and he persuaded her that she would be much happier if she married him and settled down to raise a family. Marguerite married the man and they had five children. She never regretted her decision.

As a girl, Marguerite saw the world through the eyes of an artist. While talking with her schoolgirl friends, her mind wandered into trying to imagine how she could capture in word or art the joy and excitement she felt in the way the light fell on the leaves or how a tree limb looked against the backdrop of a house. Later, even though she found fulfillment in her roles as wife and mother, Marguerite's urge to draw and write got the best of her.

Trying to combine her writing and drawing with a family that kept increasing in size proved to be a great challenge. Marguerite rose long before breakfast to put in a few hours of undisturbed work. She convinced Maurice Bower, a neighbor's son and a well-known illustrator, to give her drawing lessons. He agreed, with the condition that she give up singing and other outside activities. Between their two very hectic schedules, there were many times when the only opportunity they had to work together was after midnight. It's a wonder that Marguerite ever got any sleep.

Nothing could stop Marguerite. When one of her children, then about a year old, cried to be let into the studio room where his mother worked, she placed him in a playpen a few feet away. Soon the child became restless and his wails so disruptive that Marguerite put the playpen around herself and her easel and let the child have the run of the room.

Marguerite's energetic spirit kept pushing her into the next project, and then the next. Whenever she finished a book she'd promise her family that she would take a break, but it wasn't long before she was off and running with the next idea. She felt that everything in life contained a story and did her best to write as many of those stories as she possibly could.

Marguerite's deep humility, along with her compassion for others, made her a writer whose books often portrayed a message of understanding and open-mindedness toward all people. Many of her stories had characters that dealt with disabilities or the prejudice of others. Her groundbreaking book *Bright April* (Doubleday, 1946) is said to be the first children's book to deal directly with an African-American girl's encounter with racism. Marguerite's characters are so flawlessly developed that the reader of her books can hardly help but receive a heightened sense of compassion and tolerance for all people. This artist who became an author also continued to illustrate books by other authors, as well as a few of her own.

While most of Marguerite's earlier stories centered around the lives of children in the United States, she felt a constant nagging to write a story about medieval England. As she looked back on this, she speculated that the urge came from the many hours she spent as a young girl absorbing the drawings and paintings in a huge volume of art history that belonged to her father. The two sections she had most enjoyed were the pictures of ancient churches and the information devoted to medieval costumes.

Marguerite began reading books of English history. Her fascination with England culminated in a trip to London, where she spent two weeks exploring the nooks and crannies of the buildings and places she had read about. One of these places, St. Paul's Churchyard, had been the home of a bookshop owned by a man several centuries before. The man's name? John Newbery. Isn't it amazing that the book Marguerite eventually wrote about a boy in medieval England won the 1950 Newbery Medal, the prize named after that English bookseller who changed the course of children's literature? Marguerite wrote her autobiography, *Butter at the Old Price*, published in 1971. This book told not only the story of her life as an author and illustrator but also gave an account of the history of children's literature during the 1930s through the 1960s. Marguerite lived for another sixteen years after writing her autobiography. She published her final book, *Friendship and Other Poems* (Doubleday, 1981), at the age of ninety-two. She died six years later, when she was ninety-eight years old.

A Word to My Readers:

(Which she often said to her own children) When you come to a stone wall, if you look far enough, you will find a door in it. (Miller and Field 1955, 352)

Books by Marguerite de Angeli

Black Fox of Lorne (Doubleday, 1956).

Book of Nursery and Mother Goose Rhymes (Doubleday, 1954).

*illustrated by the author
Marguerite de Angeli also illustrated books by other authors.

Bright April (Doubleday, 1946).

Butter at the Old Price: The Autobiography of Marguerite de Angeli (Doubleday, 1971).

Copper Toed Boots (Doubleday, Doran & Co., 1938; Wayne State University Press, 1989).

The Door in the Wall (Doubleday, 1949, *1964, 1989).

Elin's Amerika (Doubleday, Doran & Co., 1941).

Fiddlestrings (Doubleday, 1974).

Friendship and Other Poems (Doubleday, 1981).

Henner's Lydia (Doubleday, Doran & Co., 1936; Herald Press, *1998).

Jared's Island (Doubleday, 1947).

Just Like David (Doubleday, 1951).

The Lion in the Box (Doubleday, 1975).

Petite Suzanne (Doubleday, Doran & Co., 1937).

A Pocket Full of Posies: A Merry Mother Goose (Doubleday, 1961).

*Skippack School (Herald Press, 1999).

Skippack School, Being the Story of Eli Shrawder and of One Christopher Dock (Doubleday, Doran & Co., 1939; Doubleday, 1961).

A Summer Day with Ted and Nina (Doubleday, Doran & Co., 1940).

Ted and Nina Go to the Grocery Store (Doubleday, Doran & Co., 1935).

Ted and Nina Have a Happy Rainy Day (Doubleday, Doran & Co., 1936).

The Ted and Nina Story Book (Doubleday, 1964).

Thee, Hannah! (Doubleday, Doran & Co., 1940; Doubleday, 1989; Herald Press, *1990).

Turkey for Christmas (Westminster Press, 1944, *1965).

Up the Hill (Doubleday, Doran & Co., 1942).

Whistle for the Crossing (Doubleday, 1977).

Yonie Wondernose (Doubleday, 1944, 1989; Herald Press, 1997).

For More Information About/by Marguerite de Angeli

Autobiography: 1971. *Butter at the Old Price: The Autobiography of Marguerite de Angeli.* Doubleday.

Miller, Bertha Mahony, and Elinor Whitney Field, eds. 1955. *Newbery Medal Books: 1922–1955.* Horn Book.

1951: Elizabeth Yates (McGreal)

Born	December 6, 1905
	Buffalo, New York
Married	William McGreal
	November 6, 1929
Died	July 29, 2001
	Concord, New Hampshire

Awards and Honors

Newbery Medal (Biography/Historical Fiction): *Amos Fortune, Free Man* (Aladdin Books, 1950)

About the Author and Her Writing

One week after Elizabeth Yates met William McGreal, the two went camping on a mountain peak in Hudson Highlands of New York. As they sat around a campfire one night, Elizabeth set down the book she had been reading, leaned back, and gazed into the fire and into her future. "That's good writing," she said. "Someday I, too, shall write something good" (Miller and Field 1955, 355). Elizabeth and William married in 1929. And twenty-five years later, the book *Amos Fortune, Free Man* won the 1951 Newbery Medal.

For Elizabeth Yates, the road to the Newbery Medal actually began years before on a farm in New York, where she grew up in a family with six brothers and sisters. Her love of letters and words took root in her at a very early age. Once, at about three years old, she sat under a tree with a picture book while her other brothers and sisters played. She loved the looks and shapes of the letters, and even though she couldn't yet read, thought that perhaps if she drew the letters, she might write a book. All she got for her efforts was a scolding for scribbling on the pages of the book.

> In pioneer days people knew what it was to share. Today is there any truth which we need more than to share what we have and what we are? (Hoffman and Samuels 1990, 425)

Elizabeth spent long hours hiding under her bed with a book, reading. She rode her horse through the countryside, weaving stories in her head. On rainy days she climbed into a deserted pigeon loft in the barn, and there put pencil to paper and wrote out the stories that had been waiting in her imagination.

At the age of ten, an older sister gave Elizabeth a list of books and told Elizabeth she should read these books before she turned eighteen. Elizabeth set about the task, and later credited her sister's assignment as the catalyst that turned her into a dedicated reader.

Elizabeth learned quickly that it would take more than copying letters to write a book. Several of her teachers recognized her gift for writing, and one insightful teacher wrote on one of her essays during her senior year of high school, "a delightful paper to read." That comment meant more to her than the "A" grade she received. It meant that she could do more than form the letters correctly and put commas in the right places; she could write something that people enjoyed reading. From then on, Elizabeth never wavered from her goal to become a writer.

After completing her schooling, Elizabeth tried unsuccessfully to convince her parents that she could make a living as a writer. Despite their hesitation she left home and went to live in New York City, where she worked a variety of odd jobs to earn money and took every writing assignment she could find. She wrote everything from newspaper and magazine articles to book reviews, short stories, and research papers. She took the advice of a friend and wrote something every single day, even if it was just a few lines.

After Elizabeth married, she and her husband lived in England for ten years, where he owned a business. Those years were happy ones, filled with traveling, mountain climbing, and trips to Switzerland, Germany, France, Spain, and Iceland. Her home away from home became the Reading Room of the British Museum, where she spent hours in the company of great books. She published a few stories, poems, and plays. Then, in 1938, her first book, *High Holiday,* was published in England. She finally felt justified in the hours she had given to her writing, and her career as a recognized author was born.

Elizabeth's happy years in England were followed by some tragic times. She and her husband returned to the United States, in part because her husband struggled with the gradual waning of his sight brought upon by an injury he had received as a younger man. Surgery relieved the terrible pain but also cost him the last of his vision. He could no longer read the stories and books that Elizabeth wrote so beautifully.

The two settled on a farm in New Hampshire. Elizabeth fashioned a studio in an upstairs room, with a long table and a couple of chairs set up so she could admire the view out the window. She wrote everything in longhand with a pad of yellow paper and a pencil, then rewrote everything again before typing the final draft.

One evening while on her way to a weekly meeting of a historical society, the Amos Fortune Forum, Elizabeth stopped at the graveyard where Amos Fortune and his wife Violet had been buried. After reading the headstones, her head began to fill with thoughts. She hardly heard a word of the lecture later that evening. Elizabeth was captivated by the quest to learn more of the life of this man who had been born a prince in Africa, sold as a slave in Boston, and bought his freedom in Massachusetts at the age of sixty. She spent the next year doing in-depth research into the history of the slave trade, digging for every detail she could find about Amos and his life. Her book *Amos Fortune, Free Man* (Aladdin Books, 1950) won the Newbery Medal 150 years after the death of this real-life American hero.

Elizabeth continued to write and to stay connected to the writing world. She was a staff member at writer's conferences at the University of New Hampshire, the University of Connecticut, and Indiana University, beginning in 1956. Starting in 1962, she served as an instructor at Christian Writers and Education conferences in Green Lake, Wisconsin. She traveled around, giving lectures, and was a regular contributor of articles, essays, and reviews to magazines and journals. Elizabeth's books have been translated into Dutch, Japanese, Israeli, German, and Sinhalese. She died at the age of ninety-five on July 29, 2001, in Concord, New Hampshire.

A poem that Elizabeth learned as a child reflected her philosophy about writing:

> The written word should be
> Clean as a bone,
> Clear as light,

Hard as stone.
Two words are not so good
As one.
(Author unknown) (Miller and Field 1955, 364)

It is good advice for a writer of any age.

A Word to My Readers:

In a world such as ours is today, with much of the best thought devoting itself to means of destruction, it is good to be reminded of a life such as Amos Fortune's. He lived the only force that is greater than any bomb: simple affection, deep-hearted love. Modes change but not values, and all that he stood for in his day is vital in ours: those "inalienable rights" whose achievement is part of the long mountain we all are climbing as we emerge from our various forms of slavery into the fullness of freedom. (Miller and Field 1955, 371)

Books by Elizabeth Yates (McGreal)

Amos Fortune, Free Man (Aladdin Books, 1950; Puffin Books, 1989).

Around the Year in Iceland (D. C. Heath & Co. 1942).

Beloved Bondage (Coward McCann, 1948).

A Book of Hours (Vineyard Books, 1976; Phoenix Press, 1984).

Call It Zest: The Vital Ingredient After Seventy (S. Greene Press, 1977).

Call It Zest: The Vital Ingredient for Everybody (G. K. Hall, 1978).

The Carey Girl (Coward McCann, 1956).

Carolina's Courage (E. P. Dutton & Co., 1964; Bob Jones University Press, 1989).

Children of the Bible (Aladdin Books, 1950; E. P. Dutton & Co., 1963; Cobblestone, 1996).

An Easter Story (E. P. Dutton & Co., 1967).

Haven for the Brave (A. A. Knopf, 1941).

High Holiday (no publishing information available).

Howard Thurman, Portrait of a Practical Dreamer (John Day Co., 1964).

Hue & Cry (Coward McCann, 1953; Bob Jones University Press, 1991).

Iceland Adventure (Journey Books, 1997).

Is There a Doctor in the Barn? (W. L. Bauhan, 1977).

The Journeyman (Bob Jones University Press, 1990).

The Lady from Vermont: Dorothy Canfield Fisher's Life and World (S. Greene Press, 1971).

The Lighted Heart (E. P. Dutton & Co., 1960; W. L. Bauhan, 1974).

Mountain Born (Coward McCann, 1943; Bob Jones University Press, Walker, 1993).

My Diary, My World (Westminster Press, 1981).

My Widening World (Westminster Press, 1983).

Nearby (Coward McCann, 1947).

New Hampshire (Coward McCann, 1969).

The Next Fine Day (John Day Co., 1962; Bob Jones University Press, 1994).

On That Night (E. P. Dutton & Co., 1969).

Once in the Year: A Christmas Story (Coward McCann, 1947; Upper Room Books, 1991).

One Writer's Way (Westminster Press, 1984).

Open the Door: A Gathering of Poems and Prose Pieces (New Hampshire Antiquarian Society, 1999).

Pebble in a Pool, the Widening Circles of Dorothy Canfield Fisher's Life (E. P. Dutton & Co., 1958).

A Place for Peter (Coward McCann, 1952; Bob Jones University Press, 1994).

Prudence Crandall, Woman of Courage (Aladdin Books, 1955).

Quest in the North Land, an Iceland Adventure (A. A. Knopf, 1940).

Rainbow Round the World: A Story of UNICEF (Bobbs Merrill, 1954).

The Road Through Sandwich Notch (S. Greene Press, 1973).

Sam's Secret Journal (Friendship Press, 1964).

Sarah Whitcher's Story (E. P. Dutton & Co., 1971; Bob Jones University Press, 1994).

The Seventh One (Walker, 1978).

Silver Lining: A Novella (Phoenix Pub., 1981).

Skeezer: Dog with a Mission (Harvey House, 1973).

Someday You'll Write (E. P. Dutton & Co., 1962; Bob Jones University Press, 1995).

Sound Friendships: The Story of Willa and Her Hearing Ear Dog (Countryman Press, 1987).

Spanning Time: A Diary Keeper Becomes a Writer (Cobblestone, 1996).

Swiss Holiday (Bob Jones University Press, 1996).

Up the Golden Stair (E. P. Dutton & Co., 1966; Upper Room Books, 1990).

We, the People (Countryman Press, 1974).

Wind of Spring (Coward McCann, 1945).

With Pipe, Paddle, and Song: A Story of the French Canadian Voyageurs (E. P. Dutton & Co., 1968; Bethlehem Books, 1998).

Your Prayers and Mine (Houghton Mifflin, 1954).

For More Information About/by Elizabeth Yates (McGreal)

Autobiographies: 1960. *The Lighted Heart.* E. P. Dutton & Co.; 1981. My *Diary, My World.* Westminster Press; 1983. *My Widening World.* Westminster Press; 1984. *One Writer's Way.* Westminster Press; 1996. *Spanning Time: A Diary Keeper Becomes a Writer.* Cobblestone; 1977. *Call It Zest: The Vital Ingredient After Seventy.* S. Greene Press; 1978. *Call It Zest: The Vital Ingredient for Everybody.* G. K. Hall.

Hoffman, Miriam, and Eva Samuels. 1990. *Authors and Illustrators of Children's Books: Writings on Their Lives and Works.* National Council of Teachers of English.

Miller, Bertha Mahony, and Elinor Whitney Field, eds. 1955. *The Newbery Medal Books: 1922–1955.* Horn Book.

Straub, Deborah A., ed. 1987. *Contemporary Authors.* New Revision Series, vol. 21. Gale Research.

1952: Eleanor Estes

Born   May 9, 1906
West Haven,
Connecticut

Married   Rice Estes,
December 8, 1932
(children: Helena)

Died   July 15, 1988

Awards and Honors

Newbery Medal (Animal Stories): *Ginger Pye* (Harcourt, Brace & Co., 1951)
Newbery Honor Book for 1943: *The Middle Moffat* (Harcourt, Brace & Co., 1942)
Newbery Honor Book for 1944: *Rufus M.* (Harcourt, Brace & Co., 1943)
Newbery Honor Book for 1945: *The Hundred Dresses* (Harcourt, Brace & Co., 1944)

About the Author and Her Writing

Eleanor Estes used to go to sleep at night imagining the speech she would give when she won the Newbery Medal one day. Once she began writing books, she gave up imagining speeches. By the time she actually won the award in 1952 for *Ginger Pye,* Eleanor wished she'd written down some of those earlier, imaginary speeches. She said, "If anything has numbed my wits ever it was the news of the Newbery Award" (Miller and Field 1955, 379).

Eleanor was born and raised in West Haven, Connecticut. In those days, the area was largely undeveloped, and the countryside provided prime space for a curious child who loved to climb trees, ice skate, swim, and explore. Her mother was a skilled dressmaker, taught dancing lessons, and sewed the costumes for most of the plays in town. A musty, old black trunk kept in the cellar held a treasure trove of colorful costumes designed and created by her mother, costumes that Eleanor used for Halloween or dress-up parties.

Eleanor's happy childhood became the backdrop for most of her books. Her beloved characters were created from composites of the people she knew as a child. In these ways she agreed that most of her writing was autobiographical.

After high school, Eleanor took a job in the children's department of the New Haven Free Public Library and became head of the department in 1928. In 1931, Eleanor won the Carolina M. Hewins scholarship for children's librarians and left New Haven to study at the Pratt Institute Library School. There she met and fell in love with a fellow student, Rice Estes. The two married on December 8, 1932. They had one daughter, Helena.

While working as a librarian, Eleanor pursued her true love: writing. When she published her first book in 1941, *The Moffats* (Harcourt, Brace & Co., 1941), she put aside her work with the books others had written and turned full-time to writing her own. *The Moffats,* her first in an ongoing, popular series of books about a fatherless family, marked her as a gifted writer for children. She bristled at the thought that children's authors were often considered less important than those who wrote for adults. For Eleanor the essence of writing lay in the quest for integrity and authenticity. She believed that the best writers for children were those who could both remember the emotions and experiences of childhood and filter all those memories through the maturity of an adult.

> With me, writing is remembering, sensing, recreating, and creating, a blending of these processes. (Miller and Field 1955, 383–84)

Eleanor was keenly aware of the Newbery Medal and the honor it was for a book to receive this award. She had come close to winning the Newbery Medal several times before 1952. For three consecutive years her books received the Newbery Honor Medal: *Middle Moffat* (1943), *Rufus M.* (1944), and *The Hundred Dresses* (1945), a touching story about a poor Polish girl seen by many to be an outcast.

Ginger Pye was actually the only character in Eleanor's books named for someone she knew in real life: a little dog that had belonged to Eleanor and her brothers when they were children. The dog got lost on Thanksgiving Day and returned in May, all grown up. At first, as Eleanor began to write the story of the little dog, she thought it might be another story centered around the Moffat family. As the story developed, so did a new family: the Pyes, as realistic and entertaining as the Moffats.

Eleanor would often say that one of her favorite pastimes was doing nothing, but that she rarely had time to pursue this hobby. She liked to draw and paint but she focused on her writing. She did the illustrations for *Ginger Pye,* simple sketches that fit the flavor of the story, but illustrating her own book was the exception rather than the rule. She kept busy and wrote all through the years. Eleanor surprised her reading audience when she wrote a sequel to the Moffats forty years after what everyone thought would be the last in the series.

She published her final book, *The Curious Adventures of Jimmy McGee* (Harcourt Brace Jovanovich, 1987) shortly before her death at the age of 82. She never lost her flair for understanding the world of children and for writing books that many generations have cherished as much as her first readers.

A Word to My Readers:

I really don't have a favorite among my books. Sometimes I like one better than another but this varies. Long after I've written a book, one like *The Moffats,* I begin to enjoy them. It's as though someone else had written them, and I laugh at the funny parts. When writing, I simply try to make the book I'm working on as good as it can possibly be; years may go by before I open its covers again. (Miller and Field 1955, 151)

Books by Eleanor Estes

The Alley (Harcourt, Brace & Co., 1964).

The Coat Hanger Christmas Tree (Atheneum, 1973).

The Curious Adventures of Jimmy McGee (Harcourt Brace Jovanovich, 1987).

The Echoing Green, a Novel (Macmillan, 1947).

Ginger Pye (Harcourt, Brace & Co., 1951; ABC Clio, 1987; Harcourt Brace Jovanovich, 1990; Harcourt, 2000).

The Hundred Dresses (Harcourt, Brace & Co., 1944; Harcourt Brace Jovanovich, 1974).

A Little Oven (Harcourt, Brace & Co., 1955).

The Lollipop Princess: A Play for Paper Dolls in One Act (Harcourt, Brace & Co., 1967).

The Lost Umbrella of Kim Chu (Atheneum, 1978).

The Middle Moffat (Harcourt, Brace & Co., 1942; Harcourt Brace Jovanovich, 1979; Harcourt, 2001).

Miranda the Great (Harcourt, Brace & Co., 1967).

The Moffat Museum (Harcourt Brace Jovanovich, 1983; Harcourt, 2001).

The Moffats (Harcourt, Brace & Co., 1941; Harcourt, 2001).

Pinky Pye (Harcourt, Brace & Co., 1958; Harcourt Brace Jovanovich, 1976; Harcourt, 2000).

Rufus M. (Harcourt Brace Jovanovich, 1943; Harcourt, Brace & Co., 1943; Harcourt, 2001).

The Sleeping Giant and Other Stories (Harcourt, Brace & Co., 1948).

The Sun and the Wind and Mr. Todd (Harcourt, Brace & Co., 1943).

The Tunnel of Hugsy Goode (Harcourt Brace Jovanovich, 1971).

The Witch Family (Harcourt, Brace & Co., 1960; Harcourt Brace Jovanovich, 1990; Harcourt, 2000).

For More Information About/by Eleanor Estes

Hopkins, Lee Bennett. 1974. *More Books by More People: Interviews with Sixty-Five Authors of Books for Children*. Citation Press.

Miller, Bertha Mahony, and Elinor Whitney Field, eds. 1955. *Newbery Medal Books: 1922–1955*. Horn Book.

*illustrated by the author

1953: Ann Nolan Clark

Born	December 5, 1896
	Las Vegas, New Mexico
Married	Thomas Patrick Clark, 1919 (children: Thomas)
Died	December 13, 1995
	Tucson, Arizona

Awards and Honors

Newbery Medal (Action and Adventure): *Secret of the Andes* (Viking Press, 1952)
Wrote the Caldecott Honor Book for 1942: *In My Mother's House* (Viking Press, 1941), illustrated by Velino Herrera

About the Author and Her Writing

Ann Nolan Clark was born and raised in Las Vegas, New Mexico, in the early years of the twentieth century. The population of her town included Native Americans, French trappers, colonial Spanish, Anglos, and a mix of races from all over the United States. This rich diversity within the town's life made it a community where harmony and acceptance was a natural way of life. Thus, her childhood set the stage for a lifetime of fostering understanding among the various cultures of the southwestern United States and of Central and South America.

Ann remembered much about her childhood, from her Irish grandfather's flowing black cape and stories to the Native American woman who raised the neighbor's children and welcomed Ann and her brother into their home. Years later she was able to describe in vivid detail the traditions and customs of her hometown, including the compassionate practice of baking bread for the poor.

Clark's idyllic childhood came to an abrupt end with the advent of World War I. Her older brother went off to war, and she took a teaching job at a one-room schoolhouse in a settlement out on the mesas. Ann was paid sixty dollars a month and given an old cow pony as transportation. She had no home, but took turns boarding on the farms, moving from place to place.

After one year she'd had enough, and the eighteen year old moved to Tacoma, Washington, where she began a series of odd jobs as an elevator attendant, a worker in a sash and door factory, and at a defense plant. She became a journalist and might have pursued that as a career, except that her family begged her to return home. Ann returned to New Mexico and took various jobs teaching in nearby mining towns. Within that first year home, she met and married her husband, Thomas Patrick Clark. She quit teaching when their son, Thomas, was born.

Her career as a stay-at-home mother ended suddenly and sadly with the death of her husband. With a two-year-old son to raise, Ann returned to teaching, this time with Native American children. She went to work for the Bureau of Indian Affairs. She began writing books, not because it was a lifelong dream but because she saw the need within her classrooms for literature written especially for Native American children. The curriculum available at that time was poor in quality and culturally inappropriate. Ann loved her students and wanted them to have a better education. She wrote her first published book, *In My Mother's House* (Viking Press, 1941), as a geography book for nine-year-old Tesuque Indian children. The book won the Book World Children's Spring Book Festival Award in 1941 and was named a Caldecott Honor Book in 1942.

> I do not like morals in stories—at least, if they show. But often I think that groups of children have messages for other groups of children and for grownups, too. (Miller and Field 1955, 401)

As part of her job, Ann taught at a Native American reservation and in their boarding schools. She traveled extensively in the southwest and in Central and South America. At the request of the Inter-Educational Foundation, Ann spent five years living in Mexico, Guatemala, Ecuador, Costa Rica, and Peru, training other teachers with the skills that came so naturally to her.

She also continued to write. Her books were published in English, Sioux, Navajo, and Spanish. The books she wrote as curriculum for the Native American schools were so skillfully done and well received that the publishers made them available to mainstream readers as well.

Ann wrote *Secret of the Andes* as part of an ongoing outreach of books that taught about native cultures and traditions. The book, which tells of an Incan boy and his quest to discover the truth of his life, won the Newbery Medal in 1953. The choice of *Andes* as the Newbery winner elicited some criticism because it won over the immensely popular book *Charlotte's Web* by E. B. White (Harper, 1952). Yet Ann Nolan Clark's books have held their place as breakthrough books in the area of Native American literature.

Although the Newbery Medal brought Clark recognition for her writing, her heart remained in teaching and writing for Native Americans. Ann retired from the Bureau of Indian Affairs in 1962. She lived on her Red Dog Ranch in Tesuque, New Mexico, where she also raised cocker spaniels.

Ann lost her only son, an Air Force pilot in World War II, when he was shot down over the Pacific. Although her life had more than its share of tragedy, Ann remained devoted and faithful to the larger family of children and adults who called her teacher and friend.

A Word to My Readers:

If I could have a wish come true for the Newbery people who follow me, it is that they do not receive this great honor too soon in their writing career, or too early in their years of living. I wish this because I believe to get its richest, headiest flavor the trail to it must have been long and rough and slow in climbing to make the thirst for its nectar deep and good. (Miller and Field 1955, 404)

Books by Ann Nolan Clark

About the Grass Mountain Mouse (Education Division, U.S. Office of Indian Affairs, 1943).

All This Wild Land (Viking Press, 1976).

Along Sandy Trails (Viking Press, 1969).

Bear Cub (Viking Press, 1965).

Blue Canyon Horse (Viking Press, 1969).

Bringer of the Mystery Dog (U.S. Department of the Interior, Bureau of Indian Affairs, 1943; Kiva, 2000).

Brother Andre of Montreal (Vision Books, 1967).

Buffalo Caller: The Story of a Young Sioux Boy of the Early 1700's, Before the Coming of the Horse (Row, Peterson, 1942).

A Child's Story of New Mexico (University Publishing Co., 1941, 1960).

Circle of Seasons (Farrar, Straus & Giroux, 1970).

The Desert People (Viking Press, 1962).

Father Kino: Priest to the Pimas (Farrar, Straus, 1963).

Hoofprint on the Wind (Viking Press, 1972).

In My Mother's House (Viking Press, 1941; Puffin Books, 1992).

In the Land of Small Dragon: A Vietnamese Folktale, told by Dang Manh Kha to Ann Nolan Clark (Viking Press, 1979).

Journey to the People (Viking Press, 1969).

Little Boy with Three Names. Stories of Taos Pueblo (Education Division, U.S. Office of Indian Affairs, 1940).

Little Herder in Autumn (Printing Department, Phoenix Indian School, 1940).

Little Herder in Autumn, in Winter (U.S. Indian Service, 1950).

Little Herder in Spring (Printing Department, Phoenix Indian School, 1940).

Little Herder in Summer (Printing Department, Phoenix Indian School, 1942).

Little Herder in Winter (Printing Department, Phoenix Indian School, 1942).

The Little Indian Basket Maker (Melmont, 1957).

The Little Indian Pottery Maker (Melmont, 1955).

Little Navajo Bluebird (Viking Press, 1943).

Little Navajo Herder (U.S. Indian Service, Haskell Institute, 1951).

Magic Money (Viking Press, 1950).

Medicine Man's Daughter (Farrar, Straus, 1963).

Paco's Miracle (Bell Books, 1962).

The Pine Ridge Porcupine (Haskell Institute Printing Department, 1941).

Santiago (Viking Press, 1955).

A Santo for Pasqualita (Viking Press, 1959).

Secret of the Andes (Viking Press, 1952; Puffin Books, 1976).

Singing Sioux Cowboy Reader (U.S. Indian Service, 1947).

The Slim Butte Raccoon (U.S. Department of the Interior, Bureau of Indian Affairs, Branch of Education, 1942, 1957).

Summer Is for Growing (Farrar, Straus & Giroux, 1968).

Sun Journey: A Story of Zuni Pueblo (U.S. Department of the Interior, Bureau of Indian Affairs, Branch of Education, 1945).

There Still Are Buffalo (Ancient City Press, 1992).

These Were the Valiant: A Collection of New Mexico Profiles (C. Horn, 1969).

Third Monkey (Viking Press, 1956).

This for That (Golden Gate Junior Books, 1965).

Tia Maria's Garden (Viking Press, 1963).

To Stand Against the Wind (Viking Press, 1978).

Who Wants to Be a Prairie Dog? (Education Division, U.S. Office of Indian Affairs, 1940; Salina Bookshelf, 1994).

World Song (Viking Press, 1960).

Year Walk (Viking Press, 1975).

Young Hunter of Picuris (U.S. Department of the Interior, Bureau of Indian Affairs, Branch of Education, 1963).

For More Information About/by Ann Nolan Clark

Kunitz, Stanley J., and Howard Haycraft, eds. 1951. *The Junior Book of Authors.* 2d ed. H. W. Wilson.

Miller, Bertha Mahony, and Elinor Whitney Field, eds. 1955. *Newbery Medal Books: 1922–1955.* Horn Book.

1954/1960: Joseph Quincy Krumgold

Born	April 9, 1908 Jersey City, New Jersey
Married	Helen Litivin, January 10, 1947 (children: Adam)
Died	July 10, 1980 Hope, New Jersey

Awards and Honors

First person to win the Newbery Medal twice.
Newbery Medal for 1954 (Adventure): *. . . And Now Miguel* (Crowell, 1953)
Newbery Medal for 1960 (Adventure): *Onion John* (Crowell, 1959)

About the Author and His Writing

The man who became the first person to win the Newbery Medal twice did not even consider himself to be a writer. Joseph Quincy Krumgold was that man.

His first and foremost love was movies and the film industry. His father built theaters. His Uncle Jules bought and sold them. Another uncle, Sigmund, an acclaimed organist, often played the organ in the big theater houses in the days before "talking pictures." By the time Joseph was twelve years old, he knew he wanted to follow in his family's footsteps and earn a living by making films.

> The stories the old men tell of how we grew out of this earth and how we can continue to grow, the legends that recount for us the history of our own humanity, if ever these get into print at all, it's in the books that we make for our children. (Miller and Field 1955, 422)

Joseph attended New York University, graduating before the age of twenty. He took his first job working for MGM Studios, although the job was in New York City working in the business department and with the exhibitors.

Joseph's big break in Hollywood came when he was offered a job working on Lon Chaney's first movie as a dialogue writer. Although the movie never made it to the big screen, Lon Chaney went on to become one of the great Hollywood stars of the time, and Joseph Krumgold found himself at the intersection of movie making and writing.

Joseph loved working on films and writing the scripts. He sought to learn every detail he could about the art of making movies. After twelve years working for studios such as Paramount, Republic, RKO, and Columbia, Joseph felt that he had learned all he needed to know, and he struck out on his own. The movies he made won awards at film festivals in Venice, Prague, and Edinburgh. Along the way, Krumgold even received an Academy Award nomination.

As creator of his own films, Joseph became especially fascinated with the documentary genre. He liked the idea of making movies about real life and real people. He lived in Israel for four years and then returned to the United States to do a film about a Mexican American boy who wanted to be a sheep farmer like his father. The contrast between the lives of the Mexican Americans living in poverty in Los Cordovas and the European Americans living in the antiseptic city of Los Alamos a few miles away (where the atom bomb was created) captured Joseph's interest. He didn't feel that the documentary alone could convey the lives of the people and all the information he had gathered in the making of the documentary, and so, at the encouragement of a publisher, Joseph wrote a book: . . . *And Now Miguel.*

Imagine his surprise to learn that he had won the Newbery Medal for the best contribution to children's literature in 1954, when he did not even think of himself as an author!

And then imagine his surprise six years later when a second book, *Onion John,* received the Newbery Medal, making Joseph the first person in history to win the award twice. Joseph already had the idea for *Onion John* when he won the first Newbery Medal but never imagined he would win the award again. In his closing comments given in his acceptance speech for the Newbery Medal in 1954, Joseph mentioned that it was with profound satisfaction that he received his only literary honor for writing a children's book. Six years later, he thanked the American Library Association for honoring his writing yet again.

All in all, Joseph wrote only four books for children. Despite the honors he received for his writing skills, his heart remained in filmmaking. He traveled extensively, continuing to make documentaries and, in between films, writing books. Along with the four children's books, he wrote a couple of books for adults but mostly stuck to screenplays and scripts. His Newbery winner . . . *And Now Miguel* has been translated into at least fifteen languages.

In 1947, Joseph married Helen Litivin, and they had one son, Adam. Helen and Adam traveled around the world along with Joseph as he made his films and wrote his books. Eventually Joseph and Helen settled in New Jersey but continued to travel with his film company for many years.

Joseph and Miguel, the young sheepherder portrayed in the Newbery–winning book, shared a common goal in life. Although both grew up in very different settings, with little else in common, they each wanted to follow in their father's footsteps. That each one did is a tribute to both families and also to the human spirit. Thanks to Joseph—and to Miguel—we know that dreams can come true.

A Word to My Readers:

I've had a new look, through the writing of this book, at the Newbery Medal. I find that the one it places under commitment is not I, but you. The writer can bring you only what he's able. You assure him that however personal is the job he does, however indifferent it is to the market and the demand, if it's truly done it will be read. (Kingman 1965, 88)

Books by Joseph Quincy Krumgold

. . . And Now Miguel (Crowell, 1953).

Henry 3 (Atheneum, 1967).

The Most Terrible Turk: A Story of Turkey (Crowell, 1969).

Onion John (Crowell, 1959).

Sweeny's Adventure (Random House, 1942).

Thanks to Murder (Vanguard Press, 1935).

For More Information About/by Joseph Quincy Krumgold

Kingman, Lee, ed. 1965. *Newbery and Caldecott Medal Books, with Acceptance Papers, Biographies and Related Material Chiefly from the Horn Book Magazine: 1956–1965*. Horn Book.

Miller, Bertha Mahony, and Elinor Whitney Field, eds. 1955. *Newbery Medal Books: 1922–1955*. Horn Book.

1955: Meindert DeJong

Born	March 4, 1906
	Wierum, Friesland, the Netherlands
Married	Hattie Overeinter, 1932
	Beatrice DeClaire McElwee, 1962
	five stepchildren
Died	July 16, 1991
	Allegan, Michigan

Awards and Honors

Newbery Medal (Action and Adventure): *The Wheel on the School* (Harper, 1954)
Newbery Honor Book for 1954: *Hurry Home, Candy* (Harper, 1953)
Newbery Honor Book for 1954: *Shadrach* (Harper, 1953)
Newbery Honor Book for 1957: *The House of Sixty Fathers* (Harper, 1956)
Newbery Honor Book for 1959: *Along Came a Dog* (Harper, 1958)
Hans Christian Andersen Medal, 1962
National Book Award for Children's Literature, 1969: *Journey from Peppermint Street* (Harper & Row, 1968)

About the Author and His Writing

The 1950s were very good years for Meindert DeJong (MINE-ert De-YOUNG). He won four Newbery Honor Awards, for *Hurry Home, Candy* (1954), *Shadrach* (1954), *House of Sixty Fathers* (1957), and *Along Came a Dog* (1959); and one Newbery Medal, in 1955 for *The Wheel on the School.* It's hard to imagine that once his parents tried to take him out of school because of his poor grades!

Meindert had struggled in school. When his brother David heard their parents' plans for removing Meindert from school, he raised such a fuss that the boy was allowed to continue. Buoyed by his brother's confidence, from then on Meindert received straight A's.

Meindert spent the first eight years of his life in a fishing town on the North Sea, Wierum, in the Netherlands. On the day of his birth, a mighty flood hit the town and the sea spilled over the dike. His father took his two older brothers to see the effects of the catastrophe, and there announced that a new baby brother had been born. Mother and baby were safe in the attic of the house, above the rising seawater.

In Holland in those days, a child took on the responsibilities of adulthood very quickly. By the age of eleven, children were expected to work. Meindert enjoyed a longer childhood than most Dutch children because at the age of eight, he and his family moved to Grand Rapids, Michigan. However, before leaving Holland Meindert nearly got lost in the shuffle of a big parade. After the ship in which they sailed landed at Ellis Island in New York City harbor, Meindert wandered off again. Fortunately, both times his family found him safe and sound.

The adjustment to life in the United States did not come easily for the DeJong family. Meindert's mother gave birth to a baby boy shortly after their arrival in the new country, but the baby died. She was so homesick that she refused to learn the English language. Meindert struggled in school because of the language problems. He longed for his beloved grandparents, who had remained in the Netherlands. The family suffered financial loss, and the boys had to do whatever odd jobs they could find to help bring a little income into the home. In later years, Meindert looked back on his life and felt fortunate to have had "two childhoods," even though each had its share of trouble and tragedy.

After Meindert finished college, he taught for a year in Iowa, but he hated teaching. He then worked a number of odd jobs from janitor to gravedigger to poultry farmer, but none of these paid enough for him to earn a living. After marrying, he became a farmer.

> I never decided to write for children. A librarian, a goose, and a duck decided it for me. I owned the goose and duck; they were wonderful pets. (Hopkins 1969, 122)

The stint on the poultry farm did provide Meindert with something perhaps more precious than money: time with animals, which gave him the inspiration for his first book. A children's librarian made the suggestion that DeJong write a book about farm life, and the resulting manuscript for *The Big Goose and the Little White Duck* (Harper & Row, 1938) was accepted for publication. DeJong decided to be a writer.

Many of Meindert's books have animals as main characters. In some stories, no human beings ever appear on the pages. So adept was he at creating realistic dialogue and believable plots that the animals did not need any human protagonists.

Meindert used the setting of the Netherlands to write *The Wheel on the School,* a story about a group of schoolchildren who work together to bring the storks back to their little village. Storks were a sign of good luck and certainly proved to be good luck for Meindert's career, as the book won the Newbery Medal in 1955.

During World War II, Meindert served in the air force. His unit was stationed in China. He returned to the United States after the war but needed time to recover from some of the emotional scars left by the violence. Eventually he was able to start writing again.

Meindert received many other literary honors during his career. In 1969, he became the first recipient of the National Book Award for Children's Literature for *Journey from Peppermint Street* (Harper & Row, 1968). He also won the Hans Christian Andersen Medal, an international award, in 1962, becoming the first U.S. citizen to be so honored. His books have been translated into Finnish, German, Swedish, Italian, Hebrew, Danish, Friesian, Afrikaans, Polish, Japanese, Portuguese, Spanish, and Czechoslovakian languages.

Meindert once said that he turned to writing for children because the magazines that published his occasional short stories went out of business during the depression. Yet he had a gift for delving into the realm of childhood. He believed that anyone writing for children needed to first peel away the layers of adulthood that blocked a true vision of how it felt to be a child, and then one could write realistically. One need only read one of his books to know that Meindert DeJong understood what he was talking, and writing, about.

DeJong retired from writing in the early 1970s. He lived for a time in Mexico and in North Carolina. He died in Michigan in 1991.

A Word to My Readers:

It seems reasonable, with a beautiful simple logic, that when writing for children you ought to write for them out of your own inner childhood, and not out of an adult remembrance. When you write for children from adult memory, you satisfy only the other adults who have also forgotten their inner childhood, and have substituted for it an adult conception of what the child needs and wants in books. (Miller and Field 1955, 434)

Books by Meindert DeJong

The Almost All White Rabbity Cat (Macmillan, 1972).

Along Came a Dog (Harper, 1958).

Bells of the Harbor (Harper & Brothers, 1941).

Bible Days (Fideler, 1948, 1949).

The Big Goose and the Little White Duck (Harper & Row, 1938, 1963).

The Cat That Walked a Week (Harper, 1943).

Dirk's Dog, Bello (Harper, 1939).

The Easter Cat (Macmillan, 1971; Aladdin Books, 1991).

Far Out the Long Canal (Harper & Row, 1964).

Good Luck Duck (Harper, 1950).

A Horse Came Running (Macmillan, 1970).

The House of Sixty Fathers (Harper, 1956).

Hurry Home, Candy (Harper, 1953).

Journey from Peppermint Street (Harper & Row, 1968).

The Last Little Cat (Harper, 1961).

The Little Cow and the Turtle (Harper, 1955).

The Little Stray Dog (Harper & Brothers, 1943).

The Mighty Ones: Great Men and Women of Early Bible Days (Harper, 1959).

Nobody Plays with a Cabbage (Harper, 1962).

Puppy Summer (Harper & Row, 1966).

Shadrach (Harper, 1953).

The Singing Hill (Harper & Row, 1962).

Smoke Above the Lane (Harper, 1951).

The Tower by the Sea (Harper, 1950).

The Wheel on the School (Harper, 1954).

The Wheels Over the Bridge (Harper & Brothers, 1941).

For More Information About/by Meindert DeJong

Hopkins, Lee Bennett. 1969. *Books Are by People: Interviews with 104 Authors and Illustrators of Books for Young Children.* Citation Press.

Miller, Bertha Mahony, and Elinor Whitney Field, eds. 1955. *Newbery Medal Books: 1922–1955.* Horn Book.

1956: Jean Lee Latham

Born	April 19, 1902 Buckhannon, West Virginia
Died	June 13, 1995
Pseudonyms	Janice Gard and Julian Lee

Awards and Honors

Newbery Medal (Fictionalized Biography): *Carry On, Mr. Bowditch* (Houghton Mifflin, 1955)

About the Author and Her Writing

Jean Lee Latham was born in Buckhannon, West Virginia, and never left the state until she had graduated from college. Yet many of her works of juvenile historical fiction take place on the sea.

Her best-known work of this kind is the book that won the Newbery Medal in 1956: *Carry On, Mr. Bowditch,* the story of an early nineteenth-century seaman and mathematical genius who wrote *The American Practical Navigator,* considered by many to be the "sailor's Bible."

Jean grew up in an area filled with open fields, trees, and hills, and she used to joke that she concentrated on studying the three R's: "readin', ritin', and runnin' " (Hopkins 1974, 250). About the only thing that could make her sit still was a good book. She often sat in the branches of a tree while she read. The one exception to this seating arrangement came when she read anything written by Edgar Allen Poe. She felt she needed to be indoors to read Poe's frightening horror stories, with a good, strong wall behind her back. Jean finished reading his complete works by the time she was ten years old.

> When it comes to doing something new, I ain't got no shame about flubbing it, so I have more fun than most people. (Hopkins 1974, 250)

Jean got early practice as a storyteller in her own home. She had two brothers and a sister, and each child had assigned chores to do around the house. Jean had the task of doing the dishes. She discovered that she could entice her younger brother, George, to dry the dishes, and sometimes even to wash them, if she told him a good story while they worked. George proved to be no easy subject to keep entertained. Being a matter-of-fact type of person, he didn't want lots of unnecessary details in the stories Jean told him. She learned quickly how to keep the attention of a young boy. Later, when she wrote children's books, she again sought to reach the mind-set of an adolescent boy.

As a child Jean didn't like the time it took to write stories down, but as the years went on, she discovered that she enjoyed the process of writing. She started writing plays in high school and continued through college and graduate school. She wrote numerous stage plays and radio dramas, including a series on Lewis and Clark that ran for 140 episodes.

Jean's study of the three R's earned her a bachelor of arts degree from West Virginia Wesleyan in 1925, a bachelor's of oral English from the drama school of Ithaca Conservatory in 1928, and a master of arts from Cornell University in 1930. She then took a job in Chicago as editor in chief of the Dramatic Publishing Company.

During World War II Jean decided to put writing aside for a while and use her hands in other ways. She went to work for the Department of Defense, helping to repair radio equipment for the Signal Corps. In 1942 she took special training in electronics at the West Virginia Institute of Technology. Jean's writing skills were put to good use when she was assigned to write inspection procedures for new equipment. Her efforts during the war earned her the War Department's Silver Wreath.

Jean resigned from the Department of Defense in 1945 so that she could return to the type of writing she preferred, but she continued to serve her country as a volunteer in the reserves. For twelve years, Jean lived in a trailer, not because she liked to travel but because there was a housing shortage during the war. She didn't like to keep a lot of "things" around, and said that if she brought something new in the front door, she threw something old out the back door. It didn't bother her not to have a lot of possessions, but when it got to the point that she had to throw out valuable research papers because of a lack of room, she decided the time had come to move to an apartment.

Jean's first book for adults was published in 1935. Her first book for children came eighteen years later in 1953. On the advice of her brother, Jean concentrated on writing historical fiction, and this is the area where her skills as a writer shine the brightest.

During the time that Jean wrote *Carry On, Mr. Bowditch,* she accumulated enough research material to fill ten books. She did thorough research, beginning with junior high school level books on mathematics, astronomy, and seamanship. She didn't want to miss a single important detail. Once she finished her research, Jean had to switch gears and become a storyteller. Keeping in mind her little brother George, standing in the kitchen drying dishes, she condensed the years and pages of research into an exciting historical novel.

Others found the novel exciting as well. The book was named the winner of the 1956 Newbery Medal. Jean was immersed in writing another novel when she got the news that she had won the Medal. She hardly had time to prepare for the announcement because she had another deadline to meet!

Latham continued to write biographical novels following the winning of the Newbery Medal. Several of these novels also had nautical themes. Her last published book was *Elizabeth Blackwell, Pioneer Woman Doctor* (Garrard, 1975; Chelsea Juniors, 1991). She was a frequent speaker at writer's conferences, sharing her wit, wisdom, and vitality with others who loved the craft of writing.

Jean sometimes wrote under the names "Janice Gard" and "Julian Lee," although she mostly used these names when writing her plays. In children's literature she will always be known as Jean Lee Latham, the woman who brought history to life.

She died in 1995, at the age of ninety-three.

A Word to My Readers:

It seems to me a writer has a personal Geiger counter that, on occasion, says to him: *Dig here for treasure.* The most unexpected things may cause that personal Geiger counter to signal that a story lies buried. (Kingman 1965, 17)

Books by Jean Lee Latham

Aladdin (Bobbs Merrill, 1961), retold by Jean Lee Latham.

Ali Baba (Bobbs Merrill, 1961), retold by Jean Lee Latham.

Anchor's Aweigh: The Story of David Glasgow Farragut (Harper & Row, 1968).

The Arms of the Law (Dramatic, 1940).

The Bed of Petunias (Dramatic, 1937).

The Brave Little Tailor, Hansel and Gretel, and Jack and the Beanstalk (Bobbs Merrill, 1962), retold by Jean Lee Latham.

Broadway Bound, a Comedy in Three Acts (Dramatic, 1933).

Carry On, Mr. Bowditch (Houghton Mifflin, 1955).

Chagres, Power of the Panama Canal (Garrard, 1964).

The Christmas Party (Dramatic, 1930), dramatized by Jean Lee Latham from the story by Zona Gale.

The Columbia, Powerhouse of North America (Garrard, 1967).

The Cuckoo That Couldn't Count (Macmillan, 1961).

David Glasgow Farragut: Our First Admiral (Garrard, 1967; Chelsea Juniors, 1991).

The Dog That Lost His Family (Macmillan, 1961).

Drake, the Man They Called a Pirate (Harper, 1960).

Earl Derr Biggers' The House Without a Key: A Charlie Chan Mystery Play in Three Acts (dramatized from the novel) (Dramatic, 1942).

Eli Whitney, Great Inventor (Garrard, 1963; Chelsea Juniors, 1991).

Elizabeth Blackwell, Pioneer Woman Doctor (Garrard, 1975; Chelsea Juniors, 1991).

Far Voyager: The Story of James Cook (Harper & Row, 1970).

555 Pointers for Beginning Actors and Directors (Dramatic, 1935).

The Frightened Hero: A Story of the Siege of Latham House (Chilton Books, 1965).

George Goethals, Panama Canal Engineer (Garrard, 1965; Chelsea Juniors, 1991).

The Ghost of Rhodes Manor, Mystery Play for Girls in Three Acts (Dramatists Play Service, 1939).

Gray Bread: A Drama in One Act (Row, Peterson, 1941).

. . . Have a Heart! (Dramatic, 1937).

Hop O' My Thumb (Bobbs Merrill, 1961), retold by Jean Lee Latham.

Jack the Giant Killer (Bobbs Merrill, 1961), retold by Jean Lee Latham.

The Magic Fishbone (Bobbs Merrill, 1961), retold by Jean Lee Latham.

Man of the Monitor: The Story of John Ericsson (Harper, 1962).

The Man Who Never Snoozed (Macmillan, 1961).

The Master of Solitaire (Dramatic, 1935).

Medals for Morse, Artist and Inventor (Aladdin Books, 1954).

Minus a Million, Comedy in Three Acts (Dramatists Play Service, 1941).

More Blessed, a Christmas Play in One Act (Dramatic, 1932).

Nine Radio Plays (Dramatic, 1940).

The Nutcracker (Bobbs Merrill, 1961).

Old Doc (Dramatic, 1940).

On Stage, Mr. Jefferson! (Harper, 1958).

Puss in Boots (Bobbs Merrill, 1961), retold by Jean Lee Latham.

Rachel Carson, Who Loved the Sea (Garrard, 1973; Chelsea Juniors, 1991).

Retreat to Glory: The Story of Sam Houston (Harper & Row, 1965).

Sam Houston, Hero of Texas (Garrard, 1965; Chelsea Juniors, 1991).

Samuel F. B. Morse, Artist-Inventor (Garrard, 1961; Chelsea Juniors, 1991).

Senor Freedom, a Drama in One Act (Row, Peterson, 1941).

Smile for the Lady! (Dramatic, 1937).

The Story of Eli Whitney: Invention and Progress in the Young Nation (Aladdin, 1953; Harper & Row, 1962).

They'll Never Look There! Comedy in One Act (Dramatists Play Service, 1939).

This Dear Bought Land (Harper, 1957).

Trail Blazer of the Seas (Houghton Mifflin, 1956).

What Tabbit the Rabbit Found (Garrard, 1974).

When Homer Honked (Macmillan, 1961).

Who Lives Here? (Garrard, 1974).

Young Man in a Hurry: The Story of Cyrus W. Field (Harper, 1958).

For More Information About/by Jean Lee Latham

Hopkins, Lee Bennett. 1974. *More Books by More People: Interviews with Sixty-Five Authors of Books for Children.* Citation Press.

Kingman, Lee, ed. 1965. *Newbery and Caldecott Medal Books, with Acceptance Papers, Biographies and Related Material Chiefly from the Horn Book Magazine: 1956–1965.* Horn Book.

1957: Virginia Sorensen

Born	February 17, 1912 Provo, Utah
Married	Frederick Sorensen, August 16, 1933 (children: Elizabeth and Frederick Walter) Alec Waugh, July 15, 1969
Died	December 24, 1991

Awards and Honors

Newbery Medal (Contemporary Life): *Miracles on Maple Hill* (Harcourt, Brace & Co., 1956)

About the Author and Her Writing

Virginia Sorensen's mother once said that her daughter's first sentence was "Tell me a story," followed by her second sentence, "*I* will tell *you* a story," which she promptly did (Kingman 1965, 35). But that was just the beginning. As a child, Virginia carried scraps of paper in her pockets, scraps upon which she had written poems that she shared at the dinner table with a captive audience of brothers and sisters who didn't always appreciate their sister's recitations.

> Storytellers are not very often people with answers, but people with questions for which they are seeking answers. (Kingman 1965, 36)

Virginia grew up in Utah. She loved to read and did so with such great concentration that she could tune out anyone and anything around her. At one point, her father worried that there might be something wrong with his daughter's hearing. He had her tested, only to find that her hearing was fine but that her skills in concentration were even better.

The young Virginia also got some practice telling stories with a childhood friend. The friend knew how to sew, and Virginia never did master the needle. While the friend sewed clothes for their dolls, Virginia kept her entertained by telling stories.

A fifth-grade teacher told the class that she believed Virginia would grow up to be a poet. Although she didn't become known as a poet as much as of a writer of novels, the gift of words and poetic phrasing graced much of her writing.

Virginia delighted in the very act of living, finding joy and fascination in everything from the beauty of a single maple leaf to the complex process of turning maple sap into syrup.

Virginia's strong religious training and work ethic provided the foundation upon which she built her life and her writing. As an adult, she lived for a brief time in both Mexico and Denmark after winning two Guggenheim Fellowships to study in these countries. Eventually, Virginia, her husband, and their two children settled in Pennsylvania.

While living in Pennsylvania, Virginia had the opportunity to observe the process of turning sugar to maple syrup, which in turn helped to generate the ideas for her book *Miracles on Maple Hill.* The book was awarded the Newbery Medal in 1957. More than just a story about the sugaring process, *Miracles on Maple Hill* tells about the transformation of a family as they begin a new life and as the father recovers from the horrors of being a former prisoner of war.

Many of Virginia's books were written in an abandoned classroom on the campus of the Indiana State Teacher's College, where her husband served on the faculty. She needed little more than an old chair, a beat-up desk, and a typewriter. The one adornment in her office was a scrap of yellow paper upon which her young daughter had written: "Dear Mama, I like you and I love you. I wish you rite [*sic*] a good book. Beth" (Kingman 1965, 44).

Write a good book she did, and many of them. Virginia couldn't help herself. Writing was for her like breathing or eating: as natural as any part of life. Along with writing books for children and teens, Virginia wrote for preschool children and adults and did all with skill and agility.

Before she won the Newbery Medal, Virginia had the joy of meeting two of the previous winners: Elizabeth Yates and Meindert DeJong. She was awed by what she believed to be in them a special "Newbery vitality," never imagining that one day she, too, would join the ranks of the Newbery Medal winners. In her acceptance speech, Virginia expressed the joy and the fear that comes in winning such an award. She said that "It is even more important than you may know for a writer to feel the existence of a great and critical and sensitive group of people whose eyes are steadily upon his work. This Medal seems to me not only a star for all of us to shoot at but a bright light for all of us to work by" (Kingman 1965, 35).

Sorensen was the writer-in-residence at the State University of Oklahoma in Edmond from 1966 to 1967. She also lived for a while in Tangier, Morocco. She continued to write and published several more books in the remaining years of her life. She died in 1991.

A Word to My Readers:

When I look back upon our Stanford days [where her first husband earned a Ph.D.] I wonder why we were so anxious to be "through." There is no being through really, and nothing in the world is so wonderful as having something before you, looming like heaven, and struggling to it. If only one could run after a star always, sensing some distance behind. (Kingman 1965, 48)

Books by Virginia Sorensen

Around the Corner (Harcourt Brace Jovanovich, 1971).

Curious Missie (Harcourt, Brace & Co., 1953).

The Evening and the Morning (Harcourt, Brace & Co., 1949; Signature Books, 1999).

Friends of the Road (Atheneum, 1978).

Kingdom Come (Harcourt, Brace & Co., 1960).

A Little Lower than the Angels (Signature Books, 1997).

Lotte's Locket (Harcourt, Brace & Co., 1964).

The Man with the Key (Harcourt Brace Jovanovich, 1974).

Many Heavens, a New Mormon Novel (Harcourt, Brace & Co., 1954).

Miracles on Maple Hill (Harcourt, Brace & Co., 1956; Harcourt Brace Jovanovich, 1988, 1990).

The Neighbors: A Novel (Reynal & Hitchcock, 1947).

On This Star (Reynal & Hitchcock, 1946).

Plain Girl (Harcourt, Brace & Co., 1955; Harcourt Brace Jovanovich, 1988).

The Proper Gods (Harcourt, Brace & Co., 1951).

Where Nothing Is Long Ago: Memories of a Mormon Childhood (Harcourt, Brace & Co., 1963; Signature Books, 1998).

For More Information About/by Virginia Sorensen

Autobiography: 1963. *Where Nothing Is Long Ago: Memories of a Mormon Childhood.* Harcourt, Brace & Co.

Kingman, Lee, ed. 1965. *Newbery and Caldecott Medal Books, with Acceptance Papers, Biographies and Related Material Chiefly from the Horn Book Magazine: 1956–1965.* Horn Book.

1958: Harold Keith

Born	April 8, 1903
	Lambert, Oklahoma
Married	Virginia Livingston, August 20, 1931
	(children: John Livingston and Kathleen Ann)
Died	February 24, 1998
	Norman, Oklahoma

Awards and Honors

Newbery Medal (Western, Historical Fiction): *Rifles for Watie* (Crowell, 1957)
Lewis Carroll Shelf Award, 1964
Western Heritage Award, 1978: *The Obstinate Land: Cherokee Strip Run of 1893* (Crowell, 1997)

About the Author and His Writing

Harold Keith was a man who knew what it meant to go the distance.

Before becoming known as a writer, Harold was one of Oklahoma's best-known athletes. He won many prizes as a long-distance runner in his younger years and beyond. In 1973 he broke the U.S. Masters National records for the two- and three-mile runs; the record for the 10,000-meter run fell a year later. Harold was in his early seventies at the time.

> In my interviews I looked mainly for suggestions out of which I might build believable characters and dramatic scenes. I rarely found them in complete form. (Fuller 1963, 121)

Sports always figured prominently in Harold's life. He grew up in a small town in Oklahoma without radio, television, or even paved roads. Each evening a small passenger train stopped in town and folks would gather to watch the well-dressed travelers descend from the train and into the hotel bus, a horse-drawn carriage. Harold often got to ride along on these trips back and forth from the train station to the hotel. He breathed in the smell of fresh-baked bread from the town bakery and heard the ringing of the blacksmith's hammer upon the iron anvil.

The biggest event in town was summer baseball. Folks rounded up their teams and began playing as soon as the weather permitted and often continued into October. The sense of teamwork developed during these games and football in particular convinced him of the necessity of people working together toward a common goal. This theme also held true later, when Harold began to write books and found that only by working in cooperation with editors and others in the publishing business could a book take form.

Along with being a recognized athlete Harold spent several decades as the sports publicity director at his alma mater, the University of Oklahoma. He often traveled with the school teams, and this was when he found time to do some research and writing on his books. Harold was asked by the managing editor of *American Boy* magazine to write the biography of Will Rogers, a famous Oklahoman who had been killed in an airplane crash. The editor knew Harold through the sports stories that the magazine had published through the years. Although he had never written a biography, Harold was ready to face a challenge and accepted the assignment.

As he researched Will's life Harold discovered an even deeper interest in Will's father, Clem, a part-Cherokee soldier and politician. So fascinated did Harold become in Clem's life that when he wrote his master's thesis a few years later, he wrote it on Clem.

One research project led to the next. During the time Harold did research for his thesis on Clem, he interviewed a number of people who had been children during the Civil War. They always had fascinating tales to tell, and this piqued Harold's interest. Thus, the seeds for *Rifles for Watie* started taking root. When he finished the thesis he decided to seek out Civil War veterans and ask them to tell their stories. He interviewed twenty-two men, all of them nearly one hundred years old.

Like a true athlete, Harold knew that even once his research was complete, he needed to keep training. He enrolled in the University of Oklahoma's professional writing school to hone his skills as a writer. He had lived just a couple of blocks from the school for nearly twenty years but never thought about attending until someone else made the suggestion. He must have received some good training because the book he subsequently wrote, *Rifles for Watie,* won the Newbery Medal in 1958. The book took him five years to finish, not counting the years of research. But Harold always lived by the old frontier philosophy: "The most important things you accomplish are done on time which you don't have" (Kingman 1965, 63).

As Harold wrote his books, he thought back on his own childhood. His father had introduced him to the world of books. Harold especially enjoyed reading *The Hound of the Baskervilles* by Sir Arthur Conan Doyle; *Tom Sawyer* by Mark Twain, and *Sea Wolf* by Jack London. As a boy he became so enthralled with these stories that he couldn't put the books down. So when he began to write his own books, he wanted to write with that same sense of immediacy, that same intensity that would draw in his young readers and keep them turning the pages.

Harold said that "There are no new plots in fiction" (Kingman 1965, 60). The same stories are told again and again, but the characters and the storyteller make them fresh and new. This athlete and author could make an old story new. Like the long-distance runner he was, Harold knew about good form, how to pace himself, and what it takes to be a winner.

Harold wrote both fiction and nonfiction for numerous magazines. He was especially interested in anything to do with his home state, Oklahoma. In his free time, he enjoyed quail hunting, trout fishing, and singing in a barbershop quartet. He died on February 24, 1998, in Norman, Oklahoma, of congestive heart failure.

A Word to My Readers:

Readers probably don't know it, but the reason they read a story is to be moved emotionally. Even though they have to turn to fiction to experience vicariously such emotions as love, hate, sorrow, hope, anger, fear and revenge, it makes them feel alive. (Kingman 1965, 58)

Books by Harold Keith

The Bluejay Boarders (Crowell, 1972).

Boys' Life of Will Rogers (Crowell, 1937).

Brief Garland (Crowell, 1971).

Chico and Dan (Eakin Press, 1998).

Forty Seven Straight: The Wilkinson Era at Oklahoma (University of Oklahoma Press, 1984).

Go, Red, Go! (T. Nelson, 1972).

Komantcia (Crowell, 1965; Levite of Apache, 1991).

The Obstinate Land (Crowell, 1997; Levite of Apache, 1993).

Oklahoma Kickoff (University of Oklahoma Press, 1978).

A Pair of Captains (Crowell, 1951).

Rifles for Watie (Crowell, 1957).

The Runt of Rogers School (Lippincott, 1971).

Shotgun Shaw, a Baseball Story (Crowell, 1949).

The Sound of Strings (Levite of Apache, 1992).

Sports and Games (Crowell, 1941, 1947, 1953, 1960, 1969, 1976).

Susy's Scoundrel (Crowell, 1974).

For More Information About/by Harold Keith

Fuller, Muriel, ed. 1963. *More Junior Authors.* H. W. Wilson.

Kingman, Lee, ed. 1965. *Newbery and Caldecott Medal Books, with Acceptance Papers, Biographies and Related Material Chiefly from the Horn Book Magazine: 1956–1966.* Horn Book.

1959/1962: Elizabeth George Speare

Born	November 21, 1908
	Melrose, Massachusetts
Married	Alden Speare, September 26, 1936 (children: Alden Jr. and Mary Elizabeth)
Died	November 15, 1994
	Tucson, Arizona

Awards and Honors

First woman to win the Newbery Medal twice.

Newbery Medal for 1959 (Historical Fiction): *The Witch of Blackbird Pond* (Houghton Mifflin, 1958)

Newbery Medal for 1962 (Historical Fiction): *The Bronze Bow* (Houghton Mifflin, 1961)

Child Study Committee Award, 1983

Scott O'Dell Award for Historical Fiction, 1983: *The Sign of the Beaver* (Houghton Mifflin, 1983)

American Library Association Notable Children's Book, 1984: *The Sign of the Beaver* (Houghton Mifflin, 1983; ABC Clio, 1988)

Newbery Honor Book for 1984: *The Sign of the Beaver* (Houghton Mifflin, 1983)

Christopher Award, 1984

Laura Ingalls Wilder Award, 1989

About the Author and Her Writing

Elizabeth George Speare remembered many lonely hours as a child, hours that she later decided had been a special gift. She grew up in Massachusetts, near Boston, where the family often attended concerts and the theater. Her family spent the summer in a house on the shore, with a beautiful view of the ocean. However, Elizabeth and her younger brother happened to be the only children in the area, and that's why she remembered the summer as being a lonely time.

All those long hours exploring, reading, daydreaming, and thinking fed the spirit of that young girl. Later, when she turned to writing, she still found herself alone for many hours at a time. Yet when writing, Elizabeth never felt lonely. "The occupation of writing can never be lonely because the solitude is so richly peopled," she said in her first Newbery Medal acceptance speech (Kingman 1965, 72). She became so wrapped up in the lives of the people in her books that she even said that she lived two lives while writing her books: one with her real-life family and one with the people in her stories.

Elizabeth's first attempt at writing came when she was eight years old, "an incredibly dull imitation of my much-loved *Babs Twins*" (Silvey 1995, 616). Her next venture into the world of words didn't come until after her children reached junior high school age. At home by herself for the first time in years, Elizabeth began to fill the hours with writing. She wrote articles about family life for *Women's Day* and *Better Homes and Gardens.*

Unlike many authors, Elizabeth did not draw on her own childhood experiences. She chose instead to write historical fiction, a peculiar focus for a person who once admitted that she had never been much interested in history.

> Children need textbooks for the heart as well as for the mind. The enduring values of life —courage, devotion, compassion, forgiveness—none of these can be absorbed entirely by the mind but must instead be received into the heart. (Kingman 1965, 77)

But people were the center of her writing. While some authors are inspired by a particular idea or incident, most of Elizabeth's books developed around a person, often an individual from history. The inspiration for her first published book, *Calico Captive* (Houghton Mifflin, 1957), came after reading about a family who had been taken captive by a tribe of Native Americans in the eighteenth century. Her second book, *The Witch of Blackbird Pond,* developed as she imagined the life of a young girl living during the infamous witch trials of early American history. The story was set in Wethersfield, Connecticut, where Elizabeth was living with her husband and two children.

The one exception to Elizabeth's usual practice of focusing on a specific character came about as she wrote *The Bronze Bow.* She had always been interested in the Middle East during the time between B.C. and A.D., an interest sparked even further when she taught a Sunday school class on heroes of history. She delved into her historical research with glee. When she finished her research, she realized she couldn't write a book. She didn't have a person to write about. She thought at first that her main protagonist would be a girl, as in her first two books, but when she began to write, she came to a dead end. Thus Daniel, the young hero of *The Bronze Bow,* was born.

After *The Bronze Bow* won Elizabeth a second Newbery Medal, she revealed the mistake she had made trying to write a book based on a time and theme rather than a character. Elizabeth had the ability not only to admit her mistakes but to make the best of them.

Elizabeth wrote slowly, about four or five pages a day. She then rewrote her books at least three times. She kept a pad of paper nearby to use for questions that might come to her, such as the cost of a particular item or the distance between two towns. Later she would do the research needed to find the answers so that her stories could be accurate and authentic.

In a writing career that spanned over thirty years, this incredible author only wrote half a dozen books. After publishing her third book, it was twenty years before she wrote another book of children's fiction. Her books were worth the wait. She was the first woman to win the Newbery Medal twice, for *The Witch of Blackbird Pond* (1959) and *The Bronze Bow* (1962). Another one of Elizabeth's books, *The Sign of the Beaver* (1983), won the Scott O'Dell Award for Historical Fiction. Interestingly enough, Scott O'Dell won the Newbery Medal in 1961, in between Elizabeth's two Newbery books.

In 1989, Elizabeth won the Laura Ingalls Wilder Award for an outstanding career as a children's writer. She lived her final years in Connecticut, enjoying watching birds but even more in watching her grandchildren grow. Speare died in Tucson, Arizona, on November 15, 1994, just six days shy of her eighty-sixth birthday.

A Word to My Readers:

There are many needful ways of equipping young people for the future. We have chosen to place books in their hands, books that will serve not only as companions and teachers but as guardians. For the world into which our children are about to step is filled with peril. And perhaps of all the dangers that lie in wait, the most terrifying is that they may settle for a world without meaning. (Kingman 1965, 115)

Books by Elizabeth George Speare

The Bronze Bow (Houghton Mifflin, 1961).

Calico Captive (Houghton Mifflin, 1957).

Child Life in New England, 1790–1840 (Old Sturbridge Village, 1961).

Life in Colonial America (Random House, 1963).

The Prospering (Houghton Mifflin, 1967).

The Sign of the Beaver (Houghton Mifflin, 1983; ABC Clio, 1988).

The Witch of Blackbird Pond (Houghton Mifflin, 1958; Cornerstone Books, 1989).

For More Information About/by Elizabeth George Speare

Kingman, Lee, ed. 1965. *Newbery and Caldecott Medal Books, with Acceptance Papers, Biographies and Related Material Chiefly from the Horn Book Magazine: 1956–1965.* Horn Book.

Silvey, Anita, ed. 1995. *Children's Books and Their Creators.* Houghton Mifflin.

1961: Scott O'Dell

Born	May 23, 1898
	Los Angeles, California

Married   Dorsa Jane Rattenbury,
1948
Elizabeth Hall, 1966
(children: Susan Andersen
and David Mason)

Died   October 15, 1989
Mt. Kisco, New York

Awards and Honors

Newbery Medal (Historical Fiction): *Island of the Blue Dolphins* (Houghton Mifflin, 1960)
American Library Association Notable Children's Book: *Island of the Blue Dolphins* (Houghton Mifflin, 1960); *Zia* (Houghton Mifflin, 1976)
The Lewis Carroll Shelf Award, 1961: *Island of the Blue Dolphins* (Houghton Mifflin, 1960)
Southern California Notable Book Award, 1961: *Island of the Blue Dolphins* (Houghton Mifflin, 1960)
William Allen White Award, 1963: *Island of the Blue Dolphins* (Houghton Mifflin, 1960)
Newbery Medal Honor Book for 1967: *The King's Fifth* (Houghton Mifflin, 1966)
Newbery Medal Honor Book for 1968: *The Black Pearl* (Houghton Mifflin, 1967)
Newbery Medal Honor Book for 1971: *Sing Down the Moon* (Houghton Mifflin, 1970)
Hans Christian Andersen Medal, 1972
Catholic Library Association Regina Medal, 1978
Scott O'Dell Award for Historical Fiction, 1987: *Streams to the River, River to the Sea* (Houghton Mifflin, 1986; G. K. Hall, 1989)

About the Author and His Writing

Scott O'Dell's first novel never made it into print. He wrote the book while living in Florence, Italy, where he had stayed after finishing work on a film with MGM studios. When he returned to his home in California, he rewrote the book, read it over, and then burned it.

Scott's first book for children almost never made it into print, either. He had read a story about an Indian girl in the late 1800s who spent eighteen years stranded on an island off the coast of California near the place where Scott grew up. After he wrote the book, narrated in the girl Karana's voice, he sent it to his literary agents in New York. The agents returned the manuscript, suggesting that Scott rewrite the book, make the hero a young boy, and place the story in a more modern setting. Scott refused to do this. Instead he made an appointment with a friend who worked for a publishing company in Boston. They met for lunch in New York, and a few days later, the friend called and said the publisher wanted to do the book.

> To say that my books were written *for* children is not exactly true. In one sense they were written for myself, out of happy and unhappy memories and a personal need. But all of them lie in the emotional area that children share with adults. (Hoffman and Samuels 1972, 344)

The author never intended to write for children, yet *Island of the Blue Dolphins* won the Southern California Notable Book Award, the Lewis Carroll Shelf Award, the William Allen White Award, and the 1961 Newbery Medal. He was fifty-nine years old when the book was published.

As a boy, Scott loved the sea. His father worked for the railroad, and the family traveled a lot but never too far from the southern California coast. This was in the days when Los Angeles was a frontier town and far different from the city it would become later in Scott's lifetime. Scott's earliest childhood memory was of the sound of a wildcat scratching on the roof of their house. The family also lived in a house on stilts on an island in San Pedro harbor. He thrilled to the sound of the waves washing up under the house.

O'Dell and his friends would take logs brought in to the harbor and ride them around the peninsula. They imagined themselves to be great adventurers, riding out among the great sailing vessels that peppered the harbor. The adventure and excitement of these days remained with Scott all his life, and the sounds and smells and sights of the sea filled many of his books.

Scott sailed through high school. His teachers told him that he was one of the smartest students they'd ever had. He headed off to college, only to find that it wasn't as easy as high school. He got discouraged taking classes in which he had no interest simply because they were required. He attended various colleges but only took classes that interested him and classes he thought would benefit his writing, which he already saw as a possible career.

For a while Scott sought to earn a living in the film industry. He went to Italy to be a cameraman during the shooting of the film *Ben Hur.* He manned the very first Technicolor camera, built by hand at the Massachusetts Institute of Technology. The footage of film never made it into the movie, but he stayed in Florence, and this was when he wrote the novel that he later burned.

After spending a year in the air force during World War II, O'Dell became a news-

paper reporter in Los Angeles. During the time he served as a reporter, he discovered a newspaper article that triggered the idea for *Island of the Blue Dolphins,* although it would be many years before he wrote the book. In fact, it was twenty-six years between the time Scott published his first novel for adults and his first book for children.

Scott enjoyed writing books that children read. He said he liked the immediate responses he received from his young readers. He also liked being able to go back into his own childhood and to resurrect many of the emotions and experiences of those earlier times that had been filled with so many happy adventures.

Scott's work did not go unrecognized. Three of his books won Newbery Honor Medals: *The King's Fifth* (1967), *The Black Pearl* (1968), and *Sing Down the Moon* (1971). In 1972, he won the Hans Christian Andersen Medal, an international award given for an author's overall contribution to literature. O'Dell said that this award meant more to him in his career as a writer than any other he received.

In 1982, Scott established the Scott O'Dell Award for Historical Fiction, an award that is considered one of the most prestigious given for a book of historical fiction. The first winner of the award was Elizabeth George Speare, the first woman to win two Newbery Medals, in 1959 and 1962 (Scott's Newbery Medal came between those years). Several other Newbery Medal winners have also been honored with the Scott O'Dell Award, which is the only award named for a Newbery Medal author.

O'Dell died on October 15, 1989, at the age of ninety-one. After his death, his wife, Elizabeth Hall, completed his novel, *Thunder Rolling in the Mountains,* a story of Chief Joseph and the Nez Perce Indians as told through the eyes of a Native American girl. The book was published in 1992.

A Word to My Readers:

It is very rewarding for me to write for children. I have a sincere feeling that I am able to say something to children, that someone is listening. I am not just entertaining them; I hope that somewhere in each of my books there is something they will take away from it that is important to them as a person. (Hoffman and Samuels 1972, 347)

Books by Scott O'Dell

Alexandra (Houghton Mifflin, 1984).

The Amethyst Ring (Houghton Mifflin, 1983).

The Black Pearl (Houghton Mifflin, 1967).

Black Star, Bright Dawn (Houghton Mifflin, 1988).

The Captive (Houghton Mifflin, 1979).

Carlota (Houghton Mifflin, 1977).

The Castle in the Sea (Houghton Mifflin, 1983).

Child of Fire (Houghton Mifflin, 1974; G. K. Hall, 1976).

The Cruise of the Arctic Star (Houghton Mifflin, 1973; G. K. Hall, 1973).

The Dark Canoe (Houghton Mifflin, 1968).

The Feathered Serpent (Houghton Mifflin, 1981).

The Hawk That Dare Not Hunt by Day (Houghton Mifflin, 1975).

Island of the Blue Dolphins (Houghton Mifflin, 1960, 1990; G. K. Hall, 1974; ABC Clio, 1987).

Journey to Jericho (Houghton Mifflin, 1969).

Kathleen, Please Come Home (Houghton Mifflin, 1978).

The King's Fifth (Houghton Mifflin, 1966).

My Name Is Not Angelica (Houghton Mifflin, 1989).

The Road to Damietta (Houghton Mifflin, 1985).

Sarah Bishop (Houghton Mifflin, 1980).

The Serpent Never Sleeps: A Novel of Jamestown and Pocahontas (Houghton Mifflin, 1987).

Sing Down the Moon (Houghton Mifflin, 1970; Cornerstone Books, 1989).

The Spanish Smile (Houghton Mifflin, 1982).

Streams to the River, River to the Sea: A Novel of Sacagawea (Houghton Mifflin, 1986; G. K. Hall, 1989).

Thunder Rolling in the Mountains (Houghton Mifflin, 1992), finished by his wife, Elizabeth Hall, after O'Dell's death.

The Treasure of Topo el Bampo (Houghton Mifflin, 1972).

The 290 (Houghton Mifflin, 1976).

Zia (Houghton Mifflin, 1976).

For More Information About/by Scott O'Dell

Fuller, Muriel, ed. 1963. *More Junior Authors.* H. W. Wilson.

Hoffman, Miriam, and Eva Samuels. 1972. *Authors and Illustrators of Children's Books: Writings on Their Lives and Works.* R. R. Bowker.

Kingman, Lee, ed. 1965. *Newbery and Caldecott Medal Books, with Acceptance Papers, Biographies and Related Material Chiefly from the Horn Book Magazine: 1956–1965.* Horn Book.

1963: Madeleine L'Engle

Born   November 29, 1918
              New York, New York

Married   Hugh Franklin,
              January 26, 1946 (chil-
              dren: Josephine, Maria,
              and Bion)

Awards and Honors

Newbery Medal (Science Fiction): *A Wrinkle in Time* (Farrar, Straus & Giroux, 1962)
American Library Association Notable Children's Book, 1981: *A Ring of Endless Light*
    (Farrar, Straus & Giroux, 1980)
Newbery Honor Book for 1981: *A Ring of Endless Light* (Farrar, Straus & Giroux, 1980)
American Library Association's Margaret A. Edwards Award, 1998

About the Author and Her Writing

If time travel were possible, Madeleine L'Engle (MAD-uh-len LENG-ul) might have chosen to skip through the many years when she couldn't find a publisher to take any of her books. It may be hard to imagine now that this popular author ever went through such a time, but she did. For ten years, she collected more rejection letters than acceptances. As incredible as it may seem, publishers repeatedly turned down her book *A Wrinkle in Time.* Over forty publishing houses said "no" before one finally said "yes."

It is also difficult to imagine Madeleine L'Engle ever doing anything but writing books, but she did. She worked in the theater for several years before she turned to writing as a career. It's hard to imagine, but all of this is true. These are facts, not fiction, the facts that led Madeleine L'Engle to becoming one of the premier writers of her time, a writer who almost single-handedly paved the way for science fiction to becoming a legitimate genre in children's literature.

Madeleine L'Engle Camp was born on November 29, 1918, the only child of Charles and Madeleine Camp. Charles Camp was a journalist, author, and playwright, and Madeleine Camp was a musician. The Camp home welcomed other musicians, artists, and writers, so Madeleine grew up surrounded by creative people and she learned to love the arts right from the start.

However, Mr. Camp, Madeleine's father, had suffered irreparable damage to his lungs from the toxic gasses he inhaled during World War I. By the time Madeleine was born, her father was already ill, and the family traveled to different parts of the world trying to find the best climate for his failing lungs. Madeleine was first sent to a boarding school in Switzerland and then to South Carolina. In 1936, her father died, when Madeleine was only seventeen years old.

> Most of what is best in writing isn't done deliberately. (Kingman 1965, 121)

From the time that she could pick up a pencil, Madeleine knew that she wanted to be a writer. She wrote her first story at age six and a novel at age twelve. In the sixth grade, she won a poetry contest. Her homeroom teacher could not believe the poem was her own and accused Madeleine of copying it. Madeleine's mother brought in a large stack of her daughter's writing and showed it to the teacher. That dispelled any doubt in the teacher's mind that Madeleine could write.

Madeleine graduated from Smith College, after which she moved with three other women to an apartment in New York. She thought that she could best learn how to write plays by working in the theater. The theater also provided a way for her to support herself and her writing. During one of her tours, she met the actor Hugh Franklin, and a year later, in 1946, they married.

Once Madeleine and Hugh began raising a family, they decided that they didn't want their children growing up in the city. They moved to Connecticut and bought an old 1770s farmhouse named Crosswicks. They bought and rejuvenated the general store, which attracted many interesting people from the small town and others as well: gypsies, carnival folk, factory workers, artists, farmers, philosophers. The business thrived, and so did the family. They had three children: Josephine, Maria, and Bion.

While everything else seemed to be going well, Madeleine's career as a writer was not. She sold her first book, *The Small Rain,* in 1945, and after that, two more books and a play. Then came a long stretch of time in which she could hardly get a publisher to look at her manuscripts. After ten years in Connecticut, Madeleine, Hugh, and their three children decided to resettle in New York. They kept the house in Connecticut, took a ten-week trip across the country, and moved to New York City. Hugh worked in the theater and then landed a role on a popular television soap opera.

Madeleine used her middle name, L'Engle, as her pen name because she wanted to establish her own identity, separate from her father who had been well known in literary circles. It seemed for a while as though asserting her independence in such a way would be unnecessary. Finally, all the years of writing and perseverance and determination paid off.

One year during a Christmas visit, Madeleine's mother hosted a tea party for some of her old friends. One of the guests at the party was a man who worked for a small publishing house run by John Farrar of Farrar, Straus & Giroux publishers. Madeleine's mother showed him the much-rejected manuscript. He liked what he read and agreed to publish the book. *A Wrinkle in Time* not only became Farrar's best-selling book of all time but also received the Newbery Medal in 1963, quite an honor for a book that many publishers said wasn't fit for children! Madeleine never went unrecognized again. The Newbery Medal was not the last award Madeleine ever won but the first of many.

Throughout her life Madeleine was always interested in the deeper questions of life. She had no time for trivia or idle chatter. Her husband, Hugh, often told about the time she took a class in college called "Survey of the Novel." On the final exam, one of the questions was "What color dress was Jane Eyre wearing when she met Mr. Rochester?" According to Hugh, Madeleine "marched to the front desk, grabbed a handful of blue books, and scrawled, 'Dear Miss C——: These are silly questions and I don't know the answer to any of them. But I have read the books, loved them, and shall now proceed to tell you what I think of them.' " Madeleine received an A in the class (Kingman 1965, 125).

> To hurt a butterfly is to shake the universe. (Silvey 1995, 402)

Having grown up an only child, often with her parents living in another part of the world, Madeleine chose a very different life as an adult. Nothing was ever more important to her than her home and family. She loved being surrounded by her children and grandchildren, and she delighted in the special qualities of each. When Hugh died of cancer in 1986, she was devastated. Then on December 17, 1999, she suffered the worst loss a mother can ever face: the death of her beloved son, Bion, at the age of forty-seven. The loss of her only son left a deep and tender wound in Madeleine's life, but her remarkable strength of spirit never diminished. Madeleine never stopped writing, whether it was an annual Christmas poem sent to family or friends or yet another book. She worked out of St. John the Divine Cathedral in New York City and divided her time between New York and the family home, Crosswicks.

Madeleine often signed her books with the inscription "Tesser Well." The phrase comes from the word *tesseract*, a time travel concept explained in Madeleine's book *A Wrinkle in Time*. To tesser is to move from one point in time to another in an extraordinary way, without the limitations of regular time. Madeleine L'Engle knew how to "tesser well," even within the constraints of this life. She took her readers on journeys back and forth in time and deep into the heart as well.

> **A Word to My Readers:**
> Unless a writer works constantly to improve and refine the tools of his trade, they will be useless instruments if and when the moment of inspiration, of revelation, does come. This is the moment when a writer is spoken through, the moment that a writer must accept with gratitude and humility, and then attempt, as best he can, to communicate to others. (Kingman 1965, 121)

Books by Madeleine L'Engle

An Acceptable Time (Farrar, Straus & Giroux, 1989).

And Both Were Young (Lothrop, Lee & Shepard, 1949; Delacorte Press, 1983).

And It Was Good, Reflections on Beginnings (H. Shaw, 1983).

The Anti Muffins (Pilgrim Press, 1980).

Anytime Prayers (H. Shaw, 1994).

The Arm of the Starfish (Ariel Books, 1965).

Bright Evening Star: Mystery of the Incarnation (H. Shaw, 1997, 2001).

Camilla (Crowell, 1965; Delacorte, 1981).

Camilla Dickinson, a Novel (Simon & Schuster, 1951).

Certain Women (Farrar, Straus & Giroux, 1992; HarperSanFrancisco, 1993).

A Circle of Quiet (Farrar, Straus & Giroux, 1972).

A Cry Like a Bell (H. Shaw, 1987).

Dance in the Desert (Farrar, Straus & Giroux, 1969).

Dragons in the Waters (Farrar, Straus & Giroux, 1976).

18 Washington Square, South: A Comedy in One Act (Baker's Plays, 1944).

Everyday Prayers (Morehouse-Barlow, 1974).

Friends for the Journey (Vine Books/Servant Publications, 1997; Thorndike Press, 1998).

A Full House: An Austin Family Christmas (H. Shaw, 1999).

The Genesis Trilogy (WaterBrook Press, 2001).

Glimpses of Grace: Daily Thoughts and Reflections (HarperSanFrancisco, 1996).

The Glorious Impossible (Simon & Schuster Books for Young People, 1990).

A House Like a Lotus (Farrar, Straus & Giroux, 1984).

Ilsa (Vanguard Press, 1946).

The Irrational Season (Seabury Press, 1977; Phoenix Press, 1984; Farrar, Straus & Giroux, 1987).

The Journey with Jonah (Farrar, Straus & Giroux, 1967).

Ladder of Angels: Scenes from the Bible (Seabury Press, 1979; Penguin, 1980; Harper & Row, 1988).

Lines Scribbled on an Envelope, and Other Poems (Farrar, Straus & Giroux, 1969).

A Live Coal in the Sea (Farrar, Straus & Giroux, 1996).

Love Letters (Farrar, Straus & Giroux, 1966; H. Shaw, 1996).

Madeleine L'Engle Herself: Reflections on a Writing Life (WaterBrook Press, 2001).

Many Waters (Farrar, Straus & Giroux, 1986).

Meet the Austins (Vanguard Press, 1960; Farrar, Straus & Giroux, 1997).

Miracle on 10th Street & Other Christmas Writings (H. Shaw, 1998).

The Moon by Night (Ariel Books, 1963).

Mothers & Daughters (H. Shaw, 1997; Gramercy Books, 2001).

Mothers & Sons (H. Shaw, 1999).

The Other Dog (SeaStar Books, 2001).

The Other Side of the Sun (Farrar, Straus & Giroux, 1971; Thorndike Press, 1993; H. Shaw, 1996).

Penguins and Golden Calves: Icons and Idols (H. Shaw, 1996).

A Prayerbook for Spiritual Friends: Partners in Prayer (Augsburg, 1999).

Prelude (Vanguard Press, 1968).

A Ring of Endless Light (Farrar, Straus & Giroux, 1980).

The Rock That Is Higher: Story as Truth (H. Shaw, 1993, 2002).

A Severed Wasp (Farrar, Straus & Giroux, 1982).

The Small Rain (Vanguard Press, 1945; Farrar, Straus & Giroux, 1984).

Sold into Egypt: Joseph's Journey into Human Being (H. Shaw Publishers, 1989).

The Sphinx at Dawn: Two Stories (Seabury Press, 1982; Harper & Row, 1989).

A Stone for a Pillow (H. Shaw, 1986).

The Summer of the Great Grandmother (Farrar, Straus & Giroux, 1974).

A Swiftly Tilting Planet (Farrar, Straus & Giroux, 1978; Thorndike Press, 1993).

Trailing Clouds of Glory: Spiritual Values in Children's Literature (Westminster Press, 1985).

Troubling a Star (Farrar, Straus & Giroux, 1994).

The Twenty Four Days Before Christmas: An Austin Family Story (Ariel Books, 1964; H. Shaw, 1984).

Two Part Invention: The Story of a Marriage (Farrar, Straus & Giroux, 1988; Harper & Row, 1989; Walker, 1991).

Walking on Water: Reflections on Faith & Art (H. Shaw, 1980, 1998; North Point Press, 1995).

The Weather of the Heart: Poems (H. Shaw, 1978).

A Wind in the Door (Farrar, Straus & Giroux, 1973; London: Methuen, 1975; Thorndike Press, 1993).

A Winter's Love (Lippincott, 1957; H. Shaw, 1999).

A Wrinkle in Time (Farrar, Straus & Giroux, 1962; Ariel Books, 1962; ABC Clio, 1987; G. K. Hall, 1998).

The Young Unicorns (Farrar, Straus & Giroux, 1968).

For More Information About/by Madeleine L'Engle

Autobiographies: 1988. *Two Part Invention: The Story of a Marriage.* Farrar, Straus & Giroux; 1974. *The Summer of the Great Grandmother.* Farrar, Straus & Giroux; 2001. *Madeleine L'Engle Herself: Reflections on a Writing Life.* Water-Brook Press.

Drew, Bernard A. 1997. *The 100 Most Popular Young Adult Authors: Biographical Sketches and Bibliographies.* Rev. ed. Libraries Unlimited.

Hopkins, Lee Bennett. 1974. *More Books by More People: Interviews with Sixty-Five Authors of Books for Children.* Citation Press.

Kingman, Lee, ed. 1965. *Newbery and Caldecott Medal Books, with Acceptance Papers, Biographies and Related Material Chiefly from the Horn Book Magazine: 1956–1965.* Horn Book.

Silvey, Anita, ed. 1995. *Children's Books and Their Creators.* Houghton Mifflin.

1964: Emily Cheney Neville

Born   December 28, 1919
            Manchester, Connecticut

Married   Glenn Neville,
            December 18, 1948
            (children: Emily Tam,
            Glenn Jr., Dessie, Marcy
            Ann, and Alexander)

Died   December 14, 1997

Awards and Honors

Newbery Medal (Contemporary Life): *It's Like This, Cat* (Harper & Row, 1963)
Jane Addams Award, 1966: *Berries Goodman* (Harper & Row, 1965)

About the Author and Her Writing

Emily Cheney Neville was born in the Cheney family home in Manchester, Connecticut. The youngest of seven children, she never had a friend outside of the family until she reached the age of ten years old. Her father and her uncles ran a family business, a silk mill. Emily, her siblings, and all their cousins attended the Cheney Family School. The school had no other students except for family members. Emily began attending a public school at the age of ten.

In her teen years, Emily sought to escape some of the small-town closeness that had governed most of her life. She left Manchester and went to Bryn Mawr College near Philadelphia. Her goal after college was to move to New York City and she did, first working as an errand girl for the New York *Daily News,* then as a columnist for the New York *Daily Mirror.*

Emily met her husband at the *Daily Mirror.* Glenn Neville was the executive editor of the newspaper. After they married and started their family, Emily quit her job on the newspaper. The Nevilles had five children: Emily Tam, Glenn Jr., Dessie, Marcy Ann, and Alexander.

Emily's writing career resumed after her youngest child started going to kindergarten. She took the two hours of the day when all the children were in school to sit at a rickety old typewriter and compose stories. Emily accumulated a pile of rejection letters for her short stories, essays, and children's tales, until her manuscript for a proposed picture book caught the attention of editor Ursula Nordstrom. Ms. Nordstrom liked the idea of the story and encouraged Emily to expand the plot into a full-length book. Emily pecked away at the old typewriter until the manuscript finally stretched into a book. The book, *It's Like This, Cat,* was her first published work for children and won the Newbery Medal in 1964. She was forty-three years old.

> There is no excitement quite as great to an author—after the pages of nearly right, or all wrong—as feeling you have finally *hit* it. It is even more exciting to a would-be author. (Kingman 1965, 132)

By the time Emily won the Newbery Medal, the honor of this award had been well established. She had grown up reading books written by previous winners, including Will James, Hugh Lofting, and Dhan Mukerji. Emily was awed by winning the Medal for her first book for children.

When the New York *Daily Mirror* went out of business, Emily and her husband moved from the city to a mountain village in Keene Valley, New York. Unfortunately, their time together in the country came to an end when her husband died that following June in 1965. Emily was only forty-six years old.

The death of her husband deeply affected Emily. "Once death happens to you," she wrote, "instead of being an accident in others' lives, you are forced to upend your values: getting and spending become accidental, and only life, death, and love matter" (de Montreville and Hill 1972, 208).

Emily could have maintained a career solely as an author but chose not to do so. With her family raised and the precious gift of time finally hers, Emily entered law school. She graduated in 1976 and was admitted to the New York bar in 1977. From then on, Neville divided her time between writing books and her law practice. It is interesting to note that the grumpy father in *It's Like This, Cat,* happened to be a lawyer. Emily more closely resembled the boy of the story, Dave Mitchell, who never let a tough situation keep him down.

Emily Cheney Neville died on December 14, 1997. Although the books she wrote are few, they continue to be read and appreciated for both their excellent writing and their insight into real-life emotions, both the sorrows and the joys.

> ## A Word to My Readers:
> This, then, is what seems to me to be the job for a writer of junior novels: to shine the flashlight on good things, and on bad things. It is not our job to preach that this is right and that is wrong. It is ours to show how and when and why Wrong can be so overwhelmingly attractive at a given moment—and how Right can be found in some very unlikely corners. (Kingman 1965, 136)

Books by Emily Cheney Neville

Berries Goodman (Harper & Row, 1965).

The Bridge (Harper & Row, 1988).

The China Year: A Novel (HarperCollins, 1991).

Fogarty (Harper & Row, 1969).

Garden of Broken Glass (Delacorte Press, 1975).

It's Like This, Cat (Harper & Row, 1963; London: Angus & Robertson, 1969).

The Seventeenth Street Gang (Harper & Row, 1966).

Traveler from a Small Kingdom (Harper & Row, 1968).

For More Information About/by Emily Cheney Neville

de Montreville, Doris, and Donna Hill, eds. 1972. *The Third Book of Junior Authors.* H. W. Wilson.

Kingman, Lee, ed. 1965. *Newbery and Caldecott Medal Books, with Acceptance Papers, Biographies and Related Material Chiefly from the Horn Book Magazine: 1956–1966.* Horn Book.

1965: Maia Wojciechowska

Born	August 7, 1927
	Warsaw, Poland
Married	Selden Rodman, 1950
	Richard Larkin, 1972
	(children: Oriana and
	Leonora)
Died	June 13, 2002

Awards and Honors

Newbery Medal (Action and Adventure, Animal Stories): *Shadow of a Bull* (Atheneum, 1964)

About the Author and Her Writing

At the tender age of six, someone accused Maia Wojciechowska (MY-a Voy-cha-HOF-ska) of being a liar. "I am a writer, not a liar," the little girl responded. "I make up stories because facts are boring" (interview, March 1996).

Maia's life was anything but boring. She was born and raised in Warsaw, Poland, along with her two brothers. Her family roots can be traced back to 1511. Her family emigrated to the United States in 1942 when her father was assigned as the air attache at the Polish Embassy in Washington.

As a child, Maia was an avid reader, using moonlight to highlight the words in her books and candles when her flashlights were taken from her. She set her bed on fire more than once, but nothing diminished her love of the written word.

Being the only girl in the family did not please Maia at all. She wanted to be a priest when she grew up, but that was not an option for a Catholic girl in Poland. She begged to play with her older brother and his friends. They tied her to a cemetery cross and left her there overnight, promising that if she did not tell on them and did not cry, they'd let her play with them. She kept her end of the bargain, but the boys did not. After that she wasn't sorry to be a girl any longer, because she felt that she had at least kept her integrity

146

intact. She gave up wanting to be a priest when she discovered that it was allowable for a girl to grow up and be a writer. This was a career she believed she could enjoy.

From early on Maia wrote stories centering on the theme of Polish exiles, people who were forced to leave the country during the war. Ruper Hughes, a novelist, read a collection of her stories. He was so moved by them that he called her on the telephone in tears to tell her so. Encouraged by this response, and so certain that her writing would be accepted as enthusiastically by a publisher, she traveled by bus to New York. She took her manuscript to Harper & Brothers publishers because she liked the look of their building. The next day she returned, ready for acceptance, only to have her manuscript returned to her without even a rejection letter. She vowed to give up writing forever. Maia was seventeen years old.

> Ideas come from the head, inspiration from the heart, and imagination is nothing more than a desire to see things as they could be, rather than as they are, or when you are really inspired to discover that you can see what nobody else had ever seen, think what nobody else had thought. (interview, March 1996)

Maia took a job as a tennis coach for fifteen dollars a week and a small room. She supplemented her income by playing pool. Later, she met and married a poet, Selden Rodman, had a daughter, and divorced. Then Maia left her daughter with her ex-husband and moved to Spain to "find herself."

It was during the years in Spain that Maia decided to go back to writing. She thought that this would force her to grow up and face the responsibilities of her life. She returned to the United States after several years and settled in Los Angeles. During this time she wrote the short story that later became the book *Shadow of a Bull*.

Maia's inspiration for the book came from living in Spain and, in an odd way, from an encounter she had with a young teenage girl on a bus. Maia watched the girl on the bus sitting quietly and wished she could find a way to reach out to her. She kept the girl in mind as she turned her thirteen-page short story into a book, believing that a good book for children could be a bridge between herself and children she would never know.

Maia's daughter chose the title for the book, which Maia sent to an editor. The editor changed the ending so much that Maia wasn't even sure she liked it anymore. She decided to submit the manuscript anyway, and the first publisher who read it bought it. The book won the 1965 Newbery Medal. The rest, as they say, is history.

But the turmoil of that history was far from over. Just when Maia thought she had her life together and was on her way, she was diagnosed with cancer. She survived the cancer, kept writing, and received good reviews for her books. After a while, she became discouraged by the criticisms of editors and vowed again to quit writing. This time, she kept her promise for five years. She married again, had another daughter, and later divorced. But the need to write won again, and Maia resumed her writing career with the zest and drive that characterized much of her life.

Maia was never one to settle for the easy way of doing things. She pushed herself as a writer and as an individual. She tried skydiving, bullfighting, and skiing, and once said that it was only in growing old that she grew up and found some of the peace she longed to discover in her life.

In the years following her Newbery Medal, Maia continued to write, although she did not always complete the books she began because, in her words, "ending something always seems to me to be the beginning of something else (for a writer it's publication). And publication does not seem to be in the cards for me" (Peacock 2000, 442). Nonetheless, she wrote several books dealing with the modern-day stresses of teenagers, including eating disorders, mental health issues, and suicide. She also wrote a series of "Dreams of" books, including *Dreams of Golf, Dreams of the Deep, Dreams of Soccer, Dreams of the Hoop*. These books were published by Pebble Beach Press, which was owned and operated by one of her brothers.

Maia once said that "If only people were not so afraid of facing (the truth). It doesn't make you blind, as some would have it. It makes you see. Very clearly. And makes you laugh. Very often. Life is good" (Peacock 2000, 444). This attitude sums up the life of Maia Wojciechowska, who truly was never afraid of facing the truth and who always found a way to enjoy life.

A Word to My Readers:

The best, the safest, the cheapest escape of all is reading. If you don't acquire that habit early in life you run the danger of being brain dead from boredom. (interview, March 1996)

Books by Maia Wojciechowska

"Don't Play Dead Before You Have To," a novel (Harper & Row, 1970).

Dreams of Baseball (Pebble Beach Press, 1997).

Dreams of the Deep (Pebble Beach Press, 1997).

Dreams of Golf (Pebble Beach Press, 1993).

Dreams of the Hoop (Pebble Beach Press, 1997).

Dreams of the Indy Five-Hundred (Pebble Beach Press, 1997).

Dreams of the Kentucky Derby (Pebble Beach Press, 1996).

Dreams of Soccer (Pebble Beach Press, 1994).

Dreams of Teaching (Pebble Beach Press, 1997).

Hey, What's Wrong with This One? (Harper & Row, 1969).

The Hollywood Kid (Harper & Row, 1966).

How God Got Christian into Trouble (Westminster Press, 1984).

A Kingdom in a Horse (Harper & Row, 1965).

The Life and Death of a Brave Bull (Harcourt Brace Jovanovich, 1972).

Market Day for Ti Andre (Viking Press, 1952).

Odyssey of Courage: The Story of Alvar Nunez Cabez de Vaca (London: Burns & Oates, 1965; Atheneum, 1967).

The People in His Life (Stein & Day, 1980).

The Rotten Years (Doubleday, 1971).

Shadow of a Bull (Atheneum, 1964; Toronto: McClelland & Stewart, 1969; Globe Books, 1975; Aladdin Books, 1987, 1992).

A Single Light (Harper & Row, 1968).

Through the Broken Mirror with Alice (Harcourt Brace Jovanovich, 1972).

Till the Break of Day (Harcourt Brace Jovanovich, 1972).

Tuned Out (Harper & Row, 1968).

Winter Tales from Poland (Doubleday, 1973).

For More Information About/by Maia Wojciechowska

Autobiography: 1972. *Till the Break of Day.* Harcourt Brace Jovanovich.

Commire, Anne, ed. *Something About the Author: Facts and Pictures About Contemporary Authors and Illustrators of Books for Young People.* Vol. 1. Gale Research.

Hoffman, Miriam, and Eva Samuels. 1972. *Authors and Illustrators of Children's Books: Writings on Their Lives and Works.* R. R. Bowker.

Kingman, Lee, ed. 1965. *Newbery and Caldecott Medal Books, with Acceptance Papers, Biographies and Related Material Chiefly from the Horn Book Magazine: 1956–1965.*Horn Book.

Peacock, Scot, ed. 2000. *Contemporary Authors.* Vol. 183. Gale Group.

Note: Indicated citations from a personal interview with the author, March 1996.

1966: Elizabeth Borton de Treviño

Born	September 2, 1904 Bakersfield, California
Married	Luis Treviño, August 10, 1935 (children: Luis Fredrico and Enrique Ricardo)

Awards and Honors

Newbery Medal (Historical Fiction): *I, Juan de Pareja* (Farrar, Straus & Giroux, 1965)

About the Author and Her Writing

Elizabeth Borton de Treviño began her journey to becoming an award-winning author in Bakersfield, California, where she grew up in a family of readers who treasured books. Her father published a number of short stories and poems before he turned his full attention to the practice of law. During dinnertime he kept a dictionary to his right and a small set of encyclopedias to his left. If the children wished to join in the conversation, they had to look up any words they didn't understand and any information that was new to them. The use of slang or poor sentence structure was all it took for one of them to be banished from the dinner table for the remainder of that particular meal.

> Children love justice and the triumph of the right. Cynicism, after all, is an adult invention. (Kingman 1976, 9)

At the age of six, Elizabeth contracted malaria, and for many summers thereafter she lived with her grandmother in her home by the shore. Elizabeth spent most of her time at the library, reading.

She began writing poetry when she was six and had her first poem published in the local newspaper when she was eight. That experience convinced her that what she wanted more than anything was to be an author.

Elizabeth always had a great love for Mexico and its people. She received a degree in Latin American history from Stanford University. For a time, she studied violin at the Boston Conservatory of Music and then went to work for the Boston *Herald* as a newspaper editor and a reporter.

One of the most important lessons Elizabeth learned about being a writer came during her painful years in college. She had a professor in whose class she wrote many plays, which were often criticized and ridiculed by both the professor and her classmates. Elizabeth left the course in tears many times. But she kept writing. The teacher later told her that he knew she could be a true writer, since she did not let criticism and discouragement keep her from doing what she loved to do.

The Great Depression put a sudden end to Elizabeth's newspaper career. She returned home to Bakersfield, California. Seeing how much his daughter yearned to write, Elizabeth's father, instead of discouraging her, set her up in an office with a table, typewriter, chair, and a small salary. His instructions were for her to write every day from 9:00 A.M. until noon, and again from 1:00 P.M. until 5:00 P.M., with Saturdays off. He wanted to teach Elizabeth that writing was hard work. One day, Elizabeth told him that she had started a novel. He responded, "Probably 5,649 other persons started novels today. Chances are that 5,640 have more talent than you. But honey, you can do what 5,000 won't do. You can finish yours" (Kingman 1976, 7).

When the *Herald* invited her back in 1931 after a year's absence, she returned to Boston. In 1934, she received the reporting assignment that she longed for, the one that changed her life. She was sent to Mexico to do a series of articles for the newspaper.

Luis Treviño, the young man assigned to be her interpreter and guide, quickly fell in love with the vivacious, pretty blonde, and vice versa. Before Elizabeth left her assignment in Mexico, she and Luis were engaged. They married a year later.

Elizabeth and Luis lived in Mexico and raised two boys, Luis Fredrico and Enrique Ricardo. Two of the biggest influences in Elizabeth's life were reflected in the lives of her sons: in Luis, whose love for painting brought his mother's attention to the story that became the basis for her Newbery Medal–winning book; and in Enrique, who became a lawyer in Mexico City as Elizabeth's father had been a lawyer for all those years in California.

It is said that a picture is worth a thousand words. This was certainly true when it came time for Elizabeth to write *I, Juan de Pareja*. Her love for Latin America and for writing made a perfect marriage in this book. Treviño painted a portrait of a particular time, place, and person.

The picture in her mind was based on a painting by the great seventeenth-century Spanish painter Diego Velásquez. Elizabeth's son Luis, who had a strong interest in art and painting, first brought to her attention the story of the painter and his slave, Juan, whom Velásquez taught to paint and later freed. When Elizabeth visited Spain, she sought out the painting that Velásquez had done of Juan. She decided then and there that someday she would tell the story of the lifelong friendship between these two men, so different and yet so alike. The book, *I, Juan de Pareja*, won the Newbery Medal for 1966.

Elizabeth Borton de Treviño continued to live in Mexico and to write books well into the 1990s. She also served as the honorary lecturer for the American Institute for Foreign Trade.

A Word to My Readers:

The longer I live, the more I am convinced that every child is born with a deep need to love and be loved, and that this longing accompanies us through life, passing through many metamorphoses, but always at the root of all our actions and hopes. (Kingman 1976, 11)

Books by Elizabeth Borton de Treviño

Among the Innocent (Doubleday, 1981).

Beyond the Gates of Hercules: A Tale of the Lost Atlantis (Farrar, Straus & Giroux, 1971).

A Carpet of Flowers (Crowell, 1955).

Casilda of the Rising Moon: A Tale of Magic and of Faith, of Knights and a Saint in Medieval Spain (Farrar, Straus & Giroux, 1967; London: Gollancz, 1968).

Even As You Love (Crowell, 1957).

The Fourth Gift (Doubleday, 1966).

The Greek of Toledo: A Romantic Narrative About El Greco (Crowell, 1959).

El Guero: A True Adventure Story (Farrar, Straus & Giroux, 1989).

The Heart Possessed: A Love Story (Doubleday, J. Curley & Associates, 1978).

The Hearthstone of My Heart (Doubleday, 1977).

The House on Bitterness Street (Doubleday, 1970).

I, Juan de Pareja (Bell Books, 1965; Farrar, Straus & Giroux, 1965; FSG Spanish Edition, 1994).

Juarez, Man of Law (Farrar, Straus & Giroux, 1974).

Leona, a Love Story (Farrar, Straus & Giroux, 1994).

The Music Within (Doubleday, 1973).

My Heart Lies South: The Story of My Mexican Marriage (Crowell, 1953; Crowell, with epilogue, 1972; Young People's Edition, Bethlehem Books, 2000).

Nacar, the White Deer (Farrar, Straus, 1963).

Our Little Aztec Cousin of Long Ago (L. C. Page, 1934).

Our Little Ethiopian Cousin: Children of the Queen of Sheba (L. C. Page, 1935).

Turi's Papa (Farrar, Straus & Giroux, 1968; London: Gollancz, 1969).

Where the Heart Is (Doubleday, 1962).

For More Information About/by Elizabeth Borton de Treviño

Autobiography: 1954. *My Heart Lies South: The Story of My Mexican Marriage.* Crowell, 1953; Crowell, with epilogue, 1972; Young People's Edition, Bethlehem Books, 2000.

Autobiography: 1977. *The Hearthshone of My Heart.* Doubleday.

Evory, Ann, and Linda Metzger, eds. 1983. *Contemporary Authors.* New Revision Series. Gale Research.

Kingman, Lee, ed. 1976. *Newbery and Caldecott Medal Books, with Acceptance Papers, Biographies and Related Material Chiefly from the Horn Book Magazine: 1966–1975.* Horn Book.

1967: Irene Hunt

Born   May 18, 1902 (although many
resources list Irene's year of
birth as 1907, her sister, Shirley
Beem, verified that the actual
year was 1902)
Pontiac, Illinois

Died   May 18, 2001
Champaign, Illinois

Awards and Honors

Newbery Medal (Contemporary Life): *Up a Road Slowly* (Follett, 1966)
Charles W. Follett Award, 1964: *Across Five Aprils* (Follett, 1964)
Newbery Honor Book for 1965: *Across Five Aprils* (Follett, 1964)
American Notable Book Award, 1965: *Across Five Aprils* (Follett, 1964)

About the Author and Her Writing

The title of Irene Hunt's 1967 Newbery Medal–winning book, *Up a Road Slowly,* could be the title of her life. The road she traveled was a long one, with twists and turns, sorrows and joys along the way. She walked that road with a steady step, able to move forward and to look back at her life.

The first big bend in the road of Irene's life came when she was seven years old. Her beloved Papa died of typhoid fever, leaving her with a sadness she never forgot. "I was hurt because I thought he didn't love me anymore," she said in an interview. "He said to my mother, 'Please take her away. I don't want her to remember me the way I am'" (interview, March 1, 1994). Only later did Irene understand that it was because her father loved her so much that he couldn't bear the thought of his precious little girl having to watch him suffer.

Irene had a gift for staying in touch with the deep sorrows of childhood while at the same time remembering the joy. Although she never forgot the loss of her father, she also remembered the wonderful closeness the two had shared. She remembered the bounce in

153

his step and the twinkle in his eye as he returned home after a day of teaching high school students. She remembered the way he used to make up his own words. Someone would ask him, "Frank, are you going to get a new car this year?" He would respond, "I'd like to have one of those beautiful new automobiles, but right now I don't have the spondulix."

"Papa made up words like that all the time," Irene recalled many years later (interview, March 1, 1994).

Irene's early memories remained vivid throughout her life. Those memories, and her ability to remember how it felt to be a child treasured dearly by a father whose life ended far too soon, formed the basis for many of her books.

After the death of her father, Irene moved with her mother and a younger sister to the farm where her maternal grandparents lived. Her grandfather loved to tell stories. He had been a young boy when the Civil War broke out, and he shared his own eyewitness perspective on those troubled times. The grief-stricken girl soaked up her grandfather's stories, along with the stories in the books that were kept in her grandparents' attic.

Irene went to college and then went on to earn her master's degree. She taught school for over thirty-five years. She loved teaching, and most of all she wanted to bring to her students the joy of learning. It was during her time as a teacher that Irene recognized that children could learn more about history by reading stories and good literature than by trying to memorize facts and figures.

> Real satisfaction for me is to step into a room where teacher and children are off together in another world, bound together by a bond made possible through the magic of a well-loved book. (Kingman 1976, 23)

"My books were generated by the needs of my students," she said (interview, March 1, 1994). Irene responded to those needs first by introducing her classes to literature that made history come alive, and later by writing her own books that did the same.

Irene's road to publication was slow. Her nephew remembered her sitting at a kitchen table with a typewriter, night after night. She compiled rejection letters as well as articles and stories. Her first publishing credits came from magazine articles, stories that helped pave the way for her to write the books that have become beloved by so many.

After she finished writing the manuscript for her first published book, *Across Five Aprils,* Irene sent it to an editor along with a note that read, "I don't know if you care to read this, but I'm sending it to you." The editor wrote back that she liked the manuscript very much, and so began Irene's career as a novelist.

Across Five Aprils drew on the stories told to her by her grandfather. The story is set during the Civil War and filled with emotions and feelings that never could be gleaned from a history textbook. This book, published in 1964 when Irene was over sixty years old, was the only Newbery Honor Book for the year. *Across Five Aprils* also won the Charles W. Follett Award and the American Notable Book Award.

Two years later, Irene published *Up a Road Slowly.* The novel tells the story of a girl who faces the death of her mother and then goes to live with her aunt, where she grows into adulthood. Again Irene drew on real life to furnish the details of the book. This time it was Irene's life that inspired the story.

Irene never "prettied up" her characters. She let them have feelings: anger, despair, joy. She also let her characters work through tough issues such as ridicule and racism, dealing honestly with the issues and the people. Irene had a gift for telling a good story without ignoring the harsh realities of life, but always in a way that left room for hope.

Irene Hunt died peacefully in her sleep on May 18, 2001, on the evening of her ninety-ninth birthday and ninety-two years after the death of her beloved Papa, whom she never, ever forgot.

A Word to My Readers:

Great books do not have to preach. But they do speak to the conscience, the imagination, and the heart of many a child. And they speak with very clear and forceful voices. (Kingman 1976, 28)

Books by Irene Hunt

Across Five Aprils (Follett, 1964; Silver Burdett, 1993).

Claws of a Young Century (C. Scribner's Sons, 1980).

The Everlasting Hills (C. Scribner's Sons, 1985).

Lottery Rose (C. Scribner's Sons, 1976).

No Promises in the Wind (Follett, 1970).

Trail of Apple Blossoms (Follett, 1968; Modern Curriculum Press, 1993).

Up a Road Slowly (Follett, 1966; Silver Burdett, 1993).

William: A Novel (C. Scribner's Sons, 1977).

For More Information About/by Irene Hunt

Kingman, Lee. 1976. *Newbery and Caldecott Medal Books, with Acceptance Papers, Biographies and Related Material Chiefly from the Horn Book Magazine: 1966–1975*. Horn Book.

Note: Indicated citations from a personal interview with the author, March 1, 1994.

1968/1997: E. L. Konigsburg

Born   February 10, 1930
            New York, New York

Married   David Konigsburg, July 6,
            1952 (children: Paul,
            Laurie, and Ross)

Awards and Honors

Newbery Medal for 1968 (Mystery, Adventure): *From the Mixed-Up Files of Mrs. Basil E. Frankweiler* (Atheneum, 1967)

Newbery Medal for 1997 (Contemporary Life, Adventure): *The View from Saturday* (Atheneum Books for Young Readers, 1996)

Newbery Honor Book for 1968: *Jennifer, Hecate, Macbeth, William McKinley, and Me, Elizabeth* (Atheneum, 1967)

Lewis Carroll Shelf Award, 1968: *From the Mixed-Up Files of Mrs. Basil E. Frankweiler* (Atheneum, 1967; Aladdin Books, 1986; ABC Clio, 1988)

American Library Association Notable Children's Book, 1980: *Throwing Shadows* (Atheneum, 1979; Collier Books, 1988); 1987: *Up from Jericho Tel* (Atheneum, 1986); 1997: *The View from Saturday* (Atheneum Books for Young Readers, 1996)

School Library Journal Best Books, 1996: *The View from Saturday* (Atheneum Books for Young Readers, 1996); 2000: *Silent to the Bone* (Atheneum Books for Young Readers, 2000; Aladdin Paperbacks, 2002)

About the Author and Her Writing

Imagine the fun of living in a magnificent museum, bathing in the fountains, sleeping in the antique beds, exploring all the nooks and crannies long after all the tourists have gone home. E. L. Konigsburg created such an adventure. She wrote about it in a book, *From the Mixed-Up Files of Mrs. Basil E. Frankweiler.* The book won the Newbery Medal for 1968.

As if winning the Newbery Medal wasn't exciting enough, E. L., or Elaine, was the first person ever to win a Newbery Honor Medal in the same year as the Newbery Medal.

156

Jennifer, Hecate, Macbeth, William McKinley, and Me, Elizabeth was actually the first book Elaine ever wrote, although the two Medal–winning books were published in the same year. When the Newbery committee called the Konigsburg home on January 13, 1968, Elaine and her family were in the middle of moving from an apartment to a new house. The thrill of that phone call made moving the many boxes a bit easier but also kept the realities of daily life in the forefront of Elaine's mind. Those two extremes are what fed Elaine's joy as a writer: the chance to experience the unbelievable while keeping one's feet firmly planted on the ground.

Elaine grew up in several small mill towns in western Pennsylvania, the second of three girls. She was an excellent student and the valedictorian of her high school class.

> I spread words on paper for the same reasons that Cro-Magnon man spread pictures on the walls of caves . . . I need to see the words to make more real that which I have experienced. (Kingman 1976, 37)

Elaine went to college planning to be a chemist, and after receiving her degree taught chemistry in a private girl's school. By that time, she had married her husband, David. With the advent of their first child, Paul, Elaine quit teaching and centered her life on her family. A second child, Laurie, and then a third, Ross, quickly joined the Konigsburg household.

During the raising of her children Elaine also pursued an interest in art. She took painting lessons whenever she could fit them into her busy schedule. She even won a prize for the art displayed in her very first exhibition.

Once her last child entered kindergarten, Elaine began to write during the few hours when she had the house to herself. She let the beds go unmade and left the dirty dishes in the sink, making the best use of her precious hours. She knew there would be time later for those chores, as indeed there was.

Elaine said she liked to think about the characters that would people her stories. She usually had a beginning, middle, and end to a story before she sat down to write. But once at the keyboard, Elaine let the characters take over and lead the way, taking the stories to places she hadn't quite imagined at the start.

It was while the Konigsburg family was on summer vacation that the concept for *From the Mixed-Up Files of Mrs. Basil E. Frankweiler* came into focus. She watched as her children squirmed with the discomforts of "roughing it" during a picnic in Yellowstone National Park where the family shared their ground space with ants and bugs. Elaine thought about how so many children, including her own, had lived fairly comfortable lives, without ever having to deal with the hardships that other children experienced daily. She figured that her kids might find it more appealing to live in the Metropolitan Museum of Art in New York City with all the advantages of home and then some, rather than in the outdoor setting of a national park.

Winning her first Newbery Medal gave Elaine the confidence to stretch her writing style. She wrote a historical novel and many other books in the next three decades of her writing career.

In 1997, twenty-nine years after winning her first Newbery Medal, Elaine won a second Newbery Medal, this time for *The View from Saturday,* a clever story about four sixth-grade students who represent their class in an academic competition. The book intertwines the students' lives in creative and unsuspecting ways. The idea for the book developed through the years as she attended lectures on the dynamics of learning and gave lectures on this topic as well. Elaine recognized the importance of experience as a necessary factor in the learning process, whether that experience was emotional, social, or educational.

Elaine began her second Newbery Medal acceptance speech with these words: "As I was saying, four days and twenty-nine years ago, thank you" (Horn Book/ALSC 2001, 267). A lot can happen in twenty-nine years, and that is true with Elaine's life. But one thing has stayed the same. From her first Newbery Medal to her second, Elaine's wit, humor, and gift with words continued to shine.

A Word to My Readers:

The difference between being a person of talent and being an author is the ability to finish. (Kovacs and Preller 1991, 107)

Books by E. L. Konigsburg

About the B'nai Bagels (Atheneum, 1969; Econo-Clad Books, 1999).

Altogether, One at a Time (Atheneum, 1971; Aladdin Books, 1989; Econo-Clad Books, 1999).

Amy Elizabeth Explores Bloomingdale's (Atheneum, 1992).

The Dragon in the Ghetto Caper (Atheneum, 1974; Econo-Clad Books, 1999).

Father's Arcane Daughter (Atheneum, 1976).

From the Mixed-Up Files of Mrs. Basil E. Frankweiler (Atheneum, 1967; Aladdin Books, 1986; ABC Clio, 1988).

(George) (Atheneum, 1970).

Jennifer, Hecate, Macbeth, William McKinley, and Me, Elizabeth (Atheneum, 1967; Cornerstone Books, 1989; Aladdin Paperbacks, 2001).

Journey to an 800 Number (Atheneum, 1982; Econo-Clad Books, 1999).

The Mask Beneath the Face: Reading About and with, Writing About and for Children (Library of Congress, 1990).

A Proud Taste for Scarlet and Miniver (Atheneum, 1973; Aladdin Books, 2001).

Samuel Todd's Book of Great Colors (Atheneum, 1990).

Samuel Todd's Book of Great Inventions (Atheneum, 1991).

The Second Mrs. Giaconda (Atheneum, 1975).

Silent to the Bone (Atheneum Books for Young Readers, 2000; Aladdin Paperbacks, 2002).

T Backs, T Shirts, COAT, and Suit (Atheneum, 1993; Hyperion Paperbacks for Children, 1995).

Talk Talk: A Children's Book Author Speaks to Grown Ups (Atheneum, 1995).

*illustrated by the author

Throwing Shadows (Atheneum, 1979; Collier Books, 1988).

Up from Jericho Tel (Atheneum, 1986).

The View from Saturday (Atheneum Books for Young Readers, 1996).

For More Information About/by E. L. Konigsburg

Horn Book and Association for Library Service to Children (ALSC), American Library Association. 2001. *The Newbery and Caldecott Medal Books, 1986–2000: A Comprehensive Guide to the Winners.* Horn Book and Association for Library Service to Children, American Library Association.

Kingman, Lee, ed. 1976. *Newbery and Caldecott Medal Books, with Acceptance Papers, Biographies and Related Material Chiefly from the Horn Book Magazine: 1966–1975.* Horn Book.

Kovacs, Deborah, and James Preller. 1991. *Meet the Authors and Illustrators: 60 Creators of Favorite Children's Books Talk About Their Work.* Scholastic.

1969: Lloyd Alexander

Born   January 30, 1924
              Philadelphia, Pennsylvania

Married   Janine Denni, 1946
              (children: Madeleine)

Awards and Honors

Newbery Medal (Science Fiction, Fantasy): *The High King* (Holt, Rinehart & Winston, 1968)

Newbery Honor Book for 1966: *The Black Cauldron* (Holt, Rinehart & Winston, 1965)

School Library Journal's Best Book of the Year Award, 1971: *Taran Wanderer* (Holt, Rinehart & Winston, 1967; H. Holt & Co., 1999); 1995: *The House Gobbaleen* (Dutton Children's Books, 1995); 2001: *The Gawgon and the Boy* (Dutton Children's Books, 2001)

National Book Award, 1971

Drexel Award for outstanding contributions to literature for children, 1972, 1976

American Book Award, 1982

Boston Globe-Horn Book Award, 1993: *The Fortune Tellers* (Dutton Children's Books, 1992)

American Library Association Notable Children's Book Award, 1982: *Westmark* (Dutton, 1981; Penguin Putnam, 2002); 1983: *The Kestrel* (Dutton, 1982; Puffin Books, 2000); 1987: *The Illyrian Adventure* (Dutton, 1986; Puffin Books, 2000); 1993: *The Fortune Tellers* (Dutton Children's Books, 1992); 1996: *The Arcadians* (Dutton Children's Books, 1995; Econoclad Books, 1999); 1998: *The Iron Ring* (Dutton Children's Books, 1997; Puffin Books, 2001); 2002: *The Gawgon and the Boy* (Dutton Children's Books, 2001)

About the Author and His Writing

Lloyd Alexander taught himself to read at the age of three. He always loved books, first reading them and eventually writing them. He knew from the time he was fifteen that he wanted to be a writer. Yet like so many others, when he first embarked on a writing career he was met with rejection and discouragement.

Lloyd knew he could not make a living as a writer when he first began, so he took a job as a bank messenger. He then decided that a life of adventure would be better preparation for a writing career and so joined the army during World War II. His time in the army gave him the opportunity to travel, first in the United States and then overseas in Wales, France, and Germany.

Lloyd found himself especially enchanted by the land of Wales, its rich history and mythology, its folktales and customs. Seeds for future books were planted during the time he lived there.

If Wales captured his writing heart, France captured his romantic heart, for it was in Paris that he met and married his wife, Janine Denni, in 1946. Janine had a young daughter, Madeleine, and the three of them moved back to Pennsylvania where Lloyd had family roots. In order to write, he felt he needed to be living in the place where he had grown up.

> I think that every creative work, on the deepest levels, is an aspect of the writer himself, and his own personal vision. (Hopkins 1974, 14)

Lloyd's books were not met with immediate enthusiasm. He spent seven years gathering rejection letters while making some money doing other kinds of writing as a copywriter, layout artist, cartoonist, and associate editor and writer for a small magazine. Finally, in 1955, Lloyd's first book was published, and for the next ten years he wrote books for adults.

He never planned to write books for children, but as time went on Lloyd recognized that the types of stories he truly wanted to write and the things he really wanted to say were best suited for children's literature. "Writing for young people became the most creative and liberating experience of my life," he once wrote (Silvey 1995, 13). Lloyd Alexander had found his niche.

He used the mythology he so loved to create a fantasy world inspired in part by the country of Wales. For six straight years his new children's books came out: in 1963, 1964, 1965, 1966, 1967, and 1968. His 1965 book, *The Black Cauldron,* was named a Newbery Honor Book and later made into a movie by Disney. But the pinnacle of that decade of writing came in 1968, when *The High King,* the final book in his tales of Prydain, won the Newbery Medal. Through these books, and others that came later, Lloyd established his reputation as one of the foremost writers of the twentieth century, particularly in the genre of fantasy for children.

While writing his books, Lloyd would imagine himself sitting in a movie theater, watching the story unfold. This gave him a clearer picture of the story, where the plot was headed, and what scenes needed to be written. Lloyd took many notes during the writing of a book and wrote and rewrote numerous times. He believed that he could learn from his mistakes and be a better writer if he kept polishing his manuscripts.

It is hard to imagine an author as prolific as Lloyd Alexander ever having writer's block, but on occasion he found it difficult to write. When this happened, Lloyd figured that the only way to break through the block was to force himself to sit down and write, a discipline he often suggested to other people who asked him what it took to be a writer.

One of Lloyd's leisure activities was playing the violin. After being notified that he won the Newbery Medal, he was so pleased and delighted that during a Sunday afternoon concert, he totally botched his violin solo. He said that the cellist responded by shaking his head and saying to Lloyd, "No doubt about it. The Newbery Medal's a wonderful thing for you. But it doesn't do anything for Johann Sebastian Bach" (Kingman 1976, 49).

One day while cleaning the attic of their house, Lloyd's wife found an old manuscript that he had written fifteen years earlier. He had set aside the manuscript in order to pursue other projects and forgotten all about it. Eventually the lost manuscript became a beautiful picture book, *The Fortune Tellers* (Dutton Children's Books, 1992).

A prolific writer, Lloyd Alexander continued to produce wonderful books, over three dozen titles in all.

A Word to My Readers:

From what I've seen during my visits to schools, what children really want to know, and I think it's important for them to know, is that writers are genuine human beings, that they're real human beings, that they're real people, with real lives, problems, ups and downs, that we aren't abstractions or textbook figures. Even though we're adults, we really are alive. (Hopkins 1974, 17)

Books by Lloyd Alexander

And Let the Credit Go (Crowell, 1955).

The Arkadians (Dutton Children's Books, 1995; Econo-Clad Books, 1999).

The Beggar Queen (Dutton, 1984; Puffin Books, 2002).

The Black Cauldron (Holt, Rinehart & Winston, 1965; H. Holt & Co., 1999).

The Book of Three (Holt, Rinehart & Winston, 1964; H. Holt & Co., 1999).

Border Hawk: August Bondi (Farrar, Straus & Cudahy, 1958).

The Castle of Llyr (Holt, Rinehart & Winston, 1966; H. Holt & Co., 1999).

The Cat Who Wished to Be a Man (Dutton, 1973; Puffin Books, 2000).

Coll and His White Pig (Holt, Rinehart & Winston, 1965).

The Drackenberg Adventure (Dutton, 1988, 2001).

The El Dorado Adventure (Dutton, 1987; Puffin Books, 2000).

Fifty Years in the Doghouse (Putnam's, 1964).

The First Two Lives of Lukas Kasha (Dutton, 1978; Puffin Books, 1998).

The Fortune Tellers (Dutton Children's Books, 1992).

The Foundling and Other Tales of Prydain (Holt, Rinehart & Winston, 1973; Puffin Books, 1996; H. Holt & Co., 1999).

The Four Donkeys (Holt, Rinehart & Winston, 1972).

The Gawgon and the Boy (Dutton Children's Books, 2001).

Gypsy Rizka (Dutton Children's Books, 1999, 2000).

The High King (Holt, Rinehart & Winston, 1968; H. Holt & Co., 1999).

The House Gobbaleen (Dutton Children's Books, 1995).

How the Cat Swallowed Thunder (Dutton Children's Books, 2000).

The Illyrian Adventure (Dutton, 1986; Puffin Books, 2000).

The Iron Ring (Dutton Children's Books, 1997; Puffin Books, 2001).

Janine Is French (Crowell, 1959).

The Jedera Adventure (Dutton, 1989; Puffin Books, 2001).

The Kestrel (Dutton, 1982; Puffin Books, 2002).

The King's Fountain (Dutton, 1971).

The Marvelous Misadventures of Sebastian (Dutton, 1970; Puffin Books, 2000; Peter Smith, 2001).

My Five Tigers (Crowell, 1956).

My Love Affair with Music (Crowell, 1960; London: Cassell, 1960, 1961).

The Philadelphia Adventure (Dutton Children's Books, 1990, 2002; Puffin Books, 2002).

The Remarkable Journey of Prince Jen (Dutton Children's Books, 1991).

Taran Wanderer (Holt, Rinehart & Winston, 1967; H. Holt & Co., 1999).

Time Cat: The Remarkable Journeys of Jason and Gareth (Holt, Rinehart & Winston, 1963; Avon Books, 1982; Puffin Books, 1996).

The Town Cats and Other Tales (Dutton, 1977; Puffin Books, 1998).

The Truthful Harp (Holt, Rinehart & Winston, 1967).

Westmark (Dutton, 1981; Penguin Putnam, 2002).

The Wizard in the Tree (Dutton, 1975).

Park Adventure Vet (Holt, Rinehart & Winston, 1962).

For More Information About/by Lloyd Alexander

Autobiography: 1959. *Janine Is French.* Crowell.

Hopkins, Lee Bennett. 1974. *More Books by More People: Interviews with Sixty-Five Authors of Books for Children.* Citation Press.

Kingman, Lee, ed. 1976. *Newbery and Caldecott Medal Books, with Acceptance Papers, Biographies and Related Material Chiefly from the Horn Book Magazine: 1966–1975.* Horn Book.

Silvey, Anita, ed. 1995. *Children's Books and Their Creators.* Houghton Mifflin.

1970: William H. Armstrong

Born   September 14, 1914
            Collierstown, Virginia

Married   Martha Stonestreet
            Williams, August 24, 1942
            (children: Christopher,
            David, and Mary)

Died   April 11, 1999
            Kent, Connecticut

Awards and Honors

Newbery Medal (Historical Fiction, Animal Stories): *Sounder* (Harper & Row, 1969)

About the Author and His Writing

When William H. Armstrong won the Newbery Medal in 1970, nobody was more surprised than the author himself. Surprised, because he had never heard of the Newbery Medal, and even more surprised because he hadn't realized that his book, *Sounder,* was a children's story.

The books of William's childhood consisted mainly of the Sears & Roebuck catalog, the Bible, the *Old Farmer's Almanac, McGuffey's Third Reader,* and his favorite, Burpee's Seed Catalog, with all its promise of spring. But even though William did not have many choices in reading material, he learned the thrill of hearing a good story and the art of storytelling from Charles Jones, an African-American man who worked on the Armstrong farm. Jones told stories while the family gathered around the dinner table.

Through Mr. Jones William first heard the tale of a faithful old raccoon hunting dog named Sounder, whose howl carried through the hills and was recognized by all who knew him. Years later, while William was walking in the moonlight one night, he heard the call of an owl, which reminded him of the voice of Sounder. He knew then and there that he had to tell the story of this wonderful dog.

William never thought of himself as a writer, although his gifts were apparent early on. He studied his final three years before college at the Augusta Military Academy. After William turned in one of his stories, his English teacher accused him of plagiarism. He didn't believe that William could write so well. When William's story was published in his college literary magazine, one of the first people to congratulate him was the same professor who had accused him of plagiarism years before.

Although William enjoyed his time working on the college magazine and newspaper, even serving as editor in chief, he chose not to go into journalism but into teaching

> I discovered that the questions of young and old were about the same, so in teaching I early became aware that the young will rise to mature stature, and if not given that challenge will become bored and indifferent to reading and learning. (de Montreville and Hill 1972, 20)

instead. He loved history, in part inspired by the Virginia countryside where he grew up, the land where Robert E. Lee had ridden his horse and where Stonewall Jackson had gone to church, the same church that the Armstrong family attended.

After college William settled in Connecticut and bought a piece of land not far from the Kent School. He cleared the land himself, built his own house, and there raised his family. Unfortunately, William's wife, Martha, died after only eleven years of marriage, leaving Armstrong with three very young children, Christopher, David, and Mary. William taught history at the Kent School for over fifty years, often bicycling the mile between his home and the school.

Even though William felt compelled to write the story of the dog, Sounder, as well as several other books that followed, he said that he never truly enjoyed the process of writing. "I really hate to write," he said, "so what I do is live with an idea for a long, long time. My favorite part of writing is going down to the basement to sharpen my pencil" (Kovacs and Preller 1991, 81). William usually wrote from the hours of 4:00 to 7:30 A.M., before going off to teach. He felt he had accomplished a great deal if he rose early and got a head start on the day.

Sounder received its share of criticism, yet it stands as a fine example of a story that does not hesitate to struggle with the tough issues of life, death, and fidelity. The book became a movie in 1972. William continued the story of the book's family in its sequel, *Sour Land* (Harper & Row, 1971).

Although William Armstrong will always be remembered for his books, he thought of himself primarily as a teacher. He died on April 11, 1999, in his home, at the age of eighty-seven.

> ## A Word to My Readers:
> I'm a loner, and the pleasures I enjoy most in life are my flock of sheep, my three children, my land, ledge and all, my house and stone walls that I built myself, and my flowers and garden. I am not an instant writer. My stories and books have been with me a long time without my knowing they were good enough to be published. (Hopkins 1974, 22–23)

Books by William H. Armstrong

Animal Tales, by Hana Doskocilova, adapted by William H. Armstrong (Doubleday, 1970).

Barefoot in the Grass: The Story of Grandma Moses (Doubleday, 1970).

The Education of Abraham Lincoln (Coward, McCann & Geoghegan, 1974).

87 Ways to Help Your Child in School (Barron's Educational Series, 1961).

Hadassah: Esther the Orphan Queen (Doubleday, 1972).

Joanna's Miracle (Broadman Press, 1977).

The Mac Leod Place (Coward, McCann & Geoghegan, 1972).

The Mills of God (Doubleday, 1973).

My Animals (Doubleday, 1974).

A Pocket Guide to Correct Study Tips (Barron's Educational Series, 1997).

Sounder (Harper & Row; Holt, Rinehart & Winston, 1969; London: Gollancz, 1971; ABC Clio, 1987; Holt, Rinehart & Winston, [1999?]; Harper Perennial, Harper-Collins, 2001).

Sour Land (Harper & Row, 1971).

Study Is Hard Work (Harper, 1956; Harper & Row, 1967; D. R. Godine, 1995/96).

Study Tactics (Barron's Educational Series, 1983).

Study Tips (Barron's Educational Series, 1983, 1990).

Study Tips: How to Study Effectively and Get Better Grades (Barron's Educational Series, 1975).

The Tale of Tawny and Dingo (Harper & Row, 1979).

Through Troubled Waters (Harper & Row, 1957, 1973).

For More Information About/by William H. Armstrong

de Montreville, Doris, and Donna Hill, eds. 1972. *The Third Book of Junior Authors.* H. W. Wilson.

Hopkins, Lee Bennett. 1974. *More Books by More People: Interviews with Sixty-Five Authors of Books for Children.* Citation Press.

Kovacs, Deborah, and James Preller. 1991. *Meet the Authors and Illustrators: 60 Creators of Favorite Children's Books Talk About Their Work.* Scholastic.

1971: Betsy Byars

Born   August 7, 1928
                     Charlotte, North Carolina

Married   Edward Ford Byars, June 24,
                     1950 (children: Laurie, Betsy
                     Ann, Nan, and Guy)

Awards and Honors

Newbery Medal (Contemporary Life): *Summer of the Swans* (Viking Press, 1970)

American Library Association Notable Children's Book, 1982: *The Cibil War* (Viking Press, 1981; Puffin Books, 1990); 1983: *The Two-Thousand Pound Goldfish* (Harper & Row, 1982; Cornerstone Books, 1989); 1986: *Cracker Jackson* (Viking Kestrel, 1985; Puffin Books, 1986); 1988: *The Blossoms and the Green Phantom* (Delacorte Press, 1987); 1991: *Bingo Brown, Gypsy Lover* (Viking Press, 1990; Puffin Books, 1992); 1992: *Wanted: Mud Blossom* (Delacorte Press, 1991); 1995: *The Golly Sisters Ride Again* (HarperCollins, 1994); 1997: *My Brother, Ant* (Viking Press, 1996)

About the Author and Her Writing

When Betsy Byars received the telephone call announcing that her book *Summer of the Swans* had won the Newbery Medal for 1971, the only family members with whom she could share this great news were two dogs and two cats. No one else was home.

"You would be amazed at how pleased dogs and cats look when you turn to them and say, 'Listen, I just won the Newbery Medal'," she said in her acceptance speech (Kingman 1975, 69).

Byars grew up in Charlotte, North Carolina, living part of the time in the city and part of the time in a nearby mill town. She learned to sew her own clothes using the scraps of fabric her father would bring home. However, she wasn't always allowed to leave her own yard with the garments she created!

In 1950 Betsy earned a degree in English from Queens College. She met her husband, Edward, who taught engineering at nearby Clemson University. They married shortly after her graduation and had four children, whom she claimed were her greatest critics whenever she wrote something new.

Betsy's first publishing credits came when she was a mother at home with young children. She enjoyed reading magazines such as the *Saturday Evening Post,* especially the back section entitled "Postscript," for which readers sent in humorous anecdotes and stories. Betsy, always one to enjoy life and to see the humor in everyday events, sent in a "Postscript." The piece was accepted, she was paid seventy-five dollars, and her writing career began.

> When I was young, I was mainly interested in having as much fun as possible . . . Enjoying things was just more important to me than taking things seriously. (Hopkins 1974, 69)

It took Betsy seven years and nine rejections before her first book was published in 1955. That was the beginning of a string of over thirty books, from picture books to fantasies, easy readers to historical fiction.

This writer once said she rarely had a lack of ideas. Even while in the middle of writing one book, she would take time to stop and jot down an idea for another. And if an idea for a later chapter in a book came before an earlier chapter, that's how she'd write it. Betsy never wanted to lose track of an idea when it was fresh.

Betsy's adolescent characters are deeply realistic. She has written about troubled teenagers with great skill, conveying the sense of isolation and loneliness that can mark the adolescent years. But Betsy doesn't just convey the difficulties of growing up. She has enabled her characters to make their own choices about their lives, rather than leaving them helpless in the face of challenges and opposition.

Betsy's process for writing starts with thinking it through from beginning to end, which often looked to her children as if she were doing nothing more than staring at the walls. Once she started to write, she could hardly tear herself away from her typewriter. She was even tempted to get up in the middle of the night and head for the typewriter, but hesitated lest she wake up her family.

The hardest part of writing for Betsy came after the story was on paper. Then she went back and read and edited and rewrote, realizing that some of her writing fell far short of the wonderful ideas she'd had flowing through her mind. She said once that "I just do not know how it is possible to have something in your mind which is so hilarious you are all but chuckling as you write, and then when you read it over, it is completely flat" (Kingman 1975, 71).

Betsy and her husband have spent much of their free time flying in gliders, soaring with the wind over the countryside. Perhaps for Betsy there is an analogy between gliding and writing: ever watchful of the landscape around her, ready and eager to spot a new vista that just might lead to a new story.

A Word to My Readers:

The words *author* and *authority* go together. When you write about what you know, you write with authority. Authority is the greatest gift a writer can have. (Kovacs and Preller 1991, 85)

Books by Betsy Byars

After the Goat Man (Viking Press, 1974; Puffin Books, 1982).

The Animal, the Vegetable, and John D. Jones (Delacorte Press, 1982).

Ant Plays Bear (Viking Press, 1997).

Beans on the Roof (Delacorte Press, 1988).

Bingo Brown and the Language of Love (Viking Kestrel, Cornerstone Books, 1989; Puffin Books, 1991).

Bingo Brown, Gypsy Lover (Viking Press, 1990; Puffin Books, 1992).

Bingo Brown's Guide to Romance (Viking Press, 1992).

A Blossom Promise (Delacorte Press, 1987).

The Blossoms and the Green Phantom (Delacorte Press, 1987).

The Blossoms Meet the Vulture Lady (Delacorte Press, 1986).

The Burning Questions of Bingo Brown (Viking Kestrel, 1988; G. K. Hall, 1989; Puffin Books, 1990).

The Cartoonist (London: Bodley Head, Viking Press, 1978; Puffin Books, 1987).

Clementine (Houghton Mifflin, 1962).

Coast to Coast (Delacorte Press, 1992).

The Computer Nut (Viking Kestrel, 1984; Puffin Books, 1986).

Cracker Jackson (Viking Kestrel, 1985; Puffin Books, 1986).

The Cybil War (Viking Press, 1981; Puffin Books, 1990).

The Dancing Camel (Viking Press, 1965).

The Dark Stairs: A Herculeah Jones Mystery (Viking Press, 1994).

Dead Letter (Viking Press, 1996).

Death's Door (Viking Press, 1997).

Disappearing Acts (Viking Press, 1998).

18th Emergency (Viking Press, 1973; Puffin Books, 1981; G. K. Hall, 1988).

The Glory Girl (Viking Press, 1983; Puffin Books, 1985).

Go and Hush the Baby (Viking Press, 1971; Puffin Books, 1982).

The Golly Sisters Go West (Harper & Row, 1985).

The Golly Sisters Ride Again (HarperCollins, 1994).

Good Bye, Chicken Little (Harper & Row, 1979).

The Groober (Harper & Row, 1967).

Hooray for the Golly Sisters! (Harper & Row, 1990).

*illustrated by the author

The House of Wings (Viking Press, 1972; Puffin Books, 1982).

The Joy Boys (Yearling First Choice Chapter Books, 1996).

*Lace Snail (Viking Press, 1975).

Little Horse (H. Holt & Co., 2001, 2002).

McMummy (Viking Press, 1993).

Me Tarzan (HarperCollins, 2000).

The Midnight Fox (Viking Press, 1968; Puffin Books, 1981).

The Moon and I (J. Messner, 1991; Beech Tree Books, 1996).

My Brother, Ant (Viking Press, 1996).

My Dog, My Hero (H. Holt & Co., 2000).

Night Swimmers (Delacorte Press, 1980; Cornerstone Books, 1990).

The Not Just Anybody Family (Delacorte Press, 1986).

The Pinballs (Harper & Row, 1977; ABC Clio, 1988).

Rama, the Gypsy Cat (Viking Press, 1966).

The Seven Treasure Hunts (HarperCollins, 1991).

Summer of the Swans (Viking Press, 1970; Puffin Books, 1981; ABC Clio, 1988).

Tarot Says Beware (Viking Press, 1995).

Tornado (HarperCollins, 1996).

Trouble River (Viking Press, 1969; Puffin Books, 1989).

The TV Kid (Viking Press, 1976).

The Two-Thousand Pound Goldfish (Harper & Row, 1982; Cornerstone Books, 1989).

Wanted: Mud Blossom (Delacorte Press, 1991).

The Winged Colt of Casa Mia (Viking Press, 1973).

For More Information About/by Betsy Byars

Autobiography: 1991. *The Moon and I.* J. Messner.

Hopkins, Lee Bennett. 1974. *More Books by More People: Interviews with Sixty-Five Authors of Books for Children.* Citation Press.

Kingman, Lee, ed. 1975. *Newbery and Caldecott Medal Books, with Acceptance Papers, Biographies and Related Material Chiefly from the Horn Book Magazine: 1966–1975.* Horn Book.

Kovacs, Deborah, and James Preller. 1991. *Meet the Authors and Illustrators: 60 Creators of Favorite Children's Books Talk About Their Work.* Scholastic.

1972: Robert C. O'Brien

Born	January 11, 1918
	Brooklyn, New York
Married	Sally McCaslin, 1943
	(children: Christopher, Jane, Sarah, and Catherine)
Died	March 5, 1973

Awards and Honors

Newbery Medal (Fantasy): *Mrs. Frisby and the Rats of NIMH* (Atheneum, 1971)
Lewis Carroll Shelf Award, 1972: *Mrs. Frisby and the Rats of NIMH* (Atheneum, 1971)

About the Author and His Writing

Robert C. O'Brien wrote a Newbery Medal–winning book but never delivered his Newbery Medal acceptance speech, due to poor health. His editor, Jean Karl, spoke for him, while he watched along with the rest of the audience. The next year he died of a heart attack at the age of fifty-five.

O'Brien was not really Robert's last name. His real name was Robert Leslie Conly, but he used his mother's maiden name as a pen name. He did this because *National Geographic* magazine, where he worked as an editor for twenty-two years, did not encourage its staff to write for any publications except their own.

> I have wondered: If we should vanish from the earth, who might survive us? What kind of civilization might follow ours? (Kingman 1975, 84)

Robert was a sickly, anxious child. He hated school and often had to be dragged there kicking and screaming. He did not get along with his brothers and sisters until later in life, and he was a constant challenge to his mother.

When he got to high school, Robert started doing better, in part because by then he had developed a strong sense of self-discipline. He often rose at 4:00 A.M. to study, practice the piano, or walk on the beach before going to school, where he served as the editor of the school newspaper.

In college, Robert was forced to take some time off due to the ongoing stress of his life. Eventually, he graduated from the University of Rochester with a degree in English. He worked as a reporter for *Newsweek* and other periodicals before becoming a full-time employee on the staff of the *National Geographic*.

One of the areas in which Robert found relief from his anxieties was in music. He could sing before he could talk. He worked out a lot of his nervous energy playing the piano. Along with words and writing, music was another language that Robert loved and understood.

In 1943, Robert married Sally McCaslin. They had four children: Christopher, Jane, Sarah, and Catherine. The entire family loved to read.

Robert began writing books in the 1960s, when a bad case of glaucoma kept him from driving at night and forced him to cut back on his hours at work. His first novel, *The Silver Crown* (Atheneum), was published in 1968.

As a writer Robert maintained the discipline that he had developed early in his life. He wrote every single day, including Sundays and holidays. He especially enjoyed writing for children, saying that these books were "the stories I most like to write, because children like a straightforward, honest plot, the way God meant plots to be, with a beginning, a middle, and an end: a problem, an attempt to solve it, and at the end, a success or a failure" (Kingman 1975, 85).

Perhaps it was because he led a somewhat troubled life as a youngster that Robert created characters who often found themselves trying to make the best out of a bad situation, even with the threat of danger lingering nearby. His characters learned to work with one another to find a solution that would, in the end, benefit everyone involved. His Newbery Medal–winning book, *Mrs. Frisby and the Rats of NIMH*, is a prime example of this technique. Mrs. Frisby, a widowed field mouse, finds the help she needs with an alliance of rats that have escaped a medical laboratory. This book smoothly combines the old tradition of stories about talking animals with science fiction and futuristic themes.

Robert was often asked why he chose to write a book about rats, creatures that not many people find attractive. He could not pinpoint the exact reason why he chose the theme for *Mrs. Frisby,* but he said "rats are tough, highly adaptable to a changing environment, and enormously prolific" (Kingman 1975, 83). It takes a remarkable writer to be able to make heroes out of rodents that many people detest or ignore!

Robert was working on a book for young adults when he died. His wife and a daughter took his notes and completed the book, which was published in 1975. *Z for Zachariah* was the final contribution of a wonderful author who gave the world of children's literature four superb books in his short career.

A Word to My Readers:

As the mind-seed wonders, it grows. Having put down roots, it opens its leaves and looks around. It learns about love, hate, fear, sadness, courage, kindness. All these things are in the world around it. But all of them come to life in books in a way that is peculiarly suitable for examination, for contemplation, and for evaluation. (Kingman 1975, 88)

Books by Robert C. O'Brien

Mrs. Frisby and the Rats of NIMH (Atheneum, 1971; Aladdin Books, 1986).

Report from Group 17 (Atheneum, 1972).

The Silver Crown (Atheneum, 1968; London: Gollancz, 1973; Collier Books, 1988).

Z for Zachariah (Atheneum, 1975; G. K. Hall, 1976; Collier Books, 1987).

For More Information About/by Robert C. O'Brien

Kingman, Lee, ed. 1975. *Newbery and Caldecott Medal Books, with Acceptance Papers, Biographies and Related Material Chiefly from the Horn Book Magazine: 1966–1975.* Horn Book.

1973: Jean Craighead George

Born   July 2, 1919
                 Washington, D.C.

Married   John George,
                 January 28, 1944
                 (children: Carolyn
                 Laura [Twig], John
                 Craighead [Craig], and
                 Thomas Lothar [Luke]

Awards and Honors

Newbery Medal (Animal Stories): *Julie of the Wolves* (Harper & Row, 1972)

Newbery Honor Book for 1960: *My Side of the Mountain* (Dutton, 1959)

Irving Kerlan Award from the University of Minnesota, 1982

De Grummond Award from the University of Southern Mississippi, 1986

The Washington Irving Children's Book Choice Award, 1990: *One Day in the Woods* (Crowell, 1987); 1992, *On the Far Side of the Mountain* (Dutton Children's Books, 1990)

Knickerbocker Award for Juvenile Literature in New York, 1991: *On the Far Side of the Mountain* (Dutton Children's Books, 1990)

About the Author and Her Writing

A child's first pet is usually one that barks, tweets, meows, or swims. Not for Jean Craighead George. Her first pet perched on the kitchen door, shoulders hunched, head hanging. His name was Nod. He was a turkey vulture.

Most people would think a turkey vulture a strange creature to have in the house, but for the Craighead family, it wasn't a bit out of the ordinary. They had falcons, raccoons, owls, opossums, and insects of all kinds come in and out the doors. All were welcome in the Craighead home.

Jean's father was an entomologist and the bureau chief of the Department of Entomology in the United States Forest Service. He took Jean and her twin brothers on outdoor adventures every weekend. Jean's parents taught their children about animals, plants, and all sorts of wildlife. More than just the facts, Jean and her brothers learned respect and love for all living creatures.

Jean's twin older brothers, Frank and John, set the pace for the family. They became known all over the United States for their wildlife expertise. Although the boys were a tough act to follow, Jean managed not only to keep up with them but to carve a path of her own as well.

> Once in print, a manuscript becomes less a part of me, and I am able to be more critical. I think some of my books would have been better if I could have rewritten them after they came out. (Hopkins 1974, 181)

Frank and John gave Jean a falcon as a pet when she was thirteen. At that time, the boys were two of the first falconers in the United States. They later became the two foremost experts on the grizzly bear.

The family spent their summers in southern Pennsylvania, on land settled by their ancestors back in 1742. Everyone was allowed to roam and explore and enjoy the setting with its varied inhabitants. This was an ideal place for a family like the Craigheads.

Along with the explorations into nature that filled her early years, Jean experimented with the world of writing. She composed poems at the age of eight. "I was writing poetry in the third grade," she recalled years later. "I loved to write. To realize what you could do with words, to make all these incredible images. When I would come back from the woods, I would go up to my room and write poetry" (interview, September 7, 1994). Poetry was a good beginning for the active naturalist and budding writer. It taught her discipline and gave her a way to express in words the beauty of nature that surrounded her.

Jean had no shortage of interests. As a child, she wanted to grow up and be an illustrator, a writer, a dancer, a mother, a poet, an ice skater, and a swimmer. Later she added politician, journalist, and scientist to her list of vocational possibilities. In college one of her professors told her that she would have to narrow down her list. Jean chose painting and writing, although she did become a mother and a journalist and she remained physically active.

Jean attended Penn State University, where she studied science and English and was voted the "Most Versatile Senior Woman" by her classmates. She became a newspaper reporter and met John George, who shared her interest in nature. They had three children: Carolyn Laura, nicknamed "Twig" because of her small size; John Craighead, or

"Craig"; and Thomas Lothar, called "Luke." (At the age of sixteen, Carolyn made "Twig" her legal name.)

In 1957, Jean published her first book as a solo author: *The Hole in the Tree* (Dutton). She and her husband, John, then coauthored several books, their first being *Vulpes, the Red Fox* (Dutton, 1948). It was through this book that Jean first learned about the Newbery Medal, when she learned that *Vulpes* had been considered for the award. Jean and her children became keenly aware of the Newbery Medal when in 1960 her book *My Side of the Mountain* was named a Newbery Honor Book.

After her divorce in 1963, Jean kept writing. She never wrote about anything she hadn't experienced herself. Her keen interest in life and her determination to live something before writing about it took Jean on many travels and opened up many new worlds that she eagerly shared in her books.

Jean was always interested in animal communication, but not in the same way as portrayed in a previous Newbery Medal book, *The Voyages of Doctor Doolittle* (Frederick A. Stokes, 1922). She loved learning how animals really do talk to one another and how they organize their lives in communities. Her growing interest in wolves took her to Alaska, along with her son Luke, to study wolf behavior and to write an article for *Reader's Digest*. Jean and Luke brought back notebooks full of information about wolf behavior and life in the frozen north. The article for *Reader's Digest* was never published, but Jean wrote and published a book called *Julie of the Wolves,* the story of a young runaway girl who lives with a pack of wolves and learns all about how they communicate and live in community with one another.

When Jean got the telephone call telling her that *Julie of the Wolves* had been named the Newbery Medal winner for 1973, Luke was still living at home. He appreciated the news almost as much as Jean, since he was the one who had spent all that time with his mother in Alaska, studying wolves.

Jean thought she took the thrilling news about the Medal in stride after she got the life-changing morning telephone call. However, that evening she discovered that she had placed the book she had been reading at the time in the freezer, and shortly thereafter she served a neighbor a celebratory feast of coffee and biscuits—dog biscuits!

Jean's books have given others a deeper insight into the mysteries of the animal world, and for many people they have removed the fear of the creatures that share our world. After reading Jean's books, a wolf can no longer be seen as a scary animal but as a beloved and wise creature to be admired. A spider is no longer something creepy crawly, but a remarkably fascinating creature. Jean's books move the reader beyond fear into understanding and respect.

In looking back on Jean's early career goals it is amazing to see how many of her dreams have been fulfilled in one way or another, often in her books. As for running out of ideas, this author's answer is simple: "I have one-hundred fifty-million species to write about. You can't go wrong with all that!" (interview, September 7, 1994).

A Word to My Readers:

On beautiful days, you should all get out of school and watch the butterflies. There are things going on around you that you should see. Sit, and look, and wonder. (interview, September 7, 1994)

Books by Jean Craighead George

Acorn Pancakes, Dandelion Salad, and 38 Other Wild Recipes (HarperCollins, 1995).

All Upon a Sidewalk (Dutton, 1974).

All Upon a Stone (Crowell, 1971).

The American Walk Book (Dutton, 1978).

Animals Who Have Won Our Hearts (HarperCollins, 1994).

Arctic Son (Hyperion Books for Children, 1997).

Autumn Moon (HarperCollins, 2001).

Beastly Inventions: A Surprising Investigation into How Smart Animals Really Are (David McKay, 1970).

The Case of the Missing Cutthroats: An Ecological Mystery (HarperCollins, 1996).

Cliff Hanger (HarperCollins Juvenile Books, 2002).

Coyote in Manhattan (Crowell, 1968).

The Cry of the Crow (Harper & Row, 1980).

Dear Katie, the Volcano Is a Girl (Hyperion Books for Children, 1998).

Dear Rebecca, Winter Is Here (HarperCollins, 1993).

**Dipper of Copper Creek* (with John George) (Dutton Children's Books, 1996).

Elephant Walk (Disney Press, 1998).

Everglades (HarperCollins, 1995).

Everglades Wildguide (National Park Service, 1972).

Exploring the Out of Doors (American Library Association, 1983).

The Fire Bug Connection: An Ecological Mystery (HarperCollins, 1993).

Firestorm (HarperCollins Juvenile Books, 2003).

The First Thanksgiving (Philomel Books, 1993).

**Frightful's Mountain* (Dutton Children's Books, 1999).

Galapagos George (HarperCollins Children's Books, 2002).

Giraffe Trouble (Disney Press, 1998).

Going to the Sun (Harper & Row, 1976).

Gorilla Gang (Disney Press, 1998).

The Grizzly Bear with the Golden Ears (Harper & Row, 1982).

Gull Number 737 (Crowell, 1964).

Hold Zero! (Crowell, 1966).

**The Hole in the Tree* (Dutton, 1957).

Hook a Fish, Catch a Mountain (Dutton, 1975).

*illustrated by the author

How to Talk to Your Animals (Harcourt Brace Jovanovich, 1985).

How to Talk to Your Cat (Warner Books, 1986; HarperCollins, 2000).

How to Talk to Your Dog (Warner Books, 1986; HarperCollins, 2000).

Incredible Animal Adventures (1st Harper Trophy, 1999).

Journey Inward (Dutton, 1982).

Julie (HarperCollins, 1994).

Julie of the Wolves (Harper & Row, 1972; G. K. Hall, 1973; London: Hamilton, 1973; Puffin Books, 1976; ABC Clio, 1987; HarperCollins, [1997?]).

Julie's Wolf Pack (HarperCollins, 1997).

Lonesome George (HarperCollins, 2001).

Look to the North: A Wolf Pup Diary (HarperCollins, 1997).

Masked Prowler, the Story of a Raccoon (Dutton, 1950).

The Missing 'Gator of Gumbo Limbo: An Ecological Mystery (HarperCollins, 1992).

The Moon of the Alligators (Crowell, 1969; HarperCollins, 1991).

The Moon of the Bears (Crowell, 1967; HarperCollins, 1993).

The Moon of the Chickarees (Crowell, 1968; HarperCollins, 1992).

The Moon of the Deer (Crowell, 1969; HarperCollins, 1992).

The Moon of the Fox Pups (Crowell, 1968; HarperCollins, 1992).

The Moon of the Gray Wolves (Crowell, 1969; HarperCollins, 1991).

The Moon of the Moles (Crowell, 1969; HarperCollins, 1992).

The Moon of the Monarch Butterflies (Crowell, 1968; HarperCollins, 1993).

The Moon of the Mountain Lions (Crowell, 1968; HarperCollins, 1991).

The Moon of the Owls (Crowell, 1967; HarperCollins, 1993).

The Moon of the Salamanders (Crowell, 1967; HarperCollins, 1992).

The Moon of the Wild Pigs (Crowell, 1968; HarperCollins, 1992).

The Moon of the Winter Bird (Crowell, 1969; HarperCollins, 1992).

Morning, Noon, and Night (HarperCollins, 1999).

My Side of the Mountain (Dutton, 1959, 1988).

My Side of the Mountain Trilogy (Dutton Children's Books, 2000).

Nutik & Amaroq Play Ball (HarperCollins, 2000).

Nutik, the Wolf Pup (HarperCollins, 2000).

On the Far Side of the Mountain (Dutton Children's Books, 1990).

One Day in the Alpine Tundra (Crowell, 1984).

One Day in the Desert (Crowell, 1983).

One Day in the Prairie (Crowell, 1986).

One Day in the Tropical Rain Forest (Crowell, 1990).

One Day in the Woods (Crowell, 1988).

Rhino Romp (Disney Press, 1998).

River Rats, Inc. (Dutton, 1979).

Shark Beneath the Reef (Harper & Row, 1989).

Snow Bear (Hyperion Books for Children, 1999).

*Snow Tracks (Dutton, 1958).

Spring Comes to the Ocean (Crowell, 1965, 1966).

Spring Moon (Harper Trophy, 2002).

Summer Moon (Harper Trophy, 2002).

The Summer of the Falcon (Crowell, 1962).

The Talking Earth (Harper & Row, 1983).

*The Tarantula in My Purse: And 172 Other Wild Pets (HarperCollins, 1996).

There's an Owl in the Shower (HarperCollins, 1995).

To Climb a Waterfall (Philomel Books, 1995).

Tree Castle Island (HarperCollins Children's Books, 2002).

*Vision, the Mink (Dutton, 1949).

*Vulpes, the Red Fox (with John George) (1948; Dutton Children's Books, 1996).

Water Sky (Harper & Row, 1987).

Wentletrap Trap (Dutton, 1978).

Who Really Killed Cock Robin? An Ecological Mystery (Dutton, 1971; Harper-Collins, 1991).

The Wild, Wild Cookbook: A Guide for Young Wild Food Foragers (Crowell, 1982).

Winter Moon (Harper Trophy, 2001).

The Wounded Wolf (Harper & Row, 1978).

For More Information About/by Jean Craighead George

Autobiography: 1982. *Journey Inward.* Dutton.

Autobiography: 1996. *The Tarantula in My Purse: And 172 Other Wild Pets.* Harper-Collins.

Cary, Alice. 1996. *Jean Craighead George.* Learning Works.

Hopkins, Lee Bennett. 1974. *More Books by More People: Interviews with Sixty-Five Authors of Books for Children.* Citation Press.

Web site: http://www.jeancraigheadgeorge.com.

Note: Indicated citations from a personal interview with the author, September 7, 1994.

1974: Paula Fox

Born	April 22, 1923
	New York, New York
Married	Richard Sigerson, 1948 (divorced 1954)
	(children: Adam and Gabriel)
	Martin Greenberg, 1962

Awards and Honors

Newbery Medal (Historical Fiction): *The Slave Dancer* (Bradbury Press, 1973)
Hans Christian Andersen Medal, 1978
Newbery Honor Book for 1985: *One Eyed Cat* (Bradbury Press, 1984)
American Library Association Notable Children's Book, 1985: *One-Eyed Cat* (Bradbury Press, 1984; Cornerstone Books, 1987); 1987: *The Moonlight Man* (Bradbury Press, 1986); 1989: *The Village by the Sea* (Orchard Books, 1988); 1992: *Monkey Island* (Orchard Books, 1991); 1996: *Eagle Kite* (Orchard Books, 1995)
Boston Globe-Horn Book Award, 1989: *The Village by the Sea* (Orchard Books, 1988)

About the Author and Her Writing

By the time she was twelve years old, Paula Fox had lived for six years with a Congregationalist minister and his ailing mother and six years with her maternal grandmother on a sugar plantation in Cuba. In those years, she attended nine different schools.

> There is mystery in all stories, I believe, especially for the writers of them. That is one reason why it is so difficult to answer the question so often asked of writers, "Where do you get your ideas?" (Hoffman and Samuels 1972, 69)

Paula's father was a "play fixer" in the 1920s, traveling with road shows and working on the scripts. Her mother was very young when Paula was born and didn't feel up to the task of raising a child, so Paula was sent to live with the local minister. Then she moved to Cuba to live with her grandmother. Those were probably the best years of Paula's childhood. She made friends, earned a spot as the only girl on the baseball team, learned fluent Spanish, and basked in the culture of the Cuban people.

During the years when Paula moved from place to place, she found peace and refuge in the library. Every one of the many schools she attended had a library, and there the solitary, young girl could immerse herself in the stories of other people. She learned a lot about writing by reading, long before she ever had the chance to make a living using words.

At the age of sixteen, Paula quit school so that she could earn a living for herself. She worked as a salesgirl, a model, and a laborer in a steel mill. She married and had two sons but by the age of thirty she was divorced and had to find work that would support her young family. Paula studied at Columbia University and then worked with emotionally disturbed children and as a schoolteacher. In whatever free moments she managed to muster, Paula turned to writing.

In 1962, Paula married Martin Greenberg, an editor and a professor. When he won a Guggenheim Fellowship and the family moved to Greece for six months, Paula received what she had wanted and needed for a long time: the opportunity to devote herself full time to writing. She wrote a television script that was accepted and articles for several magazines.

Paula completed her first novel, *Poor George* (Harcourt, Brace & Co., 1967) during her time in Greece. She also wrote a book for children, *Maurice's Room* (Macmillan, 1966). Both of these books were published, so after returning home to the United States, Paula kept writing. In 1974, Paula was awarded the Newbery Medal for *The Slave Dancer.*

The Slave Dancer tells the story of ninety-eight Africans from Ghana, captured in 1840 and shipped off to slavery. A young boy, Jessie, is kidnapped at the same time and taken on board the slave ship where he is forced to play the music that keeps the slaves dancing and active. His horror at the debasement of people at the hands of fellow human beings is told in vivid and heartbreaking detail. The book received some criticism for its topic, which Paula addressed in her acceptance speech, speaking of the ways that the institution of slavery was, and is, a crime that speaks more negatively about the perpetrators than the victims.

Paula said that "we are shaped by circumstance and we, in turn, shape it. It is in the way we do it that we make our stories" (Fox 552). In her book *One-Eyed Cat,* which was named a Newbery Honor Book in 1986, Paula drew on the memories of her own childhood to tell a story of loneliness and abandonment. As defined in her comment about fiction, the story is not literally true, but it still speaks the truth because it springs from the inner depths of a person's own soul.

"Nearly all the work of writing is silent," Paula said in her Newbery acceptance speech (Kingman 1975, 116). The work of a writer is usually done in solitude, alone. It is a wonderful kind of magic that practitioners of such an isolated profession can touch the lives of so many people of different races, cultures, social class, and intelligence. Paula's gift for writing, coupled with her ability to remember the depth of childhood emotion, allows her books to embrace a wide and varied audience.

After winning the Newbery Medal, Paula continued to write books, some based on her own memories, others growing out of her continued quest to understand and express the real-life questions and emotions of people in general.

In 1978, Paula was awarded the Hans Christian Andersen Medal for overall contribution to children's literature. It is remarkable that in the short span of eleven years, Paula's books came to be so highly regarded by the experts in the field of literature. The child who never truly had a home finally found one—among the books that once gave shelter to the fragile yet resilient spirit of a little girl.

A Word to My Readers:

The stories that come out of a writer's hard labor are efforts to understand what has happened. They engage us, our deep interest, because we are always trying to understand what has happened to us; we are always trying to see ourselves. The task is nearly impossible. (Silvey 1995, 251)

Books by Paula Fox

Amzat and His Brothers: Three Italian Tales, remembered by Floriano Vecchi and retold by Paula Fox (Orchard Books, 1993).

Blowfish Live in the Sea (Bradbury Press, 1970; Aladdin Books, 1986).

Borrowed Finery: A Memoir (H. Holt & Co., 2001).

Dear Prosper (D. White, 1968).

Desperate Characters (Harcourt, Brace & Co., 1970; Nonpareil Books, 1980; W. W. Norton, 1990).

Eagle Kite (Orchard Books, 1995).

The God of Nightmares (North Point Press, 1990; W. W. Norton, 2002).

Good Ethan (Bradbury Press, 1973).

How Many Miles to Babylon? (D. White, 1967; Bradbury Press, 1980).

Hungry Fred (Bradbury Press, 1969).

The King's Falcon (Bradbury Press, 1969).

A Likely Place (Macmillan, 1967, 1987; London: Macmillan; 1968; Simon & Schuster Books for Young Readers, 1997).

Lily and the Lost Boy (Orchard Books, 1987; G. K. Hall, 1989).

The Little Swineherd, and Other Tales (Dutton, 1978; Dutton Children's Books, 1996).

Maurice's Room (Macmillan, 1966, 1985, 1988).

Monkey Island (Orchard Books, 1991).

The Moonlight Man (Bradbury Press, 1986).

One Eyed Cat (Bradbury Press, 1984; Cornerstone Books, 1987).

A Place Apart (Farrar, Straus & Giroux, 1980).

Poor George (Harcourt, Brace & Co., 1967; W. W. Norton, 2001).

Portrait of Ivan (Bradbury Press, 1969, 1985; Aladdin Books, 1987).

Radiance Descending (DK Ink, 1997).

A Servant's Tale (North Point Press, 1984; Penguin, 1986; W. W. Norton, 2002).

The Slave Dancer (Bradbury Press, 1973; ABC Clio, 1988).

The Stone Faced Boy (Bradbury Press, 1968; Aladdin Books, 1987).

The Village by the Sea (Orchard Books, 1988).

The Western Coast (Harcourt Brace Jovanovich, 1972; W. W. Norton, 2001).

Western Wind (Orchard Books, 1993).

The Widow's Children (Dutton, 1976; North Point Press, 1986; W. W. Norton, 1999).

For More Information About/by Paula Fox

Autobiography: 2001. *Borrowed Finery: A Memoir.* H. Holt & Co.

Fox, Paula. To Write Simply. *Horn Book Magazine,* September/October 1991.

Hoffman, Miriam, and Eva Samuels. 1972. *Authors and Illustrators of Children's Books: Writings on Their Lives and Works.* R. R. Bowker.

Kingman, Lee, ed. 1975. *Newbery and Caldecott Medal Books, with Acceptance Papers, Biographies and Related Material Chiefly from the Horn Book Magazine: 1966–1975.* Horn Book.

McElmeel, Sharon L. 1999. *100 Most Popular Children's Authors: Biographical Sketches and Bibliographies.* Libraries Unlimited (quoted from *Horn Book Magazine,* September–October 1991).

Silvey, Anita, ed. 1995. *Children's Books and Their Creators.* Houghton Mifflin.

1975: Virginia Hamilton

Born   March 12, 1936
            Yellow Springs, Ohio

Married   Arnold Adoff,
            March 19, 1960
            (children: Leigh
            and Jaime)

Died   February 19, 2002
            Dayton, Ohio

Awards and Honors

Newbery Medal (Contemporary Life): *M. C. Higgins, the Great* (Macmillan, 1974)

Edgar Allan Poe Award for Best Juvenile Fiction, 1969: *House of Dies Drear* (Collier Books, 1968)

Newbery Honor Book for 1972: *The Planet of Junior Brown* (Macmillan, 1971)

Boston Globe-Horn Book Award, 1974: *M. C. Higgins, the Great* (Macmillan, 1974); 1983: *Sweet Whispers, Brother Rush* (Philomel Books, 1982); 1988: *Anthony Burns: The Defeat and Triumph of a Fugitive Slave* (A. A. Knopf, 1988)

National Book Award, 1974: *M. C. Higgins, the Great* (Macmillan, 1974)

Newbery Honor Book for 1983: *Sweet Whispers, Brother Rush* (Philomel Books, 1982)

Newbery Honor Book for 1989: *In the Beginning: Creation Stories from Around the World* (Harcourt Brace Jovanovich, 1988)

Hans Christian Andersen Medal, 1992

John D. and Catherine C. MacArthur Fellowship, 1995

Laura Ingalls Wilder Award, 1995

American Library Association Notable Children's Book, 1982: *The Gathering* (Greenwillow Books, 1981; Harcourt Brace Jovanovich, 1989); 1983: *Sweet Whispers, Brother Rush* (Philomel Books, 1982); 1984: *Willie Bea and the Time the Martians Landed* (Greenwillow Books, 1983; Aladdin Books, 1989); 1984: *The Magical Adventures of Pretty Pearl* (Harper & Row, 1983); 1986: *The People Could Fly: American Black Folktales* (Knopf/Random House, 1985); 1989: *The Gathering* (Greenwillow Books, 1981; Harcourt Brace Jovanovich, 1989); 1990: *The Bells of Christmas* (Harcourt Brace Jovanovich, 1989); 1991: *Cousins* (Philomel Books, 1990); 1994: *Plain City* (Blue Sky Press, 1993); 1996: *Her Stories* (Blue Sky Press, 1995); 1997: *When Birds Could Talk and Bats Could Sing* (Blue Sky Press, 1996)

School Library Journal Best Books, 1995: *Her Stories* (Blue Sky Press, 1995); 1996: *When Birds Could Talk and Bats Could Sing* (Blue Sky Press, 1996)

Coretta Scott King Award, 1983: *Sweet Whispers, Brother Rush* (Philomel Books, 1982); 1986: *The People Could Fly: American Black Folktales* (Knopf/Random House, 1985); 1996: *Her Stories* (Blue Sky Press, 1995)

About the Author and Her Writing

The first story Virginia Hamilton remembers hearing was the tale of a runaway slave who found his way to freedom. Virginia sat on the porch swing and listened to the comforting sound of her mother's voice as she told her daughter the story. The name of the runaway slave was Levi Perry. He was Virginia's grandfather.

Virginia grew up on the land adjacent to Levi's in Yellow Springs, Ohio, once a stopping place on the Underground Railroad. Virginia, the youngest of five children, had free roam of the area, which was populated by aunts, uncles, cousins, and other kin. Not only was Virginia's mother a marvelous storyteller, so were many of the relatives with whom she had daily contact. It could be said that Virginia was raised on storytelling.

The Depression years were hard on everyone. Virginia's family was dollar poor, but the family had twelve acres of farmland and raised enough food and hogs to feed their own family plus extra produce to sell to the townspeople. Virginia's father worked full time as assistant service manager of the dining halls in nearby Antioch. At night he soothed his youngest daughter to sleep with his mandolin melodies, which greatly helped ease the little girl's fear of the dark.

> When you're young, you think you have all the time in the world. You don't. Don't wait to be inspired. Just write. (Kovacs and Preller 1991, 102)

Virginia began to write at the age of seven. She had always hoped to continue her education after high school and after receiving a full scholarship, she attended Antioch College in Ohio. She spent the next three years there, majoring in writing, before she felt the need to get away from her hometown and test her wings elsewhere.

Virginia transferred to Ohio State University, where she continued her study of literature and composition. From there she went to the New School for Social Research in New York and took courses in novel writing. Virginia, who had a beautiful voice, also sang in clubs and for a modern dance group, and she played guitar.

While at a party in New York, Virginia met Arnold Adoff, a poet and anthologist. They married on March 19, 1960. They had two children, a daughter Leigh and a son Jaime. Eventually they moved back to Ohio and built their own home on the last acres of her mother and father's farm.

During her college years, Virginia kept a steadily growing card file on everything she learned about Africa. She wrote a short story about an African-American girl who resembled a Watusi, but she tucked the story away. One of her college friends remembered the story, and when the friend went to work for a major publishing house, she asked Virginia to redo the story as a book. Virginia had forgotten the story, but she dug it out and turned the eighteen pages into her first published novel, *Zeely* (Macmillan, 1967).

In 1972, Virginia's book *The Planet of Junior Brown* was named a Newbery Honor Book. She won another Newbery Honor in 1983 for *Sweet Whispers, Brother Rush,* and yet another in 1988 for *In the Beginning: Creation Stories from Around the World.* In

1975, Virginia won the Newbery Medal for *M. C. Higgins, the Great,* becoming the first African-American ever to win the Newbery Medal.

The awards didn't stop there. Virginia won nearly every literary award given to writers of books for young readers. Twice she won the International Board on Books for Young People (IBBY). *M. C. Higgins, The Great* won a National Book Award. Virginia's 1969 novel about the Underground Railroad, *The House of Dies Drear* (Collier Books, 1968) was awarded the Edgar Allan Poe Award for best juvenile fiction in 1969. In 1992, she received the Hans Christian Andersen Medal, and in 1995 the Laura Ingalls Wilder Medal, both for her body of work. She became the first children's author to be awarded the prestigious John D. and Catherine C. MacArthur Fellowship, often called the "genius award."

Virginia never minded the rewriting process. "Rewriting, in fact, is the activity that appeals to me most," she once wrote, "for it is in the first and second revisions that the language of the first creation begins to reveal its originality" (Gallo 1990, 91).

Virginia's stories did not evolve from a desire to document her own personal life. Instead she said that she wrote about "emotions and themes which are common to all people: family, unity, friendships, the importance of individual freedom, and the influence of our past heritage on the present. My aim is always to tell a good story" (Gallo 1990, 91).

Born among gifted storytellers, Virginia and her books honor her family heritage and that of future generations who cherish the power of words. In her words, "Language is magic to me, and words make worlds that others can understand" (Gallo 1990, 91).

Tragically, Virginia Hamilton died of breast cancer on February 19, 2002. She was sixty-five years old.

A Word to My Readers:

For children, reading is the discovery of new worlds of color and texture. For me, writing for children is the creation of worlds of darkness and light. There is an essential line between us, a line of thought and ultimately of communication. Each book must speak: "This is what I have to say," in the hope that each reader will answer: "That is what I wanted to know." (Hoffman and Samuels 1972, 192)

Books by Virginia Hamilton

The All Jahdu Storybook (Harcourt Brace Jovanovich, 1991).

Anthony Burns: The Defeat and Triumph of a Fugitive Slave (A. A. Knopf, 1988).

Arilla Sun Down (Greenwillow Books, 1976).

The Bells of Christmas (Harcourt Brace Jovanovich, 1989).

Bluish: A Novel (Blue Sky Press, 1999; Scholastic Trade, 2002).

Cousins (Philomel Books, 1990).

The Dark Way: Stories from the Spirit World (Harcourt Brace Jovanovich, 1990).

Drylongso (Harcourt Brace Jovanovich, 1992).

Dustland (Greenwillow Books, 1980, Harcourt Brace Jovanovich, 1989).

The Gathering (Greenwillow Books, 1981; Harcourt Brace Jovanovich, 1989).

The Girl Who Spun Gold (Blue Sky Press, 2000).

Her Stories: African American Folktales, Fairy Tales, and True Tales (Blue Sky Press, 1995).

The House of Dies Drear (Collier Books, 1968; Macmillan, 1984).

Illusion and Reality (Library of Congress, 1976).

In the Beginning: Creation Stories from Around the World (Harcourt Brace Jovanovich, 1988).

Jaguarundi (Blue Sky Press, 1995).

Jahdu (Greenwillow Books, 1980).

Junius Over Far (Harper & Row, 1985).

Justice and Her Brothers (Greenwillow Books, 1978; Harcourt Brace Jovanovich, 1989).

A Little Love (Philomel Books, 1984).

M. C. Higgins, the Great (Macmillan, 1974; G. K. Hall, 1976; Collier Books, 1987; ABC Clio, 1988; Aladdin Books, 1993).

The Magical Adventures of Pretty Pearl (Harper & Row, 1983).

Many Thousand Gone: African Americans from Slavery to Freedom (Knopf/Random House, 1993).

The Mystery of Drear House: The Conclusion of the Dies Drear Chronicle (Chronicle Books, 1987).

New Daughters of the Oracle: The Return of Female Prophetic Power in Our Time (New Paradigm Books, 2001).

Paul Robeson: The Life and Times of a Free Black Man (Harper & Row, 1974).

The People Could Fly: American Black Folktales (Knopf/Random House, 1985).

Plain City (Blue Sky Press, 1993).

The Planet of Junior Brown (Macmillan, 1971; Collier Books, 1986; G. K. Hall, 1988; Aladdin Books, 1993).

Ring of Tricksters: Animal Tales from America, the West Indies, and Africa (Blue Sky Press, 1997).

Second Cousins (Blue Sky Press, 1998).

Sweet Whispers, Brother Rush (Philomel Books, 1982).

Time Ago Lost; More Tales of Jahdu (Macmillan, 1973).

Time Ago Tales of Jahdu (Macmillan, 1969).

Time Pieces: The Book of Times (Blue Sky Press, 2002).

W.E.B. Du Bois: A Biography (Crowell, 1972).

Wee Winnie Witch's Skinny: An Original Scare Tale for Halloween (Blue Sky Press, 2002).

When Birds Could Talk & Bats Could Sing (Blue Sky Press, 1996).

A White Romance (Harcourt Brace Jovanovich, 1987; Philomel, 1987).

Willie Bea and the Time the Martians Landed (Greenwillow Books, 1983; Aladdin Books, 1989).

Zeely (Macmillan, 1967; Aladdin Books, 1986, 1993).

For More Information About/by Virginia Hamilton

Gallo, Donald R., ed. 1990. *Speaking for Ourselves: Autobiographical Sketches by Notable Authors of Books for Young Adults.* National Council of Teachers of English.

Hoffman, Miriam, and Eva Samuels. 1972. *Authors and Illustrators of Children's Books: Writings on Their Lives and Works.* R. R. Bowker.

Kovacs, Deborah, and James Preller. 1991. *Meet the Authors and Illustrators: 60 Creators of Favorite Children's Books Talk About Their Work.* Scholastic.

Web site: http://www.virginiahamilton.com.

1976: Susan Cooper (Cronyn)

Born   May 23, 1935
Burnham,
Buckinghamshire, England

Married   Nicholas J. Grant, August 5,
1963 (divorced 1982)
(stepchildren: Anne, Bill, and
Peter; children: Jonathan and
Katharine)
Hume Cronyn, July 1996
(died June 15, 2003)

Awards and Honors

Newbery Medal (Science Fiction, Fantasy): *The Grey King* (Atheneum, 1975)
Boston Globe-Horn Book Award, 1973; *The Dark Is Rising* (Atheneum, 1973)
Newbery Honor Book for 1974: *The Dark Is Rising* (Atheneum, 1973)
American Library Association Notable Children's Book Award, 1984: *The Silver Cow: A Welsh Tale* (Atheneum, 1983; Aladdin Books, 1991); 1994: *The Boggart* (Margaret K. McElderry Books, 1993)

About the Author and Her Writing

Susan Mary Cooper grew up in England during World War II. The sights and sounds of war were all around her but so were sights and sounds of another kind. Naturally, she saw the destruction left by bombs, but she also saw the elegant costumes and elaborate set designs of Gilbert and Sullivan operettas. She heard the shrill call of the air raid sirens but also heard the soothing voices of the storytellers on the radio show *Children's Hour.* She knew the reality of war, but she also knew the wonderful fantasy world found in the books that filled her family home.

England is the land of King Arthur and the setting of countless stories of knights and ladies and grand stone castles. These legends, and the countryside that spawned them, wove themselves into Susan's imagination along with the folktales, nursery rhymes, and poetry that were read to her as a child by her mother, a teacher.

Susan began writing at the age of eight. By the time she reached the ripe old age of ten, she had written three plays for a neighbor's puppet theater, collaborated with the son of her piano teacher on a neighborhood newspaper, and wrote and illustrated her first little book of fantasy.

Susan did her undergraduate studies at Oxford in Somerville College, concentrating on English language and literature. Two of her professors were men who made their mark in literature: J.R.R. Tolkien and C. S. Lewis. She became the first woman to edit the Oxford University newspaper.

After receiving her master's degree in 1956, she chose to work in the field of journalism, which seemed the best place for a woman who wanted to write. She wrote an article that caught the eye of Ian Fleming, one of the columnists for the Sunday *Times* in London. Fleming, the man who created James Bond, was so impressed with Susan's writing that he offered her a job. For the next half-dozen years, Susan worked as a reporter and wrote feature articles for the newspaper, including an occasional piece for the section entitled "Mainly for Children." Whenever she had an opportunity for a bit of free time, she worked on a novel for adults.

> I love being able to make magic: to make you laugh, or cry, or experience what Aristotle called a catharsis—which means, in effect, feeling better even though a story has slugged you on the back of the head. (Gallo 1990, 55)

A fellow journalist brought to Susan's attention a writing contest sponsored by the English publishing house Ernest Benn Limited, which had published the children's books of E. Nesbit. Susan began writing a story about three children, intending to submit the manuscript to the contest. But then, as she described it, the story began to take over. She found herself writing a fantasy novel, *Over Sea, Under Stone* (London: J. Cape, 1965). Even though she did not know it at the time, that book started a string of fantasy novels that eventually became the series *The Dark Is Rising*.

Later, Susan married an American scientist, gained three stepchildren, Anne, Bill, and Peter, moved to the United States, and settled in Massachusetts. She became a United States citizen. Cooper and her husband had two more children, Jonathan and Katharine (Kate). Yet Susan felt rootless and homesick for her native land.

In the midst of adjusting to a new family and a new life, Susan realized that what she really wanted to do was to write a sequel to *Over Sea, Under Stone*. She outlined a sequence of events with enough information to fill four more books. She wrote the last page of the last book before she began the first page of the second book, *The Dark Is Rising*. That book won the sole Newbery Honor Award for 1974.

When Susan received the telephone call informing her that the book had won a Newbery Honor, it was the first that she had ever heard of this award. She attended the awards ceremony that spring, and upon seeing the huge crowd of people gathered for the speeches, turned to her editor and said, "I don't believe I ever want to win a Newbery!" (Kingman 1986, 16).

Two years later Susan received another phone call, this one announcing that *The Grey King* had won the Newbery Medal for 1976. Despite her earlier fears, Susan gave an eloquent speech before the gathering of 2,000 people. She commented that it was ironic and appropriate that as the United States of America celebrated the two-hundredth anniversary of its independence from Great Britain, the Newbery Medal was awarded to a writer from Great Britain.

After her divorce in 1982, Susan continued to write books for children as well as newspaper columns, a biography, and plays for theater and television. She collaborated with the well-known and talented Canadian actor, Hume Cronyn, on a Broadway play, *Foxfire*. The two also adapted for the television screen Harriet Arnow's novel *The Doll-maker*. Susan, Hume, and his longtime wife, the actress Jessica Tandy, were close friends for more than twenty years. In 1994 Jessica died. Two years later, Susan and Hume were married.

Reflecting on creativity in her Newbery acceptance speech, Susan said: "Who knows even where the words come from, the right rhythm and meaning and music all at once? Those of us who make books out of the words and ideas have less of an answer than anyone. All we know is that marvelous feeling that comes, sometimes, like a break of sunshine in a cloud-grey sky, when through all the research and concentration and slog—suddenly you are writing, fluently and fast, with every sense at high pitch and yet in a state almost like trance" (Kingman 1986, 9–10).

Of more importance to Susan than where the ideas come from is just that they come. In Susan's own words, "I'm just grateful that by some freak of nature I am able to write the kinds of books I've always liked to read" (Silvey 1995, 168). Grateful, too, are the many readers who are fortunate to know Susan Cooper through her marvelous books.

A Word to My Readers:

Whether explicitly, or through the buried metaphor of fantasy, (writing) will be trying always to say to the reader: Look, this is the way things are. The conflict that's in this story is everywhere in life, even in your own nature. It's frightening, but try not to be afraid. Ever. Look, learn, remember, this is the kind of thing you'll have to deal with yourself, one day, out there. Perhaps a book can help with the long, hard matter of growing up, just a little. Maybe, sometimes. (Kingman 1986, 11)

Books by Susan Cooper (Cronyn)

The Boggart (Margaret K. McElderry Books, 1993).

The Boggart and the Monster (Margaret K. McElderry Books, 1997).

Danny and the Kings (Margaret K. McElderry Books, 1993).

The Dark Is Rising (Atheneum, 1973; Collier Books, 1986; Thorndike Press, 2001).

Dawn of Fear (Harcourt Brace Jovanovich, 1970; London: Chatto & Windus, 1973; Aladdin Books, 1989).

Dreams and Wishes: Essays on Writing for Children (Margaret K. McElderry Books, 1996).

Frog (Margaret K. McElderry Books, 2002).

Green Boy (Margaret K. McElderry Books, 2002).

Greenwitch (London: Chatto & Windus, 1974; Atheneum, 1974; Collier Books, 1986; Thorndike Press, 2001).

1978/1981: Katherine Paterson

Born   October 31, 1932
             Tsing Kiang Pu, China
             (now called Huaiyin)

Married   John Paterson
             (children: John Jr.,
             David, Elizabeth
             [Lin], and Mary
             Katherine)

Awards and Honors

Newbery Medal for 1978 (Contemporary Life): *Bridge to Terabithia* (Crowell, 1977)

Newbery Medal for 1981 (Historical Fiction): *Jacob Have I Loved* (Crowell, 1980)

Newbery Honor Book for 1979: *The Great Gilly Hopkins* (Crowell, 1978)

American Library Association Notable Children's Book, 1974: *Of Nightingales That Weep* (Crowell, 1974); 1976: *The Master Puppeteer* (Crowell, 1975); 1977: *Bridge to Terabithia* (Crowell, 1977; ABC Clio, 1987); 1978: *The Great Gilly Hopkins* (Crowell, 1978; ABC Clio, 1987); 1981: *Jacob Have I Loved* (Crowell, 1980; Cornerstone Books, 1990; LRS, 2000); 1986: *Come Sing, Jimmy Jo* (Dutton, 1985; Puffin Books, 1995); 1991: *The Tale of the Mandarin Ducks* (Lodestar Books, 1990); 1992: *Lyddie* (Lodestar Books, 1991; Puffin Books, 1992; Thorndike Press, 1993); 1995: *Flip-Flop Girl* (Dutton, 1994); 1997: *Jip: His Story* (Lodestar Books, 1996)

Edgar Allan Poe Special Award, 1977: *Bridge to Terabithia* (Crowell, 1997; ABC Clio, 1987)

National Book Award for Children's Literature, 1977, 1979

Lewis Carroll Shelf Award, 1978: *Bridge to Terabithia* (Crowell, 1977; ABC Clio, 1987)

Silver Medallion, 1983

Catholic Library Association Regina Medal, 1988

Boston Globe-Horn Book Picture Book Award, 1991: *The Tale of the Mandarin Ducks* (Lodestar Books, 1990)

School Library Journal's Best Books, 1996: *Jip: His Story* (Lodestar Books, 1996); 1997: *Marvin's Best Christmas Present Ever* (HarperCollins, 2001); 2002: *The Same Stuff as Stars* (Clarion, 2002)

Scott O'Dell Award for Historical Fiction, 1997: *Jip: His Story* (Lodestar Books, 1996)

Hans Christian Andersen Medal, 1998

About the Author and Her Writing

The daughter of Presbyterian missionaries, Katherine Womeldorf Paterson lived the first eight years of her life in China. That experience provided the fertile soil in which Katherine developed a deep sensitivity to the unique nature of each culture and, indeed, of every human being.

> I very often get asked the question, "Do you put real people in your books?" And I say, "Yes, it's the same one over and over again: me." (interview, December 17, 1993)

For her first four and one-half years, Katherine and her family lived in Huai'an, China. They lived in a Chinese house on the boys' school campus where her father was the principal. All their neighbors were Chinese. One of these neighbors was a widow, Mrs. Loo, who took Katherine under her wing. The little girl often visited and ate lunch with Mrs. Loo. Katherine remembers, "She was one of those adults who has total respect for children, and we were friends.

"One of my very earliest memories is at her house. She had me wash my hands before we ate. I played too long in the water and the water was cold, and my fingers wrinkled and I became very distressed. I went running out to show Mrs. Loo my fingers, which had all turned pruney. I thought it was a permanent state—I'd never seen that before. I can remember vividly, she didn't laugh at me, just explained that if you leave your hands in cold water your fingers get that way, and once they warm up they'll be okay" (interview, December 17, 1993).

When World War II broke out in China, Katherine's family was forced to leave their home and return to the United States. Katherine was eight years old at the time and had lived all her life in China. As she tried to adapt to life in America, Katherine felt like a misfit, with her strange accent and clothes that looked different from what the other boys and girls wore.

Reading was always an important part of Katherine's childhood. When she lived in China, her family owned only a few books. Her mother read these to her so many times that she memorized many of the stories. Katherine's love of books and reading never faded. When asked what she would be if not a writer, reading jumps to the top of her list. "If I could make a living reading, I'd do that. Wouldn't that be great to have a job where you could read all the time and get paid for it?" (interview, December 17, 1993).

Her first published work was a poem printed in the Shanghai American School newspaper. She was seven years old:

Pat! Pat! Pat!
There is the cat.
Where is the rat?
Pat, pat, pat.

Yet despite this early attempt at writing, Katherine's journey from reader to writer was not an obvious one. As a child she had no dreams of becoming an author. At the age of eleven, she was torn between a future as a foreign missionary and one as a movie star. "I am sure that I began to write not because of any ability real or imagined but because I loved to read, and that when

I finally began to write books, it was not so much that I wanted to be a writer but that I loved books and wanted somehow to get inside the process, to have a part in their making." (interview, December 17, 1993).

In 1954, Katherine graduated from King College. She continued her schooling and earned a master of arts from the Presbyterian School of Christian Education in 1957 and a master of religious education from Union Theological Seminary in 1962.

> I've been very fortunate in my illustrated books, with what the artists have done. It's exciting to see what another mind does, and what another artist's vision is of what you've done. It opens things up for you. (interview, December 17, 1993)

Katherine wrote for many years before her books were published. At one point, there was a seven-year stretch of rejections from editors. During this time, Katherine and her husband John began raising their four children, two of whom are adopted: one Chinese and one Native American. She kept writing until her first novel was published in 1973.

A few years later, at the age of forty-one, Katherine discovered she had cancer. She had surgery, which successfully removed all the disease. As her life began to return to normal, tragedy struck again. Her young son David's best friend, a little girl, was struck and killed by lightning. Having come so close to death herself, she struggled to help her son deal with his grief. She turned to what she knew best and began to write her fourth book. The result: *Bridge to Terabithia*, a story of friendship, death, and hope. The book was awarded the Newbery Medal in 1978.

Katherine remembers the night she got the telephone call telling her that she had won the Newbery medal. She and her husband were both sound asleep. The phone was on John's side of the bed, so when it rang, he answered it. He then handed Katherine the phone with the words, "It's for you." She figured that if the phone rang at that time of night, it had to be news of the Newbery Medal.

John went down to the kitchen and warmed up some milk and brought it to his wife. "He knew I needed something soothing for my stomach. All stress and anxiety goes directly to my stomach!" (interview, December 17, 1993).

Three years later in 1980, Katherine won a second Newbery Medal for her book *Jacob Have I Loved,* which tells of the conflict between twin sisters who are total opposites. The second medal was a complete shock to her. She couldn't believe she'd received a second Newbery Medal. The reviews for *Jacob* had not been as uniformly wonderful as they'd been for *Bridge to Terabithia.*

Although Katherine figured out the first Newbery phone call, she was unprepared for the second. By that time, the Newbery committee had decided not to call people in the middle of the night. She was walking past the phone when it rang at 9:30 one morning. She took the call, and it was a woman for whom Katherine was going to make a speech later in the year, so she assumed that that was what the call was all about.

Katherine was deeply honored to have won the Newbery Medal two times. "It's a wonderful honor. It is very affirming, but you also have to realize that in any given year, any given committee might have chosen somebody else" (interview, December 17, 1993).

Katherine never let the notoriety of winning the Newbery Medal affect her writing. When she is working on a book, she doesn't think about the Medal. "You care about this particular book and you know it's going to be different from the others, and you want it to be a good book. You can't be really worried about how other people are going to see it" (interview, December 17, 1993).

Katherine never minded rewriting her stories. "Where else can you turn spilt milk into ice cream?" she often said. When asked if she ever had times when she couldn't think of what to write, she is quick to tell people that "writer's block is not a fatal disease. You need to look at the symptom and see what it's telling you" (interview, December 17, 1993).

Whatever the symptoms told Katherine, she knew how to listen. Her books are read and loved by all ages. Her characters are as genuine as anyone in real life. Perhaps the secret is that Katherine loves her stories as much as her readers do. "I don't publish things I don't love," she said. "I don't have to think they're perfect, but I still love them, and I'm proud they belong to me" (interview, December 17, 1993).

In 1998, Katherine was awarded the Hans Christian Andersen Medal for her life-time of work. She had come a long way from the little girl who had no thought of being a writer. But it is the books themselves, not the awards, that endear her to the hearts of her many readers.

A Word to My Readers:

When you pick up a piece of music, it's nothing but a bunch of black squiggles on a page. It doesn't become music until someone sings it or plays it. A book is black squiggles on a page. It doesn't become a story until someone picks it up and reads it. The writer is totally dependent on the reader for the magic to happen. I have great respect for my readers. I couldn't get along without them! (interview, December 17, 1993)

Books by Katherine Paterson

The Angel and the Donkey (Clarion, 1996).

Angels and Other Strangers: Family Christmas Stories (Crowell, 1979).

Bridge to Terabithia (Crowell, 1977; ABC Clio, 1987).

Celia and the Sweet, Sweet Water (Clarion, 1998).

Come Sing, Jimmy Jo (Dutton, 1985; Puffin Books, 1995).

Consider the Lilies: Plants of the Bible (with John Paterson) (Crowell, 1986; Clarion, 1998).

The Field of the Dogs (HarperCollins, 2001).

Flip Flop Girl (Dutton, 1994).

Gates of Excellence: On Reading and Writing Books for Children (Elsevier/Nelson Books, 1981).

The Great Gilly Hopkins (Crowell, 1978; ABC Clio, 1987).

Images of God (Clarion, 1998).

The Invisible Child: On Reading and Writing Books for Children (Dutton, 2001).

Jacob Have I Loved (Crowell, 1980; Cornerstone Books, 1990; LRS, 2000).

Jip: His Story (Lodestar Books, 1996).

The King's Equal (HarperCollins, 1992; Harper Trophy, 1999).

Lyddie (Lodestar Books, 1991; Puffin Books, 1992; Thorndike Press, 1993).

Marvin One Too Many (HarperCollins, 2001).

Marvin's Best Christmas Present Ever (HarperCollins, 1997).

The Master Puppeteer (Crowell, 1975).

A Midnight Clear: Stories for the Christmas Season (Lodestar Books, 1995).

Of Nightingales That Weep (Crowell, 1974).

Park's Quest (Lodestar Books, 1988).

Parzival: The Quest of the Grail Knight (Lodestar Books, 1998).

Preacher's Boy (Clarion, 1999).

Rebels of the Heavenly Kingdom (Dutton, 1983).

A Sense of Wonder: On Reading and Writing Books for Children (Plume, 1995).

The Sign of the Chrysanthemum (Crowell, 1973).

The Smallest Cow in the World (Vermont Migrant Education Program, 1988; Harper-Collins, 1991).

The Spying Heart: More Thoughts on Reading and Writing Books for Children (Lodestar Books, 1989).

The Same Stuff as Stars (Clarion, 2002).

The Tale of the Mandarin Ducks (Lodestar Books, 1990).

Who Am I? (W. B. Eerdmans, 1992).

The Wide Awake Princess (Clarion, 2000).

For More Information About/by Katherine Paterson

Kingman, Lee, ed. 1986. *Newbery and Caldecott Medal Books with Acceptance Papers, Biographies and Related Material Chiefly from the Horn Book Magazine: 1976–1985.* Horn Book.

Kovacs, Deborah, and James Preller. 1991. *Meet the Authors and Illustrators: 60 Creators of Favorite Children's Books Talk About Their Work.* Scholastic.

McElmeel, Sharon L. 1999. *100 Most Popular Children's Authors: Biographical Sketches and Bibliographies.* Libraries Unlimited.

Paterson, Katherine. 1988. *Gates of Excellence.* Dutton Children's Books.

Silvey, Anita, ed. 1995. *Children's Books and Their Creators.* Houghton Mifflin.

Note: Indicated citations from a personal interview with the author, December 17, 1993.

Web site: http://www.terabithia.com

1979: Ellen Raskin

Born	March 13, 1928 Milwaukee, Wisconsin
Married	Dennis Flanagan, August 1, 1960 (children: Susan Beth Kuhlman)
Died	August 4, 1984

Awards and Honors

Newbery Medal (Mystery): *The Westing Game* (Dutton, 1978)
Newbery Honor Book for 1975: *Figgs & Phantoms* (Dutton, 1974)
Edgar Allan Poe Special Award, 1975: *The Tattooed Potato and Other Clues* (Dutton, 1975)
Boston Globe-Horn Book Award, 1978: *The Westing Game* (Dutton, 1978)

About the Author and Her Writing

One of Ellen Raskin's main goals in writing for children was to create stories with happy endings.

Ellen hated growing up during the depression. She was short, shy, brilliant, Jewish, and lonely. Although her parents doted on her, she felt she never fit in with the rest of the world. She submerged herself in music, learning to play the piano at the age of four. She practiced for hours and hours every day for five years until the piano was taken away by the finance company because the family no longer had the money to pay their bills.

Ellen also had a keen mind for numbers and calculations. She accompanied her father on his excursions to neighborhood crap (dice) games, keeping a running calculation in her head of his winnings and losings. When he got to a point where he was ahead in the game, Ellen would whine and cry that she wanted to go home. That was his cue to quit while he was ahead.

Ellen studied art at the University of Wisconsin. She bought a printing press, printed some woodblocks, and made a couple of sample books. Then she hit the streets, going from business to business until she drummed up enough commissions to earn a living. She designed calendars, advertisements, and posters, but her primary focus was illustrating book jackets, of which she designed over one thousand.

Growing a bit weary of interpreting the ideas of other people, Ellen decided to take a month off from her illustrating career to see if she could write a book for children. She loved the way words, like an artist's brush strokes, came alive when placed on a page. The month turned into three months, and Ellen worked on two books. She enjoyed writing for children so much that she decided to keep at it.

Both of the books Ellen began writing during her "month off" were eventually published: *Nothing Ever Happens on My Block* (Atheneum, 1966), a picture book that she also illustrated; and a book of songs and piano accompaniments.

Ellen's books combined her skills as an artist with her gifts as a writer. She wanted her books for children "to look like a wonderful place to be" (Kingman 1986, 53) and very carefully laid out each page to include wide margins and breaks between paragraphs as room for her readers to slow down and enjoy every moment in her books. Her books indeed are works of art.

> The last thing I want is for people to think all my books are the same. I want them to be surprises. Each of the books is of itself. That's what's so nice about doing books. (Roginski 1985, 169)

When Ellen won the Newbery Medal in 1979 for *The Westing Game,* she admitted in her acceptance speech that she had imagined winning not the Newbery Medal but the Caldecott Medal for her art. Her book *Figgs & Phantoms* had been awarded a Newbery Honor Medal in 1975 as well as the Mystery Writers of America's Edgar Allan Poe Special Award. Still, she was delighted to win the Newbery Medal but made it clear that it was the book, not the writer, that had won the award.

Although Ellen wanted all of her books to have happy endings, she didn't want to know what those endings were while she was in the midst of writing the book. Often it wasn't until the fourth draft of a book that the ending started to come together. She liked being as surprised as her readers, trying to figure out how a story might unfold and how it would all end. She shared with her readers the element of surprise in trying to solve her mysteries.

Ellen usually wrote far more than she could squeeze into one book, often ending up with five times more material than could be published. She wrote and rewrote and rewrote again. Ellen thoroughly enjoyed the process because each time she rewrote, the characters and plot developed more fully, and she was fascinated as both took shape.

Ellen loved word plays and puzzles and she incorporated these into her stories, which sometimes made them complicated for her younger readers but always a delight and a joy. Her sense of humor shines in her stories and is contagious to all who read her books.

The Westing Game was Ellen's last novel. This engaging story centers around a group of people trying to solve the mystery behind a millionaire's strange death. The happy ending: the book received the Newbery Medal, a fitting, final tribute to the life and gifts of Ellen Raskin.

She died in 1984 at the age of fifty-six.

A Word to My Readers:

It is the book that is the important thing, not who I am or how I did it, but the book. Not me, the book. I fear for the book in this age of inflated personalities, in which the public's appetite for an insight into the lives of the famous has been whetted by publicity-puffers and profit-pushers into an insatiable hunger for gossip. I worry that who-the-writer-is has become more of interest than what-the-writer writes. I am concerned that this dangerous distortion may twist its way into children's literature. (Kingman 1986, 57)

Books by Ellen Raskin

A & The; or, Willia T.C.C. Baumgarten Comes to Town (Atheneum, 1970).

And It Rained (Atheneum, 1969).

Figgs & Phantoms (Dutton, 1974; Puffin Books, 1989).

Franklin Stein (Atheneum, 1972).

Ghost in a Four Room Apartment (Atheneum, 1969).

*Moe Q. McGlutch, He Smoked Too Much (Parents' Magazine Press, 1973).

*Moose, Goose, and Little Nobody (Parents' Magazine Press, 1974; Four Winds Press, 1980).

The Mysterious Disappearance of Leon (I Mean Noel) (Dutton, 1971; Puffin Books, 1989).

Nothing Ever Happens on My Block (Atheneum, 1966; Aladdin Books, 1989).

Silly Songs and Sad (Crowell, 1967).

Spectacles (Atheneum, 1968; Aladdin Books, 1988).

The Tattooed Potato and Other Clues (Dutton, 1975; Puffin Books, 1989).

Twenty Two, Twenty Three (Atheneum, 1976).

The Westing Game (Dutton, 1978; ABC Clio, 1988; Puffin Books, 1992).

Who, Said Sue, Said Whoo? (Atheneum, 1973).

The World's Greatest Freak Show (Atheneum, 1971).

For More Information About/by Ellen Raskin

Kingman, Lee, ed. 1986. *Newbery and Caldecott Medal Books with Acceptance Papers, Biographies and Related Material Chiefly from the Horn Book Magazine: 1976–1985.* Horn Book.

Roginski, Jim, ed. 1985. *Behind the Covers: Interviews with Authors and Illustrators of Books for Children and Young Adults.* Libraries Unlimited.

*illustrated by the author
Ellen Raskin also illustrated books by other authors.

1980: Joan Blos

Born   December 9, 1928
                New York, New York

Married   Peter Blos Jr., 1953
                (children: Stephen and Sarah)

Awards and Honors

Newbery Medal (Historical Fiction): *A Gathering of Days: A New England Girl's Journal, 1830–1832* (C. Scribner's Sons, 1979)

American Library Association Notable Children's Book, 1980: *A Gathering of Days: A New England Girl's Journal, 1830–1832* (C. Scribner's Sons, 1979)

About the Author and Her Writing

Joan Blos grew up as an only child. But that does not mean she was a lonely child. Born December 9, 1928, in New York, New York, Joan and her parents lived in the same building as her two aunts and their families. Her three cousins were constant playmates. "We spent summers together, we went to school together, we argued, we fought, we complained about our parents," Joan later remembered fondly. "We really grew up as a family, even though we had our own parents to go back to" (interview, February 11, 1994).

Joan's father, Max, was a physician, and her mother, Charlotte, a teacher. Both of her parents often read aloud to her. They also wrote down poems that young Joan composed before she could write for herself.

Beginning at the age of seven, Joan attended the experimental school where her mother taught. The school was not typical for its time. Students learned mostly by doing. They loved learning this way so much that the worst punishment was being told they had to stay home from school.

As part of their studies on the Middle Ages, the older children learned to do illuminated writing, set type, and run a printing press. A yearly project was the school magazine, in which a poem of Joan's was published when she was seven years old.

When Joan was in high school during World War II, a teacher suggested that she submit a short story in a writing contest. The story won first prize and was published in a national magazine that paid Joan twenty-five dollars. Joan invested $18.50 in a war bond, which was considered a very patriotic thing to do at that time. Later she couldn't remember how she spent the rest of the money, but the larger portion of her earnings was certainly put to good use.

In 1953, Joan married Peter Blos Jr. They had two children, Stephen and Sarah. The family was deeply saddened when Stephen died of cancer while he was still a young man.

Joan's introduction to children's literature began in 1954 when she became a volunteer reviewer of books for very young children. From 1958 to 1980 Joan taught children's literature at Bank Street College of Education in New York City and then at the University of Michigan in Ann Arbor. In the 1960, Joan's friends and colleagues at Bank Street encouraged her to begin writing her own stories for children. For the next twenty years Joan combined teaching about children's books with writing them. She was pleased when she realized that writing for children gave her a way to combine her interests in child development, language, and literature. It was also a way that she could reach out to children with whom she never would have connected otherwise.

> I am less worried about reader awareness, in the sense of articulate response, than hopeful that the inner story will generate understanding of others and of the self. (Kingman 1986, 68)

Joan never minded being asked where she got her ideas. She believed that this question came from an interest in the mystery of creativity: "How can there be something where there wasn't anything before? How can you just 'make up' a book?" (interview, February 11, 1994).

The author's reply to this question was that her ideas for a book often began with a question. Her Newbery award–winning novel, *A Gathering of Days: A New England Girl's Journal, 1830–1832*, was born out of questions she asked about an old New Hampshire farm house that belonged to her husband's parents. What was it like when the house was new? Who had first lived in it? What did those people do? Joan immersed herself in research, learning all that she could about how people thought, spoke, and lived in the early 1800s. She created a family to write about. As the characters developed, Joan's imaginary people seemed as real to her as any living person.

Winning the Newbery Medal came as a total surprise to Joan. She received the telephone call informing her that she had won late at night. "Next morning when I woke up, I was the winner of the Newbery Medal, not only from that day to this, but happily ever after" (interview, February 11, 1994). She tried to explain to others the utter astonishment of winning the Medal. She likened the experience to the mother of a seven-month-old baby waking up to the shock of finding out that she's the mother of a seven-month-old baby (Kingman 1986, 65).

Joan said that the award brought some changes in how people looked at her and her work; she discovered that once she became a Newbery winner, what she had to say about children's literature was suddenly of much more interest to other people!

Joan thoroughly enjoyed doing the research that is essential for a writer of historical fiction. When she got to the point where she had a hard time tearing herself away from the research, she knew it was time to stop researching and start writing.

"There is no such thing as rewriting," Joan once said. "Writing means finding the words for what you want to say, doing it over and over again until you come upon just the right word. Some parts you have to try more times than others. That is writing, the whole of it." Joan engaged in a lot of this "over and over again" part of writing. "If someone were ever to draw a cartoon of me after I've just put a new manuscript in the mail, it would be of me running after the mailman with a pencil in my hand shouting, 'Wait! One more thing!' " (interview, February 11, 1994).

Joan is best known for her historical fiction. These stories give her readers a rich and rewarding glimpse into life as it used to be. These books also remind us of the ways in which people from the past shared similar hopes, dreams, fears, joys, and disappointments to those we do today. Yet though her books often focus on the past, Joan claimed that if she could live in another time and place, she would choose the future. "I think I'd like to see what is yet to come," she once said. Then she added, "I write historical fiction because I care about the future; I write for young people because they are the future" (interview, February 11, 1994).

> What we authors are doing when we write a story is to make up an experience through which the characters grow or learn something, so that a little bit of that same experience becomes part of the reader's lives as they grow up. (interview, February 11, 1994)

Joan's twin vocations of teacher of and author of children's literature came full circle in May 2001 when the Bank Street College of Education bestowed on her an honorary doctorate of humane letters. Bank Street was where she did her first ten years of teaching, and it was as a member of the publications division and associate editor of the Bank Street/Macmillan Readers that she did her first writing for children.

In 1998, Joan was asked to create an original play for the Wild Swan Theater in Ann Arbor, Michigan. She wrote a script based on her book, *Brothers of the Heart* (C. Scribner's Sons, 1985), about a pioneer family in Michigan. In the process Joan delighted in finding a strong parallel between writing plays and picture books. "Both depend on action and dialogue. Both proceed by scenes. Neither is allowed descriptive passages. Once said, it's obvious. But to paraphrase the slogan of the United States Army Service Forces, 'the difficult we understand immediately. The obvious takes a little longer' " (interview, January 18, 2001).

For Joan, "writing has to do with a special kind of caring—caring about the world and all that goes on in it, about language and about the people who will read your words" (interview, February 11, 1994). In contrast to her paraphrase about the U.S. Army, it isn't difficult at all to recognize that Joan Blos cares deeply about the people she writes for and about. It's quite obvious to anyone who knows her or her books.

A Word to My Readers:

"Don't be scared and don't hang back," Catherine says in my book *A Gathering of Days*. That pretty much sums it up. (interview, February 11, 1994)

Books by Joan Blos

Bedtime! (Simon & Schuster Books for Young Readers, 1998).

Brooklyn Doesn't Rhyme (C. Scribner's Sons, 1994).

Brothers of the Heart: A Story of the Old Northwest, 1837–1838 (C. Scribner's Sons, 1985 Aladdin Books, 1987, 1993).

The Days Before Now: An Autobiographical Note, by Margaret Wise Brown, adapted by Joan W. Blos (Simon & Schuster Books for Young Readers, 1994).

A Gathering of Days: A New England Girl's Journal, 1830–1832 (C. Scribner's Sons, 1979; Aladdin Books, 1987, 1990).

The Grandpa Days (Simon & Schuster Books for Young Readers, 1989).

Hello, Shoes! (Simon & Schuster Books for Young Readers, 1999).

The Heroine of the Titanic: A Tale Both True and Otherwise of the Life of Molly Brown (Morrow Junior Books, 1991).

The Hungry Little Boy (Simon & Schuster Books for Young Readers, 1995).

"It's Spring," She Said (A. A. Knopf, 1968).

Just Think (with Betty Miles) (A. A. Knopf, 1971).

Lottie's Circus (Morrow Junior Books, 1989).

Martin's Hats (William Morrow, 1984).

Nellie Bly's Monkey: His Remarkable Story in His Own Words (Morrow Junior Books, 1996).

Old Henry (William Morrow, 1987).

One Very Best Valentine's Day (Little Simon, 1989).

A Seed, a Flower, a Minute, an Hour (Simon & Schuster Books for Young Readers, 1992).

For More Information About/by Joan Blos

H. W. Wilson. 1983. *The Fifth Book of Junior Authors and Illustrators.* H. W. Wilson.

Kingman, Lee, ed. 1986. *Newbery and Caldecott Medal Books with Acceptance Papers, Biographies and Related Material Chiefly from the Horn Book Magazine: 1976–1985.* Horn Book

Note: Indicated citations from a personal interview with the author, February 11, 1994.

1982: Nancy Willard

Born   June 26, 1936

Married   Eric Lindbloom, 1964
            (children: James)

Awards and Honors

Newbery Medal (Historical Fiction): *A Visit to William Blake's Inn: Poems for Innocent and Experienced Travelers* (Harcourt Brace Jovanovich, 1981). Also named a Caldecott Honor Book for 1982

Creative Artists Public Service Award

National Endowment for the Arts

Boston Globe-Horn Book Award, 1982: *A Visit to William Blake's Inn: Poems for Innocent and Experienced Travelers* (Harcourt Brace Jovanovich, 1981)

American Library Association Notable Children's Book, 1992: *Pish, Posh, Said Hieronymus Bosch* (Harcourt Brace Jovanovich, 1991)

About the Author and Her Writing

Nancy Willard was born during the Great Depression and grew up during World War II. For her, the delightful world of imagination gave life and meaning to the harsher realities around her.

Nancy and her family lived in an old house peopled by her extended family: a grandfather, a grandmother, cousins, her sister, and her parents. Anyone who needed a place had a place with the Willard family, and all were welcome.

Nancy's parents encouraged her creativity. If a crack appeared in the plaster of one of the walls, Nancy got out her paintbrush and she and her mother discussed the possibilities of what that crack might become. Often the cracks turned into beautiful angels that Nancy painted in the guestroom and the bathroom and the hallway. Nobody noticed the cracks anymore. How could they, when they had become angels?

Nancy also learned the stories of her neighbors, even though they didn't know it at the time. Her family had a "party line" telephone. Seven different families in the neighborhood shared the same phone line, and each family had its own code designated by the number of times the telephone rang. Four short and one long ring meant the call was for them. Nancy quickly learned that she could pick up the phone even when the call was for someone else and listen in to the conversations. Her mother, of course, discouraged such behavior, but the inquisitive child could not resist such a temptation.

Nancy's family spent the summers in a lakeside cottage, where she and her sister were encouraged to draw, paint, and write. The two girls wrote and edited their own neighborhood newspaper, traveling around to the nearby houses and talking to the residents in hopes of gleaning some bit of gossip for their newspaper.

> The poet writes poems for people to listen to, poems to be heard as well as read. Skipping rope or trading taunts on the jungle gym, children know the importance of hearing and saying poetry. But do we ever really outgrow that wish to hear a story, to say a poem? (Kingman 1986, 96–97)

At the age of seven, Nancy had her first poem published in a church magazine. An aunt submitted the poem for her. During that same year Nancy contracted a severe case of the measles and spent many hours in bed. Her babysitter recited poems written by the poet William Blake. She loved the rhythms and the words. Later the same babysitter sent her a book of poetry by Blake, inscribed by the man himself: "Poetry is the best medicine," he wrote, and for a sick little girl, those words rang true.

While a senior in high school, Nancy wrote and illustrated a miniature picture book. This was reproduced and published in the *Horn Book* magazine, one of the top journals of children's literature. The editor, Bertha Mahony Miller, wrote to Nancy and asked if she could use one of her drawings on the Miller family Christmas card that year. Nancy willingly gave permission and earned ten dollars for her art.

Later, Nancy earned her B.A. from the University of Michigan, where her father had taught. She then earned a master's from Stanford in medieval literature and a Ph.D. in modern literature from the University of Michigan. During her undergraduate years, Nancy earned five Hopwood Awards for poetry and essays. She later received a Creative Artists Public Service Award as well as the highly regarded National Endowment for the Arts Award. Nancy also studied art in Oslo and Paris.

One night, Nancy began building a cardboard structure with many of the scraps, odds and ends, and bits and pieces that she had collected. The structure soon turned into an inn, boarding the family cat whose weight collapsed the place more than once. A neighbor who built homes for a living saw what the cat had done and offered to rebuild the inn out of wood, which he did. Once complete, the new structure stood seven feet high. Nancy kept adding to the inn, and when her editor asked her to write a book of poetry, the inn became the imaginary residence of William Blake and a menagerie of varied but welcome guests, much like Nancy's childhood home.

The book, *A Visit to William Blake's Inn,* won the Newbery Medal in 1982 and was also named a Caldecott Honor Book the same year. All the bits and pieces and odds and ends of Nancy's experiences came to life in that book, from the many characters who peopled the family home, to the secret conversations heard on the party line, to the angels painted over cracked plaster, to the poetry and drawings and glorious imagination of Nancy Willard. The world of imagination and the world of reality had become one.

> ### A Word to My Readers:
> Reading, drawing, doing my homework, I listened and noted in the margins of my books and math papers and class schedules whatever seemed worth the saving: a fragment of speech, a line of poetry. Years later, I was reading the poetry of William Carlos Williams and suddenly felt that he was speaking directly to me. "What do I do?" wrote Williams. "I listen . . . This is my entire occupation." (Kingman 1986, 96)

Books by Nancy Willard

All on a May Morning (Putnam's, 1975).

An Alphabet of Angels (Blue Sky Press, 1994).

Among Angels: Poems (with Jane Yolen) (Harcourt, Brace & Co., 1995).

Angel in the Parlor: 5 Stories and 8 Essays (Harcourt Brace Jovanovich, 1983).

The Ballad of Biddy Early (Random House, 1989).

Beauty and the Beast (Harcourt Brace Jovanovich, 1992).

Carpenter of the Sun: Poems (Liveright, 1974).

Childhood of the Magician (Liveright, 1973).

Cracked Corn and Snow Ice Cream: A Family Almanac (Harcourt, Brace & Co., 1997).

East of the Sun & West of the Moon: A Play (Harcourt Brace Jovanovich, 1989).

Firebrat (Knopf/Random House, 1988).

The Good Night Blessing Book (Blue Sky Press/Scholastic, 1996).

Gutenburg's Gift (Wild Honey, Harcourt, Brace & Co., 1995).

The High Rise Glorious Skittle Skat Roarious Sky Pie Angel Food Cake (Harcourt Brace Jovanovich, 1990).

The Highest Hit (Harcourt Brace Jovanovich, 1978).

Household Tales of Moon and Water (Harcourt Brace Jovanovich, 1982).

In His Country: Poems (Generation, 1966).

The Island of the Grass King: The Further Adventures of Anatole (Harcourt Brace Jovanovich, 1979).

The Lively Anatomy of God: Stories (Eakin Press, 1968).

The Magic Cornfield (Harcourt, Brace & Co., 1997).

*illustrated by the author
Nancy Willard also illustrated books by other authors.

The Marzipan Moon (Harcourt Brace Jovanovich, 1981).

The Merry History of a Christmas Pie: With a Delicious Description of a Christmas Soup (Putnam's, 1974).

The Moon and Riddles Diner and the Sunnyside Cafe (Harcourt, 2001).

Mountains of Quilt (Harcourt Brace Jovanovich, 1987).

The Mouse, the Cat, and Grandmother's Hat (Little, Brown, 2002).

A Nancy Willard Reader: Selected Poetry and Prose (Hanover, 1991).

A New Herball: Poems (Ferdinand Roten Galleries, 1968).

Night Story (Harcourt Brace Jovanovich, 1986).

The Nightgown of the Sullen Moon (Harcourt Brace Jovanovich, 1983).

19 Masks for the Naked Poet (Kayak Books, 1971; Harcourt Brace Jovanovich, 1984).

Papa's Panda (Harcourt Brace Jovanovich, 1979).

Pish, Posh, Said Hieronymus Bosch (Harcourt Brace Jovanovich, 1991).

Poem Made of Water (Brighton Press, 1992).

Raggedy Ann and the Christmas Thief (Simon & Schuster Books for Young Readers, 1999).

Sailing to Cythera, and Other Anatole Stories (Harcourt Brace Jovanovich, 1974).

Shadow Story (Harcourt, Brace & Co., 1999).

Shoes Without Leather (Putnam's, 1976).

Simple Pictures Are Best (Harcourt Brace Jovanovich, 1977, 1978).

Sister Water (Knopf/Random House, 1993).

Skin of Grace: Poems (University of Missouri Press, 1967).

The Snow Rabbit (Putnam's, 1975).

The Sorcerer's Apprentice (Blue Sky Press, 1993).

A Starlit Somersault Downhill (Little, Brown, 1993).

Strangers' Bread (Harcourt Brace Jovanovich, 1977).

Swimming Lessons: New and Selected Poems (Knopf/Random House, 1996).

The Tale I Told Sasha (Little, Brown, 1999).

Telling Time: Angels, Ancestors, and Stories (Harcourt, Brace & Co., 1993).

Testimony of the Invisible Man (University of Missouri Press, 1970).

Things Invisible to See (Knopf/Random House, 1984).

The Tortilla Cat (Harcourt, Brace & Co., 1998).

Uncle Terrible: More Adventures of Anatole (Harcourt Brace Jovanovich, 1982).

A Visit to William Blake's Inn: Poems for Innocent and Experienced Travelers (Harcourt Brace Jovanovich, 1981).

The Voyage of the Ludgate Hill: Travels with Robert Louis Stevenson (Harcourt Brace Jovanovich, 1987).

Water Walker (A. A. Knopf, 1989).

The Well Mannered Balloon (Harcourt Brace Jovanovich, 1976).

For More Information About/by Nancy Willard

Kingman, Lee, ed. 1986. *Newbery and Caldecott Medal Books with Acceptance Papers, Biographies and Related Material Chiefly from the Horn Book Magazine: 1976–1985.* Horn Book.

1983: Cynthia Voigt

Born   February 25, 1942
                Boston, Massachusetts

Married   1964 (children:
                Jessica)
                Walter Voigt, 1974
                (children: Peter)

Awards and Honors

Newbery Medal (Contemporary Life): *Dicey's Song* (Atheneum, 1982)
Newbery Honor Book for 1984: *A Solitary Blue* (Atheneum, 1983)
Edgar Allan Poe Award for Best Juvenile Mystery, 1984: *The Callender Papers* (Atheneum, 1983)
ALAN Award, 1989
American Library Association Margaret A. Edwards Award, 1995
American Library Association Notable Children's Book, 1983: *Dicey's Song* (Atheneum, 1982); 1984: *A Solitary Blue* (Atheneum, 1983)

About the Author and Her Writing

Cynthia Voigt once said that she grew up in the shadow of her older sister. "In nursery school, she was Miss Muffet, and I was the Spider. When we got to dancing school, she was a Sweet Pea, and I was a Head of Cabbage" (Kingman 1986, 116). Whether or not the comparison is accurate, one could certainly say that the girl who thought she was an ugly duckling grew up to be a beautiful swan.

Better yet, Cynthia can be compared to her favorite bird, the great blue heron. Herons love the water: Cynthia always loved the water. The heron, a patient, graceful bird, can spend an eternity waiting in a pool of water for a fish to swim into just the right spot. Cynthia had the patience to let an idea ripen and mature until it panned out into a full-fledged story. The great blue heron is eventually rewarded for its patience. Although it took a while, Cynthia finally received the acclaim she deserved for her writing.

Cynthia knew that she wanted to be a writer from the age of twelve. She wrote short stories and poetry while in high school and college, mostly for fun. After graduating from Smith College she worked at the J. Walter Thompson Advertising Agency. Then she turned to teaching, the one profession she was sure she'd detest. Much to her surprise, Cynthia discovered that not only was she good at teaching, she loved it.

For many years, Cynthia taught school, every grade from second through twelfth with the exception of third grade. She served as chair of the English department from 1971 to 1979 at the Key School in Annapolis, Maryland.

Cynthia married and had a daughter, Jessica. Later, she divorced, then married Walter Voigt in 1974 and had a son, Peter. She once equated the seemingly endless length of time it took from signing a contract on a book to seeing the book in print with becoming a mother. She could give birth to two children, she said, in the length of time it took for one book to move to publication.

> While a book may be out, that doesn't mean necessarily that I am finished with it, or it with me; and perhaps that is why I have never had the impulse to type "the end" at the conclusion of a story. (Kingman 1986, 109)

If one watches a great blue heron as it fishes, it appears as though the bird is just standing on its long, bent legs, doing nothing. Cynthia once said the same thing about writers. "From the outside, if, say, a movie camera were focused on the writer at work, the words *boring* and *dull* would spring to mind. This is, however, only true from the outside. Inside, secretly, invisibly, the right writing of a paragraph or a good telling of a story tastes like an adventure as exciting as any I've heard about, taken part in, or imagined" (Gallo 1990, 217).

Cynthia first began writing for younger readers. She shifted to writing young adult fiction because those were the books she had enjoyed while growing up.

Cynthia said she liked having an object with her that represented the current book she was writing. She also used drawings to help her plot out the development of a book. She felt that if she could sketch out visually the scene in a particular room, it would help her focus on writing the scenes that took place in that room and keep the details accurate.

The Tillerman family, four fatherless children left in a car and abandoned by their mother, first took form in her book *Homecoming* (Atheneum, 1981). The book became the prequel to *Dicey's Song,* which won the Newbery Medal in 1983. The stories of the family continue through several more books, of which *A Solitary Blue* won a Newbery Honor Medal in 1984. What is a "solitary blue"? A great blue heron!

When Cynthia got the phone call telling her that she had won the Newbery Medal, she went into a state of shock. "I did not know good news could pack such a wallop," she admitted in her acceptance speech (Kingman 1986, 107). Next, she said she had to be sure to learn how to spell the name "Newbery," as she was certain she had misspelled the word during her many years as a teacher, on her reading lists and curriculum suggestions. How do you spell "Newbery?" In the year 1983, the word was spelled "V-o-i-g-t."

Cynthia became one of the most popular and well-recognized writers for young adults. In 1984, Cynthia won the Edgar Allan Poe Award for Best Juvenile Mystery for *The Callender Papers* (Atheneum, 1983). In 1989, she received the ALAN Award, given by the Assembly on Literature for Adolescents by the National Council of Teachers of English for significant contribution to the field of adolescent literature. And in 1995, Cynthia won the Margaret A. Edwards Award for her contributions to the field of young adult literature.

Like the patient, great blue heron waiting for the right fish, good things finally came to Cynthia Voigt.

A Word to My Readers:

In my life, I have three jobs, all of which I like. I have the job of wife-and-mother, where you build relationships that you hope will last all your life long. I have the job of teacher, where you think about really substantial books, like *Hamlet,* and think also about who the students are and how they can make themselves better at being what they are. I have the job of writer, which is one of the world's strangest occupations, full of contradictions, intensely interesting. (H. W. Wilson 1983, 320)

Books by Cynthia Voigt

Bad, Badder, Baddest (Scholastic, 1997).

Bad Girls (Scholastic, 1996).

Bad Girls in Love (Atheneum, 2002).

Building Blocks (Atheneum, 1984; Aladdin Paperbacks, 2002).

The Callender Papers (Atheneum, 1983; Aladdin Paperbacks, 2000).

Come a Stranger (Atheneum, 1986).

David and Jonathan (Scholastic, 1992).

Dicey's Song (Atheneum, 1982; Cornerstone Books, 1990; Pocket Books, 2002).

Elske (Atheneum, 1999; Pocket Books, 2001).

Glass Mountain: A Novel (Harcourt Brace Jovanovich, 1991; Thorndike Press, 1992).

Homecoming (Atheneum, 1981; Pocket Books, 2002).

It's Not Easy Being Bad (Atheneum Books for Young Readers, 2000, 2002).

Izzy, Willy Nilly (Atheneum, 1986).

Jackaroo (Atheneum, 1985).

On Fortune's Wheel (Atheneum, 1990).

Orfe (Atheneum, 1992; Pulse, 2002).

The Runner (Atheneum, 1985).

Seventeen Against the Dealer (Atheneum, 1989; Pocket Books, 2002).

A Solitary Blue (Atheneum, 1983).

Sons from Afar (Atheneum, 1987).

Stories About Rosie (Atheneum, 1986).

Tell Me if the Lovers are Losers (Atheneum, 1982).

Tree by Leaf (Atheneum, 1988; Aladdin Paperbacks, 2000).

The Vandemark Mummy (Atheneum, 1991; Aladdin Paperbacks, 2001).

When She Hollers (Scholastic, 1994).

The Wings of a Falcon (Scholastic, 1993).

For More Information About/by Cynthia Voigt

Gallo, Donald R., ed. 1990. *Speaking for Ourselves: Autobiographical Sketches by Notable Authors of Books for Young Adult.* National Council of Teachers of English.

H. W. Wilson. 1983. *The Fifth Book of Junior Authors and Illustrators.* H. W. Wilson.

Kingman, Lee, ed. 1986. *Newbery and Caldecott Medal Books with Acceptance Papers, Biographies and Related Material Chiefly from the Horn Book Magazine: 1976–1985.* Horn Book.

1984: Beverly Cleary

Born	April 12, 1916 McMinnville, Oregon
Married	Clarence T. Cleary, 1940 (children: twins Marianne Elizabeth and Malcolm James)

Awards and Honors

Newbery Medal (Contemporary Life): *Dear Mr. Henshaw* (William Morrow, 1983)
Newbery Honor Book for 1978: *Ramona and Her Father* (William Morrow, 1977)
Newbery Honor Book for 1982: *Ramona Quimby, Age 8* (William Morrow, 1981)
Laura Ingalls Wilder Award, 1975
Catholic Library Association Regina Medal, 1980
University of Southern Mississippi's Silver Medallion, 1982
Golden Kite Award, 1982: *Ralph S. Mouse* (William Morrow, 1982)
American Library Association Notable Children's Book Award, 1980: *Ramona and Her Mother* (William Morrow, 1979); 1982: *Ramona Quimby, Age 8* (William Morrow, 1981; Clio, 1987); 1984: *Dear Mr. Henshaw* (William Morrow, 1983); 1985: *Ramona Forever* (William Morrow, 1984; Dell, 1985; Cornerstone Books, 1989)

About the Author and Her Writing

From Ribsy to Ralph to Ramona the Pest, for decades Beverly Cleary's beloved characters have been cherished companions of countless children.

Beverly spent the first six years of her life in a thirteen-room house built by pioneers, on a large farm in Yamhill, Oregon. When the farm failed, Beverly and her parents moved to the city of Portland. The change to city life was a rude awakening to the little girl who had been free to run and play and learn from the natural world around her.

Beverly's mother was an enthusiastic reader and often told her only child that "reading is to the mind as exercise is to the body" (Kingman 1986, 123). Yet Beverly had problems learning to read. Even once she mastered the skill, she didn't much care for the books that were available. She wanted to read books about children who lived everyday lives like herself, not the simplified folktales that she had heard many times before. She longed for books with a sense of humor and stories that reflected the way she thought.

In first grade, Beverly had a teacher who was a strict disciplinarian. She punished children by making them sit under her desk or by rapping their knuckles with a metal-tipped stick. Second grade turned out to be a much better experience, and Beverly's teacher was kinder and gentler than the first one. By third grade, Beverly discovered books about children that connected with her life. Reading, which had once been a chore, became great fun. Beverly became such an avid reader that the school librarian suggested

> The library was my best friend, too, and still is. (Kingman 1986, 128)

that she should write children's books when she grew up. The thought appealed to her, but her parents wanted her to learn a practical vocation that could support her. Once Beverly became an established writer, her advice to others seeking to make a career in the field echoed her parents' advice: "If you're serious about becoming a professional writer, prepare to have some other way of earning a living. Many fine writers don't earn enough to live on" (Kovacs and Preller 1991, 87).

Beverly studied library science at the University of California and later at the University of Washington. She met Clarence Cleary, an accountant, while at school, and the two eloped in 1940. They were married for fifteen years before their twins Marianne and Malcolm were born. The children later served as models for several of the characters in Beverly's books.

During World War II Beverly served as post librarian at the Oakland Army Hospital. After the war and her ten years experience as a librarian, Beverly chose to work from her home and to concentrate on her writing. She began writing *Henry Huggins* (William Morrow) on January 2, 1950. The book was published in 1950, and Beverly spent the next twenty-five years writing an average of one book a year.

When Beverly first started writing books, she remembered how she felt as a child, wanting to read books about children to whom she could relate. The author was also inspired by a group of young boys she had known who resisted reading because they longed for books about kids like themselves. Beverly's books are populated with characters that deal with everyday issues of life, from a pesky little sister to the fear of losing a beloved pet.

Two of Cleary's books won Newbery Honor Medals, *Ramona and Her Father,* in 1978, and *Ramona Quimby, Age 8,* in 1982.

In the 1980s, as Beverly moved into her seventies, she began to slow her diligent pace just a bit. She took on fewer speaking engagements but continued to receive a huge amount of fan mail from her readers. She sometimes received one hundred letters a day, and thousands per year. Cleary found some of the letters deeply moving. These many "fan" letters motivated her to write a book very different in style from the ones that had made her such a popular and well-read author. *Dear Mr. Henshaw* centered on a lonely boy suffering through the divorce of his parents. Through his letters to an adventurous and caring author, the boy, Leigh Botts, is able to grow to some maturity and self-confidence.

Dear Mr. Henshaw won the Newbery Medal in 1984. This book was so unlike her others it surprised many that this was the title that finally earned Beverly a Newbery Medal. In this book, Beverly was able to address many of the issues brought to her attention by the real-life children who wrote to her. She dealt with the realities of a child growing up in a broken home, a theme she had not specifically addressed before but which she found more and more prevalent in the lives of her readers.

One of the greatest honors ever given to Beverly came on April 8, 1977, when the Central Library in Portland was rededicated and renamed in her honor. Her mother, who started the library in Yamhill half a century before, would have loved knowing that her only child learned not only to appreciate reading but also to share the joy of reading with generations of children through her own legacy of books.

Throughout the 1970s and 1980s, Beverly received the recognition she undeniably deserved. She received the Laura Ingalls Wilder Award in 1975, the Catholic Library Association Regina Medal in 1980, and in 1982 the University of Southern Mississippi's Silver Medallion.

On October 13, 1995, the Beverly Cleary Sculpture Garden for Children was dedicated in her honor. The garden, located in Portland, Oregon, contains enchanting statues of Ramona, Henry, and Ribsy, now immortalized in bronze as well as in print.

The awards and honors did not mark the end of Beverly Cleary's writing career. The girl who had a hard time learning to read continued to write books that will be read for many years to come.

A Word to My Readers:

Although I am deeply touched that my books have reached two generations of children, popularity has never been my goal. (Kingman 1986, 131)

Books by Beverly Cleary

Beezus and Ramona (William Morrow, 1955).

Dear Mr. Henshaw (William Morrow, 1983; ABC Clio, 1987).

Ellen Tebbits (William Morrow, 1951).

Emily's Runaway Imagination (William Morrow, 1961).

Fifteen (William Morrow, 1956).

A Girl from Yamhill: A Memoir (William Morrow, 1988).

The Growing Up Feet (William Morrow, 1987).

Henry and Beezus (William Morrow, 1952).

Henry and Ribsy (William Morrow, 1954).

Henry and the Clubhouse (Morrow, 1962).

Henry and the Paper Route (Morrow, 1957).

Henry Huggins (Morrow, 1950; Cornerstone Books, 1989; HarperCollins, 2000).

The Hullabaloo ABC (Parnassus Press, 1960; Morrow, 1998).

Janet's Thingamajigs (Morrow, 1987).

Jean and Johnny (Morrow, 1959).

The Luckiest Girl (William Morrow, 1958).

Lucky Chuck (William Morrow, 1984).

Mitch and Amy (William Morrow, 1967; Morrow Junior Books, 1991).

The Mouse and the Motorcycle (William Morrow, 1965; Cornerstone Books, 1989).

Muggie Maggie (Morrow Junior Books, 1990).

My Own Two Feet: A Memoir (Morrow Junior Books, 1995).

Otis Spofford (William Morrow, 1953).

Petey's Bedtime Story (Morrow Junior Books, 1993).

Ralph S. Mouse (William Morrow, 1982; Cornerstone Books, 1989).

Ramona and Her Father (William Morrow, 1977; ABC Clio, 1988).

Ramona and Her Mother (William Morrow, 1979).

Ramona Forever (William Morrow, 1984; Dell, 1985; Cornerstone Books, 1989).

Ramona Quimby, Age 8 (William Morrow, 1981; ABC Clio, 1987).

Ramona the Brave (William Morrow, 1975; Cornerstone Books, 1990).

Ramona the Pest (William Morrow, 1968; Cornerstone Books, 1990).

Ramona's World (Morrow Junior Books, 1999).

Real Hole (William Morrow, 1960, 1986).

Ribsy (William Morrow, 1964).

Runaway Ralph (William Morrow, 1970).

Sister of the Bride (William Morrow, 1963).

Socks (William Morrow, 1973).

Strider (Morrow Junior Books, 1991).

Two Dog Biscuits (William Morrow, 1961, 1986).

For More Information About/by Beverly Cleary

Autobiography: 1995. *My Own Two Feet: A Memoir.* Morrow Junior Books; 1988. *A Girl from Yamhill: A Memoir.* William Morrow.

Kingman, Lee, ed. 1986. *Newbery and Caldecott Medal Books with Acceptance Papers, Biographies and Related Material Chiefly from the Horn Book Magazine: 1976–1985.* Horn Book.

Kovacs, Deborah, and James Preller. 1991. *Meet the Authors and Illustrators: 60 Creators of Favorite Children's Books Talk About Their Work.* Scholastic.

1985: Robin McKinley

Born	November 16, 1952
	Warren, Ohio
Married	Peter Dickinson, January 3, 1992

Awards and Honors

Newbery Medal (Fantasy): *The Hero and the Crown* (Greenwillow Books, 1984)

Newbery Honor Book for 1983: *The Blue Sword* (Greenwillow Books, 1982)

American Library Association Best Book for Young Adults, 1978: *Beauty: A Retelling of the Story of Beauty and the Beast* (Harper & Row, 1978; Econo-Clad Books, 1999); 1982: *The Blue Sword* (Greenwillow Books, 1982; Puffin Books, 2000); 1988: *The Outlaws of Sherwood* (Greenwillow Books, 1988); 1989: *The Hero and the Crown* (Greenwillow Books, 1984; ABC Clio, 1988; Puffin Books, 2000); 1994: *Deerskin* (Ace Books, 1994)

American Library Association Notable Children's Book, 1983: *The Blue Sword* (Greenwillow Books, 1982; Puffin Books, 2000); 1985: *The Hero and the Crown* (Greenwillow Books, 1984)

About the Author and Her Writing

Robin McKinley grew up an only child who wasn't quite sure what "home" meant, except that it was where her parents lived at any one time. Her father served in the navy, and the family was constantly on the move. Robin quickly discovered that the most reliable friends in her world were the books that could be found at libraries wherever the family happened to be, books in which she could lose herself and enter other, more fantastic worlds. Although as an adult, Robin was able to put down some roots and develop long-standing friendships, books have never lost their role as faithful companions in her life.

Along with books, Robin loved horses. She took her first riding lessons in Tokyo during the time that her father was stationed in Japan. The instructor did not speak English, but despite this and a few well-earned blisters, Robin learned to ride.

Robin loved the writing of J.R.R. Tolkien and Rudyard Kipling. Yet in her reading of diverse types of literature, she was troubled by the traditional roles assigned to women. Robin was particularly bothered by the way the boys and men got to be the heroes while the girls and women were cast as inferior or supportive characters. Why should boys have all the fun? Why should they get to be the ones who rode off into the wild, slaying dragons and saving the world from the clutching claws of evil?

Robin longed to read about "Girls Who Do Things," things besides sit at home and wait for their heroes to return. So she grew up and became a "Girl Who Wrote About Girls Who Do Things." She discovered that there were plenty of people who were hungry and thirsty for the same kind of heroines she had longed for as a child.

From the time Robin discovered that a person could grow up and be a writer, that was her goal. It wasn't as though she decided to "become a writer." She had been writing stories since she first learned the alphabet. In college she majored in English literature. Then she worked as an editorial assistant at Little, Brown Publishers in Boston. After marrying and divorcing, Robin kept writing. She did a lot of work as a freelance editor. It wasn't until fifteen years after graduation that she could afford to become a full-time writer.

Once a story grabbed Robin's attention, she said it was as if the story compelled her to write and wouldn't leave her alone until she did. After she began to write, it was easy for her to get lost in the writing. "When a story wants out of my skull and onto paper, it lets me know. It keeps me awake at night, makes me forget to pay overdue bills, renders me incapable of holding a rational conversation with old friends" (H. W. Wilson 1983, 212). As for where those ideas came from in the first place, Robin claimed it was as if they came from someplace beyond her. It was as simple, and as complex, as that.

> The story is *always* better than your ability to write it. (Robin McKinley's Web site, accessed December 29, 2000)

Frequently, the ideas that have grabbed hold of Robin and wouldn't shake loose were the ideas that centered around "Girls Who Do Things." A number of Robin's books are retellings of classic folktales such as "Beauty and the Beast" or "Robin Hood." But in Robin's stories the women are more fully alive and central to the telling of the story than in the traditional versions. Robin's skill in weaving a new story out of an old one makes her retelling as fresh as the originals and more suited to the tastes of contemporary readers.

Robin married Peter Dickinson, an English author whom she had long admired, on J.R.R. Tolkien's birthday. They settled in a centuries-old family home in England, where there was plenty of space for both of them to write. Robin found the English countryside a perfect settling place. There, in the land where so much mythology and so many folktales came to life, Robin found the home where her roots could sink into the ground along with the several hundred rose bushes flourishing in the gardens.

Never considering herself a "Girl Who Writes Children's Books," Robin once said that "I don't write 'children's books.' I write my books for anyone who wants to read them" (Kingman 1986, 151). Her advice to aspiring writers is to "Write what *you* want to read. The person you know best in this world is *you*. Listen to yourself. If you are excited by what you are writing, you have a much better chance of putting that excitement over to a reader" (Robin McKinley's Web site, accessed December 29, 2000).

Robin was certainly successful in putting her own excitement about a story into the hands of her readers. *The Blue Sword* was named a Newbery Honor Book in 1983, and two years later in 1985, the next book in the series, *The Hero and the Crown,* was awarded the Newbery Medal. The award recognized not only a wonderful writer but also one who validated the growing genre of stories about strong, active girls.

Robin's first reaction to being awarded the Newbery Medal was, "Oh, no!" She remembered a number of well-intentioned librarians back in grade school who insisted she read Newbery Medal books in order to broaden her horizons. Some of the books did not interest her at all, and she grew up believing that Newbery books were boring. Winning the Newbery Medal herself may have changed her mind about that, at least in part.

After winning the Newbery Medal, Robin continued to write books of fantasy. *The Outlaws of Sherwood* (Greenwillow Books, 1988) was named an American Library Association Best Book for Young Adults, as was *Deerskin* (Ace Books, 1993).

In her Newbery Medal acceptance speech, Robin said that "I can't remember a time when the stories I told myself weren't about shy, bumbling girls who turned out to be heroes" (Kingman 1986, 143). She could have been speaking about herself. For the many who have read her books she has proven that a shy, awkward girl can indeed turn out to be a hero, or heroine: "A Girl Who Does Things That Others Only Dared to Dream About."

A Word to My Readers:

I hope some of my [stories] may inspire more girls, both young and grown-up, to do more things they want to do and haven't been quite sure they dared; and more boys not to think it odd that they should want to do them. (Kingman 1986, 148)

Books by Robin McKinley

Beauty: A Retelling of the Story of Beauty and the Beast (Harper & Row, 1978; Econo-Clad Books, 1999).

Black Beauty, by Anna Sewell, adapted by Robin McKinley (Random House, 1986).

The Blue Sword (Greenwillow Books, 1982; Puffin Books, 2000).

Deerskin (Ace Books, 1993; Econo-Clad Books, 1999).

The Door in the Hedge (Greenwillow Books, 1981; Ace Books, 1997).

The Hero and the Crown (Greenwillow Books, 1984; ABC Clio, 1988; Puffin Books, 2000).

A Knot in the Grain and Other Stories (Greenwillow Books, 1994).

The Light Princess, by George MacDonald, adapted by Robin McKinley (Harcourt Brace Jovanovich, 1988).

My Father Is in the Navy (Greenwillow Books, 1992).

The Outlaws of Sherwood (Greenwillow Books, 1988; Firebird, 2002).

Rose Daughter (Greenwillow Books, 1997; Econo-Clad Books, 1999).

Rowan (Greenwillow Books, 1992).

Spindle's End (Putnam's, 2000; Puffin Books, 2002).

The Stone Fey (Harcourt, Brace & Co., 1998).

Tales from the Jungle Book, by Rudyard Kipling, adapted by Robin McKinley (Random House, 1985).

Water: Tales of Elemental Spirits (Putnam Publishing Group Juvenile, 2002), coauthored with her husband, Peter Dickinson.

For Information About/by Robin McKinley

H. W. Wilson. 1983. *The Fifth Book of Junior Authors and Illustrators.* H. W. Wilson.

Kingman, Lee, ed. 1986. *Newbery and Caldecott Medal Books with Acceptance Papers, Biographies and Related Material Chiefly from the Horn Book Magazine: 1976–1985.* Horn Book.

Web site: http://www.robinmckinley.com; Web site used for research (now defunct): http://www.sff.net/people/robin-McKinley/RM_FAQ.htp.

1986: Patricia MacLachlan

Born   March 3, 1938
            Cheyenne, Wyoming

Married   Robert MacLachlan,
            April 14, 1962 (children:
            John, Jamie, and Emily)

Awards and Honors

Newbery Medal (Historical Fiction): *Sarah, Plain and Tall* (Harper & Row, 1985)
American Library Association Notable Children's Book, 1981: *Arthur, For the Very First Time* (Harper & Row, 1980; Cornerstone Books, 1990; Econo-Clad Books, 1999); 1985: *Unclaimed Treasures* (Harper & Row, 1984; Econo-Clad Books, 1999); 1986: *Sarah, Plain and Tall* (Harper & Row, 1985); 1989: *The Facts and Fictions of Minna Pratt* (Harper & Row, 1988; Econo-Clad Books, 1999)
Golden Kite Award, 1980: *Arthur, for the Very First Time* (Harper & Row, 1980); 1985: *Sarah, Plain and Tall* (Harper & Row, 1985)
Scott O'Dell Award for Historical Fiction, 1985: *Sarah, Plain and Tall* (Harper & Row, 1985)
Christopher Award, 1986: *Sarah, Plain and Tall* (Harper & Row, 1985)

About the Author and Her Writing

Somewhere around the third grade, Patricia MacLachlan (Mick-LOCK-lin) wrote a story for a school assignment. The teacher told the students that their stories had to have a beginning, a middle, an end, and that they should be about their pets. Patricia wrote her entire story on a three-inch by five-inch index card: "My cats have names and seem happy. Often they play. The end."

The teacher was not impressed. Patricia went home and wrote in her diary, "I shall try not to be a writer" (Commire 1990, 62:117–18). Fortunately, she changed her mind.

Patricia was born March 3, 1938, in Cheyenne, Wyoming, an only child. She spent a lot of time with her parents and peopled her childhood with imaginary brothers and sisters,

224

as well as a very good imaginary friend, Mary, who was always suggesting some kind of mischief. Patricia insisted that her parents set a place at the dinner table for Mary. Once she even got upset when her father accidentally sat down on the couch—on top of Mary.

Patricia's parents were open-minded and imaginative, and they loved books. Her mother frequently took her to the library. Patricia would be so busy reading her books while walking back to the house that even before they returned home, she had finished the stack she had just checked out and was ready to go back to the library for more. Her father sometimes acted out characters in the stories, making them seem to come alive.

Patricia's father had taught school in a one-room schoolhouse when he was nineteen. Patricia decided to follow in her father's footsteps and become an educator, but then came the priority of family life. She met Robert MacLachlan while studying at the University of Connecticut and they married on April 14, 1962. Three children were born: John, Jamie, and Emily. As the children grew older and became involved in their own activities, Patricia decided it was time to do something new. She thought about going back to graduate school or teaching. Then it dawned on her that what she really wanted to do was write.

> I can't write about anything that doesn't have some connection to what I care about. (Kovacs and Preller 1991, 116)

Patricia was fortunate to live in an area of the northeast populated by terrific writers. She took a class on writing taught by Jane Yolen, a well-known children's author who encouraged her every step of the way. In time Patricia joined a writing group with Jane and several other published authors. Every week they met and read their latest work, offering honest feedback and allowing room for each to explore the craft of writing in a supportive and honest setting.

As Patricia's books were published and she became a more recognized name in children's literature, kids began asking her the same questions they asked other writers. Where did she get her ideas? Were her stories true? Did she ever get writer's block?

"I use my life a whole lot as starting places in books," was Patricia's answer. "It's important for children to know that they have amazing stories in their family. You don't have to be rich and exciting and adventurous to be a writer. The good stories come out of everyday life" (interview, May 1994).

Patricia's stories start with a central character or characters. At times she has had to cut characters from her manuscripts, but these have a way of appearing later in another book of their own.

> My greatest fear is being stuck somewhere without a book. (Kovacs and Preller 1991, 117)

As for writer's block, Patricia never believed in it. She claimed that if she had trouble writing, it usually meant that something in the story needed to be changed. At those times Patricia would walk away from a manuscript for a while and do something physical like take a walk before returning to her writing. Usually, after the break, the problem would become more apparent, and she would be able to make the necessary changes.

The heroine in her Newbery Medal–winning book, *Sarah, Plain and Tall,* came from the story of a real-life relative who had journeyed from Maine to the prairie as a mail order bride. Patricia remembered her mother talking about this lady when Patricia was a child. She wrote *Sarah* in part for her mother, who by that time was beginning to suffer from Alzheimer's disease.

Patricia also wrote the screenplay for the television movie of *Sarah, Plain and Tall*. She found the work to be rewarding but difficult. Trying to fit the story into a two-hour time slot forced her to do some rewriting of the original story. She likened the process of making a movie to writing a book, and said that when she writes, she imagines looking through a camera lens in order to visualize the scenes and the characters.

In reverse, writing a picture book is also like making a film. "You get another very important person's view mixed in with it," she said, referring to the illustrator's work. "That's kind of the exciting thing about writing picture books. You give up all your control, and that's a good thing for people to do sometimes" (interview, May 1994).

After winning the Newbery Medal, Patricia continued to write novels and picture books. She also collaborated with her son on several books. In one she wrote about the lives of writers and he took the photographs. Patricia said that they enjoyed working together and hoped to do so again.

A sense of "place" has always been a key to Patricia's life and writing. For her the place she has always felt most drawn to is the prairie, even though she has spent many years living on the East Coast. Like *Sarah*, who always remembered the sea, Patricia's heart finds its home among the waves of golden grain and the wide-open skies, the place where she was born, the place where Sarah, too, found a home.

A Word to My Readers:

There is an entire world, complex and layered and full, behind each word or between words, that is often present but not spoken. And it is often what is left unsaid that shapes and empowers a moment, an experience, a book. Or a life. Actors know this. Musicians know it, too. (Horn Book/ALSC 2001, 41)

Books by Patricia MacLachlan

All the Places to Love (HarperCollins, 1994).

Arthur, for the Very First Time (Harper & Row, 1980; Cornerstone Books, 1990; Econo-Clad Books, 1999).

Baby (Delacorte Press, 1993; Econo-Clad Books, 1999).

Caleb's Story (HarperCollins, 2001; Harper Trophy, 2002).

Cassie Binegar (Harper & Row, 1982; Econo-Clad Books, 1999).

The Facts and Fictions of Minna Pratt (Harper & Row, 1988; Econo-Clad Books, 1999).

Journey (Delacorte Press, 1991; Econo-Clad Books, 1999).

Letter Perfect: A Guide to Practical Proofreading (Econo-Clad Books, 1999).

Mama One, Mama Two (Harper & Row, 1982).

Moon, Stars, Frogs, and Friends (Pantheon, 1980).

Painting the Wind (Joanna Cotler Books, 2003).

Sarah, Plain and Tall (Harper & Row, 1985).

Seven Kisses in a Row (Harper & Row, 1983; Econo-Clad Books, 1999).

The Sick Day (Pantheon Books, 1979; Random Library, 2001).

Skylark (HarperCollins, 1994).

Three Names (HarperCollins, 1991; Econo-Clad Books, 1999).

Through Grandpa's Eyes (Harper & Row, 1980; Econo-Clad Books, 1999).

Tomorrow's Wizard (1982; Harcourt, Brace & Co., 1996; Econo-Clad Books, 1999).

Unclaimed Treasures (Harper & Row, 1984; Econo-Clad Books, 1999).

What You Know First (HarperCollins, 1995; HarperCollins Juvenile Books, 1998).

For More Information About/by Patricia MacLachlan

Commire, Anne, ed. 1990. *Something About the Author: Facts and Pictures About Contemporary Authors and Illustrators of Books for Young People.* Vol. 62. Gale Research.

Horn Book and Association for Library Service to Children (ALSC), American Library Association. 2001. *Newbery and Caldecott Medal Books, 1986–2000: A Comprehensive Guide to the Winners.* Horn Book and Association for Library Service to Children, American Library Association.

Kovacs, Deborah, and James Preller. 1991. *Meet the Authors and Illustrators: 60 Creators of Favorite Children's Books Talk About Their Work.* Scholastic.

Note: Indicated citations from a personal interview with the author, May 1994.

1987: Albert Sidney "Sid" Fleischman

Born   March 16, 1920
            Brooklyn, New York

Married   Betty Taylor,
            January 25, 1942
            (three children: Jane,
            Paul, and Anne)

Awards and Honors

Newbery Medal (Action and Adventure; Historical Fiction): *The Whipping Boy* (Greenwillow Books, 1986)

School Library Journal's Best Books, 1996: *The Abracadabra Kid: A Writer's Life* (Greenwillow Books, 1996; Econo-Clad Books, 1999)

Spur Award, Western Writers of America, 1963: *By the Great Horn Spoon!* (Little, Brown, 1963; Econo-Clad Books, 1999)

Lewis Carroll Shelf Award, 1969

Southern California Council on Literature for Children Award, 1964: *By the Great Horn Spoon!* (Little, Brown, 1963; Econo-Clad Books, 1999); 1997: *The Abracadabra Kid: A Writer's Life* (Greenwillow Books, 1996; Econo-Clad Books, 1999)

American Library Association Notable Children's Book, 1987: *The Whipping Boy* (Greenwillow Books, 1986); 1991: *The Midnight Horse* (Greenwillow Books, 1990; Econo-Clad Books, 1999); 1993: *Jim Ugly* (Greenwillow Books, 1992; Econo-Clad Books, 1999); 1999: *Bandit's Moon* (Greenwillow Books, 1998; Yearling Books, 2000); 1999: *Jingo Django* (Little, Brown, 1971; Econo-Clad Books, 1999)

American Library Association Notable Book for Young Adults, 1997: *The Abracadabra Kid: A Writer's Life* (Greenwillow Books, 1996; Econo-Clad Books, 1999)

Boston Globe-Horn Book Award, 1979: *Humbug Mountain* (Little, Brown, 1978)

About the Author and His Writing

Albert Sidney "Sid" Fleischman was born on March 16, 1920, in Brooklyn, New York. Shortly thereafter, the family moved to San Diego, California, where he grew up.

228

As a boy, he became fascinated with the art of magic. He began learning magic tricks in fifth grade and wrote a book about magic that was published when he was in his teens.

Sid left high school and entered the world of vaudeville, performing on the stage as a magician. He lived a life of adventure, traveling on the road, and even panned for gold in California. Many of his adventures later found a home within the plots of his books. With the advent of "talking pictures," vaudeville quickly lost its shine as a primary form of entertainment.

Then World War II broke out and the young magician went to war, serving on a destroyer escort in the United States Navy. When the war ended, Sid returned to San Diego and attended college, graduating in 1949. He and his wife, Betty Taylor, married in 1942 and had three children: Jane, Paul, and Anne. Paul grew up to be a writer and won the Newbery Medal himself in 1989. Sid and Paul are the only Newbery Medal winners from the same family.

> Writing one book doesn't teach you how to write the next one. (Kovacs and Preller 1993, 88)

For a time Sid worked as a reporter for the San Diego *Daily Journal*. When the newspaper went out of business, he started writing fiction, mostly suspense and mystery thrillers. Some of his manuscripts were purchased by motion picture companies and turned into films. This led Sid into writing screenplays, which he continued to do throughout his career in writing.

Motivated in part by his own children, Sid wrote and published his first children's book in 1961. *Mr. Mysterious & Company* (Little, Brown, 1962) was about a magician, a character dear to Sid's heart.

Sid had a gift for writing with humor and one for creating colorful, memorable characters that his readers gobbled up. He didn't set out to write a series, but one of the characters from his books for children, a fellow by the name of McBroom, became so popular that Sid wrote a dozen novels with McBroom as the central figure.

Sid never liked writing a first draft of a novel and then rewriting it. Instead he preferred to rewrite his books a page at a time, before moving on to the next page. There were times he rewrote the same page over and over again before he felt that he had gotten it just right. By the time Sid finished a book, it was ready to be sent to the publisher.

When Sid visited schools and talked with children, he always made sure to tell them that writing was hard work. He said it took practice, like learning a musical instrument or perfecting a magic trick.

There is another kind of magic in the way Sid wrote his books. He never knew how the stories would end. He didn't use outlines and never wanted to have the whole story figured out before he wrote it. "I am audience as well as author," he wrote (Silvey 1994, 246). Sid didn't want to know if he was going to pull a rabbit out of his writing hat or some other character he hadn't even thought about. He said he liked the excitement of learning the story as he wrote, just as the reader does.

Sid took lots of notes when he was working on a book. He discovered everything he could about a topic. Even though much of the research material didn't end up in a particular book, it sometimes turned up in another story.

Sid originally envisioned his book *The Whipping Boy* as a picture book. As he gathered the material about a prince and his "whipping boy," a child chosen to take any punishment earned by the prince, he realized that the story needed more room to be told. He ended up writing the book as a novel. In 1987 the book won the Newbery Medal. The story, witty and skillfully written, is often used by schools to teach students about a time and place very different from our more modern age.

In 1969, Sid was awarded the Lewis Carroll Shelf Award, and in 1979, the Boston Globe-Horn Book Award for fiction. He received many other awards for his writing.

Sid's autobiography, *The Abracadabra Kid: A Writer's Life,* was published in 1996. The title sums up the two facets of Sid's life that he so successfully combines: the magician and the writer, whose books are indeed a kind of magic in their own right.

A Word to My Readers:

Novels are written in the dark. At least, mine are. Unlike more sensible authors, I start Chapter One with rarely a notion of the story that's about to unfold. It's like wandering into a pitch-black theater and groping around for the lights. One by one, the spots and footlights come on, catching a character or two against a painted backdrop. I sit back and enjoy the show. When the final curtain falls a year or two later, the stage is ablaze with lights, and I have a new novel. (Silvey 1994, 246)

Books by Albert Sidney "Sid" Fleischman

The Abracadabra Kid: A Writer's Life (Greenwillow Books, 1996; Econo-Clad Books, 1999).

Bandit's Moon (Greenwillow Books, 1998; Yearling Books, 2000).

The Bloodhound Gang in the Case of Princess Tomorrow (Random House/Children's Television Workshop, 1981).

The Bloodhound Gang in the Case of the Cackling Ghost (Random House/Children's Television Workshop, 1981).

The Bloodhound Gang in the Case of the Flying Clock (Random House/Children's Television Workshop, 1981).

The Bloodhound Gang in the Case of the Secret Message (Random House/Children's Television Workshop, 1981).

The Bloodhound Gang in the Case of the 264 Pound Burglar (Random House/Children's Television Workshop, 1982).

The Bloodhound Gang's Secret Code Book: With Five Stories (Random House/Children's Television Workshop, 1983).

Bo and Mzzz Mad (Greenwillow Books, 2001).

By the Great Horn Spoon! (Little, Brown, 1963; Econo-Clad Books, 1999).

A Carnival of Animals (Greenwillow Books, 2000).

Chancy and the Grand Rascal (Little, Brown, 1966; Greenwillow Books, 1997; Econo-Clad Books, 1999).

Counterspy Express (Ace Books, 1954).

The Ghost in the Noonday Sun (Little, Brown, 1965; Greenwillow Books, 1989; Laureleaf, 1999).

The Ghost on Saturday Night (Little, Brown, 1974; Greenwillow Books, 1997; Econo-Clad Books, 1999).

Here Comes McBroom: Three More Tall Tales (Greenwillow Books, 1992; Peter Smith, 1999).

The Hey Hey Man (Little, Brown, 1979).

Humbug Mountain (Little, Brown, 1978; Peter Smith, 1999).

Jim Bridger's Alarm Clock and Other Tall Tales (Dutton, 1978).

Jim Ugly (Greenwillow Books, 1992; Econo-Clad Books, 1999).

Jingo Django (Little, Brown, 1971; Econo-Clad Books, 1999).

Kate's Secret Riddle Book (Watts, 1977).

Longbeard the Wizard (Little, Brown, 1970).

McBroom and the Beanstalk (Little, Brown, 1978).

McBroom and the Big Wind (W. W. Norton, 1967; Little, Brown, 1982).

McBroom and the Great Race (Little, Brown, 1980).

McBroom Tells a Lie (Little, Brown, 1976; Price Stern Sloan, 1999).

McBroom Tells the Truth (W. W. Norton, 1966; Little, Brown, 1981; Price Stern Sloan, 1998; Econo-Clad Books, 1999).

McBroom the Rainmaker (Little, Brown, 1982; Price Stern Sloan, 1999).

McBroom's Almanac (Little, Brown, 1984).

McBroom's Ear (W. W. Norton, 1969; Little, Brown, 1982).

McBroom's Ghost (Grosset & Dunlap, 1971; Little, Brown, 1981; Price Stern Sloan, 1998; Econo-Clad Books, 1999).

McBroom's Wonderful One Acre Farm: Three Tall Tales (Greenwillow Books, 1992; Econo-Clad Books, 1999).

McBroom's Zoo (Grosset & Dunlap, 1972; Little, Brown, 1982).

Me and the Man on the Moon Eyed Horse (Little, Brown, 1977).

The Midnight Horse (Greenwillow Books, 1990; Econo-Clad Books, 1999).

Mr. Mysterious & Company (Little, Brown, 1962; Joy Street Books, 1990; Greenwillow Books, 1997; Econo-Clad Books, 1999).

Mr. Mysterious's Secrets of Magic (Little, Brown, 1975).

The Scarebird (Greenwillow Books, 1988; Mulberry Books, 1994; Econo-Clad Books, 1999).

The Straw Donkey Case (Phoenix Press, 1948).

The Thirteenth Floor: A Ghost Story (Greenwillow Books, 1995; Econo-Clad Books, 1999).

The Whipping Boy (Greenwillow Books, 1986; Cornerstone Books, 1989; Econo-Clad Books, 1999).

The Wooden Cat Man (Little, Brown, 1972).

For More Information About/by Albert Sidney "Sid" Fleischman

Autobiography: 1996. *The Abracadabra Kid, A Writer's Life.* Greenwillow Books, 1996.

Kovacs, Deborah, and James Preller. 1993. *Meet the Authors and Illustrators: 60 Creators of Favorite Children's Books Talk About Their Work.* Vol. 2. Scholastic.

Silvey, Anita, ed. 1994. *Children's Books and Their Creators.* Houghton Mifflin.

1988: Russell Freedman

Born   October 11, 1929
                  San Francisco,
                  California

Awards and Honors

Newbery Medal (Non-Fiction, Biography): *Lincoln: A Photobiography* (Clarion, 1987)

Newbery Honor Book for 1992: *The Wright Brothers: How They Invented the Airplane* (Holiday House, 1991)

Newbery Honor Book for 1994: *Eleanor Roosevelt: A Life of Discovery* (Clarion, 1993)

Golden Kite Award, 1991: *The Wright Brothers: How They Invented the Airplane* (Holiday House, 1991); 1993: *Eleanor Roosevelt: A Life of Discovery* (Clarion, 1993); 1994: *Kids at Work: Lewis Hine and the Crusade Against Child Labor* (Clarion, 1994); 1998: *Martha Graham: A Dancer's Life* (Clarion, 1998)

Knickerbocker Award for Juvenile Literature, 1993 (body of work)

Boston Globe-Horn Book Award, 1994

School Library Journal's Best Books, 1996: *The Life and Death of Crazy Horse* (Holiday House, 1996); 1998: *Martha Graham: A Dancer's Life* (Clarion, 1998); 1999: *Babe Didrikson Zaharias: The Making of a Champion* (Clarion, 1999); 2001: *Give Me Liberty! The Story of the Declaration of Independence* (Holiday House, 2000, 2001)

Laura Ingalls Wilder Award, 1998

About the Author and His Writing

Russell Freedman had a streak of mischief in him when he was a boy. A visit to the office of Mrs. Koeppe, the elementary school principal, was not an unusual event in his life. The many hours spent in the little waiting room outside her office weren't entirely wasted, for they gave Russell time to study the portrait of Abraham Lincoln that hung on the wall.

Russell and Mr. Lincoln must have connected in a special way. Nearly half a century after those many office visits to the principal, Russell presented the world of literature with another portrait of Abraham Lincoln: the 1988 Newbery Medal Book, *Lincoln: A Photobiography.*

In the intervening years, the name Russell Freedman became synonymous with excellent biographies on famous people written for young readers. His book *The Wright Brothers: How They Invented the Airplane* won a Newbery Honor Award in 1992. *Eleanor Roosevelt: A Life of Discovery* also won a Newbery Honor Award in 1994.

Books were part of Russell's family history even before he was born. Russell's father, a representative for Macmillan Publishing Company, met his future wife on a visit to the bookstore where she worked as a sales clerk. The Freedman home was filled with books, and authors frequently came to visit. When Russell's father traveled to various bookstores and libraries as part of his job, Russell often got to tag along.

> Writing a biography is like getting to know a person. You get to know that person better than you know yourself. (Kovacs and Preller 1991, 91)

Getting into mischief wasn't Russell's only pursuit during his school years. He also wrote a comic strip for his grade school newspaper and had samples of his writing in every school publication. He wrote fiction and poetry in both high school and college. From the start, Russell loved to write so he experimented with different forms of the craft. He worked as a reporter and editor at the Associated Press and also as a publicity writer for several network television shows.

Russell received encouragement to pursue his dream of being a writer from his mother and from a fifth-grade teacher, Miss Tennessee Kent. Miss Kent was the first person outside of his family who made him feel as if he had some talent. Along with that talent, Russell learned a lot about writing by doing it. At first he simply liked the idea of being a writer. The more he wrote, the more he discovered that it took more than just dreaming about being a writer to be one. "Along the way," he said, "you discover that there's a huge gap between thinking and writing, between those luminous images dancing around in your imagination and the cold reality of words on paper" (interview, February 2001).

Russell read a variety of books while he was growing up: novels, short stories, history, biography, science. He read anything that caught his eye. Two of his favorites were *Treasure Island* by Robert Louis Stevenson, and Ernest Thompson Seton's *Wild Animals I Have Known.* His literary hero was Howard Pease, who wrote adventure novels often based on the sea. He said he reads *Charlotte's Web* by E. B. White once every year, just to remind him what good writing is.

Russell didn't set out to be a writer of nonfiction books for young readers. "I wandered into the field by chance and immediately felt right at home," he wrote. "I couldn't wait to get started on my next book. It was as if I had found myself, even though I hadn't known that I had been lost" (Silvey 1995, 254). Once at home in the world of children's literature, Russell never felt the urge to leave.

Getting the facts straight is extremely important to Russell. Sometimes he studies rooms where people lived, so that he can describe those rooms right down to the smallest detail. Along with ensuring that his visual descriptions are accurate, Russell works hard to get a true sense of the personality of an individual. By combining facts, photographs, and personal attributes, Russell's books give a full and well-rounded picture of a person's life, which bring that person alive for Russell and for his readers.

Russell finds that writing nonfiction is exciting, and he seeks to convey this excitement in his books. He wants to capture the attention of his readers, to draw them into the remarkable experience of learning about ordinary people who made a mark on the world. "The task of the nonfiction writers is to find the story—the narrative line—that exists in nearly every subject, be it the life of a person or the life of a cell," Russell once said (Silvey 1995, 254).

While working on his biographies, Russell became an expert on the lives of his subjects. He read over thirty books about Eleanor Roosevelt before writing about her life. He enjoyed the research that took him around the country and around the world, studying the places where his subjects lived and worked. Russell saw firsthand many amazing artifacts, from an actual letter written by Abraham Lincoln to the house in France where Louis Braille was born.

Russell once said that he enjoyed writing so much that when he worked on a book, he wrote seven days a week. He didn't feel the need for hobbies, because he had no desire to get away from his writing, which he found much more satisfying than any hobby. He does, however, take time off in between the writing of books to travel, and often returns from his journeys with an idea for his next book.

Coming up with new ideas was never a problem, according to Russell. One of his joys in writing nonfiction is that he can write about any subject that interests him, believing that a topic that he finds intriguing will be of interest to others, too.

Russell would write the first draft of his books with a pencil and legal pad. This gave him time to think about the subject as he worked. He typed the second draft on an old manual typewriter because he liked the sound and feel of the machine. By the end of the second draft, he felt that the book was still in the beginning stages, so he retyped the manuscript several more times. This process helped him recognize the places where the language or material needed work. He said that if he rewrote a book five times, it had to be pretty good. If he rewrote it six times, it would be even better. So he rewrote it seven times.

Russell once described the experience of winning the Newbery Medal as "riding a rainbow to the moon!" (interview, February 2001). He couldn't believe the news when he was first informed. It had been over thirty years since a nonfiction book had been awarded the Medal, and it took a while for the reality to sink in. Russell said that winning the Newbery Medal was a wonderful gift for a writer because it gave a writer the freedom to pursue new ideas without financial pressures and constraints. Winning the Medal gave Russell the opportunity to realize a childhood dream: to travel throughout mainland China.

Russell Freedman will be remembered as an author who excelled at writing biographies of other people. Suppose some day someone writes a biography of him? What would be the one thing he would most want it to say? His answer: "More than anything, I would want it to say that my books are still being read!" (interview, February 2001). There is little doubt that Russell Freedman's books will always find a place on a bookshelf or in an eager reader's hands. Those readers may well include a few mischievous children sitting in the waiting room of a principal's office.

A Word to My Readers:

I've always found that a good book is like a lifelong friend, for it lives in your mind and imagination forever after. (interview, February 2001)

Books by Russell Freedman

Animal Architects (Holiday House, 1971).

Animal Fathers (Holiday House, 1976).

Animal Games (Holiday House, 1976).

Animal Instincts (Holiday House, 1970).

Animal Superstars: Biggest, Strongest, Fastest, Smartest (Prentice Hall, 1981).

Babe Didrikson Zaharias: The Making of a Champion (Clarion, 1999).

The Brains of Animals and Man (Holiday House, 1972).

Buffalo Hunt (Holiday House, 1988).

Can Bears Predict Earthquakes? Unsolved Mysteries of Animal Behavior (Prentice Hall, 1982).

Children of the Wild West (Clarion, 1983; Econo-Clad Books, 1999).

Confucius: The Golden Rule (Arthur A. Levine Books, 2002).

Cowboys of the Wild West (Clarion, 1985; Econo-Clad Books, 1999).

Dinosaurs and Their Young (Holiday House, 1983).

Eleanor Roosevelt: A Life of Discovery (Clarion, 1993; Econo-Clad Books, 1999).

Farm Babies (Holiday House, 1981).

First Days of Life (Holiday House, 1974).

Franklin Delano Roosevelt (Clarion, 1990; Econo-Clad Books, 1999).

Getting Born (Holiday House, 1978).

Give Me Liberty! The Story of the Declaration of Independence (Holiday House, 2000, 2001).

Growing Up Wild: How Young Animals Survive (Holiday House, 1975).

Hanging On: How Animals Carry Their Young (Holiday House, 1977).

Holiday House, the First Fifty Years (Holiday House, 1985).

Holiday House, the First Sixty Five Years (Holiday House, 2000).

How Animals Defend Their Young (Dutton, 1978).

How Animals Learn (Holiday House, 1969).

How Birds Fly (Holiday House, 1977).

Immigrant Kids (Dutton, 1980; Puffin Books, 1995; Econo-Clad Books, 1999).

In the Days of the Vaqueros: America's First True Cowboys (Clarion, 2001).

Indian Chiefs (Holiday House, 1987).

Indian Winter (Holiday House, 1992).

Jules Verne, Portrait of a Prophet (Holiday House, 1965).

Kids at Work: Lewis Hine and the Crusade Against Child Labor (Clarion, 1994; Econo-Clad Books, 1999).

Killer Fish (Holiday House, 1982).

Killer Snakes (Holiday House, 1982).

The Life and Death of Crazy Horse (Holiday House, 1996).

Lincoln: A Photobiography (Clarion, 1987; Econo-Clad Books, 1999).

Martha Graham: A Dancer's Life (Clarion, 1998).

Out of Darkness: The Story of Louis Braille (Clarion, 1997; Houghton Mifflin, 1999).

Rattlesnakes (Holiday House, 1984).

Scouting with Baden Powell (Holiday House, 1967).

Sharks (Holiday House, 1985).

Teenagers Who Made History (Holiday House, 1961).

They Lived with the Dinosaurs (Holiday House, 1980).

Thomas Alva Edison: A Concise Biography (American R.D.M. Corp., 1966).

Tooth and Claw: A Look at Animal Weapons (Holiday House, 1980).

2000 Years of Space Travel (Holiday House, 1963).

When Winter Comes (Dutton, 1981).

The Wright Brothers: How They Invented the Airplane (Holiday House, 1991; Econo-Clad Books, 1999).

For More Information About/by Russell Freedman

Kovacs, Deborah, and James Preller. 1991. *Meet the Authors and Illustrators: 60 Creators of Favorite Children's Books Talk About Their Work.* Scholastic.

Silvey, Anita, ed. 1995. *Children's Books and Their Creators.* Houghton Mifflin.

Note: Indicated citations from a personal interview with the author, February 2001.

1989: Paul Fleischman

Born   September 5, 1952
                Monterey, California

Married   Becky Mojica,
                December 15, 1978
                (children: Dana and Seth)

Awards and Honors

Newbery Medal (Poetry): *Joyful Noise: Poems for Two Voices* (Harper & Row, 1988)
Newbery Honor Book for 1982: *Graven Images: 3 Stories* (Harper & Row, 1982)
School Library Journal's Best Books, 1997: *Seedfolks* (HarperCollins, 1997); 1998: *Whirligig* (H. Holt & Co., 1998); 1999: *Weslandia* (Candlewick Press, 1999; Scholastic Trade, 2000); 2001: *Seek* (Cricket Books, 2001)
American Library Association Notable Children's Book Award, 1983: *Graven Images: 3 Stories* (Harper & Row, 1982; Harper Trophy, 1999); 1991: *Saturnalia* (Harper & Row, 1990); 1992: *The Borning Room* (HarperCollins, 1991); 2000: *Weslandia* (Candlewick Press, 1999; Scholastic Trade, 2000); 2002: *Seek* (Cricket Books, 2001)

About the Author and His Writing

Many children grow up hearing their parents read them books aloud. Very few grow up hearing the books their own parents have written and published.

Paul Fleischman and his brother and sister were often the first audience for their father's current book in progress. Sid Fleischman was a prolific writer of books for children, and the winner of the Newbery Medal in 1987 for *The Whipping Boy*.

Paul's first venture into the world of print came when his parents brought home a printing press. He enjoyed making cards and stationery for his parents and their friends.

But music was what really touched Paul's heart. He lay in bed at night, listening to a short-wave radio he earned in the fifth grade. That radio in particular gave him access to music from around the world, with a wide variety of expression. The sounds and music of other countries soothed and fascinated him, Arabic music in particular.

Paul also listened to baseball games, learning the cadence of Vin Scully's distinctive voice as he announced the ups and downs of the Los Angeles Dodgers. On Saturday evenings he basked in the melodious voice of the gifted radio host and storyteller Garrison Keillor on *Prairie Home Companion.* Paul even skipped classes in high school in order to hibernate in the local public library, reading and listening to classical music.

After two years in college at the University of Berkeley, Paul dropped out. He rode his bicycle north to Vancouver, Washington, then caught a train to New Hampshire, where he settled for a while. Growing up in California, Paul said he didn't know much about eastern winters and he arrived in New Hampshire totally unprepared, without even a hat or a pair of gloves.

> Every chapter, every paragraph, every sentence, I discovered, has an arc to it like a musical phrase. Every word has both a meaning and a music. (Horn Book/ALSC 2001, 94)

At a local college he discovered a group of people who played the recorder, a medieval musical instrument that Paul had mastered. It was then that he began to realize how music was a lot like writing prose, with its distinctive rhythms and flow.

Paul returned to college in a warmer climate and graduated from the University of New Mexico in 1977.

Soon he began to try his own hand at writing. He wrote a book, *The Birthday Tree* (Harper & Row), and showed it to his father, who liked the story, as did the editor to whom Paul sent the manuscript. The book, Paul's first, was published in 1979.

Paul combined his love of birds and music in *I Am Phoenix: Poems for Two Voices* (Harper & Row, 1985). In a sense, the book was the prelude to *Joyful Noise: Poems for Two Voices,* which won the Newbery Medal in 1989, the second book of poetry to ever win a Newbery Medal.

When Paul's book was named the Newbery winner, he and his father, Sid, became the first parent and child in the same family to both win the prestigious award. Paul's book *Graven Images* had been named a Newbery Honor Book in 1982. After the 1989 Newbery Medal announcement, when people told Sid that his son was following in his footsteps, Sid's response was, "No, I'm following in his!" (Patrick 1999, 121).

Some people wonder where Paul got the idea to write a book about the music and poetry of insects. *Joyful Noise* began first as two separate poems that Paul had once written: "The Moth's Serenade" and "Requiem." Paul had intended to write a novel, but the two he began didn't seem to go anywhere. He returned to his poems, wrote twelve more, and put them all together in a book. Insects have never been more appealing than they are in *Joyful Noise.*

Paul said that he got his ideas from a variety of sources. One book was inspired by an ancient Roman festival in which masters and their slaves exchanged places for a time. The genesis for another came as he accumulated knowledge about the therapeutic value of plants and gardens. The resulting *Seedfolks* (HarperCollins, 1997) was written in thirteen different voices, each distinct and captivating.

Paul maintained an interest in studies of contrasts, such as the differences between light and dark, good and evil, innocence and danger. Though father and son, Paul and Sid are another contrast, this one in writing styles. Both are gifted in their own way. Whether another parent and child will win the Newbery Medal some day remains to be seen. Even if that happens, Paul and Sid will always have a unique place in the history of children's literature.

A Word to My Readers:

What can you make out of a handful of sticks? How can you connect a half-dozen characters? It's much the same problem and the same joy: the joy involved in joining both post to lintel and hero to villain; in rummaging for supplies at the beach or among books, in watching a wall go up or a paragraph. The joy found in making has begotten all my books. (Horn Book/ALSC 2001, 95)

Books by Paul Fleischman

The Animal Hedge (Dutton, 1983).

Big Talk: Poems for Four Voices (Candlewick Press, 2000).

The Birthday Tree (Harper & Row, 1979).

The Borning Room (HarperCollins, 1991).

Bull Run (HarperCollins, 1993).

Cannibal in the Mirror, edited by Paul Fleischman (Twenty-First Century Books, 2000).

Coming-and-Going-Men: Four Tales (Harper & Row, 1985).

Copier Creations (HarperCollins, 1993).

Dateline: Troy (Candlewick Press, 1996).

A Fate Totally Worse Than Death (Candlewick Press, 1995).

Finzel the Farsighted (Dutton, 1983).

Ghosts' Grace: A Poem of Praise for Four Voices (Laura Geringer Books, 1996).

Graven Images: 3 Stories (Harper & Row, 1982; HarperTrophy, 1999).

The Half-a-Moon Inn (Harper & Row, 1980).

I Am Phoenix: Poems for Two Voices (Harper & Row, 1985).

Joyful Noise: Poems for Two Voices (Harper & Row, 1988).

Lost!: A Story in String (H. Holt & Co., 2000).

Mind's Eye (H. Holt & Co., 1999; Laureleaf, 2001).

Path of the Pale Horse (Harper & Row, 1983).

Phoebe Danger, Detective, in The Case of the Two Minute Cough (Houghton Mifflin, 1983).

Rear-View Mirrors (Harper & Row, 1986).

Rondo in C (Harper & Row, 1988).

Saturnalia (Harper & Row, 1990).

Seedfolks (HarperCollins, 1997).

Seek (Cricket Books, 2001).

Shadow Play: Story (Harper & Row, 1990).

Time Train (HarperCollins, 1991).

Townsend's Warbler (HarperCollins, 1992).

Weslandia (Candlewick Press, 1999; Scholastic Trade, 2000).

Whirligig (H. Holt & Co., 1998).

For More Information About/by Paul Fleischman

Horn Book and Association for Library Service to Children (ALSC), American Library Association. 2001. *The Newbery and Caldecott Medal Books, 1986–2000: A Comprehensive Guide to the Winners.* Horn Book and Association for Library Service to Children, American Library Association.

Patrick, Diane. 1999. A Living Legacy. *Publishers Weekly,* 8 February, 121.

1990/1994: Lois Lowry

Born   March 20, 1937
                   Honolulu, Hawaii

Married   Donald Lowry, 1956
                   (children: Alix,
                   Kristin, Donald
                   [Grey], and Benjamin)

Awards and Honors

Newbery Medal for 1990 (Historical Fiction): *Number the Stars* (Houghton Mifflin, 1989)

Newbery Medal for 1994 (Science Fiction, Fantasy): *The Giver* (Houghton Mifflin, 1993)

Golden Kite Award, 1987: *Rabble Starkey* (Houghton Mifflin, 1987)

School Library Journal's Best Books, 1996: *See You Around, Sam* (Houghton Mifflin, 1996; Econo-Clad Books, 1999)

Boston Globe-Horn Book Award, 1987: *Rabble Starkey* (Houghton Mifflin, 1987; G. K. Hall, 1989; Econo-Clad Books, 1999)

American Library Association Notable Children's Book, 1981: *Autumn Street* (Houghton Mifflin, 1980; Econo-Clad Books, 1999); 1982: *Anastasia Again!* (Houghton Mifflin, 1981; Econo-Clad Books, 1999); 1984: *The One-Hundredth Thing about Caroline* (Houghton Mifflin, 1983; Econo-Clad Books, 1999); 1994: *The Giver* (Houghton Mifflin, 1993); 2003: *Gooney Bird Breen* (Houghton Mifflin, 2002)

About the Author and Her Writing

Lois Lowry was one of the last people to learn that she had won the Newbery Medal for the second time.

"I was on a ship in Antarctica when the announcement was made," she said. "Of course, I had no access to newspapers, phones, TV, or radio, so I didn't know it had happened. A cable was finally sent to me on board the ship. There I was, with all the icebergs and penguins, feeling on top of the world when I was actually at the bottom of the world" (interview, September 22, 1994).

In 1990, Lois won her first Newbery Medal for *Number the Stars,* a story about how a Danish girl and her family helped save their Jewish neighbors from the Nazis during World War II. She was at home when the call came from the Newbery committee: "I was sitting at my desk when they called me and said that they had selected me for the Medal. I didn't realize this at the time, but apparently they have a speaker phone there so that the entire committee can hear the conversation. (Rumor even has it that they have a bottle of champagne and that some newly notified recipients have heard them pop the cork!) Anyway, I think they would have enjoyed it if I had shrieked and been babbling and stammering in my surprise. And certainly I *was* surprised. But I tend to become silent in the throes of astonishment. And so, although I was very, very honored and pleased, and surprised, I simply gulped and fell silent. I was probably a disappointment to them in my reaction" (interview, November 6, 1993). When Lois won her second Newbery in 1994 for *The Giver,* she became only the fourth person to win the medal twice.

Lois was born in Hawaii. Her father, a career Army officer, was sent to the Pacific shortly after World War II began. Lois, her older sister, and her mother went to live in Carlisle, Pennsylvania, with her mother's parents. They moved into their own home a few houses away after the birth of Lois's brother. Most of Lois's childhood memories came from those years spent in Pennsylvania.

> I read a whole lot, although I don't read children's books. My favorite books tend to be collected letters of writers. I think there will be fewer and fewer of these, because nobody writes letters any more, except people like me. (interview, November 6, 1993)

"I remember those years as very happy times," she said. "My grandmother bought this three story stone building that had been an old flour mill. It had burned, so it was just the walls, and she had made it into a summer home. The Appalachian Trail went right past it, so when we were up there in the summer, we would see people hiking up the paths that walked up from as far away as Georgia" (interview, November 6, 1993).

At the age of eleven, Lois and her family moved to Tokyo, Japan, where her father was stationed. A few years later, the family returned to the United States.

Lois attended a private high school in New York. The teachers there took her to the opera and to music recitals and exposed her to a variety of books. One teacher in particular had an important influence on her writing: "I wrote a poem," Lois recalled, "and the teacher had written on it, 'Be sure you keep on writing. I think there's a real possibility that you may do something with it' " (interview, November 6, 1993).

Although Lois always wanted to write, her marriage at the age of nineteen and the births of her four children delayed that goal for a number of years. As her children grew and her marriage ended, Lois returned to college. She began to send articles to magazines and to have them published. An editor who read one of these articles encouraged Lois to try writing for children. Lois took her advice.

Lois said that many of her ideas came from scraps of conversations heard through the years. "Some of them stay with me, and I'll try and use them in my writing. I don't forget them" (interview, November 6, 1993).

Lois once called herself "a very self-disciplined person who is also very flexible." She said she writes almost every day when she is at home. "It's not possible to be creative eight hours a day. I sit at my desk for five hours, and part of that time is creative. I also answer a lot of mail, write essays for journals. I probably spend three hours a day on fiction" (interview, November 6, 1993). Always a hard worker, Lois knew when to take a break to go to the movies with a friend.

> If I could live in another time, I would live in the turn of the century New England. I know there are a lot of drawbacks, but it was such a leisurely time. You went to visit other people and sat and talked and stayed for three weeks. (interview, November 6, 1993)

When Lois would begin to write a book, she already had in mind the beginning and the end. The middle of the story was not always clear at first, but developed when she got to the point of writing it.

Lois claimed that she wasn't bothered by momentary lapses in the writing process. "I get bored with a story sometimes," she once said, "so I set it aside, and go back to it. I guess I don't get panicky if I'm not being creative. I can cook, or go plant flowers" (interview, November 6, 1993).

One time a friend of Lois's asked her what she would be if she weren't a writer. "I told him I'd always had this secret fantasy about being a filmmaker. I'd like to write the screenplay but also do the set design, the casting, the cinematography, the directing, all of it. My friend said, 'Sounds like you already do all that!' He was right. I sit down at my desk, and I create a cast, I choose a set, I design the costumes, I choose the camera angle, and I write the dialogue. His comment lifted a great burden from me. I always thought, if I were just younger, I could start filmmaking. Now I don't feel as if I have to do that" (interview, November 6, 1993).

Along with being an excellent writer, Lois learned to be an accomplished photographer. She took the photographs that became the illustrations for a number of book jackets, including both of her Newbery Medal winners.

In 1995, Lois received a phone call with some very sad news. On the other end of the phone line was her daughter-in-law, Margaret, who was married to Lois's son Grey. They lived with their young daughter in Germany, where Grey served in the United States Air Force. Margaret was calling with the news that Grey had been killed in a plane crash. He was only thirty-six years old. Grief stricken, Lois's writing gave her a way to cope with her son's tragic death.

The Giver, a fantasy, tells the tale of Jonas, a young boy who lives in what seems to be a perfect world. At the age of twelve, Jonas is given the job of Receiver, the one who holds all the memories of his community.

Like Jonas from *The Giver,* Lois, too, is a keeper of memories. Her words and stories have brought comfort and hope as well as joy to her many readers.

A Word to My Readers:

Take hold of the power that you have as an individual. Follow what your heart tells you. Believe in yourself. That's what I try to say in my books. (interview, November 6, 1993)

Books by Lois Lowry

All About Sam (Houghton Mifflin, 1988; Econo-Clad Books, 1999).

Anastasia, Absolutely (Houghton Mifflin, 1995; Econo-Clad Books, 1999).

Anastasia Again! (Houghton Mifflin, 1981; Econo-Clad Books, 1999).

Anastasia, Ask Your Analyst (Houghton Mifflin, 1984; Cornerstone Books, 1989; Econo-Clad Books, 1999).

Anastasia at This Address (Houghton Mifflin, 1991).

Anastasia at Your Service (Houghton Mifflin, 1982, 1989; Econo-Clad Books, 1999).

Anastasia Has the Answers (Houghton Mifflin, 1986; Econo-Clad Books, 1999).

Anastasia Krupnik (Houghton Mifflin, 1979, 1988; Econo-Clad Books, 1999).

Anastasia on Her Own (Houghton Mifflin, 1985; Cornerstone Books, 1989; Econo-Clad Books, 1999).

Anastasia's Chosen Career (Houghton Mifflin, 1987; Econo-Clad Books, 1999).

Attaboy, Sam! (Houghton Mifflin, 1992; Econo-Clad Books, 1999).

Autumn Street (Houghton Mifflin, 1980; Econo-Clad Books, 1999).

Enchantress from the Stars (Walker, 2002).

Find a Stranger, Say Goodbye (Houghton Mifflin, 1978; Econo-Clad Books, 1999).

Gathering Blue (Houghton Mifflin, 2000; Thorndike Press, 2000; Laureleaf, 2002).

The Giver (Houghton Mifflin, 1993; Thorndike Press, 1993).

Gooney Bird Green (Houghton Mifflin, 2002).

Here in Kennebunkport (Durrell Publications, 1978).

Looking Back: A Book of Memories (Houghton Mifflin, 1998; Delacorte Press, 2000).

Number the Stars (Houghton Mifflin, 1989).

The One-Hundredth Thing About Caroline (Houghton Mifflin, 1983; Econo-Clad Books, 1999).

Rabble Starkey (Houghton Mifflin, 1987; G. K. Hall, 1989; Econo-Clad Books, 1999).

See You Around, Sam! (Houghton Mifflin, 1996; Econo-Clad Books, 1999).

Stay! Keeper's Story (Houghton Mifflin, 1997; Econo-Clad Books, 1999).

A Summer to Die (Houghton Mifflin, 1977; Econo-Clad Books, 1999).

Switcharound (Houghton Mifflin, 1985; Econo-Clad Books, 1999; Econo-Clad Books, 1999).

Taking Care of Terrific (Houghton Mifflin, 1983; Cornerstone Books, 1989).

Us and Uncle Fraud (Houghton Mifflin, 1984).

Your Move, J.P.! (Houghton Mifflin, 1990; Econo-Clad Books, 1999).

Zooman Sam (Houghton Mifflin, 1999; Young Yearling, 2001).

For More Information About/by Lois Lowry

Autobiography: 1998. *Looking Back: A Book of Memories.* Houghton Mifflin; Delacorte Press, 2000.

Horn Book and Association for Library Service to Children (ALSC), American Library Association. 2001. *Newbery and Caldecott Medal Books, 1986–2000: A Comprehensive Guide to the Winners.* Horn Book and Association for Library Service to Children, American Library Association.

H. W. Wilson. 1983. *The Fifth Book of Junior Authors and Illustrators.* H. W. Wilson.

Note: Indicated citations from personal interviews with the author, November 6, 1993, and September 22, 1994.

1991: Jerry Spinelli

Born   February 1, 1941
                  Norristown, Pennsylvania

Married   Eileen Mesi, May 21, 1977
                  (children: Kevin, Barbara,
                  Jeffrey, Molly, Sean,
                  and Ben)

Awards and Honors

Newbery Medal (Contemporary Life): *Maniac Magee* (Little, Brown, 1990)

Newbery Honor Book for 1998: *Wringer* (HarperCollins, 1997)

Boston Globe-Horn Book Award, 1990: *Maniac Magee* (Little, Brown, 1990)

D. C. Fisher Award, 1992 *Maniac Magee* (Little, Brown, 1990)

School Library Journal's Best Books, 1996: *Crash* (Knopf/Random House, 1996; Econo-Clad Books, 1999); 1997: *Wringer* (HarperCollins, 1997; Thorndike Press, 2000)

American Library Association Notable Children's Book, 1991: *Maniac Magee* (Little, Brown, 1990); 1998: *Wringer* (HarperCollins, 1997; Thorndike Press, 2000)

About the Author and His Writing

You don't have to be an avid reader as a child to grow up and write great books. You could spend your youth playing sports, dreaming about becoming a shortstop for a major league baseball team, like Jerry Spinelli did.

Jerry was born in Norristown, Pennsylvania. He lived in a brick row house in a neighborhood that later became a model for Two Mills, the town in *Maniac Magee*. Jerry didn't read much as a kid, except for comic books and sports novels. He preferred grabbing a baseball glove or bat or basketball and heading outdoors for the day.

Although Jerry remembers his childhood as a happy one, if he could change one thing, it would be to go back and read more books. That might be why the main character in his 1991 Newbery Medal book, *Maniac Magee,* always has a book in hand. "I think maybe it was the closest I can come to going back and doing it right and putting some more balance into my younger years," Jerry once said with a touch of regret (interview, April 6, 1994).

The lack of reading didn't hurt Jerry when he decided to write. In fact, all those experiences from his childhood inspired the stories that have secured him a place as a much-beloved author of books for young readers.

He got his first taste of writing for publication when the local newspaper published a poem he composed in high school after a victory by the home team. "I dropped my bat and picked up a pencil and started to think of myself as a writer," he recalled, remembering back to the thrill of seeing his words in print (interview, April 6, 1994). Little did he know that it would be a quarter of a century before his first book was published, twenty-five years during which he wrote constantly, athough not the kind of writing he longed to do.

After earning an undergraduate degree from Gettysburg College in 1963 and a master's from Johns Hopkins University, Jerry tried a couple different jobs before settling in at Chilton, a company that published journals and manuals for a variety of businesses. Jerry spent his workdays writing descriptions of automotive items for department store catalogs that were published by Chilton. He purposely chose a job that didn't take a lot of energy so that he could devote his lunch hours, evenings, and weekends to writing novels.

Jerry wrote four books for adults. Each time he completed one, he began sending the manuscripts to publishers, waiting eagerly for the day when the letter of acceptance would arrive in the mailbox. Letters came, but not acceptance letters. He collected one rejection letter after another. He began to wonder if he should keep on writing.

> I write, among other things, to touch the reader. A writer does his thing and then it doesn't even come out until a year later. Who knows, someone might be rejoicing over what they're reading in Madison, Wisconsin, but you don't know it. (interview, April 6, 1994)

"I felt like giving up about every other day. When year after year goes by and you keep looking in the mailbox and all you get are rejection slips . . . I could have papered a house with the number of rejection slips that I got. There was a lot of discouragement" (interview, April 6, 1994).

But Jerry kept trying. "It's not so much that I became immune to discouragement. It's just that the next day would dawn, and as each day would go by, I'd feel a bit better. After several days, I'd figure, Well, I might as well put it back in the mail one more time'" (interview, April 6, 1994).

Then Jerry got the urge to write a book about a thirteen-year-old boy who kept tugging at his inner muse. He sent the book to his agent, who shopped it around the major publishers. The word came back: this book isn't a book for adults, it's a book for young readers. The agent started marketing it as a book for a younger audience. The book, *Space Station Seventh Grade* (Little, Brown, 1982), was eventually accepted for publication. Jerry became a children's writer without even intending to do so.

Still, Jerry kept his day job. By then he had married Eileen Mesi, another writer whom he'd met early on at Chilton's. The marriage brought to Jerry not only a wife who understood about writing but six children as well. Suddenly, the former bachelor's life was filled with the everyday experiences of living in a house full of young people, experiences that served to draw Jerry back into the memories of his own childhood as he and Eileen grappled with the major and minor crises of family life. In the midst of it all, Jerry kept writing and publishing books.

One night about 12:30 A.M., Jerry got a phone call. Certain that someone had been hurt, he rushed to the phone only to hear the words "Newbery Medal." When his wife heard him repeat the word, "medal," she thought for a moment he'd said, "metal," and wondered who'd been injured with a piece of metal!

Jerry referred to his year after winning the Newbery as his "Miss America" year. "You go to take your raincoat to the cleaners, and everybody knows you all of a sudden" (interview, April 6, 1994). Like the boy Maniac Magee, Jerry was on the run, talking to groups of children at schools, giving speeches, fulfilling the many requests that come to those who are catapulted into the spotlight once a book has that shiny, foil sticker placed on the cover that says "Newbery Medal."

Winning a Newbery Medal gave Jerry the freedom to become a full-time writer. He quit the job at Chilton's where he had worked for twenty-three years and devoted himself to doing what he loved: writing.

Writing is work, and there was never any doubt about that in Jerry's mind. He refused to acknowledge that condition often referred to as "writer's block," in which a lapse of inspiration is used as an excuse to avoid working on a book, saying, "Teachers don't have teacher's block and taxi drivers don't have taxi's block to keep them from working." He preferred thinking of those moments when the words don't flow as "snags." When Jerry ran into a snag, he said he might take a short break, go to lunch, or talk it over with Eileen, but then he would always go back to work. He equated the process to jump-starting a stalled car. "I keep pushing the pencil across the page, like you would push a car downhill. Once it gets moving, it starts to run again" (interview, April 6, 1994).

Although Jerry didn't set out to be a writer of books for children, he found his niche and has no regrets. "Beyond the more spectacular fallouts is the occasional letter that comes and indicates that something that you've written has really made a difference to someone. There's no price on that" (interview, April 6, 1994).

Jerry Spinelli, popular children's author and Newbery Medal winner. Not bad for a shortstop who didn't read very many books.

A Word to My Readers:

Let's concentrate more on our similarities than on our differences. It's such a waste that the human race has spent so much of its time and energy quarreling with itself. We seem to have this mania for picking out the differences among ourselves. Maybe it's time we spent more effort on getting along. (interview, April 6, 1994)

Books by Jerry Spinelli

The Bathwater Gang (Little, Brown, 1990; Econo-Clad Books, 1999).

The Bathwater Gang Gets Down to Business (Little, Brown, 1992).

Blue Ribbon Blues: A Tooter Tale (Random House, 1997; Econo-Clad Books, 1999).

Crash (Knopf/Random House, 1996; Econo-Clad Books, 1999).

Do the Funky Pickle (Scholastic, 1992; Econo-Clad Books, 1999).

Dump Days (Little, Brown, 1988).

Fourth Grade Rats (Scholastic, 1991; Econo-Clad Books, 1999).

Jason and Marceline (Little, Brown, 1986).

Knots in My Yo-Yo String: The Autobiography of a Kid (A. A. Knopf, 1998).

The Library Card (Scholastic, 1997; Econo-Clad Books, 1999).

Loser (Joanna Cotler Books, 2002).

Maniac Magee (Little, Brown, 1990; Thorndike Press, 1993).

Night of the Whale (Little, Brown, 1985).

Picklemania (School Daze) (Scholastic, 1993).

Report to the Principal's Office (School Daze) (Scholastic, 1991; Econo-Clad Books, 1999).

Space Station Seventh Grade (Little, Brown, 1982; Peter Smith, 2001).

Stargirl (Knopf/Random House, 2000, 2002).

There's a Girl in My Hammerlock (Simon & Schuster, 1991; Econo-Clad Books, 1999).

Tooter Pepperday (Random House, 1995; Econo-Clad Books, 1999).

Who Put That Hair in My Toothbrush? (Little, Brown, 1984; Little, Brown & Co., Juvenile Paperbacks, 2000).

Wringer (HarperCollins, 1997; Thorndike Press, 2000).

For More Information About/by Jerry Spinelli

Autobiography: 1998. *Knots in My Yo-Yo String: The Autobiography of a Kid.* A. A. Knopf.

Holtze, Sally Holmes, ed. 1989. *The Sixth Book of Junior Authors and Illustrators.* H. W. Wilson.

Horn Book and Association for Library Service to Children (ALSC), American Library Association. 2001. *Newbery and Caldecott Medal Books, 1986–2000: A*

Comprehensive Guide to the Winners. Horn Book and Association for Library Service to Children, American Library Association.

Telgen, Diane, ed., 1993. *Something About the Author: Facts and Pictures About Contemporary Authors and Illustrators of Books for Young People*. Vol. 71. Gale Research.

Note: Indicated citations from a personal interview with the author, April 6, 1994.

1992: Phyllis Reynolds Naylor

Born   January 4, 1933
                Anderson, Indiana

Married   Rex Naylor, 1960
                (children: Jeffrey
                and Michael)

Awards and Honors

Newbery Medal (Animal Stories): *Shiloh* (Atheneum Books for Young Readers, 1991)

Golden Kite Award, 1978: *How I Came to Be a Writer* (Atheneum Books for Young Readers, 1978)

American Library Association Notable Children's Book Award, 1986: *The Agony of Alice* (Atheneum Books for Young Readers, 1985); 1987: *The Keeper* (Atheneum Books for Young Readers, 1986); 1993: *All but Alice* (Atheneum Books for Young Readers, 1992); Aladdin Paperbacks, 2002)

About the Author and Her Writing

Phyllis Reynolds Naylor was in high school when she earned her first paycheck for her writing. The amount: four dollars and sixty-seven cents.

A former Sunday school teacher had encouraged Phyllis to send one of her stories to a children's church magazine. That was the story that brought her the first check and her first published work. She continued to write for that magazine, then "began, very slowly, branching out to other denominational magazines. I learned a great deal that way. I have great respect for the religious editors" (interview, February 22, 1994). Phyllis discovered that she could sell the same story to twenty different religious magazines and get paid each time. Soon she started writing for secular magazines as well. Her writing career had begun.

Phyllis's life began in Anderson, Indiana, where she was born January 4, 1933. The depression was in full swing, and Phyllis's family felt its impact. "I was very small at the time," she later remembered. "I guess if you have to be poor, the best time is when you're really young, because you don't care what you put on your back. In kindergarten, I had two dresses, and my mother made both of them. She would tell me that if I alternated, wore one dress one day, and the other the next, it would appear that I had more clothes. I thought, 'Isn't that intelligent of mother?' " (interview, February 22, 1994).

Phyllis' mother, a college graduate, took in laundry to help earn money for the family. Phyllis and her sister had the job of carrying the baskets of freshly ironed clothes back to the owners. The worst part was that her older sister "insisted on taking the baskets back after dark, because she didn't want her friends to see her. I was afraid of the dark and thought that was ridiculous" (interview, February 22, 1994).

Reading, writing, and books were all part of Phyllis's life from an early age. But the few books her family owned weren't just used for reading. "We had a set of old Mark Twain books," she recalled, "and a set of Collier's Encyclopedias. We built tunnels out of these books, and houses. In the evening when Dad read to us, we had to take apart all our tunnels and houses!" (interview, February 22, 1994).

In college Phyllis studied psychology and planned to be a clinical psychologist. She paid for her tuition in part by writing and selling short stories and soon realized that what she really wanted to do was to write. She gave up plans for graduate school and began writing full time. Afterward, Phyllis could not imagine being anything but a writer. She gave up many of her hobbies in order to have the time to write. "I used to sing in a madrigal group. I used to do oil painting and be in dramatics. As more and more plot ideas came to me, I wanted to write more. I thought, 'I can't afford to lose one day of writing.' I still like to hike, walk, swim, and do things with the family. That and writing has really become my life" (interview, February 22, 1994).

> Writing is not a lonely profession. I don't know who started that idea. My head is so full of characters arguing back and forth that it seems like a very noisy and busy profession! (interview, February 22, 1994)

Phyllis said she never has a shortage of ideas. When she is be working on one book and ideas for another story start to intrude, she writes down her thoughts in a notebook. "That way they won't disappear and I don't have to keep worrying about losing them" (interview, February 22, 1994).

Her writing time begins early in the morning, when she is at her best, and continues into the afternoon. "Learning that point at which you should stop, when the words are going flat," was something she taught herself as a way of deciding when to quit for the day.

Phyllis was not aware of the Newbery Medal until she was in her thirties and became involved in the Children's Book Guild of Washington, D.C. In 1992, when she won the medal for her book *Shiloh,* her reaction was one of stunned delight. "I didn't even know it was being considered," she said. "I got the call about nine in the morning when I was eating my shredded wheat. My husband was out jogging, so I had no one to tell when I got the news and began to wonder if I'd imagined the whole thing. The phone rang again, and it was the *Today Show* asking me to come to New York for their show the next morning" (interview, February 22, 1994).

Shiloh is the name of a beagle who is abused by his owner. The dog escapes, and Marty Preston, a young boy, struggles to find a way to save Shiloh's life. The book is based on a real dog that Phyllis found while visiting friends in West Virginia. Phyllis wrote two more books about Shiloh: *Shiloh Season* (Atheneum Books for Young Readers, 1996), and *Saving Shiloh* (Atheneum Books for Young Readers, 1997).

As a well-known author, Phyllis got asked the same questions over and over. But one question she was never asked but wanted to answer was, "Does your husband help you?"

Phyllis replied, "He's excellent. I often think that if I were ever to lose Rex, the people who would miss him most, next to me and the children, would be my editors. I don't think they realize what a more polished manuscript they get from me because he has read through everything and made suggestions" (interview, February 22, 1994).

Did the Newbery medal change her life? "Of course. Not only *Shiloh* but all of my books have received more attention, and there are more speaking requests than I can possibly handle. The down side is that there is less time to write" (interview, February 22, 1994). Phyllis also spent a lot of time defending some of the ideas and words used in her books against would-be censors.

Despite some of the difficulties she's faced in life, Phyllis remains cheerful. She claims that growing up during the depression may have helped that. "We started out with so little, but every year, we had slightly more, or something new, so that as time went on, my life was more positive." Perhaps she put it best in her own summary of herself: "I'm a worrier, but at the same time I'm a very hopeful person, not a cynic. And because of that, I'm happy" (interview, February 22, 1994).

A Word to My Readers:

There are all kinds of solutions to every problem. As a writer, you learn that there are many possible endings. Sometimes, you decide to use your second or your third choice, and then you think, 'This is so much better than the first.' Same with life. Often the tragedies that happen to us seem at the time like the worst things we've ever experienced. But they may open a door to something that's better than what we had before. Life has so many possibilities. (interview, February 22, 1994)

Books by Phyllis Reynolds Naylor

Achingly Alice (Atheneum Books for Young Readers, 1998).

Agony of Alice (Atheneum Books for Young Readers, 1985).

Alice Alone (Atheneum Books for Young Readers, 2001).

Alice in April (Atheneum Books for Young Readers, 1993).

Alice In-Between (Atheneum Books for Young Readers, 1994).

Alice in Lace (Atheneum Books for Young Readers, 1996).

Alice in Rapture, Sort Of (Atheneum Books for Young Readers, 1989).

Alice on the Outside (Atheneum Books for Young Readers, 1999).

Alice the Brave (Atheneum Books for Young Readers, 1995; Aladdin Books, 1996).

All Because I'm Older (Atheneum Books for Young Readers, 1981).

All but Alice (Atheneum Books for Young Readers, 1992; Aladdin Paperbacks, 2002).

An Amish Family (J. P. O'Hara, 1974).

The Baby, the Bed, and the Rose (Clarion, 1987).

Beetles, Lightly Toasted (Atheneum Books for Young Readers, 1987).

Being Danny's Dog (Atheneum Books for Young Readers, 1995).

Bernie and the Bessledorf Ghost (Atheneum Books for Young Readers, 1990).

Bernie Magruder and the Bats in the Belfry (Atheneum, 2003).

Bernie Magruder & the Case of the Big Stink (Thorndike Press, 2001).

Bernie Magruder and the Disappearing Bodies (Aladdin Paperbacks, 2001).

Bernie Magruder and the Parachute Peril (Aladdin Paperbacks, 2001).

Bernie Magruder and the Pirate's Treasure (Aladdin Paperbacks, 2001).

The Bodies in the Bessledorf Hotel (Atheneum Books for Young Readers, 1986).

The Bomb in the Bessledorf Bus Depot (Atheneum Books for Young Readers, 1996).

The Boy with the Helium Head (Atheneum Books for Young Readers, 1982; Bantam Doubleday Dell Publishing Group, 1998).

Boys Against Girls (Delacorte Press, 1994; Random House, 2000).

The Boys Return (Delacorte Press, 2001).

The Boys Start the War (Delacorte Press, 1993; Yearling Books, 2002).

Carlotta's Kittens (The Club of Mysteries) (Atheneum Books for Young Readers, 2000; Aladdin Paperbacks, 2002).

Change in the Wind (Augsburg, 1980).

The Craft of Writing the Novel (Writer, Inc., 1989).

Crazy Love: An Autobiographical Account of Marriage and Madness (William Morrow, 1977).

Danny's Desert Rats (Atheneum Books for Young Readers, 1998).

The Dark of the Tunnel (Atheneum Books for Young Readers, 1985).

The Dark Side of the Moon: Stories (Fortress Press, 1969).

Ducks Disappearing (Atheneum Books for Young Readers, 1997).

Eddie, Incorporated (Atheneum Books for Young Readers, 1980).

The Face in the Bessledorf Funeral Parlor (Atheneum Books for Young Readers, 1993).

Faces in the Water (Atheneum Books for Young Readers, 1981; Aladdin Paperbacks, 2002).

The Fear Place (Atheneum Books for Young Readers, 1994).

Footprints at the Window (Atheneum Books for Young Readers, 1981; Aladdin Paperbacks, 2002).

The Galloping Goat (Abingdon Press, 1965).

Getting Along in Your Family (Abingdon Press, 1976).

Getting Along with Your Friends (Abingdon Press, 1980).

Getting Along with Your Teachers (Abingdon Press, 1981).

The Girls Get Even (Delacorte Press, 1993; Yearling Books, 2002).

The Girls' Revenge (Delacorte Press, 1998).

The Girls Take Over (Delacorte Press, 2002).

The Grand Escape (Atheneum Books for Young Readers, 1993).

Grasshoppers in the Soup (Fortress Press, 1965).

The Great Chicken Debacle (Marshall Cavendish, 2001).

The Grooming of Alice (Atheneum Books for Young Readers, 2000; Pocket Books, 2001).

The Healing of Texas Jake (Atheneum Books for Young Readers, 1997).

How I Came to Be a Writer (Atheneum Books for Young Readers, 1978; Aladdin Books, 1987).

How Lazy Can You Get? (Atheneum Books for Young Readers, 1979).

How to Find Your Wonderful Someone: How to Keep Him/Her if You Do, How to Survive if You Don't (Fortress Press, 1971).

"I Can't Take You Anywhere!" (Atheneum Books for Young Readers, 1997).

Ice (Atheneum Books for Young Readers, 1995).

In Small Doses (Atheneum Books for Young Readers, 1979).

Jade Green: A Ghost Story (Atheneum Books for Young Readers, 2000; Thorndike Press, 2000).

Jennifer Jean, the Cross Eyed Queen (Lerner Publications, 1967; Carolrhoda Books, 1993).

Josie's Troubles (Atheneum Books for Young Readers, 1992).

The Keeper (Atheneum Books for Young Readers, 1986).

Keeping a Christmas Secret (Atheneum Books for Young Readers, 1989; Macmillan/Aladdin, 1993).

King of the Playground (Atheneum Books for Young Readers, 1991; Aladdin Books, 1994).

Knee Deep Ice Cream and Other Stories (Fortress Press, 1967).

The Mad Gasser of Bessledorf Street (Atheneum Books for Young Readers, 1983).

Making It Happen (Follett, 1970).

Maudie in the Middle (Atheneum Books for Young Readers, 1988).

Meet Murdock (Follett, 1969).

Never Born a Hero (Augsburg, 1982).

The New Schoolmaster (Silver Burdett, 1967).

A New Year's Surprise (Silver Burdett, 1967).

Night Cry (Atheneum Books for Young Readers, 1984).

No Easy Circle (Follett, 1972).

Old Sadie and the Christmas Bear (Atheneum Books for Young Readers, 1984).

One of the Third Grade Thonkers (Atheneum Books for Young Readers, 1988).

Outrageously Alice (Atheneum Books for Young Readers, 1997).

Percy's Picnic (Atheneum Books for Young Readers, 2002).

Peril in the Bessledorf Parachute Factory (Atheneum Books for Young Readers, 1999).

The Picnic (Atheneum, 2001).

The Private I, and Other Stories (Fortress Press, 1969).

Reluctantly Alice (Atheneum Books for Young Readers, 1991; Aladdin Paperbacks, 2000).

Revelations (St. Martin's Press; 1979).

Sang Spell (Atheneum Books for Young Readers, 1998).

Saving Shiloh (Atheneum Books for Young Readers, 1997).

Send No Blessings (Atheneum Books for Young Readers, 1990; Puffin Books, 1992).

Shadows on the Wall (Atheneum Books for Young Readers, 1980; Aladdin Paperbacks, 2002).

Shiloh (Atheneum Books for Young Readers, 1991).

Shiloh Season (Atheneum Books for Young Readers, 1996).

Ships in the Night (Fortress Press, 1971).

Simply Alice (Atheneum Books for Young Readers, 2002).

The Solomon System (Atheneum Books for Young Readers, 1983; Aladdin Books, 1987).

A Spy Among the Girls (Delacorte Press, 2000; Yearling Books, 2002).

Starting with Alice (Atheneum Books for Young Readers, 2002).

A String of Chances (Atheneum Books for Young Readers, 1982).

Sweet Strawberries (Atheneum Books for Young Readers, 1999).

To Make a Wee Moon (Follett, 1969).

To Shake a Shadow (Abingdon Press, 1967).

To Walk the Sky Path (Follett, 1973).

A Traitor Among the Boys (Delacorte Press, 1999; Young Yearling, 2001).

The Traitor of Bessledorf Hill (Atheneum Books for Young Readers, 1997).

A Triangle Has Four Sides (Augsburg, 1984).

Unexpected Pleasures (Putnam's, 1986).

Walker's Crossing (Atheneum Books for Young Readers, 1999).

Walking Through the Dark (Atheneum Books for Young Readers, 1976).

What the Gulls Were Singing (Follett, 1967).

When Rivers Meet (Friendship Press, 1968).

The Witch Herself (Atheneum Books for Young Readers, 1979).

The Witch Returns (Delacorte Press, 1992).

Witch Water (Atheneum Books for Young Readers, 1977).

Witch Weed (Delacorte Press, 1991).

The Witch's Eye (Delacorte Press, 1990).

Witch's Sister (Atheneum Books for Young Readers, 1975).

Wrestle the Mountain (Follett, 1971).

The Year of the Gopher (Atheneum Books for Young Readers, 1987).

For More Information About/by Phyllis Reynolds Naylor

Autobiographies: 1977. *Crazy Love: An Autobiographical Account of Marriage and Madness.* William Morrow; 1978. *How I Came to Be a Writer.* Atheneum Books for Young Readers.

Commire, Anne, ed. 1991. *Something About the Author: Facts and Pictures About Contemporary Authors and Illustrators of Books for Young People.* Vol. 66. Gale Research.

Horn Book and Association for Library Service to Children (ALSC), American Library Association. 2001. *Newbery and Caldecott Medal Books, 1986–2000: A Comprehensive Guide to the Winners.* Horn Book and Association for Library Service to Children, American Library Association.

H. W. Wilson. 1983. *The Fifth Book of Junior Authors and Illustrators.* H. W. Wilson.

Note: Indicated citations from a personal interview with the author, February 22, 1994.

1993: Cynthia Rylant

Born   June 6, 1954
                  Hopewell, Virginia

Children   Nathaniel

Awards and Honors

Newbery Medal (Contemporary Life): *Missing May* (Orchard Books, 1992)

Newbery Honor Book for 1987: *A Fine White Dust* (Bradbury Press, 1986)

Wrote the Caldecott Honor Book for 1983: *When I Was Young in the Mountains* (Dutton, 1982), illustrated by Diane Goode

Wrote the Caldecott Honor Book for 1986: *The Relatives Came* (Bradbury Press, 1985), illustrated by Stephen Gammell

American Library Association Notable Children's Book, 1983: *When I Was Young in the Mountains* (Dutton, 1982); 1986: *The Relatives Came* (Bradbury Press, 1985; Aladdin Books, 1993); *A Blue-Eyed Daisy* (Bradbury Press, 1985); 1988: *Henry and Mudge under the Yellow Moon* (Simon & Schuster Books, 1987; Aladdin Books, 1992); 1991: *Henry and Mudge and the Happy Cat* (Simon & Schuster, 1990; Bradbury Press, 1994); 1993: *An Angel for Solomon Singer* (Orchard Books, 1992); 1993: *Missing May* (Orchard Books, 1992); 1996: *Mr. Putter & Tabby Pick the Pears* (Harcourt, Brace & Co., 1995); 1996: *The Van Gogh Cafe* (Harcourt Brace, and Co., 1995)

American Library Association Best Books for Young Adults, 1987: *A Fine White Dust* (Bradbury Press, 1986); 1988: *A Kindness* (Orchard Books, 1988)

Boston Globe-Horn Book Award, 1991: *Appalachia: The Voices of Sleeping Birds* (Harcourt Brace Jovanovich, 1991); 1992: *Missing May* (Orchard Books, 1992)

About the Author and Her Writing

Cynthia Rylant's life as an author reads like a writer's dream. She wrote her first book, *When I Was Young in the Mountains,* in practically one sitting, mailed it off to a publisher, and it was quickly accepted for publication. She can write a picture book in an hour, rarely rewrites, and published over seventy-five books in the first decade of her career. Cynthia even illustrated several of her picture books and has won numerous honors and awards for her books.

Cynthia's life as a child, however, was not the stuff of dreams. Born in Hopewell, Virginia, on June 6, 1954, her parents split when she was four, and she was raised for the next four years by her grandparents. She lived in a house without indoor plumbing, had no brothers or sisters, never again saw her father after the divorce, and did not set foot in a public library until she went to college. She didn't have books, television, or the material luxuries that most people think of as necessities. But she did have grandparents who gave her stability and love. And she had the natural world to explore. As far as Cynthia was concerned, she had everything she needed.

> The more I write, it seems the more willing I am to get closer to my real life today, who I am today. (Holtze 1989, 256)

"I was raised in at atmosphere of forgiveness, and this may be the finest gift God has given me on this earth," Cynthia said in her Newbery acceptance speech. "Knowing that I would be forgiven by my mother, my family, if I ever failed at anything I tried gave me the courage to be a writer, the courage to place my work in the world for judgment, and the courage to keep on trying to say something important in my books" (Horn Book/ALSC 2001, 191).

The small town of Cool Ridge, West Virginia, did not have a bookstore or a library. Cynthia's reading consisted mostly of comic books and later of paperback romances. She didn't know the great writers and never read the classics until she went away to school. After majoring in English in college, Cynthia waitressed for a while and then took a job as a clerk in a public library. Cynthia's son, Nathaniel, was born in 1979. Then she wrote a book. Both events changed her life forever.

With the advent of motherhood and publication, Cynthia discovered the two great joys of her life. Along with the many picture books, Cynthia wrote chapter books, novels, and poetry. She wrote an autobiography of her early years in part as an attempt to answer the many questions that children asked her on school and library visits. She found those visits emotionally draining and sought a way to reach out to her readers in a personal way through the book, rather than in person. Cynthia was surprised to discover that many of the people who read the autobiography and wrote to her were adults.

Cynthia said she never wrote with a specific age group in mind. Instead, she wrote what she enjoyed writing and then figured out where it fit. Cynthia said that she blessed with wonderful editors who encouraged her as a writer. They allowed her to use her own voice, and eventually, even her own paintbrush.

Cynthia turned to illustrating some of her picture books after writing *Dog Heaven* (Blue Sky Press, 1995), which was inspired by the death of her best friend's dog. Cynthia knew that it would be frustrating to wait for an illustrator to do the artwork for the book, so she decided to do it herself. She stood at a table and painted, and the pictures began to flow. They fit the text perfectly. Cynthia illustrated several other of her books, including *Cat Heaven* (Blue Sky Press, 1997), which came out a few years after the one about dogs.

Cynthia's first book, *When I Was Young in the Mountains,* was named a Caldecott Honor Book in 1983. Another of her books, *The Relatives Came* (Bradbury Press, 1985) won the Caldecott Honor in 1986. In 1987, her novel *A Fine White Dust* was given a Newbery Honor Award, and in 1993, *Missing May* won the Newbery Medal.

Writing flowed from Cynthia like one of the rippling brooks in the mountains of West Virginia, with a poetry and music all its own. Yet she has always recognized that writing is hard work. Cynthia said she could never be someone who wrote just for the sheer joy of it. "Writing is very hard. That doesn't mean that I don't love my work. But, I view it as exactly that: it *is* work, and there has to be more reward than just me reading it and putting it in the drawer" (Antonucci 1993, 4).

A Word to My Readers:

The most important thing I learned (while working in a library) is that they are free. That any child from any kind of house in any kind of neighborhood in this whole vast country may walk into a building which has a room full of books meant just for him and may choose whichever ones he wants to read and may take them home because they are free. And they are not free in a way which might diminish the child . . . They are free in the most democratic and humane way. Both the poor child and the wealthy child are privileged with free libraries. (Horn Book/ALSC 2001, 192)

Books by Cynthia Rylant

All I See (Orchard Books, 1988).

An Angel for Solomon Singer (Orchard Books, 1992).

Appalachia: The Voices of Sleeping Birds (Harcourt Brace Jovanovich, 1991).

Bear Day (Harcourt, Brace & Co., 1998).

Best Wishes (R. C. Owen Publishers, 1992).

The Bird House (Blue Sky Press, 1998).

Birthday Presents (Orchard Books, 1987).

Bless Us All: A Child's Yearbook of Blessings (Simon & Schuster Books for Young Readers, 1998).

A Blue Eyed Daisy (Bradbury Press, 1985).

The Blue Hill Meadows (Harcourt, Brace & Co., 1997).

The Blue Hill Meadows and the Much Loved Dog (Harcourt, Brace & Co., 1997).

The Bookshop Dog (Blue SkyPress/Scholastic, 1996).

Bunny Bungalow (Harcourt, Brace & Co., 1999).

But I'll Be Back Again (Beech Tree Books, 1993).

But I'll Be Back Again: An Album (Orchard Books, 1989).

Cat Heaven (Blue Sky Press, 1997).

Children of Christmas: Stories for the Season (Orchard Books, 1987).

Christmas in the Country (Blue Sky Press, 2002).

The Cookie Store Cat (Blue Sky Press, 1999).

*illustrated by the author

A Couple of Kooks and Other Stories About Love (Orchard Books, 1990).

*Dog Heaven (Blue Sky Press, 1995).

The Dreamer (Blue Sky Press, 1993).

Every Living Thing (Bradbury Press, 1985; Aladdin Books, 1988).

An Everyday Book (Simon & Schuster Books for Young Readers, 1997).

A Fine White Dust (Bradbury Press, 1986).

Give Me Grace: A Child's Daybook of Prayers (Simon & Schuster Books for Young Readers, 1999).

Good Morning Sweetie Pie and Other Poems for Little Children (Simon & Schuster Books for Young Readers, 2002).

Gooseberry Park (Harcourt, Brace & Co., 1995).

The Great Gracie Chase (Blue Sky Press, 2001).

The Heavenly Village (Blue Sky Press, 1999).

Henry and Mudge (Bradbury Press, 1987; Aladdin Books, 1990).

Henry and Mudge and a Very Special Merry Christmas (Simon & Schuster Books for Young Readers, 1999).

Henry and Mudge and Annie's Good Move (Simon & Schuster Books for Young Readers, 1998).

Henry and Mudge and Annie's Perfect Pet (Simon & Schuster Books for Young Readers, 2000).

Henry and Mudge and a Very Merry Christmas (Simon & Schuster Books for Young Readers, 1999).

Henry and Mudge and Mrs. Hopper's House (Simon & Schuster Books for Young Readers, 1999).

Henry and Mudge and the Bedtime Thumps (Bradbury Press, 1991).

Henry and Mudge and the Best Day of All (Bradbury Press, 1995).

Henry and Mudge and the Big Sleepover (Simon & Schuster Books for Young Readers, 1999).

Henry and Mudge and the Careful Cousin (Bradbury Press, 1994).

Henry and Mudge and the Forever Sea (Bradbury Press, 1989; Aladdin Books, 1993).

Henry and Mudge and the Funny Lunch (Simon & Schuster Books for Young Readers, 1999).

Henry and Mudge and the Great Grandpas (Simon & Schuster Books for Young Readers, 1999).

Henry and Mudge and the Happy Cat (Simon & Schuster Books, 1990; Bradbury Press, 1994).

Henry and Mudge and the Long Weekend (Bradbury Press, 1992).

Henry and Mudge and the Sneaky Crackers (Simon & Schuster Books for Young Readers, 1998).

Henry and Mudge and the Snowman Plan (Simon & Schuster Books for Young Readers, 1999).

Henry and Mudge and the Starry Night (Simon & Schuster Books for Young Readers, 1998).

Henry and Mudge and the Tall Tree House (Simon & Schuster Books for Young Readers, 1999).

Henry and Mudge and the Tumbling Trip (Simon & Schuster Books for Young Readers, 1999).

Henry and Mudge and the Wild Goose Chase (Simon & Schuster Books for Young Readers, 1999).

Henry and Mudge and the Wild Wind (Bradbury Press, 1992).

Henry and Mudge Get the Cold Shivers (Bradbury Press, 1989).

Henry and Mudge in Puddle Trouble (Aladdin Books, 1990).

Henry and Mudge in the Family Trees (Simon & Schuster Books for Young Readers, 1997).

Henry and Mudge in the Green Time (Aladdin Books, 1992).

Henry and Mudge in the Sparkle Days (Macmillan, 1993).

Henry and Mudge Take the Big Test (Bradbury Press, 1991).

Henry and Mudge Under the Yellow Moon (Simon & Schuster Books, 1987; Aladdin Books, 1992).

Henry's Puppy Mudge Has a Snack (Simon & Schuster Books for Young Readers, 2001).

Henry's Puppy Mudge Takes a Bath (Simon & Schuster Books for Young Readers, 2001).

The High Rise Private Eyes: The Case of the Climbing Cat (Greenwillow Books, 2000).

The High Rise Private Eyes: The Case of the Puzzling Possum (Greenwillow Books, 2001).

The High Rise Private Eyes: The Case of the Troublesome Turtle (Greenwillow Books, 2001).

I Had Seen Castles (Harcourt, Brace & Co., 1993).

In Aunt Lucy's Kitchen (Simon & Schuster Books for Young Readers, 1998).

In November (Harcourt, Brace & Co., 2000).

The Islander (DK Ink, 1998).

A Kindness (Orchard Books, 1988).

Let's Go Home: The Wonderful Things About a House (Simon & Schuster Books for Young Readers, 2000).

A Little Shopping (Simon & Schuster Books for Young Readers, 1998).

Little Whistle (Harcourt, Brace & Co., 2000).

Little Whistle's Dinner Party (Harcourt, Brace & Co., 2001).

Little Whistle's Medicine (Harcourt, Brace & Co., 2001).

Margaret, Frank, and Andy: Three Writers' Stories (Harcourt, Brace & Co., 1996).

Miss Maggie (Dutton, 1983).

Missing May (Orchard Books, 1992).

Mr. Grigg's Work (Orchard Books, 1989).

Mr. Putter & Tabby Bake the Cake (Harcourt, Brace & Co., 1994).

Mr. Putter & Tabby Feed the Fish (Harcourt, 2001).

Mr. Putter & Tabby Fly the Plane (Harcourt, Brace & Co., 1997).

Mr. Putter & Tabby Paint the Porch (Harcourt, 2000).

Mr. Putter & Tabby Pick the Pears (Harcourt, Brace & Co., 1995).

Mr. Putter & Tabby Pour the Tea (Harcourt, Brace & Co., 1994).

Mr. Putter & Tabby Row the Boat (Harcourt, Brace & Co., 1997).

Mr. Putter & Tabby Take the Train (Harcourt, Brace & Co., 1998).

Mr. Putter & Tabby Toot the Horn (Harcourt, Brace & Co., 1998).

Mr. Putter & Tabby Walk the Dog (Harcourt, Brace & Co., 1994).

Night in the Country (Bradbury Press, 1986; Aladdin Books, 1991).

Old Town in the Green Groves (HarperCollins, 2002).

The Old Woman Who Named Things (Harcourt, Brace & Co., 1996).

Poppleton (Blue Sky Press, 1997).

Poppleton and Friends (Blue Sky Press, 1997).

Poppleton Everyday (Blue Sky Press, 1998).

Poppleton Forever (Blue Sky Press, 1998).

Poppleton Has Fun (Blue Sky Press, 2000).

Poppleton in Fall (Blue Sky Press, 1999).

Poppleton in Spring (Scholastic, 1999).

Poppleton in Winter (Blue Sky Press, 2001).

The Relatives Came (Bradbury Press, 1985; Aladdin Books, 1993).

Scarecrow (Harcourt, Brace & Co., 1998).

Silver Packages: An Appalachian Christmas Story (Orchard Books, 1997).

Soda Jerk (Beech Tree Books, 1993).

Soda Jerk: Poems by Cynthia Rylant (Orchard Books, 1999).

Some Good News (Simon & Schuster Books for Young Readers, 1999).

Special Gifts (Simon & Schuster Books for Young Readers, 1999).

Summer Party (Simon & Schuster Books for Young Readers, 2001).

Thimbleberry Stories (Harcourt, Brace & Co., 2000).

This Year's Garden (Bradbury Press, 1984; Aladdin Books, 1987).

The Ticky Tacky Doll (Harcourt, Brace & Co., 2002).

Tulip Sees America (Blue Sky Press, 1998).

The Van Gogh Cafe (Harcourt, Brace & Co., 1995).

Waiting to Waltz, a Childhood: Poems (Bradbury Press, 1984).

Wedding Flowers (Simon & Schuster Books for Young Readers, 2002).

The Whales (Blue Sky Press, 1996).

When I Was Young in the Mountains (Dutton, 1982).

Wonderful Happens (Simon & Schuster Books for Young Readers, 2000).

For More Information About/by Cynthia Rylant

Autobiography: 1993. *But I'll Be Back Again.* Beech Tree Books.

Antonucci, Ron. 1993. Rylant on Writing: A Talk with Newbery Medalist Cynthia Rylant. *School Library Journal,* May.

Holtze, Sally Holmes, ed. 1989. *The Sixth Book of Junior Authors and Illustrators.* H. W. Wilson.

Horn Book and Association for Library Service to Children (ALSC), American Library Association. 2001. *The Newbery and Caldecott Medal Books, 1986–2000: A Comprehensive Guide to the Winners.* Horn Book and Association for Library Service to Children, American Library Association.

1995: Sharon Creech (Rigg)

Born   July 29, 1945
             Cleveland, Ohio

Married   1967 (children: Karin
             and Rob)
             Lyle Rigg, 1982

Awards and Honors

Newbery Medal (Contemporary Life): *Walk Two Moons* (HarperCollins, 1994)

Newbery Honor Book for 2001: *The Wanderer* (HarperCollins, 2000)

American Library Association Notable Children's Book, 1995: *Walk Two Moons* (HarperCollins, 1994); 2001: *The Wanderer* (HarperCollins, 2000); 2002: *Love That Dog* (HarperCollins, 2001); 2003: *Ruby Holler* (Joanna Cotler/HarperCollins, 2002; Thorndike Press, 2003)

Heartland Award for Excellence in Young Adult Literature, 1997: *Walk Two Moons* (HarperCollins, 1994)

School Library Journal's Best Book of the Year Award, 2001: *The Wanderer* (Harper-Collins, 2000, 2002); 2001: *Love That Dog* (HarperCollins, 2001); 2002: *Ruby Holler* (Joanna Cotler/HarperCollins, 2002; Thorndike Press, 2003)

Christopher Award, 2001: *The Wanderer* (HarperCollins, 2000, 2002); 2002: *Love That Dog* (HarperCollins, 2001)

Carnegie Medal, 2003: *Ruby Holler* (Joanna Cotler/HarperCollins, 2002; Thorndike Press, 2003)

About the Author and Her Writing

When asked what she would want to be if not a writer, Sharon Creech had a quick answer: Estsanatlehi.

Estsanatlehi is the Navajo woman in Sharon's Newbery Medal–winning book *Walk Two Moons*. Estsanatlehi never dies but lives a thousand, thousand lives. "I can remember, in college," Sharon wrote, "bemoaning the fact that we seemed expected to choose only one occupation. I told a roommate that I wanted to try every job there was for three months at a time. It was all sorts of jobs I was interested in: writing, painting, house-building, tree-trimming, teaching, acting" (interview, March 2, 1998).

She continued: "I wonder if writing is the closest I can come to that wish to be Estsanatlehi and to have every job there is, because through writing you can become whoever your characters are" (interview, March 2, 1998).

In fact, Sharon did have several other jobs before becoming a full-time writer. She taught, a profession she loved. She raised two children, Karin and Rob. She did all the things expected of a wife whose husband is headmaster at an English boarding school and did them all very well.

> Come along and walk with us awhile, slip into our moccasins so that you might see what we think and feel, and so that you might understand why we do what we do, and so that you might glimpse the larger world outside your own. (Horn Book/ALSC 2001, 232)

But Sharon was also fascinated with writing. As a child her favorite day of the year was the first day of school, when all the paper, pens, pencils, and notebooks were perfect and new. She loved the freshness of each item, the unknown possibilities that could leap into life as pen met paper.

A car trip from Cleveland, Ohio, to Lewiston, Idaho, in the summer of 1957, when Sharon turned twelve, began the journey that later found new expression in *Walk Two Moons*. Packed in a car with her father, her pregnant mother, an older sister, and two younger brothers, Sharon could hardly sit still, but not because she was bored. "I think I must have been in a state of hyper-excitement the whole time. I just couldn't get enough of this new, vast world" (interview, March 2, 1998).

During the trip, Sharon celebrated her twelfth birthday. To honor the occasion, the family stopped at a Native American reservation and Sharon got to choose her gift: a pair of leather moccasins.

Sharon took her first writing class in college. She received a bachelor of arts from Hiram College and a master of arts from George Mason University. She married, had two children, then divorced. With two small children to support and a desire to see more of the world, Sharon applied for a teaching position at an American School in Surrey, England. The headmaster was reluctant to hire a single mother, but her letter to him was so convincing, he finally agreed to give her a chance.

On her first day at the school Sharon met Lyle Rigg, a fellow American from Ohio who was also teaching at the school. She asked to borrow some ice. Three years later, the two were married. They celebrated with a party on a riverboat floating down the River Thames.

When Sharon's husband was appointed headmaster at the American School in Switzerland, the family packed their bags and moved to Lugano, a town in the foothills of the Alps. Two years later, the family moved back to England when Lyle was named headmaster at the school there. The family lived in a cottage that was over four hundred years old.

Then in 1980, Sharon's father had a stroke. The suddenness of his illness made her think about the need to live each day, not knowing what might come next. She had always wanted to be a writer. Why put it off any longer? Besides, she says, "There was also a feeling of wanting to use all those words that my father could not use during his last six years, or after his death, ever again" (interview, March 2, 1998).

In 1988, Sharon's poem "Cleansing" won the Billee Murray Denny Poetry Award, sponsored by Lincoln College in Illinois. Like the eye-opening car ride thirty-one years before, winning the award affirmed for Sharon that she was, indeed, a writer. She wrote and published two books for adults under her married name, Rigg, and one children's book under the name Sharon Creech. These first three books were published in England. She then began a new novel.

This fourth book did not come easily. She rewrote the manuscript twice but still wasn't satisfied. Then one night a meal of Chinese food brought the spark she needed in the form of a fortune cookie. Her fortune read, "Don't judge a man until you've walked two moons in his moccasins" (Horn Book/ALSC 2001, 231). The American Indian proverb wasn't a message she expected to find in a Chinese restaurant in England, but the spark became a flash of light, and *Walk Two Moons,* a story about a young Native American girl seeking to find her lost mother, was on its way.

When Sharon received the telephone call telling her that *Walk Two Moons* had been named the Newbery Medal Book for 1995, she couldn't believe it. She waited for the call to come telling her it was a mistake. That call never came, but many other phone calls did. Sharon learned quickly that being a Newbery Medalist had its ups and downs. The ups: the affirmation as a writer, a wider audience of readers, and meeting the children, teachers, and librarians who read her books. The downside: trying to keep up with all the fan mail and finding time to write in the midst of the inevitable speeches and interviews that come with being a Newbery Medal winner.

Asked many times where she found her ideas, Sharon was reluctant to give too precise of an answer. "For me, the greatest interest is in the process of writing and discovery, and I'm uncomfortable trying to nail down the sources for such mysterious, abstract things as ideas and inspiration" (interview, March 2, 1998). In 2003, Sharon won The Carnegie Medal, the United Kingdom's equivalent to the Newbery Medal and became the first author ever to win both The Carnegie Medal and The Newbery Medal.

Everything, according to Sharon, feeds the imagination. Car trips. Moccasins. Fortune cookies. Who knows where ideas will turn up next?

A week after Sharon received the life-changing phone call about the Newbery Medal, her husband called her from the United States, where he was spending a couple of weeks. It was Valentine's Day. He told her to look in the sock drawer for her gift. When Sharon opened the present, she found that the gift was a miniature egg made of enamel, decorated with pictures of the various phases of the moon. Inscribed around the top were these words: "May all your dreams come true " (Horn Book/ALSC 2001, 238).

A Word to My Readers:

I hope that you have easy access to good books, that you enjoy reading and writing and the worlds you enter through books. I hope you explore all kinds of books and if you want to write, then write, write, write. Try all forms and styles and have fun with it. (interview, March 2, 1998)

Books by Sharon Creech (Rigg)

Absolutely Normal Chaos (HarperCollins, 1995; Econo-Clad Books, 1999).

Bloomability (HarperCollins, 1998).

Chasing Redbird (HarperCollins, 1997).

A Fine, Fine School (Joanna Cotler/HarperCollins, 2001).

Fishing in the Air (Joanna Cotler/HarperCollins, 2000).

Love That Dog (HarperCollins, 2001).

Pleasing the Ghost (HarperCollins, 1996).

Ruby Holler (Joanna Cotler/HarperCollins, 2002; Thorndike Press, 2003).

Walk Two Moons (HarperCollins, 1994).

The Wanderer (HarperCollins, 2000, 2002).

For More Information About/by Sharon Creech (Rigg)

Horn Book and Association for Library Service to Children (ALSC), American Library Association. 2001. *The Newbery and Caldecott Medal Books, 1986–2000: A Comprehensive Guide to the Winners.* Horn Book and Association for Library Service to Children, American Library Association.

Note: Indicated citations from a personal interview with the author, March 2, 1998.

1996: Karen Cushman

Born   October 4, 1941
              Chicago, Illinois

Married   Philip Cushman,
              September 6, 1969
              (children: Leah)

Awards and Honors

Newbery Medal (Historical Fiction): *The Midwife's Apprentice* (Clarion, 1995)

Newbery Medal Honor Book for 1995: *Catherine, Called Birdy* (Clarion, 1994)

Carl Sandburg Award for Literary Excellence, 1994: *Catherine, Called Birdy* (Clarion, 1994)

The Golden Kite Award, 1994: *Catherine, Called Birdy* (Clarion, 1994)

American Library Association Notable Children's Book, 1996: *The Midwife's Apprentice* (Clarion, 1995)

School Library Journal's Best Books, 1996: *The Ballad of Lucy Whipple* (Clarion, 1996); 2000: *Matilda Bone* (Clarion, 2000)

About the Author and Her Writing

What if?

That's the question Karen Cushman asks herself before starting a book. What if there was a girl who lived in medieval England? What if she didn't have a home? What if someone found her sleeping in a dung heap and offered to train her as a midwife?

What if . . . ? It's a good question to ask about Karen Cushman's life.

What if a little girl born near Chicago had never moved to California at the age of ten?

What if she hadn't been born in a time when women didn't have the career options they have today?

What if she hadn't married a rabbinical student named Philip who believed she could write books and supported her in doing so?

What if Karen Cushman had never tried writing a book?

Karen always loved to write, but she didn't think of herself as a writer, and she didn't think that a woman could grow up and actually earn a living writing books. When

270

she was in elementary school, she wrote a story about Santa Claus going down the wrong chimney and ending up in a Jewish home. At thirteen, she began an epic poem about Elvis Presley. Neither of these early attempts made it into the public arena. They did show that she had the heart of a writer long before the rest of the world discovered this.

When Karen was about eleven years old, her family moved from their home near Chicago, Illinois, to a suburb in California. The move was traumatic for her, not only because she had to leave behind her grandparents and her pet dog but also because she lost the freedom she'd had to walk down the street to the public library and into the marvelous world of books. In California, the library was much farther away, and Karen had to ask her mother or father to drive her there. It just wasn't the same.

> It's not enough to have an idea. You have to make a commitment, take a stand, write it down. (Holtze 1989, 72)

After high school, Karen won a scholarship to Stanford University and earned a degree in English and Greek in 1963. While in college she wrote depressing poems and parodies of school songs. She thought the creative writing classes she took seemed geared to squelch creativity rather than to encourage it.

Karen worked at a number of odd jobs and then took an administrative position at the Hebrew Union College in northern California. There she met Philip Cushman, a young man studying to be a rabbi. They discovered that they shared many of the same goals, and they also fell in love. They married in 1968 and moved to Oregon for several years, making blackberry jam from the berries they grew in their garden and creating a family with the birth of their daughter, Leah.

Eventually the Cushman family moved to San Diego, where Karen and Philip both earned master's degrees in counseling and human behavior from the U.S. International University. Then Philip received a doctorate in psychology and Karen a master's in museum studies at John F. Kennedy University in Orinda, California. While Philip worked as a psychotherapist and teacher, Karen spent ten years working in the graduate department of museum studies at JFK University, editing journals and teaching classes.

Leah grew up and went off to college. Karen was still trying to figure out what it was she really wanted to do, especially now that Leah was gone and she had time to fill. What if . . .

What if she really could write a book?

Whenever Karen had an idea for a book, she shared the idea with her husband. Nothing more came of these conversations until the day she told Philip her idea about a young girl living in the Middle Ages. Philip was so intrigued he said to his wife, "Don't tell me. Write it down." So she did. Karen titled the book *Catherine, Called Birdy* (Holtze 1989, 72).

Karen's first book was named a Newbery Honor Book in 1995. It won the Carl Sandburg Award for Children's Literature from the Friends of the Chicago Public Library and a Golden Kite Award from the Society of Children's Book Writers and Illustrators.

Even while writing *Birdy,* Karen had the idea for another book. She wrote the title *Midwife's Apprentice* on a scrap of paper and put it in a file. When she finished her first book, she started the second.

The Midwife's Apprentice was awarded the Newbery Medal in 1996. Karen had found her life's work, and thousands of readers found Karen and her books.

Again comes the question, "what if?" What if Karen had listened to the many people who, through the years, told her that writing was a waste of time, and that she should give her time and attention to more secure vocations? What if she had listened to the people who said that if she still insisted on writing she should write what would sell, not what came from her heart?

"As a writer, I whisper in children's ears. And they talk back," Karen said in an interview for *Publishers Weekly* magazine (Lodge 1995, 46). In Karen's books those whispers have found a voice that speaks loud and clear.

Many believe that the life of an award-winning author is filled with glamour. True, there is a lot of joy in meeting one's readers, knowing that one's books are being read by people all over the world. But, says Karen, "I'm still the same person who has to empty the cat box and do the dishes, and it's strange to me that people are standing in line to have me sign my books. On the other hand, I feel pride and I feel a certain responsibility" (Lodge 1995, 46).

What if Karen Cushman had never written books?

Thank goodness, that is a question nobody ever has to ask.

A Word to My Readers:

As children are what they eat and hear and experience, so too they are what they read. This is why I write what I do, about strong young women who in one way or another take responsibility for their own lives, about tolerance, thoughtfulness, and caring; about choosing what is life affirming and generous; about the ways that people are the same and the ways they are different and how rich that makes us all. (Horn Book/ALSC 2001, 250)

Books by Karen Cushman

The Ballad of Lucy Whipple (Clarion, 1996).

Catherine, Called Birdy (Clarion, 1994).

Matilda Bone (Clarion, 2000).

The Midwife's Apprentice (Clarion, 1995).

For More Information About/by Karen Cushman

Holtze, Sally Holmes, ed. 1989. *The Seventh Book of Junior Authors and Illustrators.* H. W. Wilson.

Horn Book and Association for Library Service to Children (ALSC), American Library Association. 2001. *Newbery and Caldecott Medal Books, 1986–2000: A Comprehensive Guide to the Winners.* Horn Book and Association for Library Service to Children, American Library Association.

Lodge, Sally. 1995. A Talk with Karen Cushman. *Publishers Weekly,* 26 August.

1998: Karen Hesse

Born	August 29, 1952 Baltimore, Maryland
Married	Randy Hesse, November 27, 1971 (children: Kate and Rachel)

Awards and Honors

Newbery Medal (Historical Fiction): *Out of the Dust* (1997, Scholastic Press)

Christopher Award, 2002: *Witness* (Scholastic, 2001)

School Library Journal's Best Book of the Year Award, 1996: *The Music of Dolphins* (Scholastic, 1996); 1997: *Out of the Dust* (Scholastic, 1997); 2000: *Stowaway* (Margaret K. McElderry Books, 2000; Aladdin Paperbacks, 2002); 2001, *Witness* (Scholastic, 2001)

American Library Association Notable Children's Book, 1993: *Letters from Rifka* (H. Holt & Co., 1992; Puffin Books, 1993, 2001); 1995: *Phoenix Rising* (H. Holt & Co., 1994, Puffin Books, 1995); 1998: *Out of the Dust* (Scholastic, 1997); 2002: *Witness* (Scholastic, 2001)

Scott O'Dell Award, 1998: *Out of the Dust* (Scholastic, 1997)

American Library Association Best Book for Young Adults, 2002: *Witness* (Scholastic, 2001)

John D. and Catherine C. MacArthur Fellowship, 2002

About the Author and Her Writing

Not much is written about Karen Hesse's childhood. Rather than dwell on her own past, she chose to move forward. Karen is a writer who doesn't like to see people suffer, either in life or in her books. Yet because her stories are true to reality, the pain and hardship that are part of daily life are not ignored but lived out through the characters she so honestly brings to life in her books. Sorrow and joy live side by side, but ultimately, there is always the opportunity to find transformation and hope.

Karen began her writing life as a poet, publishing many of her poems while in college at the University of Maryland, where she graduated in 1975. She married young, and soon after graduation, she and her husband Randy moved to Vermont, where they settled and later welcomed their two daughters, Kate and Rachel.

During her first pregnancy Karen found that the creative energies she had given to her poetry were now turned toward the new life forming within. She could not write poetry anymore. Before her first daughter was born, Karen began reading what were then current works of children's literature. She could hardly believe how much the field had changed since she was a child. She fell in love with the writing of Katherine Paterson (Newbery Medal winner in 1978 and 1981) and read everything that Katherine had written. Years later the two became friends, a special bonus for the young author who had once devoured Katherine's books, hungry for good literature.

After her daughter's birth, Karen wrote while the baby napped. She did freelance writing: typesetting, proofreading, odd jobs that helped supplement the family income.

> Reading historical fiction gives us perspective. It gives us respite from the tempest of our present day lives. It gives us a safe place in which we can grow, transform, transcend. It helps us understand that sometimes the questions are too hard, that sometimes there are no answers, that sometimes there is only forgiveness. (Horn Book/ALSC 2001, 301)

When the baby went to bed at 7:00 P.M., Karen did, too. She woke up around 1:00 to 2:00 A.M. and then wrote for the next five or six hours until the baby woke up. Karen admitted that she was sleep deprived and probably cranky during those years, but said that she would have been even harder to live with if she hadn't gotten her writing time. But she also discovered she had a talent for writing prose. She wrote several books and began the arduous process of becoming a published author.

Karen wrote and wrote but was rejected time and again. Often, however, the rejection letters she received had personal notes that complimented her style and let her know that at least she was getting closer to getting published.

When Karen's beloved grandmother was dying, Karen carefully observed the tender care she received through hospice, a service that enables the terminally ill to die with grace and dignity, often in their own home. Touched by what she saw happen with her grandmother, Karen trained to be a hospice volunteer. She credited this training and experience with helping her discover more about her own inner workings and appreciate the intricacies of life and death. Karen's time with hospice deepened her gifts as a writer, as she even more thoroughly delved into the personalities of her characters and their ability to face even the most devastating of circumstances.

Karen had sent a manuscript to Brenda Bowen, who, as an editor at Four Winds Press, saw promise in Karen's writing. The manuscript was not accepted, but Brenda invited Karen to submit other manuscripts when she had them. Six years later Brenda, now working at the publishing company Henry Holt, received a packet of short manuscripts submitted through an agent. The author of the material: Karen Hesse.

One of the brief manuscripts centered around a unicorn. Brenda asked Karen to rewrite and lengthen the manuscript, which Karen gratefully did. Brenda asked her to rewrite it again. Again, Karen complied. Eventually, the four-page story became a full-fledged novel, and *Wish on a Unicorn* (H. Holt & Co., 1991) became Karen Hesse's first published book.

A strong sense of place, culture, and history are built into Karen's writing. This comes in part from her love of history, her delight and joy in researching and sifting through the past. Her books draw readers into a setting that might be far different from their own but feels deeply real.

On a car trip to Colorado in 1993, Karen fell in love with the state of Kansas. She walked through a small, nameless town blown about by the ceaseless winds, witnessed her first tornado, and marveled at the beauty of a land and sky that stretched into infinity. As she worked on her next picture book, a story about rain, she found herself drawn back in time to the 1930s and the dust bowl catastrophe of the Great Plains.

Karen spent months researching this time period via microfilm newspaper articles written during the years of devastation. She used a photograph of a young girl named Lucille Burroughs, taken by photographer Walker Evans, to inspire her as she wrote about the main character, Billie Jo. Later, when Karen's editor chose a photograph for the dust jacket of her book, she chose the same photograph, not realizing it was the one Karen had used while writing the book.

Karen wrote *Out of the Dust* in free-flowing verse. It seemed the only way the story could be told, a story of sparse times, a story in which an economy of words reflected the desolate economy that caused many people to give up and even to take their own lives. Yet more than anything, *Out of the Dust* is a story about forgiveness, between parent and child and between people and the land that has forsaken them.

Out of the Dust won the Newbery Medal in 1998. The story, which deals head on with tragedy and redemption, could be a reflection of Karen's life. She turned the sadness of her own childhood into the triumph of words that bring hope to people of all ages who find, in her stories, that even the darkest of times can fill us with the promise of a new beginning.

A Word to My Readers:

I love my characters too much to hurt them deliberately, even the prickly ones. It just so happens that in life, there's pain; sorrow lives in the shadow of joy, joy in the shadow of sorrow. The question is, do we let pain reign triumphant, or do we find a way to grow, to transform, and ultimately transcend our pain. (Horn Book/ALSC 2001, 297–98)

Books by Karen Hesse

Come On, Rain (Scholastic, 1999).

First Light (Hyperion, 2002).

Just Juice (Scholastic, 1998, 2001).

Lavender (H. Holt & Co., 1993).

Lester's Dog (Crown, 1993).

Letters from Rifka (H. Holt & Co., 1992; Puffin Books, 1993, 2001).

A Light in the Storm: The Civil War Diary of Amelia Martin (Scholastic, 1999).

The Music of Dolphins (Scholastic, 1996).

Out of the Dust (Scholastic, 1997).

Phoenix Rising (H. Holt & Co., 1994; Puffin Books, 1995).

Poppy's Chair (Macmillan, 1993; Scholastic, 2001).

Sable (H. Holt & Co., 1994).

The Stone Lamp (Hyperion, 2002).

Stowaway (Margaret K. McElderry Books, 2000; Aladdin Paperbacks, 2002).

A Time of Angels (Hyperion Books for Children, 1995, 2000).

Wish on a Unicorn (H. Holt & Co., 1991; Puffin Books, 1993).

Witness (Scholastic, 2001).

For More Information About/by Karen Hesse

Devereaux, Elizabeth. 1999. Karen Hesse: A Poetics of Perfectionism. *Publishers Weekly,* 8 February.

Horn Book and Association for Library Service to Children (ALSC), American Library Association. 2001. *The Newbery and Caldecott Medal Books, 1986–2000: A Comprehensive Guide to the Winners.* Horn Book and Association for Library Service to Children, American Library Association.

1999: Louis Sachar

Born   March 20, 1954
              East Meadow, New York

Married   Carla Askew, 1985 (children:
              Sherree)

Awards and Honors

Newbery Medal (Contemporary Life): *Holes* (Farrar, Straus & Giroux, 1998)

Children's Choice Book Award, 1987: *There's a Boy in the Girl's Bathroom* (Knopf: Random House, 1987; Cornerstone Books, 1990); 1990: *Wayside School Is Falling Down* (Lothrop, Lee & Shepard, 1989)

School Library Journal's Best Book of the Year Award, 1998: *Holes* (Farrar, Straus & Giroux, 1998)

Boston Globe-Horn Book Award, 1999: *Holes* (Farrar, Straus & Giroux, 1998)

Christopher Award, 1999: *Holes* (Farrar, Straus & Giroux, 1998)

American Library Association Notable Children's Book, 1999: *Holes* (Farrar, Straus, & Giroux, 1998)

About the Author and His Writing

Like the title of his popular series *Sideways School,* Louis Sachar (LOO-iss SACK-er) took a sideways route to becoming an author.

Louis was born in New York in 1954, but when he turned nine, his family moved to Tustin, California. Louis was a good student and especially enjoyed math. He began to truly enjoy reading when he was in high school.

Later he moved to Ohio to attend Antioch College, but soon after his father died suddenly. Louis took time off to return home and be with his mother. When he returned to college, it was to the University of California at Berkeley, where he majored in economics. He then worked for a while in a sweater factory in Connecticut before enrolling at the Hastings College of the Law in San Francisco, where he earned a law degree.

Perhaps the most important class he took during his years of education was the class he fell into backward and almost didn't take at all. During his undergraduate studies, Louis decided to take a class in Russian so he could read some of his favorite books in their original language. After a few weeks, he knew this plan wasn't going to work, so he dropped the class. In order to fill the space and earn the required credits, Louis agreed to volunteer as a teacher's aide at a local elementary school. That blossomed into a paid job as a playground supervisor. The kids called him "Louis, the yard teacher." Those same kids were some of the ones that inspired him to write *Sideways Stories from Wayside School* (Follett, 1978), his first book, published during his first year in law school.

> Mostly, when I write, I'm just trying to please one reader: myself. I try to write a story I like. And knowing myself as I do, I would not presume to try to teach myself a lesson. (Horn Book/ALSC 2001, 327)

Louis took classes at the law school for six years and also wrote more books. When he learned that he had passed the bar exam and could begin practicing law, Louis wasn't sure if he was happy about that or not. He now had the training to become a lawyer, but his heart was in writing books.

For a while, Louis combined both. He practiced law in the mornings and wrote in the afternoons. His books were not hugely popular at first, although they were extremely clever and unique. Then a reading specialist named Jim Trelease started using the *Sideways* stories as read-alouds during his many reading sessions. The book became a favorite with teachers and students. By 1995, it had sold over one million copies.

The increasing popularity of Louis's books had more than one advantage. Now he could afford to devote more time to his writing. He also met some interesting people. One class of students in Plano, Texas, loved his books and wrote to ask him to come for a visit. They slyly suggested that he might like meeting their teacher, who was single. Louis took the class up on the invitation, and although he did like the teacher, he met someone else he liked even more: the school counselor, Carla Askew, who became his wife in 1985.

The couple moved to San Francisco, where Carla taught and Louis wrote. They had a daughter, Sherree, and eventually settled back in Texas. Living in a one-room apartment, Carla left early each morning so Louis could have the solitude he needed to write, but Carla and Sherree were the first people Louis allowed to read his new books. Even they had to wait until the book had gone through the first three, four, or five drafts before they were allowed to take a peek at his latest work.

After spending two years working on novels that never got off the ground, Louis had the idea for a new book. He had never liked the heat. The seemingly endless Texas summers made him miserable. He began to think that one of his worst nightmares would be to have to labor out in the blinding heat, digging holes. The idea for *Holes* started to formulate in his mind. This new book was very different from the *Wayside School* and *Marvin Redpost* stories that had gained him so many devoted readers. It did have the elements of a puzzle, something Louis had always enjoyed. The book took him eighteen months to write.

On February 1, 1999, Louis received a phone call at 7:00 A.M., telling him he had won the Newbery Medal for *Holes*. Later, in his acceptance speech, he apologized to the committee that had selected the book for not responding to the news by screaming. "I could tell I was on a speaker phone, and I knew they were eagerly awaiting my reaction. I felt I was letting everyone down by not screaming. Sorry" (Horn Book/ALSC 2001, 326).

People often assume that those who write for children always have a hidden moral or lesson they want to convey. Not so, according to Louis, even with *Holes*. "The book was written for the sake of the book, and nothing beyond that. If there's any lesson at all, it is that reading is fun" (Horn Book/ALSC 2001, 326).

Reading for fun? There's nothing sideways about that!

A Word to My Readers:

Usually I spend up to a month brainstorming. I'll get an idea, write a few words on my computer, think, "That's stupid!" and delete it. I'll try something else: "That's dumb!" and try again. Sometimes I may get an idea that intrigues me, and I may work on it for a week before realizing it isn't going anywhere. Than at some point I'll get an idea that may not seem very special at first; however, as I write, it immediately starts to grow. One idea leads to another idea, and that idea leads to another idea, and that idea leads to another idea, until I have a story going. (Horn Book/ALSC 2001, 323)

Books by Louis Sachar

The Boy Who Lost His Face (A. A. Knopf, 1989).

Dogs Don't Tell Jokes (A. A. Knopf, 1991).

Holes (Farrar, Straus & Giroux, 1998).

Johnny's in the Basement (Avon Books, 1981; Knopf/Random House, 1981, 1990; Morrow Junior Books, 1998).

Le Passage (Archimede Editions, 2002).

A Magic Crystal? (Random House, 2000).

Marvin Redpost: A Flying Birthday Cake (Random House, 1999).

Marvin Redpost: Alone in His Teacher's House (Random House, 1994).

Marvin Redpost: Class President (Random House, 1999).

Marvin Redpost: Is He a Girl? (Random House, 1993).

Marvin Redpost: Kidnapped at Birth? (Random House, 1992).

Marvin Redpost: Super Fast, Out of Control! (Random House, 2000).

Marvin Redpost: Why Pick on Me? (Random House, 1993).

Monkey Soup (A. A. Knopf, 1992).

Sideways Stories from Wayside School (Follett, 1978; A. A. Knopf, 1990; Morrow Junior Books, 1998).

Sixth Grade Secrets (Scholastic, 1987).

Someday Angeline (Avon, 1983; Knopf, 1983, 1990; Morrow Junior Books, 1998).

There's a Boy in the Girl's Bathroom (Knopf: Random House, 1987; Cornerstone Books, 1990).

Wayside School Gets a Little Stranger (Morrow Junior Books, 1995).

Wayside School Is Falling Down (Lothrop, Lee & Shepard, 1989).

For More Information About/by Louis Sachar

Holtze, Sally Holmes, ed. 1986. *The Seventh Book of Junior Authors and Illustrators.* H. W. Wilson.

Horn Book and Association for Library Service to Children (ALSC), American Library Association. 2001. *The Newbery and Caldecott Medal Books, 1986–2000: A Comprehensive Guide to the Winners.* Horn Book and Association for Library Service to Children, American Library Association.

2000: Christopher Paul Curtis

Born   May 10, 1953
           Flint, Michigan

Married   Kaysandra Sookram
           (children: Steven and
           Cydney)

Awards and Honors

Newbery Medal (Contemporary Life): *Bud, Not Buddy* (Delacorte Press, 1999)

Newbery Honor Book for 1996: *The Watsons Go to Birmingham, 1963* (Delacorte Press, 1995)

Golden Kite Award, 1995: *The Watsons Go to Birmingham, 1963* (Delacorte Press, 1995)

American Library Association Notable Children's Book, 1996: *The Watsons Go to Birmingham, 1963* (Delacorte Press, 1995); 2000: *Bud, Not Buddy* (Delacorte Press, 1999)

American Library Association Best Book for Young Adults, 1996: *The Watsons Go to Birmingham, 1963* (Delacorte Press, 1995)

Coretta Scott King Honor Book, 1996: *The Watsons Go to Birmingham, 1963* (Delacorte Press, 1995)

School Library Journal's Best Book of the Year Award, 1999: *Bud, Not Buddy* (Delacorte Press, 1999)

Coretta Scott King Award, 2000: *Bud, Not Buddy* (Delacorte Press, 1999)

About the Author and His Writing

Every week while he was growing up, Christopher Paul Curtis spent Saturday morning with his family at the public library in Flint, Michigan. The Curtis children stayed in the children's section while their father browsed through the books for adults.

One Saturday morning, Christopher's father took his brother and sister to the youth section. He told Christopher to come with him. Together father and son crossed the hall

281

into the section marked "Adult Fiction." "You're a good enough reader to start here now," his father said (*Newbery and Caldecott Medal Books: 1986–2000,* pg. 346). The sense of pride at being "promoted" to the adult section of the library made a lasting impression.

Yet Christopher always felt most at home in the children's section. A table in the children's room served as his first office when he began writing full time.

The journey from reading in the library to writing in one took more than a few years. Although Christopher was accepted to the University of Michigan at Flint, he decided to work in the local automobile factory along with his father. For thirteen years, he worked on an assembly line hanging car doors until he couldn't stand it any more. Christopher also worked as a census taker, a political campaigner, and a garbage collector.

> Rules and Things Number 541: Don't Worry about Getting a Big Head. Friends, Family, and Total Strangers Will See to It That There Is No Way in the World You Will Be Allowed to Become Too Full of Yourself. (Horn Book/ALSC 2001, 353)

While working at the automobile factory, Christopher and a coworker arranged it so that they could each work for half an hour straight and then have a half-hour break. Christopher used this time to write, as a way of escaping the noise of the factory and keeping his sanity. He also attended school at night, married his wife, Kaysandra, and had two children: a son, Steven, and a daughter, Cydney.

It was his wife, Kaysandra, who first encouraged Christopher to try writing full time. She had been telling him for years that he was a good writer. She knew from the letters he'd written to her while they were dating and from journal entries he'd kept through the years that he had a gift with words. She gave him the freedom and the challenge to take a year and write full time. After years of hanging doors on cars and dumping garbage, it sounded like a good idea.

It was a good idea, but a scary one. Christopher wondered what would happen if he couldn't write. He didn't want to waste the year. In 1993 Christopher won two Hopwood Awards from the University of Michigan, one for an essay and one for a draft of a book about an African-American family traveling to Birmingham, Alabama, at the height of the Civil Rights movement in 1963. Christopher took this early draft and spent his days in the library, reworking the manuscript in longhand. At night his son Steven would read, edit, and type the manuscript into their computer.

When the manuscript was complete, Christopher called it *The Watsons Go to Birmingham—1963.* He submitted the book to a contest for a first young adult novel. Although it turned out that the manuscript didn't quite fit the guidelines of the contest, the title caught the attention of an editor. When she read the manuscript, one of hundreds submitted, she knew she'd found a writer, and a winner.

The Watsons Go to Birmingham, 1963 was a huge hit. It was named a Newbery Honor Book and a Coretta Scott King Honor Book for 1996. The Coretta Scott King award is given to an African-American author or illustrator whose work promotes appreciation and understanding of all cultures.

Christopher didn't let the overwhelming success of his first book keep him from writing another. He discovered that writing was fun and said that if he'd known that before, he would have started at age four!

Christopher's second book was based in Flint. This story was about a boy intent on finding the father he'd never known. In part, Christopher was inspired by several of his own relatives: his two grandfathers, Earl "Lefty" Lewis, a Negro Baseball League pitcher, and Herman E. Curtis Sr., a musician with the band "Herman Curtis and the Dusky Devastators of the Depression." Christopher titled this book *Bud, Not Buddy*.

At 9:16 A.M. on Monday, January 17, 2000, the phone rang at the Curtis home. It was the Coretta Scott King Award committee calling to tell him he'd won the prize again. This time, however, his book was not named as an honor book but as the winner of the award. Sixteen minutes later, at 9:32 A.M., Christopher received another telephone call. It was the Newbery committee informing him that he'd won the Newbery Medal for 2000. In two years' time, Christopher became the first writer to have his first book named as a Newbery Honor Book and a Coretta Scott King Honor Book and his second book named as the winner of the Newbery Medal and Coretta Scott King Award.

In his acceptance speech, Christopher thanked many people with a line from a popular song: "I want to thank you for letting me be myself." It is a statement of gratitude that scores of grateful readers can offer in return. Thank you, Christopher Paul Curtis, for being yourself, and for sharing that in your books.

A Word to My Readers:

The best practice for writing is to do it at every opportunity. Many times young people feel that writing is, or should be, the result of a consultation with some mysterious, hard-to-find muse. I think in many ways writing is much like learning a second language or playing a sport or mastering a musical instrument: the more you do it, the better you become at it. That's why I think keeping a daily journal should be high on the list of priorities for every young writer. (Rockman 2000, 106)

Books by Christopher Paul Curtis

Bud, Not Buddy (Delacorte Press, 1999; Thorndike Press, 1999).

The Watsons Go to Birmingham, 1963 (Delacorte Press, 1995; Holt, Rinehart & Winston, 1995; Thorndike Press, 2000).

For More Information About/by Christopher Paul Curtis

Horn Book and Association for Library Service to Children (ALSC), American Library Association. 2001. *The Newbery and Caldecott Medal Books, 1986–2000: A Comprehensive Guide to the Winners*. Horn Book and Association for Library Service to Children, American Library Association.

Rockman, Connie C., ed. 2000. *The Eighth Book of Junior Authors*. H. W. Wilson.

2001: Richard Peck

Born   April 5, 1934
            Decatur, Illinois

Awards and Honors

Newbery Medal (Contemporary Life): *A Year Down Yonder* (Dial Books for Young Readers, 2000)

Newbery Honor Book for 1999: *A Long Way from Chicago: A Novel in Stories* (Dial Books for Young Readers, 1998)

Friends of American Writers Award, 1976: *The Ghost Belonged to Me* (Viking Press, 1975)

Edgar Allan Poe Award, 1977: *Are You in the House Alone?* (Viking Press, 1976; Puffin Books, 2000)

Illinois Writer of the Year by Illinois Association of Teachers of English, 1977

American Library Association Best Book for Young Adults, 1981

American Library Association Margaret A. Edwards Award, 1990

American Library Association Notable Children's Book, 1986: *Remembering the Good Times* (Delacorte Press, 1985); 1987: *Blossom Culp and the Sleep of Death* (Delacorte Press, 1986); 1999: *A Long Way from Chicago* (Dial Books for Young Readers, 1998)

School Library Journal Best Books, 2000: *A Year Down Yonder* (Dial Books for Young Readers, 2000); 2001: *Fair Weather* (Dial Books for Young Readers, 2001)

About the Author and His Writing

Richard Peck was once a ghostwriter who ended up writing about ghosts. During his time in the United States Army, from 1956 to 1958, Richard was stationed in Stuttgart, Germany. He wrote the sermons that the chaplains preached at their chapel services, a process known as "ghost writing." But ghosts were not the first topic that Richard chose to write about, nor were ghost stories something he wrote all the time. He made a mark as one of the foremost authors for young adults, an author who came into this genre at the very time it was beginning to form.

During the 1960s and 1970s the books written for young people began to address the issues growing out of the cultural revolution that was taking place in the United States. Teens were being faced with freedoms that hadn't existed before, and issues that had been less visible became more and more apparent. This is the arena in which Richard found his niche. He not only wrote for young adults, he helped shaped the direction of this genre.

> Possibly the greatest role a book can play in the lives of young readers is to assure them they're not alone. (Silvey 1995, 513)

Don't Look and It Won't Hurt (Holt, Rinehart & Winston, 1972), his first published book, dealt with an unwanted teen pregnancy. He also wrote about suicide, rape, death, peer pressure, single parenting, and censorship. Richard wasn't afraid to bring these issues into the light; in fact, his goal was to provide books that might even encourage young people to talk more openly with each other as well as with their parents and teachers.

Richard grew up in Decatur, Illinois, where he was born on April 5, 1934. His mother was a dietician and his father owned a gas station, which was the local hangout for a wide variety of people: elderly men who sat and talked, railroad workers, truck drivers, newspaper carriers, people passing through town. Richard got an earful listening in on conversations that weren't always appropriate for a young boy's ears. These years helped shape him into a person who knew how to listen and how to tap into the insights and emotions of other people, skills that would serve him well as a writer.

Although Richard enjoyed writing, he didn't consider earning a living from it. He felt that teaching was the closest he could come to being a writer. He majored in English at DePauw University, attending on a scholarship. He also studied at Exeter University in Devon, England, and earned a master's in 1959 from Southern Illinois University, Carbondale. He did more postgraduate work and became an English instructor at Southern Illinois University. He also taught high school.

At the age of thirty-seven, Richard decided he needed to devote all his time to writing. The philosophy of education had changed since he first began, and he felt the need to make a change. Fortunately for all, he realized that he could use what he had learned from his students to write books. His first book was published in 1971. In thirty years, he wrote and published thirty books.

The author enjoyed visiting classrooms and talking to young people about writing. He was inspired by hearing their ideas and learning about the latest fads and challenges. The ideas for his books came directly from his contacts with the young people who were his readers. In Richard they had an advocate, a friend, and someone who understood the demands and joys they were experiencing.

In both his conversations and his books, Richard shared his insights into the time and place where he grew up. He wanted his readers to catch a glimpse of life during World War II and the Great Depression and the excitement and monotony of coming of age in a small town.

A number of the characters in Richard's novels are inspired by real-life people. His great-uncle, Miles Peck, is one example. At the age of eighty, Miles rode around the countryside in his old Model A Ford. His life of total freedom had great appeal to Richard as a child. Uncle Miles played a part in the novel *The Ghost Belonged to Me* (Viking

Press, 1975). This book and its filming by Disney were so popular that Richard wrote three more books with the same characters introduced in *Ghost.*

In 1999, Richard's novel *A Long Way from Chicago* was named a Newbery Honor Book. The book tells the story of a brother and sister from the Chicago area who spend the summers with their grandmother, who lives in a small town in central Illinois. Grandma Dowdel is unlike anyone the siblings have ever met before. She packs a shotgun and has no time for gossip and trivia. She catches catfish to feed a mysterious old woman. Each year during their visits, the children learn more not only about their grandmother but also about life and about themselves.

A Long Way from Chicago was met with such enthusiasm by readers that Richard's editor asked if he could write a sequel. He tackled the project with some apprehension, not sure a sequel was possible. He needn't have worried. *A Year Down Yonder* won the Newbery Medal for 2001. This book continues the adventures of Grandma Dowdel and her granddaughter, Mary Alice, who visits her year after year. The story is so well done it stands on its own, not dependent on the book that led to its being written.

Richard also published essays, poetry, adult novels, and short stories. He received numerous awards for his books, including two Edgar Allan Poe Awards and the Margaret A. Edwards Lifetime Achievement Award given by both the *School Library Journal* and the Young Adult Library Services Association of the American Library Association.

The theme that informs Richard's books is that "you never grow up until you declare your independence from your peers" (Silvey 1995, 513). His poem "A Teenager's Prayer" states this in simple eloquence: "Give me the understanding that nobody ever grows up in a group so I may find my own way." Many young people have found, and will continue to find, their own way through the books of Richard Peck.

A Word to My Readers:

The world is my classroom. I'm always looking for a story. (talk given September 26, 2001, at Crocodile Pie children's book store in Libertyville, Illinois)

Books by Richard Peck

Amanda/Miranda (Viking Press, 1980; Dial Books for Young Readers, 1999).

Anonymously Yours (Beech Tree Books, 1995).

Are You in the House Alone? (Viking Press, 1976; Puffin Books, 2000).

Bel Air Bambi and the Mall Rats (Delacorte Press, 1993).

Blossom Culp and the Sleep of Death (Delacorte Press, 1986).

Close Enough to Touch (Delacorte Press, 1981).

Don't Look and It Won't Hurt (Holt, Rinehart & Winston, 1972; H. Holt & Co., 1999).

The Dreadful Future of Blossom Culp (Delacorte Press, 1983; Puffin Books, 2001).

Dreamland Lake (Holt, Rinehart & Winston, 1973; Puffin Books, 2000).

Fair Weather (Dial Books for Young Readers, 2001).

Father Figure (Viking Press, 1978).

The Ghost Belonged to Me (Viking Press, 1975; Cornerstone Books, 1989).

Ghosts I Have Been (Viking Press, 1977).

The Great Interactive Dream Machine: Another Adventure in Cyberspace (Dial Books for Readers, 1996).

Invitations to the World: Reflections on Teaching and Writing for Young Adults (Dial Press, 2002).

The Last Safe Place on Earth (Delacorte Press, 1995).

London Holiday (Viking Press, 1998; Thorndike Press, 1998; Penguin, 1999).

A Long Way from Chicago: A Novel in Stories (Dial Books for Young Readers, 1998).

Lost in Cyberspace (Dial Books for Young Readers, 1995).

Love and Death at the Mall: Teaching and Writing for the Literate Young (Delacorte Press, 1994).

Mindscapes: Poems for the Real World (Delacorte Press, 1971).

Monster Night at Grandma's House (Viking Press, 1977).

New York Time (Delacorte Press, 1981).

Princess Ashley (Delacorte Press, 1987).

Remembering the Good Times (Delacorte Press, 1985).

Representing Super Doll (Viking Press, 1974).

Secrets of the Shopping Mall (Delacorte Press, 1979).

Sounds and Silences (Delacorte Press, 1970).

Strays Like Us (Dial Books for Young Readers, 1998).

This Family of Women (Delacorte Press, 1983; G. K. Hall, 1983).

Those Summer Girls I Never Met (Delacorte Press, 1988).

Through a Brief Darkness (Viking Press, 1973).

Transitions: A Literary Paper Casebook (Random House, 1974).

Unfinished Portrait of Jessica (Delacorte Press, 1991).

Urban Studies: A Research Paper Casebook (Random House, 1974).

Voices After Midnight (Delacorte Press, 1989).

A Year Down Yonder (Dial Books for Young Readers, 2000).

For More Information About/by Richard Peck

Autobiography: 1995. *Anonymously Yours*. Beech Tree Books.

Drew, Bernard A. 1997. *The 100 Most Popular Young Adult Authors: Biographical Sketches and Bibliographies*. Rev. ed. Libraries Unlimited.

Silvey, Anita, ed. 1995. *Children's Books and Their Creators*. Houghton Mifflin.

2002: Linda Sue Park

Born   March 25, 1960
              Urbana, Illinois

Married   Ben Dobbin, 1984
              (children: Sean and Anna)

Awards and Honors

Newbery Medal (Historical Fiction): *A Single Shard* (Clarion, 2001)
School Library Journal's Best Books, 2001: *A Single Shard* (Clarion, 2001); 2002: *When My Name Was Keoko* (Clarion, 2002)
American Library Association Notable Children's Book, 2002: *A Shingle Shard* (Clarion, 2001); 2003: *When My Name Was Keoko* (Clarion, 2002)

About the Author and Her Writing

In 1922, history was made in the field of children's literature with the awarding of the first Newbery Medal. Eighty years later, in 2002, Linda Sue Park made history again by becoming the first Korean American to win this prestigious award.

When Linda Sue was still a young child, there were indications that this girl who loved to read books would one day become an adult who wrote books for children. She earned her first income as a writer at the age of nine when *Trailblazer* magazine paid her one dollar to publish a haiku poem. The poem shows her early talent and gift with words:

> In the green forest
> A sparkling, bright blue pond hides.
> And animals drink.
>   (*Trailblazer* magazine, Winter 1969)

Rather than cashing the check, Linda Sue gave it to her father for a Christmas present. He framed the check and hung it on the wall above his desk.

Through the years, Linda Sue continued to publish poems in magazines for children and young adults. She attended college at Stanford University in California, where she earned a degree in English. Following graduation, she went to work for a major oil company. Her work consisted of writing public-relations information, which she did for two years.

Then Linda Sue's life took an interesting twist. She moved to Ireland and then to London to study literature. She worked at an advertising agency and later as a food journalist. She married an Irishman and had two children. Linda Sue also found a niche for her talents by teaching English as a Second Language to college students.

> For me, writing is a way of exploring the world. (interview, May 6, 2002)

In 1990, Linda Sue and her family moved back to the United States. She raised her children and continued to teach. Her life was full and happy, but her schedule left no time for writing. Instead, Linda concentrated on reading. Before she wrote her first middle-grade novel, she read hundreds of books in this genre. When Linda Sue advises would-be writers to read as much as possible, she knows what she's talking about!

In 1997, Linda Sue's first book, *Seesaw Girl,* was accepted for publication and published in 1999. *The Kite Fighters* came out a year later in 2000. The next year, her Newbery Medal–winning book, *A Single Shard,* was published.

A Single Shard tells the story of Tree-ear, a young Korean orphan living in the twelfth century. Tree-ear's name comes from a mushroom that grows on its own from rotten tree trunks. He lives under a bridge with an older man who also has no family and who befriends the boy. Tree-ear is captivated by the work of Min, a renowned potter. He eventually convinces the aging man to take him on as an apprentice.

> I became a writer because I was a reader first. (interview, May 6, 2002)

Linda Sue found the inspiration for writing *A Single Shard* while researching her earlier books. She discovered that twelfth-century Korea was considered the best in the world in pottery, a fact that immediately captured her interest. Tree-ear and his story grew like the mushroom for which he is named, seemingly out of nowhere but rooted in reality and truth.

Winning the Newbery Medal changed Linda Sue's life overnight. She was so surprised when she got the phone call telling her that *A Single Shard* had won the award that at first she couldn't believe it and had to ask the committee chair to repeat herself. Within just a few weeks, Linda Sue began traveling throughout the United States visiting schools and conferences to talk about her books and writing. She also received an invitation to visit Korea.

Linda Sue Park has lived in many places in this world. Her books, too, have found a home in the hearts of readers from all walks of life.

A Word to My Readers:

I truly believe that reading can help dreams come true. Whatever you want to become in your life, whatever you want to do, reading can help you get there! (interview, May 6, 2002)

Books by Linda Sue Park

The Kite Fighters (Houghton Mifflin, 2000).

Seesaw Girl (Houghton Mifflin, 1999).

A Single Shard (Clarion, 2001).

When My Name Was Keoko (Clarion, 2002).

For More Information About/by Linda Sue Park

Web site: www.lindasuepark.com.

Note: Indicated citations from an e-mail interview with the author, May 6, 2002.

Chronological Listing of Newbery Medalists

2002	*A Single Shard*	Linda Sue Park	Clarion
2001	*A Year Down Yonder*	Richard Peck	Dial Books for Young Readers
2000	*Bud, Not Buddy*	Christopher Paul Curtis	Delacorte Press
1999	*Holes*	Louis Sachar	Frances Foster Books/Farrar, Straus & Giroux
1998	*Out of the Dust*	Karen Hesse	Scholastic
1997	*The View from Saturday*	E. L. Konigsburg	Jean Karl/ Atheneum Books for Young Readers
1996	*The Midwife's Apprentice*	Karen Cushman	Clarion
1995	*Walk Two Moons*	Sharon Creech	HarperCollins
1994	*The Giver*	Lois Lowry	Houghton Mifflin
1993	*Missing May*	Cynthia Rylant	Jackson/Orchard Books
1992	*Shiloh*	Phyllis Reynolds Naylor	Atheneum Books for Young Readers
1991	*Maniac Magee*	Jerry Spinelli	Little, Brown
1990	*Number the Stars*	Lois Lowry	Houghton Mifflin
1989	*Joyful Noise: Poems for Two Voices*	Paul Fleischman	Harper & Row
1988	*Lincoln: A Photobiography*	Russell Freedman	Clarion
1987	*The Whipping Boy*	Albert Sidney "Sid" Fleischman	Greenwillow Books
1986	*Sarah, Plain and Tall*	Patricia MacLachlan	Harper & Row
1985	*The Hero and the Crown*	Robin McKinley	Greenwillow Books
1984	*Dear Mr. Henshaw*	Beverly Cleary	William Morrow
1983	*Dicey's Song*	Cynthia Voigt	Atheneum
1982	*A Visit to William Blake's Inn: Poems for Innocent and Experienced Travelers*	Nancy Willard	Harcourt Brace Jovanovich
1981	*Jacob Have I Loved*	Katherine Paterson	Crowell
1980	*A Gathering of Days: A New England Girl's Journal, 1830–1832*	Joan Blos	C. Scribner's Sons

1979	*The Westing Game*	Ellen Raskin	Dutton
1978	*Bridge to Terabithia*	Katherine Paterson	Crowell
1977	*Roll of Thunder, Hear My Cry*	Mildred D. Taylor	Dial Press
1976	*The Grey King*	Susan Cooper (Cronyn)	Atheneum
1975	*M. C. Higgins, the Great*	Virginia Hamilton	Macmillan
1974	*The Slave Dancer*	Paula Fox	Bradbury Press
1973	*Julie of the Wolves*	Jean Craighead George	Harper & Row
1972	*Mrs. Frisby and the Rats of NIMH*	Robert C. O'Brien	Atheneum
1971	*Summer of the Swans*	Betsy Byars	Viking Press
1970	*Sounder*	William H. Armstrong	Harper & Row
1969	*The High King*	Lloyd Alexander	Holt, Rinehart & Winston
1968	*From the Mixed-Up Files of Mrs. Basil E. Frankweiler*	E. L. Konigsburg	Atheneum
1967	*Up a Road Slowly*	Irene Hunt	Follett
1966	*I, Juan de Pareja*	Elizabeth Borton de Trevino	Farrar, Straus & Giroux
1965	*Shadow of a Bull*	Maia Wojciechowska	Atheneum
1964	*It's Like This, Cat*	Emily Cheney Neville	Harper & Row
1963	*A Wrinkle in Time*	Madeleine L'Engle	Farrar, Straus & Giroux
1962	*The Bronze Bow*	Elizabeth George Speare	Houghton Mifflin
1961	*Island of the Blue Dolphins*	Scott O'Dell	Houghton Mifflin
1960	*Onion John*	Joseph Quincy Krumgold	Crowell
1959	*The Witch of Blackbird Pond*	Elizabeth George Speare	Houghton Mifflin
1958	*Rifles for Watie*	Harold Keith	Crowell
1957	*Miracles on Maple Hill*	Virginia Sorensen	Harcourt, Brace & Co.
1956	*Carry On, Mr. Bowditch*	Jean Lee Latham	Houghton Mifflin
1955	*The Wheel on the School*	Meindert DeJong	Harper
1954	*. . . And Now Miguel*	Joseph Quincy Krumgold	Crowell
1953	*Secret of the Andes*	Ann Nolan Clark	Viking Press
1952	*Ginger Pye*	Eleanor Estes	Harcourt, Brace & Co.
1951	*Amos Fortune, Free Man*	Elizabeth Yates (McGreal)	Dutton
1950	*The Door in the Wall*	Marguerite de Angeli	Doubleday
1949	*King of the Wind*	Marguerite Henry	Rand McNally

1948	*The Twenty-One Balloons*	William Pène du Bois	Viking Press
1947	*Miss Hickory*	Carolyn Sherwin Bailey (Hill)	Viking Press
1946	*Strawberry Girl*	Lois Lenski	Lippincott
1945	*Rabbit Hill*	Robert Lawson	Viking Press
1944	*Johnny Tremain, a Novel for Old and Young*	Esther Forbes	Houghton Mifflin
1943	*Adam of the Road*	Elizabeth Janet Gray (Vining)	Viking Press
1942	*The Matchlock Gun*	Walter Edmonds	Dodd, Mead
1941	*Call It Courage*	Armstrong Sperry	Macmillan
1940	*Daniel Boone*	James Daugherty	Viking Press, Junior Literary Guild
1939	*Thimble Summer*	Elizabeth Wright Enright	Farrar & Rinehart
1938	*The White Stag*	Kate Seredy	Viking Press
1937	*Roller Skates*	Ruth Sawyer	Viking Press
1936	*Caddie Woodlawn*	Carol Ryrie Brink	Macmillan
1935	*Dobry*	Monica Shannon	Viking Press
1934	*Invincible Louisa: The Story of the Author of Little Women*	Cornelia Meigs	Little, Brown
1933	*Young Fu of the Upper Yangtze*	Elizabeth Foreman Lewis	Winston
1932	*Waterless Mountain*	Laura Adams Armer	Longmans, Green & Co.
1931	*The Cat Who Went to Heaven*	Elizabeth Coatsworth	Macmillan
1930	*Hitty, Her First Hundred Years*	Rachel Field	Macmillan
1929	*The Trumpeter of Krakow, a Tale of the Fifteenth Century*	Eric P. Kelly	Macmillan
1928	*Gay Neck, the Story of a Pigeon*	Dhan Gopal Mukerji	Dutton
1927	*Smoky, the Cowhorse*	Will James	C. Scribner's Sons
1926	*Shen of the Sea: A Book for Children*	Arthur Bowie Chrisman	Dutton
1925	*Tales from Silver Lands*	Charles Joseph Finger	Doubleday, Page & Co.
1924	*The Dark Frigate*	Charles Boardman Hawes	Little, Brown
1923	*The Voyages of Doctor Dolittle*	Hugh Lofting	Lippincott
1922	*The Story of Mankind*	Hendrik van Loon	Boni & Liveright

Alphabetical Listing of Newbery Medalists

Alexander, Lloyd	*The High King*	1969
Armer, Laura Adams	*Waterless Mountain*	1932
Armstrong, William H.	*Sounder*	1970
Bailey (Hill), Carolyn Sherwin	*Miss Hickory*	1947
Blos, Joan	*A Gathering of Days: A New England Girl's Journal, 1830–1832*	1980
Brink, Carol Ryrie	*Caddie Woodlawn*	1936
Byars, Betsy	*Summer of the Swans*	1971
Chrisman, Arthur Bowie	*Shen of the Sea: A Book for Children*	1926
Clark, Ann Nolan	*Secret of the Andes*	1953
Cleary, Beverly	*Dear Mr. Henshaw*	1984
Coatsworth, Elizabeth	*The Cat Who Went to Heaven*	1931
Cooper (Cronyn), Susan	*The Grey King*	1976
Creech, Sharon	*Walk Two Moons*	1995
Curtis, Christopher Paul	*Bud, Not Buddy*	2000
Cushman, Karen	*The Midwife's Apprentice*	1996
Daugherty, James	*Daniel Boone*	1940
de Angeli, Marguerite	*The Door in the Wall*	1950
DeJong, Meindert	*The Wheel on the School*	1955
du Bois, William Pène	*The Twenty-One Balloons*	1948
Edmonds, Walter	*The Matchlock Gun*	1942
Enright, Elizabeth Wright	*Thimble Summer*	1939
Estes, Eleanor	*Ginger Pye*	1952
Field, Rachel	*Hitty, Her First Hundred Years*	1930
Finger, Charles Joseph	*Tales from Silver Lands*	1925
Fleischman, Paul	*Joyful Noise: Poems for Two Voices*	1989
Fleischman, Albert Sidney "Sid"	*The Whipping Boy*	1987
Forbes, Esther	*Johnny Tremain, a Novel for Old and Young*	1944
Fox, Paula	*The Slave Dancer*	1974
Freedman, Russell	*Lincoln: A Photobiography*	1988
George, Jean Craighead	*Julie of the Wolves*	1973
Gray (Vining), Elizabeth Janet	*Adam of the Road*	1943
Hamilton, Virginia	*M. C. Higgins, the Great*	1975
Hawes, Charles Boardman	*The Dark Frigate*	1924
Henry, Marguerite	*King of the Wind*	1949

Hesse, Karen	*Out of the Dust*	1998
Hunt, Irene	*Up a Road Slowly*	1967
James, Will	*Smoky, the Cowhorse*	1927
Keith, Harold	*Rifles for Watie*	1958
Kelly, Eric P.	*The Trumpeter of Krakow, a Tale of the Fifteenth Century*	1929
Konigsburg, E. L.	*From the Mixed-Up Files of Mrs. Basil E. Frankweiler*	1968
	The View from Saturday	1997
Krumgold, Joseph Quincy	*. . . And Now Miguel*	1954
	Onion John	1960
Latham, Jean Lee	*Carry On, Mr. Bowditch*	1956
Lawson, Robert	*Rabbit Hill*	1945
L'Engle, Madeleine	*A Wrinkle in Time*	1963
Lenski, Lois	*Strawberry Girl*	1946
Lewis, Elizabeth Foreman	*Young Fu of the Upper Yangtze*	1933
Lofting, Hugh	*The Voyages of Doctor Dolittle*	1923
Lowry, Lois	*Number the Stars*	1990
	The Giver	1994
MacLachlan, Patricia	*Sarah, Plain and Tall*	1986
McKinley, Robin	*The Hero and the Crown*	1985
Meigs, Cornelia	*Invincible Louisa: The Story of the Author of Little Women*	1934
Mukerji, Dhan Gopal	*Gay Neck, the Story of a Pigeon*	1928
Naylor, Phyllis Reynolds	*Shiloh*	1992
Neville, Emily Cheney	*It's Like This, Cat*	1964
O'Brien, Robert C.	*Mrs. Frisby and the Rats of NIMH*	1972
O'Dell, Scott	*Island of the Blue Dolphins*	1961
Park, Linda Sue	*A Single Shard*	2002
Paterson, Katherine	*Bridge to Terabithia*	1978
	Jacob Have I Loved	1981
Peck, Richard	*A Year Down Yonder*	2001
Raskin, Ellen	*The Westing Game*	1979
Rylant, Cynthia	*Missing May*	1993
Sachar, Louis	*Holes*	1999
Sawyer, Ruth	*Roller Skates*	1937
Seredy, Kate	*The White Stag*	1938
Shannon, Monica	*Dobry*	1935
Sorensen, Virginia	*Miracles on Maple Hill*	1957
Speare, Elizabeth George	*The Witch of Blackbird Pond*	1959
	The Bronze Bow	1962
Sperry, Armstrong	*Call It Courage*	1941

Newbery Medalists Who Have Won a Newbery Honor Award

2001	Sharon Creech (Rigg)	*The Wanderer*
1999	Richard Peck	*A Long Way from Chicago: A Novel in Stories*
1998	Jerry Spinelli	*Wringer*
1996	Christopher Paul Curtis	*The Watsons Go to Birmingham, 1963*
1995	Karen Cushman	*Catherine, Called Birdy*
1994	Russell Freedman	*Eleanor Roosevelt: A Life of Discovery*
1992	Russell Freedman	*The Wright Brothers: How They Invented the Airplane*
1989	Virginia Hamilton	*In the Beginning: Creation Stories from Around the World*
1987	Cynthia Rylant	*A Fine White Dust*
1985	Paula Fox	*One Eyed Cat*
1984	Elizabeth George Speare	*The Sign of the Beaver*
1984	Cynthia Voigt	*A Solitary Blue*
1983	Virginia Hamilton	*Sweet Whispers, Brother Rush*
1983	Robin McKinley	*The Blue Sword*
1982	Beverly Cleary	*Ramona Quimby, Age 8*
1982	Paul Fleischman	*Graven Images: 3 Stories*
1981	Madeleine L'Engle	*A Ring of Endless Light*
1979	Katherine Paterson	*The Great Gilly Hopkins*
1978	Beverly Cleary	*Ramona and Her Father*
1975	Ellen Raskin	*Figgs & Phantoms*
1974	Susan Cooper (Cronyn)	*The Dark Is Rising*
1972	Virginia Hamilton	*The Planet of Junior Brown*
1971	Scott O'Dell	*Sing Down the Moon*
1968	E. L. Konigsburg	*Jennifer, Hecate, Macbeth, William McKinley, and Me, Elizabeth*
1968	Scott O'Dell	*The Black Pearl*
1967	Scott O'Dell	*The King's Fifth*
1966	Lloyd Alexander	*The Black Cauldron*
1965	Irene Hunt	*Across Five Aprils*
1960	Jean Craighead George	*My Side of the Mountain*
1959	Meindert DeJong	*Along Came a Dog*
1958	Elizabeth Wright Enright	*Gone Away Lake*
1958	Robert Lawson	*The Great Wheel*
1957	Marguerite de Angeli	*Black Fox of Lorne*

1957	Meindert DeJong	*The House of Sixty Fathers*
1954	Meindert DeJong	*Hurry Home, Candy*
1954	Meindert DeJong	*Shadrach*
1948	Marguerite Henry	*Misty of Chincoteague*
1946	Marguerite Henry	*Justin Morgan Had a Horse*
1945	Eleanor Estes	*The Hundred Dresses*
1944	Eleanor Estes	*Rufus M.*
1943	Eleanor Estes	*The Middle Moffat*
1942	Lois Lenski	*Indian Captive: The Story of Mary Jemison*
1940	Kate Seredy	*The Singing Tree*
1939	Elizabeth Janet Gray (Vining)	*Penn*
1937	Lois Lenski	*Phoebe Fairchild: Her Book*
1936	Elizabeth Janet Gray (Vining)	*Young Walter Scott*
1936	Kate Seredy	*The Good Master*
1936	Armstrong Sperry	*All Sail Set: A Romance of the Flying Cloud*
1933	Cornelia Meigs	*Swift Rivers*
1932	Rachel Field	*Calico Bush*
1931	Elizabeth Janet Gray (Vining)	*Meggy MacIntosh*
1929	Cornelia Meigs	*Clearing Weather*
1922	Charles Boardman Hawes	*The Great Quest*
1922	Cornelia Meigs	*The Windy Hill*

Newbery Medalists Who Have Won the Laura Ingalls Wilder Award

Awarded triennially to the author or illustrator whose works have made a lasting contribution to the field of children's literature.

1998	Russell Freedman
1995	Virginia Hamilton
1989	Elizabeth George Speare
1975	Beverly Cleary
1965	Ruth Sawyer

Newbery Medalists Who Have Won the Hans Christian Andersen Medal

Awarded every two years to one author and one illustrator in recognition of his or her entire body of work. Established in 1956.

1998	Katherine Paterson
1992	Virginia Hamilton
1978	Paula Fox
1972	Scott O'Dell
1962	Meindert DeJong

Newbery Medalists Who Have Won the Coretta Scott King Award or a Coretta Scott King Honor Book

Presented annually to authors and illustrators of African descent whose distinguished books promote an understanding and appreciation of the "American Dream." Awarded by the Coretta Scott King Task Force of the American Library Association's Social Responsibilities Round Table.

2002	*The Land* (Phyllis Fogelman Books)	Mildred D. Taylor
2000	*Bud, Not Buddy* (Delacorte Press)	Christopher Paul Curtis
1996	*Her Stories* (Scholastic/Blue Sky Press)	Virginia Hamilton
1996	Honor Book, *The Watsons Go to Birmingham, 1963* (Delacorte Press)	Christopher Paul Curtis
1991	*The Road to Memphis* (Dial Books)	Mildred D. Taylor
1990	Honor Book: *The Bells of Christmas* (Harcourt)	Virginia Hamilton
1989	Honor Book: *Anthony Burns: The Defeat and Triumph of a Fugitive Slave* (Knopf)	Virginia Hamilton
1988	*The Friendship* (Dial)	Mildred D. Taylor
1986	*The People Could Fly: American Black Folktales* (Knopf)	Virginia Hamilton
	Honor Book: *Junius Over Far* (Harcourt)	Virginia Hamilton
1985	Honor Book: *A Little Love* (Philomel)	Virginia Hamilton
1984	Honor Book: *The Magical Adventures of Pretty Pearl* (Harper)	Virginia Hamilton
1983	*Sweet Whispers, Brother Rush* (Philomel)	Virginia Hamilton
1982	*Let the Circle Be Unbroken* (Dial)	Mildred D. Taylor
1979	Honor Book: *Justice and Her Brothers* (Greenwillow)	Virginia Hamilton

Newbery Medalists Who Have Won the Boston Globe-Horn Book Award

The Boston Globe-Horn Book Award was started in 1967 and is cosponsored by the Boston *Globe* and the Horn Book, Inc. The award is given for excellence in literature for children and young adults. The awards are considered among the most prestigious in the nation. Eligible books must be published in the United States, although citizens of any country may have their book considered for the award.

Year	Category	Author	Title
1999	Fiction	Louis Sachar	*Holes*
1994	Non-Fiction	Russell Freedman	*Eleanor Roosevelt: A Life of Discovery*
1993	Picture Book	Lloyd Alexander	*The Fortune Tellers*
1992	Fiction	Cynthia Rylant	*Missing May*
1991	Picture Book	Katherine Paterson	*The Tale of the Mandarin Ducks*
1991	Non-Fiction	Cynthia Rylant	*Appalachia: The Voices of Sleeping Birds*
1990	Fiction	Jerry Spinelli	*Maniac Magee*
1989	Fiction	Paula Fox	*The Village by the Sea*
1988	Fiction	Mildred D. Taylor	*The Friendship*
1988	Non-Fiction	Virginia Hamilton	*Anthony Burns: The Defeat and Triumph of a Fugitive Slave*
1987	Fiction	Lois Lowry	*Rabble Starkey*
1983	Fiction	Virginia Hamilton	*Sweet Whispers, Brother Rush*
1982	Picture Book	Nancy Willard	*A Visit to William Blake's Inn*
1979	Fiction	Albert Sidney "Sid" Fleischman	*Humbug Mountain*
1978	Fiction	Ellen Raskin	*The Westing Game*
1974	Fiction	Virginia Hamilton	*M.C. Higgins, the Great*
1973	Fiction	Susan Cooper (Cronyn)	*The Dark Is Rising*

Newbery Medalists Who Have Won the Golden Kite Award

The Golden Kite Award is an award presented annually by the Society of Children's Book Writers and Illustrators for excellence in the field of children's books. This is the only award given to children's book authors and artists that are chosen by their fellow authors and artists. The recipients of the award, for fiction, non-fiction, picture book text, and picture-illustration, are members of the Society of Children's Book Writers and Illustrators.

1998	Non-Fiction	Russell Freedman	*Martha Graham: A Dancer's Life*
1995	Fiction	Christopher Paul Curtis	*The Watsons Go to Birmingham, 1963*
1994	Fiction	Karen Cushman	*Catherine, Called Birdy*
1994	Non-Fiction	Russell Freedman	*Kids at Work: Lewis Hine and the Crusade Against Child Labor*
1993	Non-Fiction	Russell Freedman	*Eleanor Roosevelt: A Life of Discovery*
1991	Non-Fiction	Russell Freedman	*The Wright Brothers: How They Invented the Airplane*
1987	Fiction	Lois Lowry	*Rabble Starkey*
1985	Fiction	Patricia MacLachlan	*Sarah, Plain and Tall*
1982	Fiction	Beverly Cleary	*Ralph S. Mouse*
1980	Fiction	Patricia MacLachlan	*Arthur, for the Very First Time*
1978	Non-Fiction	Phyllis Reynolds Naylor	*How I Came to Be a Writer*

Partial Listing of Autobiographies by Newbery Medalists

Betsy Byars	*The Moon and I*
Beverly Cleary	*A Girl from Yamhill: A Memoir*
Beverly Cleary	*My Own Two Feet: A Memoir*
Elizabeth Coatsworth	*Personal Geography: Almost an Autobiography*
Marguerite de Angeli	*Butter at the Old Price: The Autobiography of Marguerite de Angeli*
Albert Sidney "Sid" Fleischman	*The Abracadabra Kid: A Writer's Life*
Paula Fox	*Borrowed Finery: A Memoir*
Jean Craighead George	*The Tarantula in My Purse: And 172 Other Wild Pets*
Elizabeth Janet Gray (Vining)	*Being Seventy: The Measure of a Year*
Will James	*Lone Cowboy: My Life Story*
Madeleine L'Engle	*The Summer of the Great Grandmother*
Madeleine L'Engle	*Two Part Invention: The Story of a Marriage*
Lois Lenski	*Journey into Childhood*
Lois Lowry	*Looking Back: A Book of Memories*
Dhan Mukerji	*Caste and Outcast*
Phyllis Reynolds Naylor	*Crazy Love: An Autobiographical Account of Marriage and Madness*
Phyllis Reynolds Naylor	*How I Came to Be a Writer*
Richard Peck	*Anonymously Yours: A Memoir by the Author of Ghosts I Have Been*
Cynthia Rylant	*But I'll Be Back Again*
Virginia Sorensen	*Where Nothing Is Long Ago: Memoirs of a Mormon Childhood*
Jerry Spinelli	*Knots in My Yo-Yo String: The Autobiography of a Kid*
Elizabeth Borton de Treviño	*My Heart Lies South: The Story of My Mexican Marriage*
	The Hearthstone of My Heart
Hendrik van Loon	*Invasion*
Hendrik van Loon	*Report to St. Peter, Upon the Kind of World in Which Hendrik Willem van Loon Spent the First Years of His Life*
Maia Wojciechowska	*Till the Break of Day*

Elizabeth Yates (McGreal)	*The Lighted Heart*
Elizabeth Yates (McGreal)	*My Diary, My World*
Elizabeth Yates (McGreal)	*My Widening World*
Elizabeth Yates (McGreal)	*One Writer's Way*
Elizabeth Yates (McGreal)	*Spanning Time: A Diary Keeper Becomes a Writer*

Fun Facts About the Newbery Medalists

Can you name the Newbery Medalist who . . .

1. Was the first woman to win the Newbery Medal?

2. Won the Newbery Medal and Newbery Honor in the same year?

3. Was the first person to win the Newbery Medal twice?

4. Used the letters he wrote home to his children during World War I as the basis for his Newbery Medal book?

5. Taught history at the same school for fifty years?

6. Wrote and illustrated in one week the book that won the Newbery Medal?

7. Was inspired to write her Newbery–winning book because of a picture on some letterhead stationery?

8. For twenty-five straight years wrote an average of one book a year?

9. Was a tutor for the crown prince of Japan following World War II?

10. Had a pet turkey vulture and falcon as pets?

11. Won the Newbery Medal two years after his father, making them the first and only father and son to win the Medal?

12. Was awarded the Order of the Netherlands Lion from Queen Wilhelmina, the highest honor given by his native country?

13. Was orphaned at the age of eight and raised by her grandmother and an aunt; the grandmother's life became the basis for the author's Newbery Medal book?

14. Learned to read as soon as he could crawl and to write as soon as he could walk?

15. Wrote about an animal that is now extinct?

16. Is the first and only person to win both a Newbery Medal and a Caldecott Medal?

17. After winning the medal, wrote ten books in the next ten years?

18. Wrote her last book at the age of ninety-two, sixteen years after writing her autobiography?

19. Had a St. Bernard dog as a guardian?

20. Used to imagine the speech she'd give if she ever won the Newbery Medal?

21. Was awarded the Newbery Medal after his death?

22. Wrote and illustrated two Newbery Honor Books and illustrated two other Newbery Honor Books and a Caldecott Honor Book?

23. Won the Pulitzer Prize in History two years before winning the Newbery Medal?

24. Spent summers at the home of her uncle, the famous architect Frank Lloyd Wright, and wrote her Newbery Medal book during one of those visits?

25. Was inspired to write his Newbery Medal book after living on a South Seas island?

26. Wrote all night while her baby slept?

27. Had a book, *Drums Along the Mohawk,* made into a movie?

28. Once lived on a house on stilts on the shore of the Pacific Ocean?

29. Wrote over 100 books and illustrated over fifty by other authors?

30. Had a daughter who married Caldecott Medal–winner Robert McCloskey?

31. As a child, used to hide under her bed and read where nobody could find her?

32. Was orphaned at the age of four and raised by his father's friend, a fur trapper and prospector?

33. Began writing books to provide quality literature for her Native American students?

34. Rarely ever read as a child?

35. While working on a poultry farm, got the idea for his first children's book?

36. Read the complete works of Edgar Allan Poe by the age of ten?

37. Designed over 1,000 book jackets?

38. Said "Tell me a story" as her first sentence?

39. Wrote and illustrated a Caldecott Honor Book the year before he won the Newbery Medal?

40. Was the first woman to win the Newbery Medal twice?

41. Served as a missionary in China?

42. Had her Newbery Medal book rejected over twenty times before it was accepted by a publisher; the book went on to become their best-selling book of all time?

43. Read E. B. White's book *Charlotte's Web* every year just to remind himself what good writing was?

44. Quit his job at the age of fifty to spend time with his family and become a writer?

45. Was the first African-American woman to win the Newbery Medal?

46. Was one of Oklahoma's star athletes before becoming a writer?

47. Worked as a reporter for the Sunday *Times* in London?

48. As a child, attended the circus an average of thirty times a year?

49. Was inspired by a famous painting, which led her to write her Newbery Medal book?

50. Had his wife and daughter complete his last book after his death?

51. Grew up on a family farm and never had a friend outside of her family until she was ten?

52. Was the first Korean American to win the Newbery Medal?

53. Used to set her bed on fire when she tried to read at night by candlelight?

54. Wrote the screenplay for the televised version of her Newbery Medal book?

55. Took the photographs that are used on the book covers of her Newbery Medal books?

56. Began publishing articles in children's church magazines while still in high school?

57. Was educated at home until the age of twelve?

58. Wasn't sure she wanted to win the Newbery Medal because she always thought the books were boring?

59. Published his first book during his first year in law school?

60. Published her first book when she was over sixty years old?

61. Did not set foot in a library until she was in her early twenties because there were none in the town where she grew up?

62. Taught himself to read at the age of three?

63. Received the phone call informing her that she had won the Newbery Medal while nobody else was home, so she told the news to her pets?

64. Wrote an epic poem about Elvis Presley while she was in high school?

65. Won first prize in a short story contest while still in high school?

66. Got the inspiration for her Newbery Medal book during a cross country car trip when she was twelve years old?

67. Had a career as a vaudeville magician?

68. At the age of thirty-seven, quit teaching to devote himself full time to writing?

69. Lived the first years of her life in China, where her parents were missionaries?

70. Often used drawings to help her visualize the plot of a book?

71. Lived with her grandmother for six years on a sugar plantation in Cuba?

72. Worked in a car factory for thirteen years and wrote books during his breaks?

73. Grew up in an old house and painted angels on the walls to cover up the cracks?

74. Cowrote and edited a book on the history of children's literature?

75. Painted thirty murals of the Navajo Indians before writing a book about them, which then won the Newbery Medal?

76. Had thirty family members attend the Newbery Medal awards ceremony?

Answers to Fun Facts About the Newbery Medalists

1. Rachel Field, 1930

2. E. L. Konigsburg, 1968

3. Joseph Krumgold, 1954, 1960

4. Hugh Lofting, 1923

5. William Armstrong, 1970

6. Elizabeth Coatsworth, 1931

7. Marguerite Henry, 1949

8. Beverly Cleary, 1984

9. Elizabeth Janet Gray, 1943

10. Jean Craighead George, 1973

11. Paul Fleischman, 1989

12. Hendrik van Loon, 1922

13. Carol Ryrie Brink, 1936

14. Arthur Chrisman, 1926

15. Dhan Mukerji, 1928

16. Robert Lawson, Newbery Medal: 1945; Caldecott Medal: 1940

17. Eric Kelly, 1929

18. Marguerite de Angeli, 1950

19. Monica Shannon, 1935

20. Eleanor Estes, 1952

21. Charles Hawes, 1924

22. Kate Seredy, 1938

23. Esther Forbes, 1944

24. Elizabeth Enright, 1939

25. Armstrong Sperry, 1941

26. Karen Hesse, 1998

27. Walter Edmonds, 1942

28. Scott O'Dell, 1961

29. Lois Lenski, 1946

30. Ruth Sawyer, 1937

31. Elizabeth Yates, 1951

32. Will James, 1927

33. Ann Nolan Clark, 1953

34. Jerry Spinelli, 1991

35. Meindert DeJong, 1955

36. Jean Lee Latham, 1956

37. Ellen Raskin, 1979

38. Virginia Sorensen, 1957

39. James Daugherty, 1940

40. Elizabeth George Speare, 1959, 1962

41. Elizabeth Lewis, 1933

42. Madeleine L'Engle, 1963

43. Russell Freedman, 1988

44. Charles Finger, 1925

45. Virginia Hamilton, 1975

46. Harold Keith, 1958

47. Susan Cooper, 1976

48. William Pène du Bois, 1948

49. Elizabeth Borton de Trevino, 1966

50. Robert C. O'Brien, 1972

51. Emily Neville, 1964

52. Linda Sue Park, 2002

53. Maia Wojciechowska, 1965

54. Patricia MacLachlan, 1986

55. Lois Lowry, 1990, 1994

56. Phyllis Reynolds Naylor, 1992

57. Carolyn Sherwin Bailey, 1947

58. Robin McKinley, 1985

59. Louis Sachar, 1999

60. Irene Hunt, 1967

61. Cynthia Rylant, 1993

62. Lloyd Alexander, 1969

63. Betsy Byars, 1971

64. Karen Cushman, 1996

65. Joan Blos, 1980

66. Sharon Creech, 1995

67. Sid Fleischman, 1987

68. Richard Peck, 2001

69. Katherine Paterson, 1978, 1981

70. Cynthia Voigt, 1983

71. Paula Fox, 1974

72. Christopher Paul Curtis, 2000

73. Nancy Willard, 1982

74. Cornelia Meigs, 1934

75. Laura Adams Armer, 1932

76. Mildred D. Taylor, 1977

PHOTOGRAPHY CREDITS

Photograph of Lloyd Alexander, courtesy of Sarah Henry of Penguin Putnam Books for Young Readers, and reprinted with permission.

Photograph of William Armstrong, courtesy of Rebecca Grose and Dana Schwartz of HarperCollins Publishers, and reprinted with permission.

Photograph of Joan Blos, Peter Blos, Jr. (photographer), courtesy of Joan Blos and Peter Blos, and reprinted with permission.

Photograph of Betsy Byars, courtesy of Alison Root, Melanie Chang, and Random House Children's Books, and reprinted with permission.

Photograph of Beverly Cleary, Alan McEwen (photographer), courtesy of Rebecca Grose and Dana Schwartz of HarperCollins Children's books, and reprinted with permission.

Photograph of Susan Cooper, Jeffrey Hornstein (photographer), courtesy of Susan Cooper, and reprinted with permission.

Photograph of Sharon Creech, Matthew Self (photographer), courtesy of Sharon Creech, and reprinted with permission.

Photograph of Christopher Paul Curtis, James Keyser (photographer), courtesy of Alison Root and Melanie Chang, Random House Children's Books, and reprinted with permission.

Photograph of Karen Cushman, Fred Mertz (photographer), courtesy of Clarion Books, a Houghton Mifflin Company Imprint, and reprinted with permission.

Photographs of Eleanor Estes, courtesy of Helena Estes, and reprinted with permission.

Photograph of Paul Fleischman, courtesy of Paul Fleischman, and reprinted with permission.

Photograph of Sid Fleischman, courtesy of Sid Fleischman, and reprinted with permission.

Photograph of Russell Freedman, Carlo Ontal (photographer), courtesy of Marjorie Naughton of Clarion Books, a Houghton Mifflin Company Imprint, and reprinted with permission.

Photograph of Jean Craighead George, Martha Holmes (photographer), courtesy of Sarah Henry of Penguin Putnam Books for Young Readers and reprinted with permission. Childhood photographs of Jean Craighead George, courtesy of Jean Craighead George, and reprinted with permission. Childhood photo, 1923, Ottawa, Canada.

Photograph of Virginia Hamilton, Jim Callaway (photographer), courtesy of Virginia Hamilton and Arnold Adoff, and reprinted with permission.

Photograph of Karen Hesse, Andrew Kennery (photographer), courtesy of Karen Hesse, and reprinted with permission.

Photograph of Irene Hunt, courtesy of Shirley Beem, and reprinted with permission. Photo taken 1945.

Photograph of Elaine Konigsburg, Ron Kunzman (photographer), courtesy of Simon & Schuster Children's Publishing Division, and reprinted with permission.

Photograph of Madeleine L'Engle, Kenneth S. Lewis (photographer), and reprinted with permission. Photo © Kenneth S. Lewis.

Photographs of Lois Lowry, courtesy of Lois Lowry, and reprinted with permission. Childhood photo, 1947, age 10.

Photograph of Patricia MacLachlan, John MacLachlan (photographer), courtesy of Patricia MacLachlan, and Bantam Doubleday Dell Books for Young Readers, and reprinted with permission.

Photograph of Phyllis Reynolds Naylor, Katherine Lambert Photography, and reprinted with permission. Childhood photograph of Phyllis Reynolds Naylor, courtesy of Phyllis Reynolds Naylor, and reprinted with permission.

Photograph of Emily Neville, R.J. Levison (photographer), courtesy of Rebecca Gross and Dana Schwartz of HarperCollins Publishers, and reprinted with permission.

Photographs of Scott O'Dell, courtesy of Elizabeth Hall, and reprinted with permission.

Photograph of Linda Sue Park, Klaus Pollmeier (photographer), courtesy of Debra Shapiro of Clarion Books, and reprinted with permission.

Photograph of Katherine Paterson, Samantha Loomis Paterson (photographer), courtesy of Katherine Paterson, and reprinted with permission.

Photograph of Katherine Paterson, courtesy of Katherine Paterson and reprinted with permission. Childhood photo, 1935, Hwainfu, China; siblings Ray and Liz in background.

Photograph of Richard Peck, Don Lewis (photographer), courtesy of Random House, and reprinted with permission.

Photograph of Ellen Raskin, courtesy of Sarah Henry of Penguin Putnam Books for Young Readers, and reprinted with permission.

Photograph of Cynthia Rylant, courtesy of Stephanie Wimmer of Scholastic, Inc., and reprinted with permission.

Photograph of Louis Sachar, Sonya Sones (photographer), courtesy of Penguin Putnam Books for Young Readers, and reprinted with permission.

Photographs of Jerry Spinelli, courtesy of Jerry Spinelli, and reprinted with permission. Childhood photo, February 1945.

Photograph of Mildred D. Taylor, courtesy of Sarah Henry of Penguin Putnam Books for Young Readers, and reprinted with permission.

Photographs of Cynthia Voigt, Tillman Crane (photographer), courtesy of Scholastic, Inc. and reprinted with permission.

Photograph of Nancy Willard, Eric Lindbloom (photographer), courtesy of Kristin Marley of Harcourt Children's Books, and reprinted with permission.

Photograph of Maia Wojciechowska, Kate Schermerhorn (photographer), courtesy of Maia Wojciechowska, and reprinted with permission.

Annotated Bibliography

Alderson, Brian. *Sing a Song for Sixpence: The English Picture Book Tradition & Randolph Caldecott.* Cambridge, England: Press Syndicate of the University of Cambridge, 1986.

Berger, Laura Standley, ed. *Twentieth-Century Children's Writers.* 4th ed. Detroit: St. James Press, 1955.

Blackstock, Josephine. *Songs for Sixpence.* New York: Follet, 1955. A fictionalized story of John Newbery's life, based on actual facts and real people.

Brown, Muriel W., Rita Schoch Foudray, and Jim Roginski, eds. *Newbery and Caldecott Medalists and Honor Book Winners.* 2d ed. New York: Neal-Schuman Publishers, 1993. Bibliographies and resource material including background reading.

Byars, Betsy. *The Moon and I.* New York: J. Messner, 1991.

Cary, Alice. *Jean Craighead George.* Santa Barbara, Calif.: Learning Works, 1996.

Cleary, Beverly. *A Girl from Yamhill.* New York: Bantam Doubleday Dell Publishing Group, 1988.

————. *My Own Two Feet: A Memoir.* New York: Avon Books, 1995.

Comfort, Claudette Hegel. *Distinguished Children's Literature: The Newbery & Caldecott Winners—The Books and Their Creators.* Minneapolis: T. S. Denison & Co., 1990. A listing of the Medalists, including brief facts, and a synopsis and review of each book.

Commire, Anne, ed. *Something About the Author: Facts and Pictures About Contemporary Authors and Illustrators of Books for Young People.* Vols. 1 (1971), 11 (1977), 13 (1978), 14 (1978), 15 (1979), 18 (1980), 23 (1981), 27 (1982), 42 (1986), 62 (1990). Detroit: Gale Research.

Contemporary Authors. Vols. 107 (1983), 147 (1995), 162 (1998). Detroit: Gale Research.

Dalgliesh, Alice. *A Book for Jennifer.* New York: C. Scribner's Sons, 1940. A fictionalized story of a little girl and her two brothers who buy books from Mr. Newbery's shop.

de Montreville, Doris, and Elizabeth D. Crawford, eds. *The Fourth Book of Junior Authors and Illustrators.* New York: H. W. Wilson, 1978.

de Montreville, Doris, and Donna Hill, eds. *The Third Book of Junior Authors.* New York: H. W. Wilson, 1972.

Drew, Bernard A. *The 100 Most Popular Young Adult Authors: Biographical Sketches and Bibliographies.* Rev. ed. Englewood, Colo.: Libraries Unlimited, 1997. Includes Newbery Medalists Lloyd Alexander, Betsy Byars, Susan Cooper, Paula Fox, Jean Craighead George, Virginia Hamilton, E. L. Konigsburg, Madeleine L'Engle, Lois Lowry, Robin McKinley, Phyllis Reynolds Naylor, Scott O'Dell, Katherine Paterson, Richard Peck, Cynthia Rylant, Jerry Spinelli, Mildred D. Taylor, and Cynthia Voigt.

Duhl, Gregory. *The Newbery Reviews.* Highland Park, Ill.: Edgewood School, 1983. A thirteen-year-old boy summarizes the plots to the Newbery books; includes titles, authors, publishers, and number of pages in each.

Edgar, Kathleen J., ed. *Contemporary Authors.* Vol. 147. Detroit,: Gale Research, 1995.

Evory, Ann, and Linda Metzger, eds. *Contemporary Authors.* Detroit: Gale Research, 1983.

Fleischman, Sid. *The Abracadabra Kid: A Writer's Life.* New York: Greenwillow Books, 1996.

Fuller, Muriel, ed. *More Junior Authors.* New York: H. W. Wilson, 1963.

Gallo, Donald R., ed. *Speaking for Ourselves: Autobiographical Sketches by Notable Authors of Books for Young Adults.* Urbana, Ill.: National Council of Teachers of English, 1990.

Hile, Kevin S., ed. *Something About the Author: Facts and Pictures About Contemporary Authors and Illustrators of Books for Young People.* Vols. 81 (1995), 83 (1995). Detroit: Gale Research.

Hoffman, Miriam, and Eva Samuels. *Authors and Illustrators of Children's Books: Writings on Their Lives and Works.* New York: R. R. Bowker, 1972.

Holtze, Sally Holmes, ed. *The Seventh Book of Junior Authors and Illustrators.* New York: H. W. Wilson, 1989.

————.*The Sixth Book of Junior Authors and Illustrators.* New York: H. W. Wilson, 1989.

Hopkins, Lee Bennett. *Books Are by People: Interviews with 104 Authors and Illustrators of Books for Young Children.* New York: Citation Press, 1969. Includes Newbery Medalists James Daugherty, Lois Lenski, and Ellen Raskin.

————. *More Books by More People: Interviews with Sixty-Five Authors of Books for Children.* New York: Citation Press, 1974. Includes Newbery Medalists Lloyd Alexander, William Armstrong, Carol Ryrie Brink, Betsy Byars, Ann Nolan Clark, Beverly Cleary, Elizabeth Coatsworth, Marguerite de Angeli, Meindert DeJong, Elizabeth Borton de Trevino, Walter D. Edmonds, Eleanor Estes, Jean Craighead George, Virginia Hamilton, Irene Hunt, Harold Keith, E. L. Konigsburg, Jean Lee Latham, Madeleine L'Engle, Emily Neville, Virginia Sorensen, Elizabeth George Speare, Maia Wojciechowska, and Elizabeth Yates.

H. W. Wilson. *The Fifth Book of Junior Authors and Illustrators.* New York: H. W. Wilson, 1983.

Kingman, Lee, ed. *Newbery and Caldecott Medal Books, with Acceptance Papers, Biographies and Related Material Chiefly from the Horn Book Magazine: 1956–1965.* Boston: Horn Book, 1965.

————. *Newbery and Caldecott Medal Books, with Acceptance Papers, Biographies and Related Material Chiefly from the Horn Book Magazine: 1966–1975.* Boston: Horn Book, 1976.

————. *Newbery and Caldecott Medal Books with Acceptance Papers, Biographies and Related Material Chiefly from the Horn Book Magazine: 1976–1985.* Boston: Horn Book, 1986.

Kirkpatrick, D. L., ed. *Twentieth-Century Children's Writers.* New York: St. Martin's Press, 1978.

Kovacs, Deborah, and James Preller. *Meet the Authors and Illustrators: 60 Creators of Favorite Children's Books Talk About Their Work.* New York: Scholastic, 1991. Brief profiles on sixty authors and illustrators of children's books, including a few Newbery medalists.

————. *Meet the Authors and Illustrators: 60 Creators of Favorite Children's Books Talk About Their Work.* Vol. 2. New York: Scholastic, 1993.

Kunitz, Stanley J., and Howard Haycraft, eds. *The Junior Book of Authors.* 2d ed. New York: H. W. Wilson, 1951.

Lowry, Lois. *Looking Back: A Book of Memories.* Boston: Walter Lorraine Books, 1998.

May, Hal, ed. *Contemporary Authors.* Vol. 107. Detroit: Gale Research, 1983.

McElmeel, Sharon L. *100 Most Popular Children's Authors: Biographical Sketches and Bibliographies.* Englewood, Colo.: Libraries Unlimited, 1999. Includes Newbery Medalists Lloyd Alexander, Betsy Byars, Beverly Cleary, Eleanor Estes, Paul Fleischman, Sid Fleischman, Paula Fox, Russell Freedman, Jean Craighead George, Virginia Hamilton, Marguerite Henry, Irene Hunt, E. L. Konigsburg, Madeleine L'Engle, Robert Lawson, Lois Lowry, Patricia MacLachlan, Phyllis Reynolds Naylor, Scott O'Dell, Katherine Paterson, Richard Peck, Cynthia Rylant, Louis Sachar, Elizabeth George Speare, Jerry Spinelli, Mildred D. Taylor, Cynthia Voigt, and Elizabeth Yates.

Miller, Bertha Mahony, and Elinor Whitney Field, eds. *Newbery Medal Books: 1922–1955.* Boston: Horn Book, 1955.

Newbery, John. *A Little Pretty Pocket-Book.* With an introductory essay and bibliography by M. F. Thwaite. New York: Harcourt, Brace & Co., 1966. A reproduction of John Newbery's book, with an extensive introduction and bibliography.

The Newbery and Caldecott Awards: A Guide to the Medal and Honor Books. Chicago: American Library Association and Association for Library Service to Children, 1999.

The Newbery and Caldecott Medal Books, 1986–2000: A Comprehensive Guide to the Winners. Chicago: Horn Book and Association for Library Service to Children, American Library Association, 2001.

Paterson, Katherine. *Gates of Excellence.* New York: Dutton Children's Books, 1988.

Peacock, Scot, ed. *Contemporary Authors.* New Revision Series. Vols. 62 (1998), 84 (2000), 183 (2000). Farmington Hills, Mich.: Gale Group.

Peterson, Linda Kauffman, and Marilyn Leathers Solt. *Newbery and Caldecott Medal and Honor Books: An Annotated Bibliography.* Boston: G. K. Hall, 1982. Includes a history of the Newbery and Caldecott Medals; a listing of the winning books and honor books; characteristics and trends; and author, illustrator, and title index.

Rockman, Connie C., ed. *The Eighth Book of Junior Authors.* New York: H. W. Wilson, 2000.

Roginski, Jim, ed. *Behind the Covers: Interviews with Authors and Illustrators of Books for Children and Young Adults.* Bibliographies compiled by Muriel Brown. Littleton, Colo.: Libraries Unlimited, 1985 (Vol. 1); 1989 (Vol. 2). Interviews with children's book authors and illustrators, including biographical notes; personal impressions of the interviewees; bibliography of books, awards, and honors; and additional sources. Includes Newbery winner Ellen Raskin (Vol. 1, pp. 167–76).

Silvey, Anita, ed. *Children's Books and Their Creators.* New York: Houghton Mifflin, 1995. A comprehensive overview of the history and content of children's literature, including biographies and personal reflections by numerous Newbery Medalists.

Spinelli, Jerry. *Knots in My Yo-Yo String: The Autobiography of a Kid.* New York: A. A. Knopf, 1998.

Straub, Deborah A., ed. *Contemporary Authors.* New Revision Series. Vol. 21. Detroit: Gale Research, 1987.

Telgen, Diana, ed. *Something About the Author: Facts and Pictures About Contemporary Authors and Illustrators of Books for Young People.* Vols. 71 (1993), 72 (1993), 87 (1996). Detroit: Gale Research.

Trelease, Jim, ed. *Hey, Listen to This! Stories to Read Aloud.* New York: Viking Penguin, 1992. Consists of stories to be read aloud to children ages 5–9; including an introduction and brief profile of each author and a story about how each book came to be written. Includes Newbery Medalists Beverly Cleary (pp. 35–44), Arthur Bowie Chrisman (pp. 148–56), and Elizabeth George Speare (pp. 321–24).

Waugh, Charles G., and Martin H. Greenburg, eds. *The Newbery Award Reader.* New York: Harcourt Brace Jovanovich, 1974. A collection of short fiction by eighteen winners of the Newbery Medal.

Woolman, Bertha, and Patricia Litsey. *The Newbery Award Winners: The Books and Their Authors.* Rev. ed. Minneapolis: T. S. Denison &Co., 1985. A brief listing of facts and "clues" about each of the Newbery Medal books.

Author/Title Index

The names of the Newbery Medal authors and the titles of the Newbery Medal winning books are in bold print, as are the main page numbers for each author. Information included in the book prior to the beginning of the author chapters, and information contained in the indexes following the author chapters has not been included in this index.

About the Author

Kathleen Long Bostrom is a Presbyterian minister and the author of a growing number of books for children. Her first book was published in 1997; her most recent publication is *Mary's Happy Christmas Day* (Zonderkidz, 2003). Kathy has won awards for preaching and has published numerous articles in various journals and newspapers. She is included in an edition of *Something About the Author* (vol. 139) and *Contemporary Authors* (vol. 210), published 2003.

Kathy earned a Master of Arts in Christian Education (1980) and a Master of Divinity (1983) from Princeton Theological Seminary, and a Doctor of Ministry in Preaching degree from McCormick Theological Seminary in Chicago (2000).

Kathy currently serves as co-pastor along with her husband, Greg, at a church in Wildwood, Illinois. They have three children, Christopher, Amy, and David.

Do you have a question or comment for the author? You can write to the Kathleen Long Bostrom in care of:
Libraries Unlimited
88 Post Road West
Westport, CT 06881